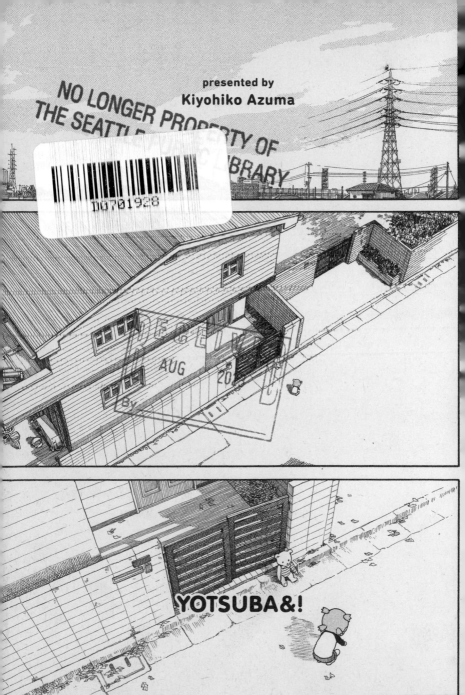

presented by
**Kiyohiko Azuma**

**YOTSUBA&!**

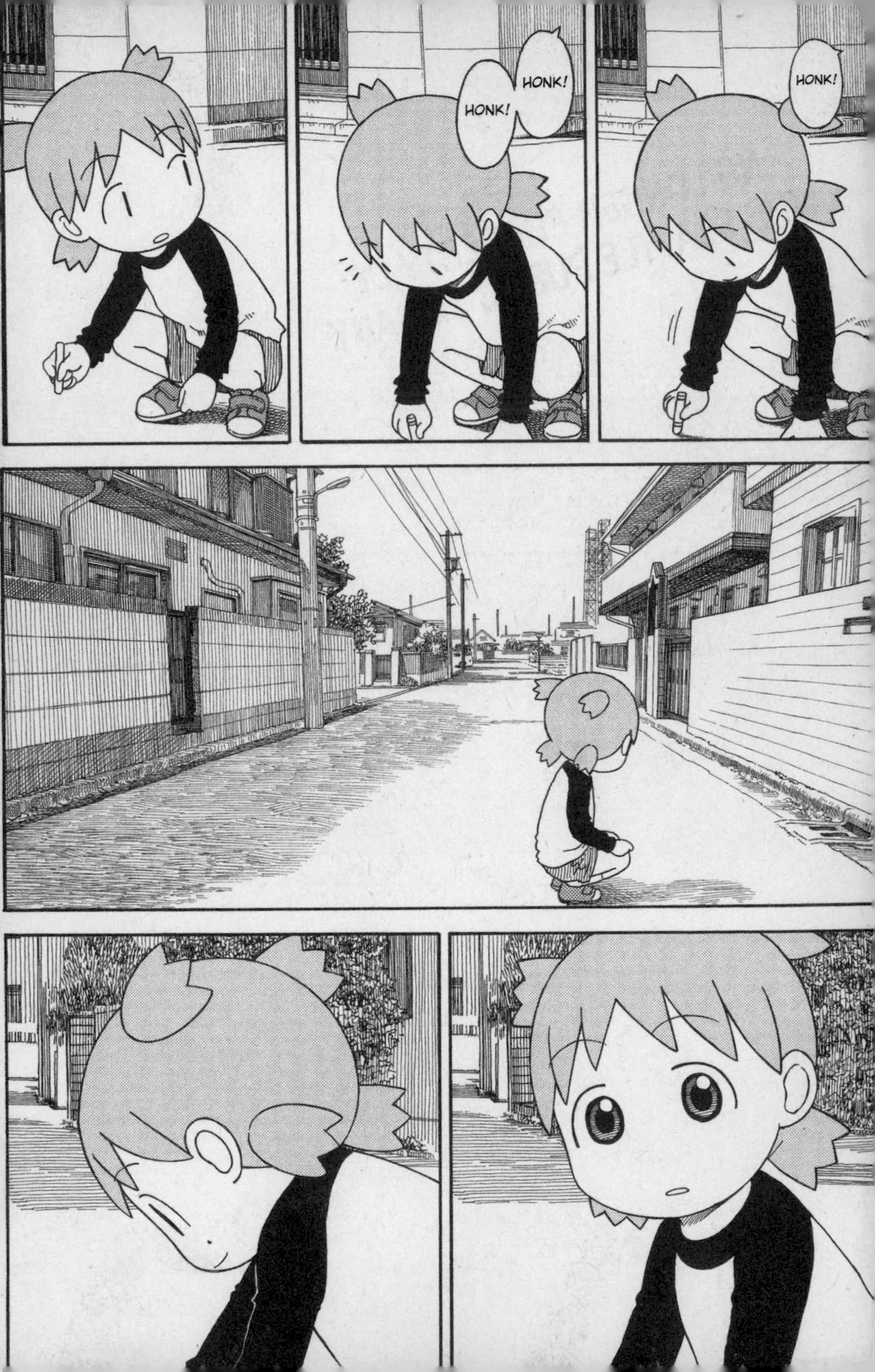
HONK!
HONK!
HONK!

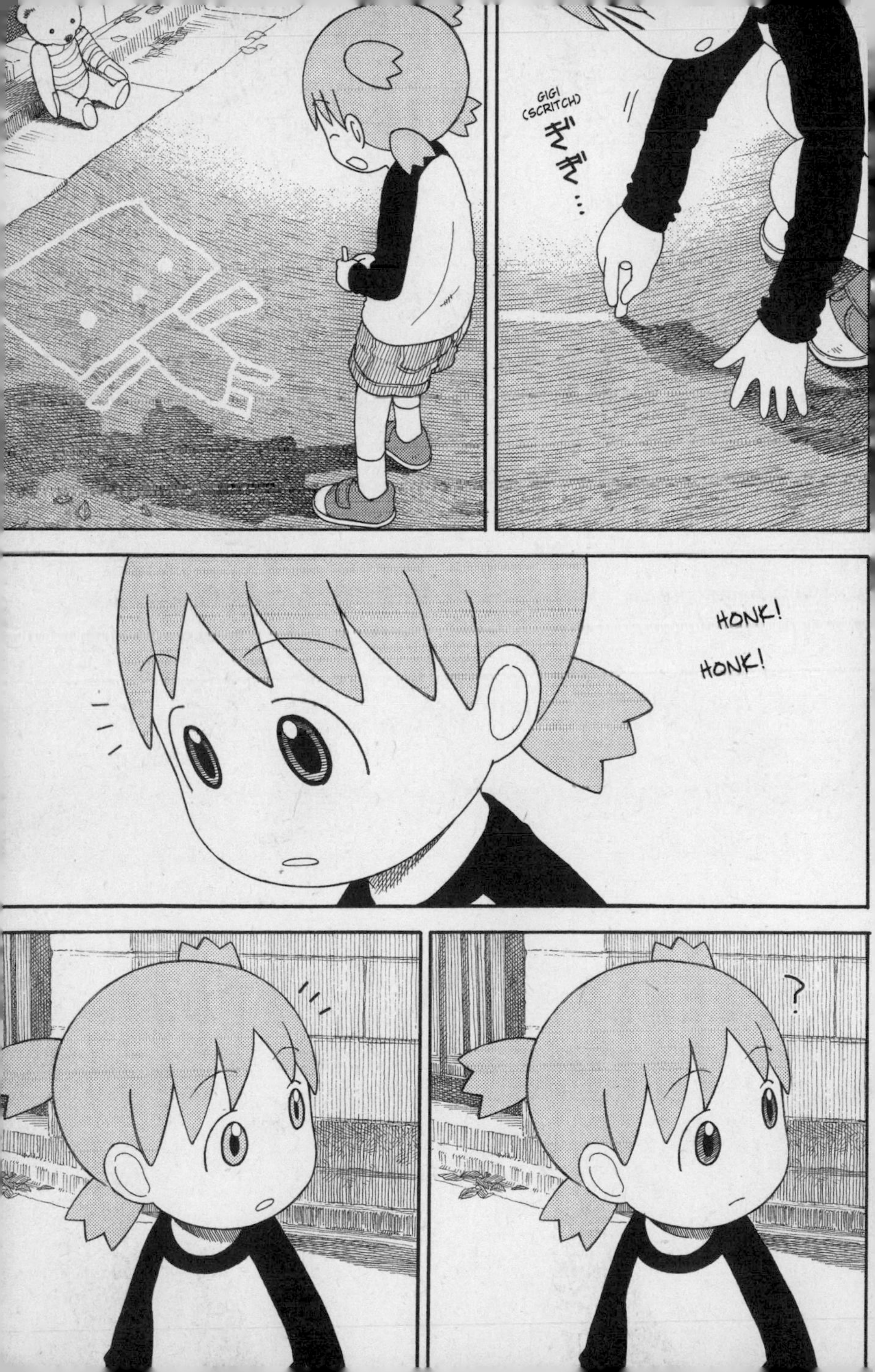
GIGI (SCRITCH)
ぎぎ…
HONK!
HONK!

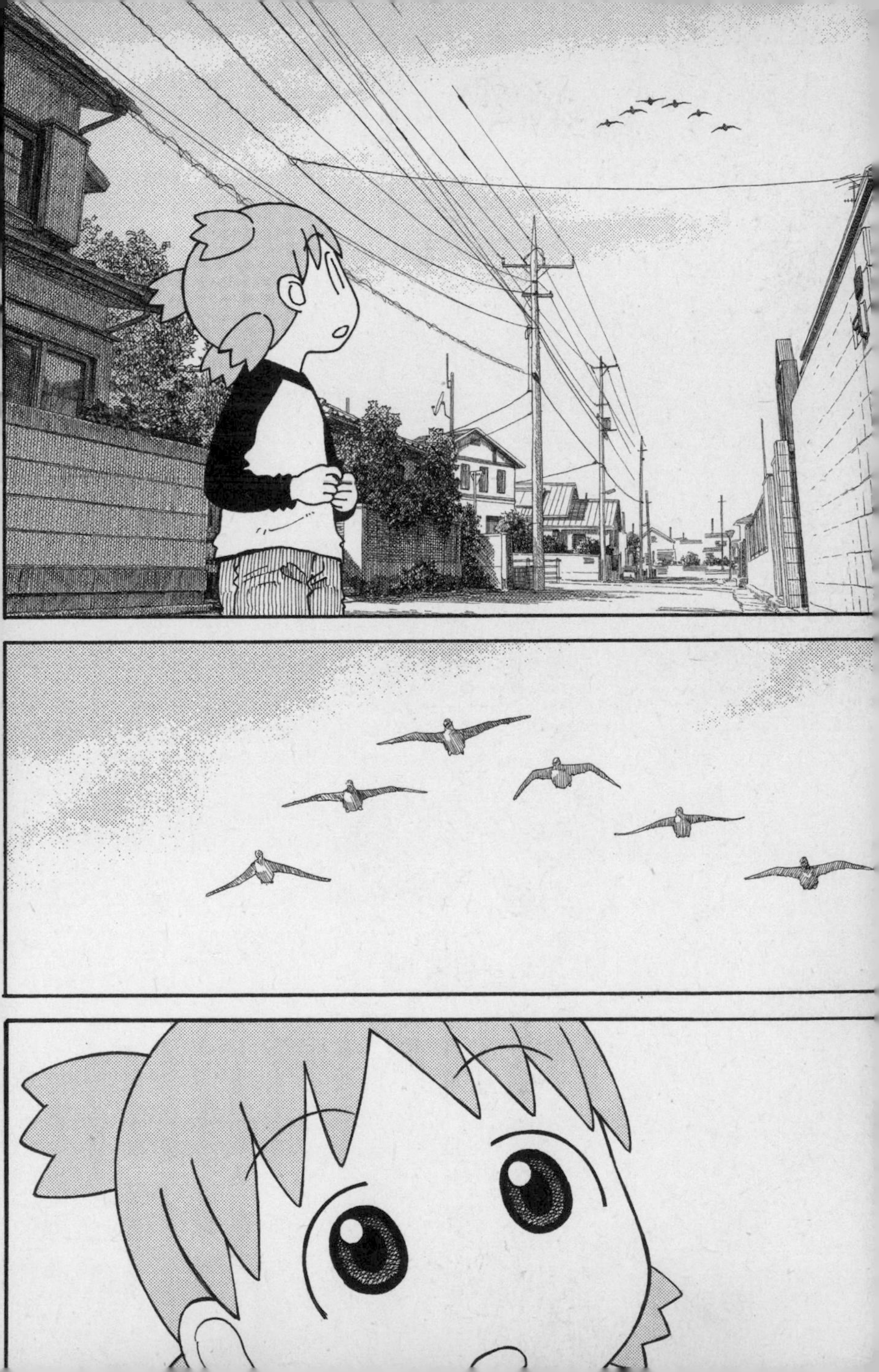

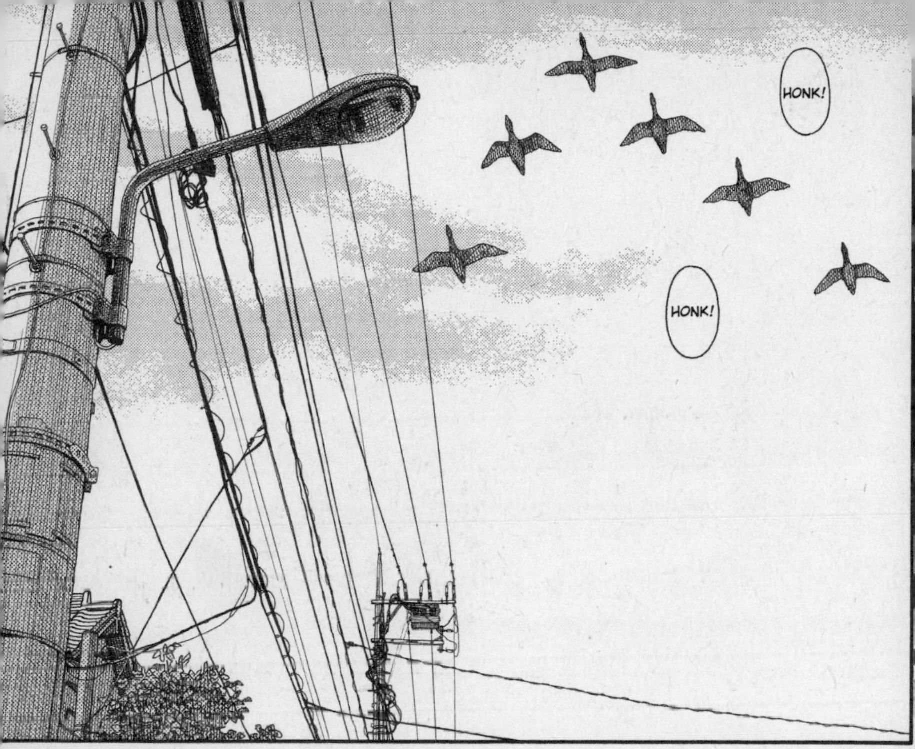
HONK!
HONK!
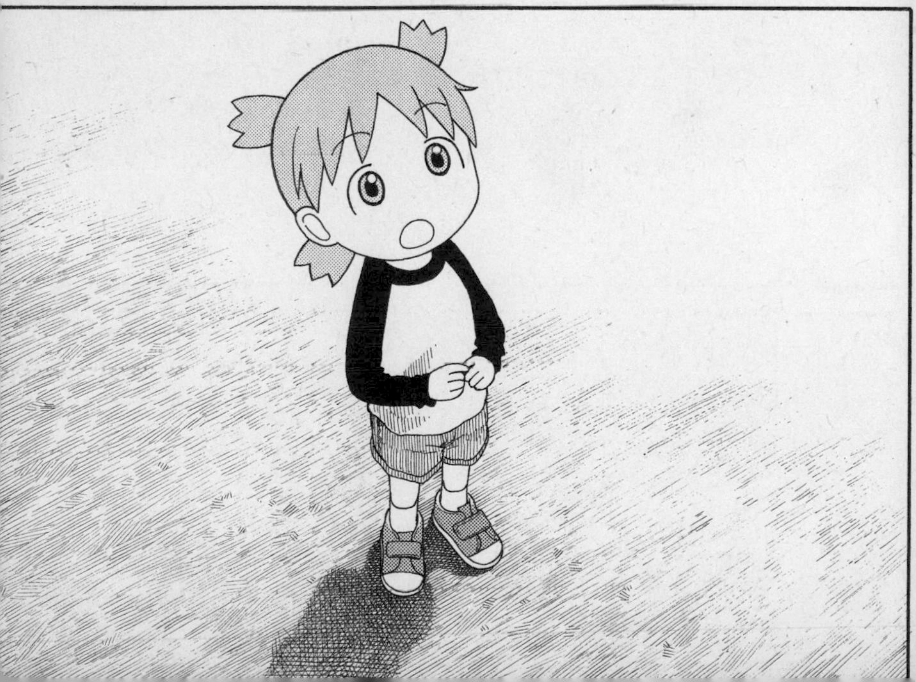

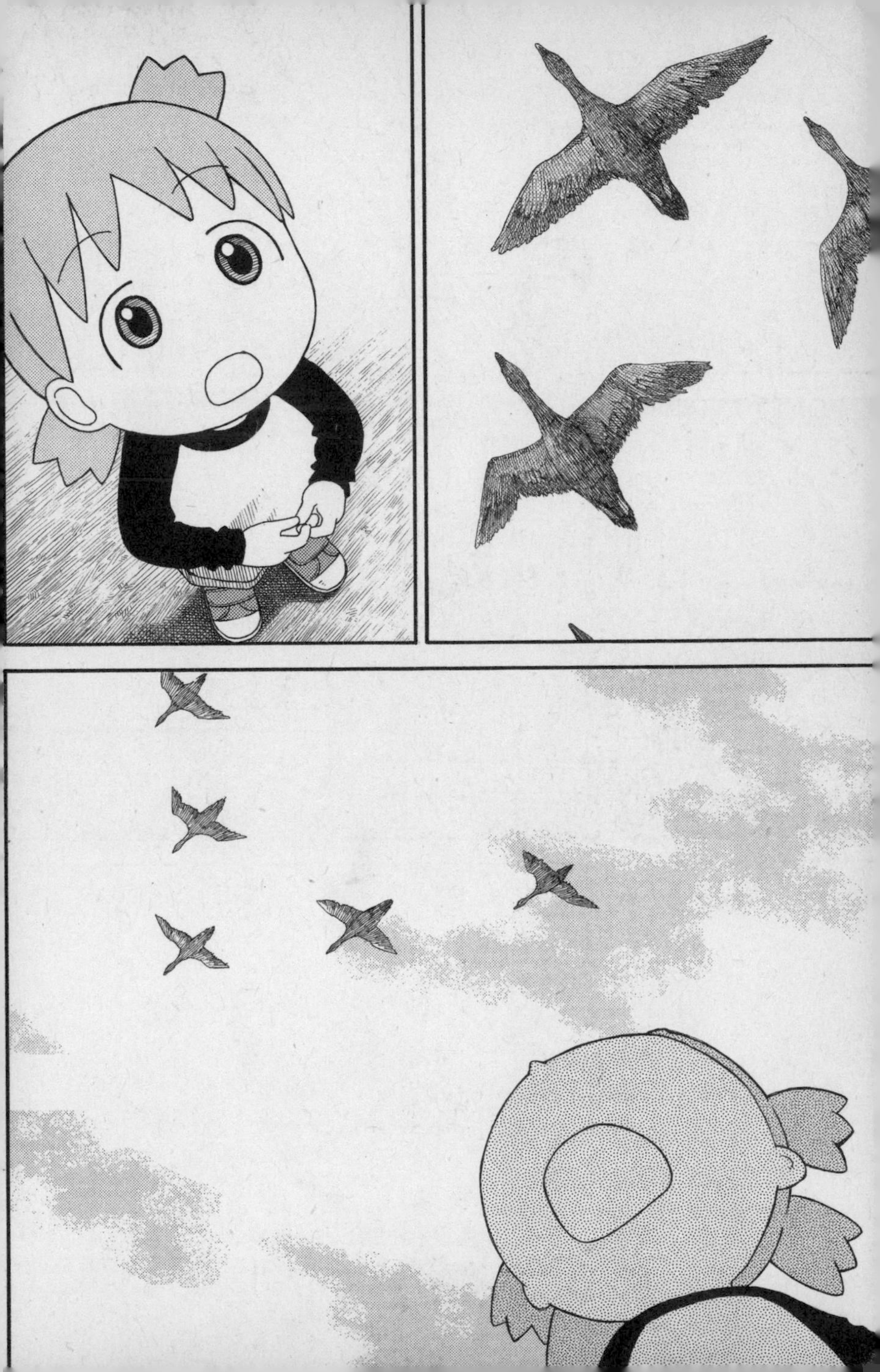

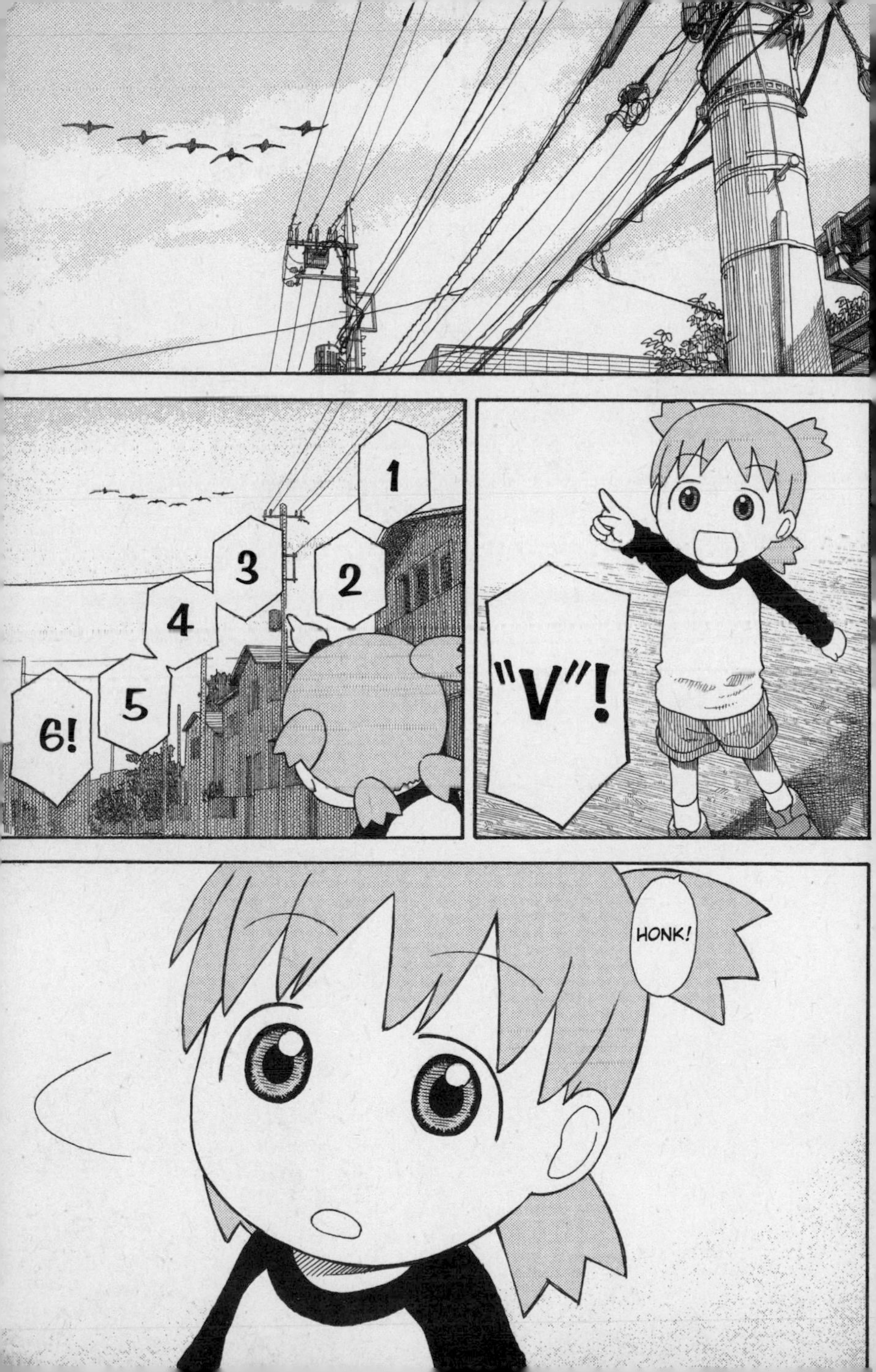
"V"!
1
2
3
4
5
6!
HONK!

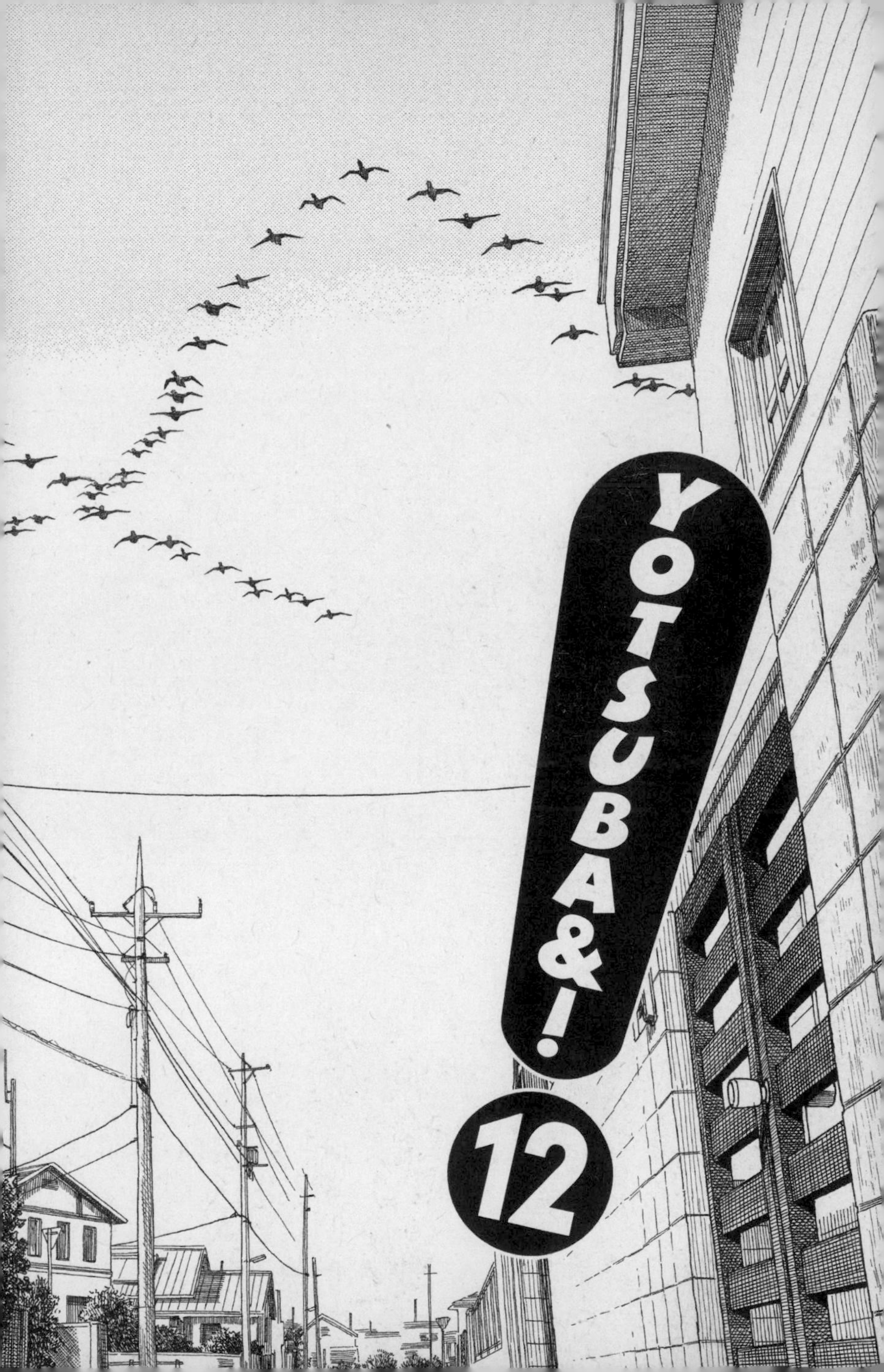
YOTSUBA&!
12

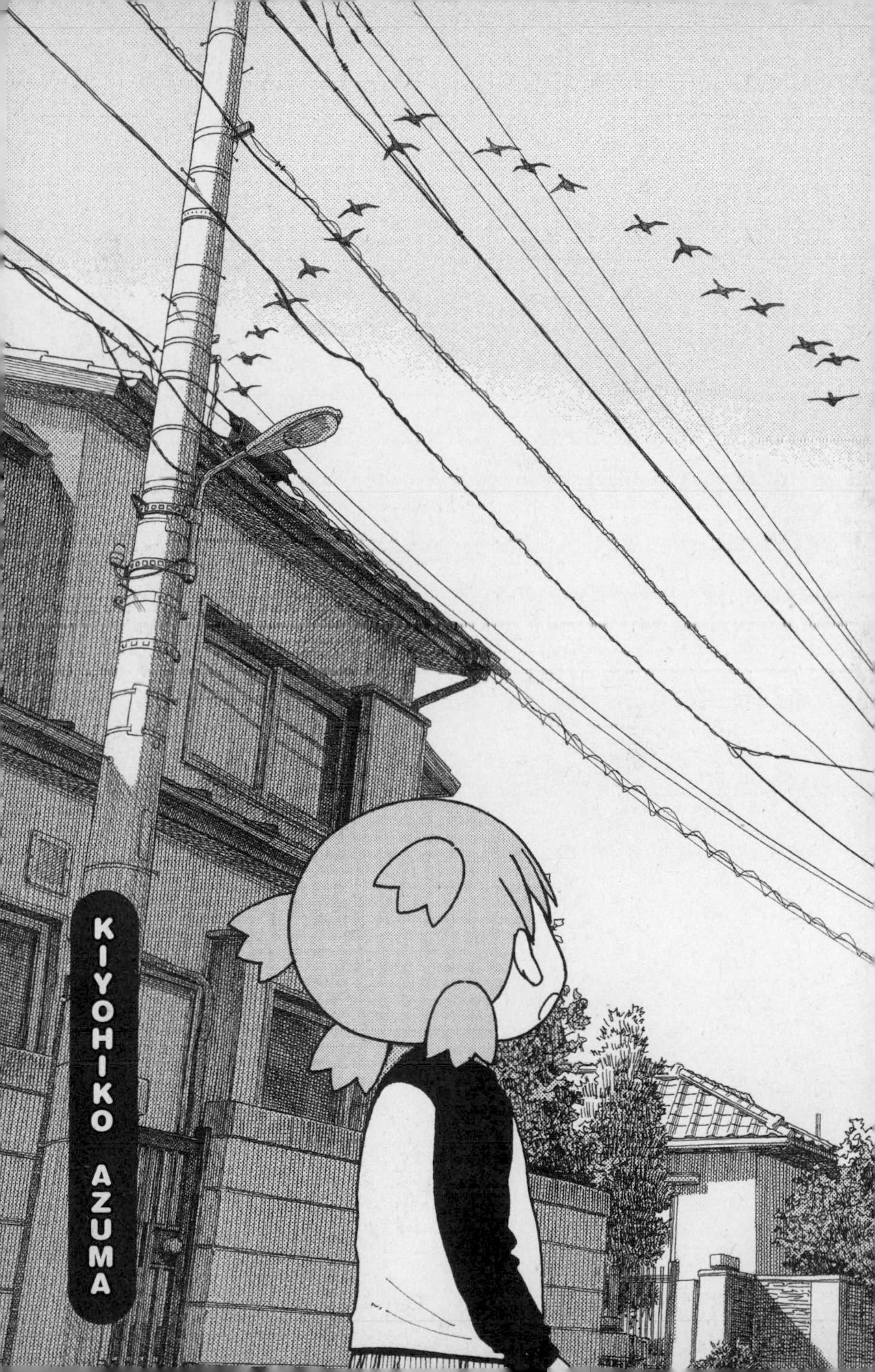
KIYOHIKO AZUMA

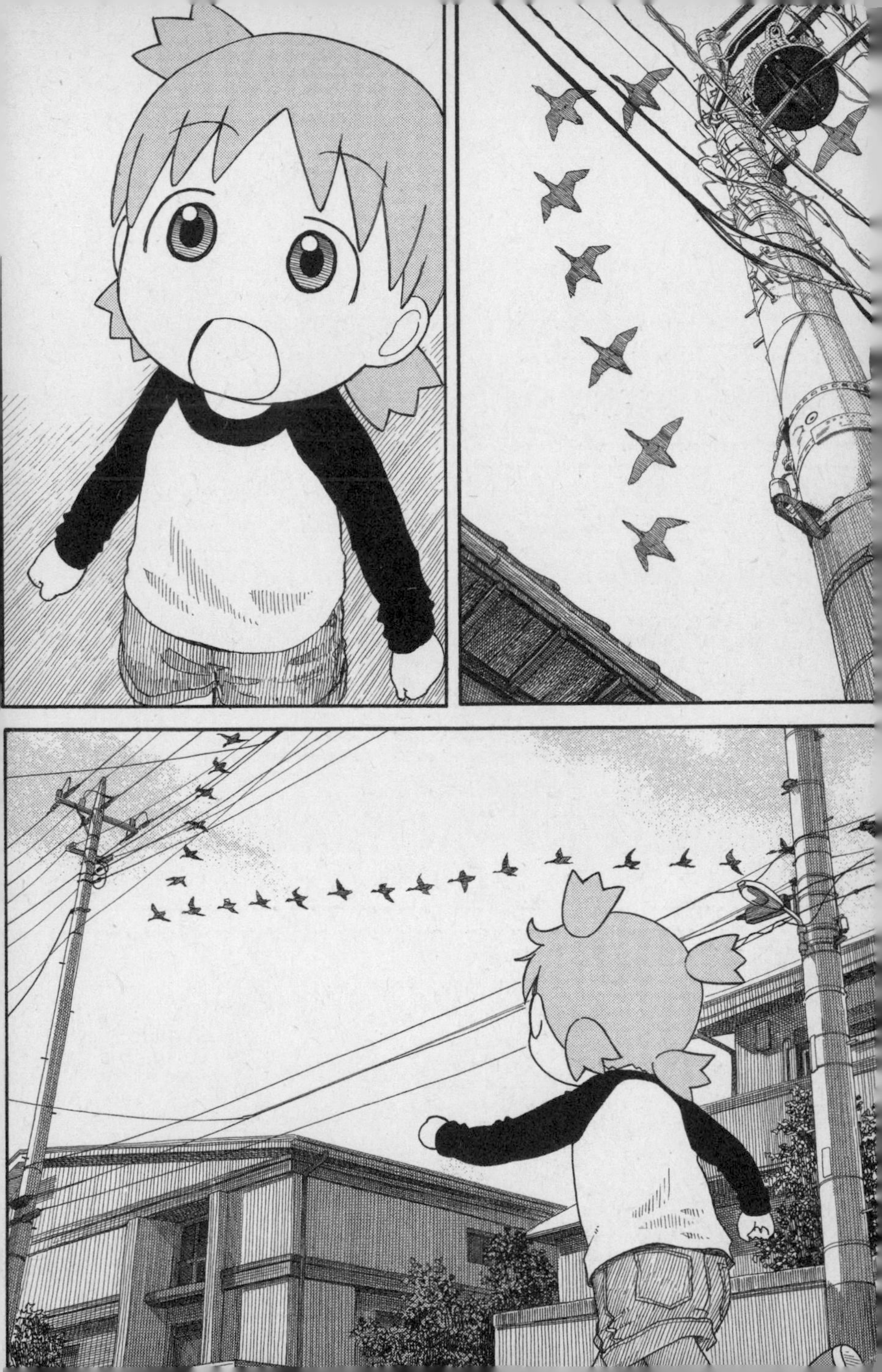

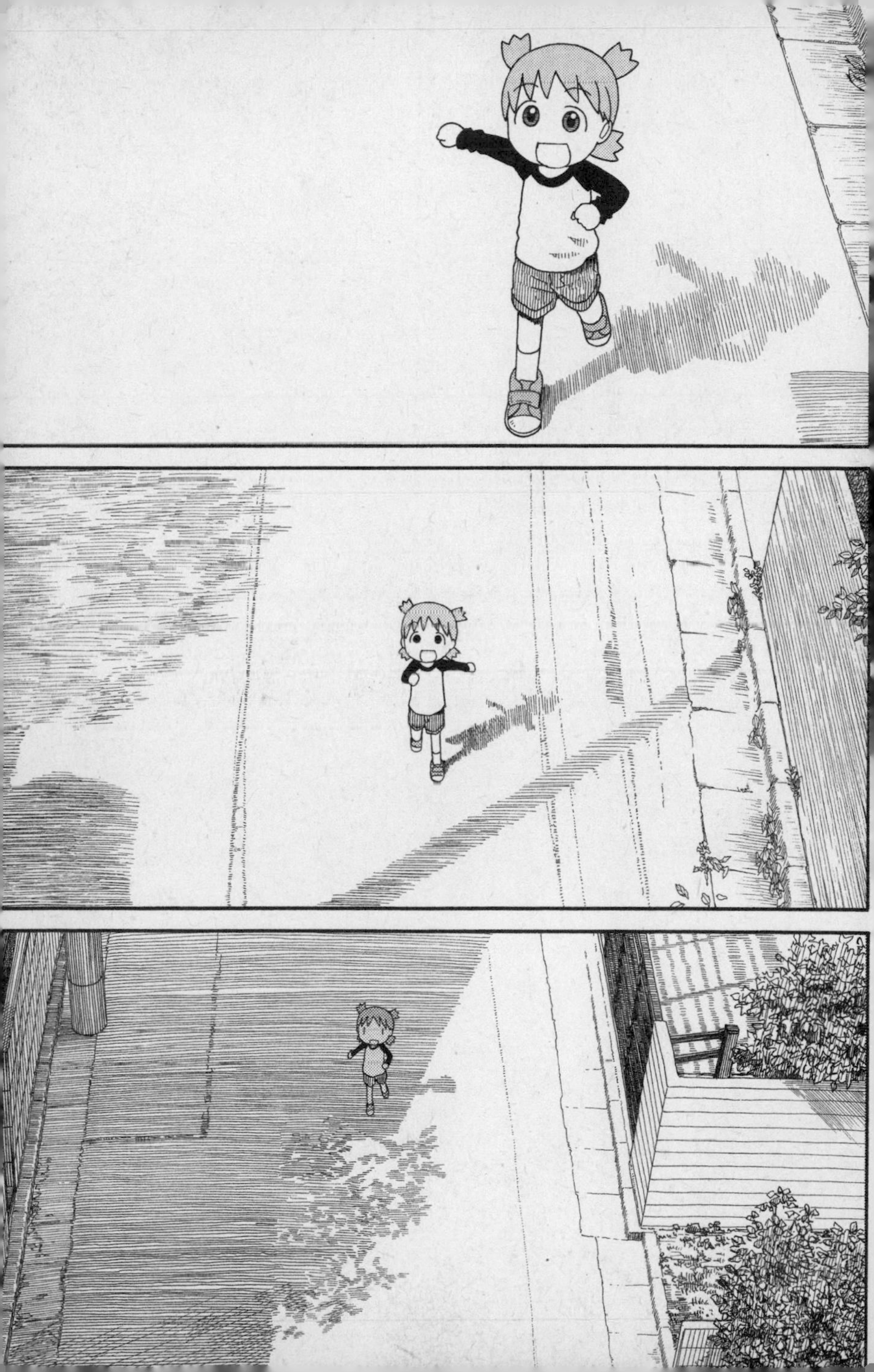

# CONTENTS

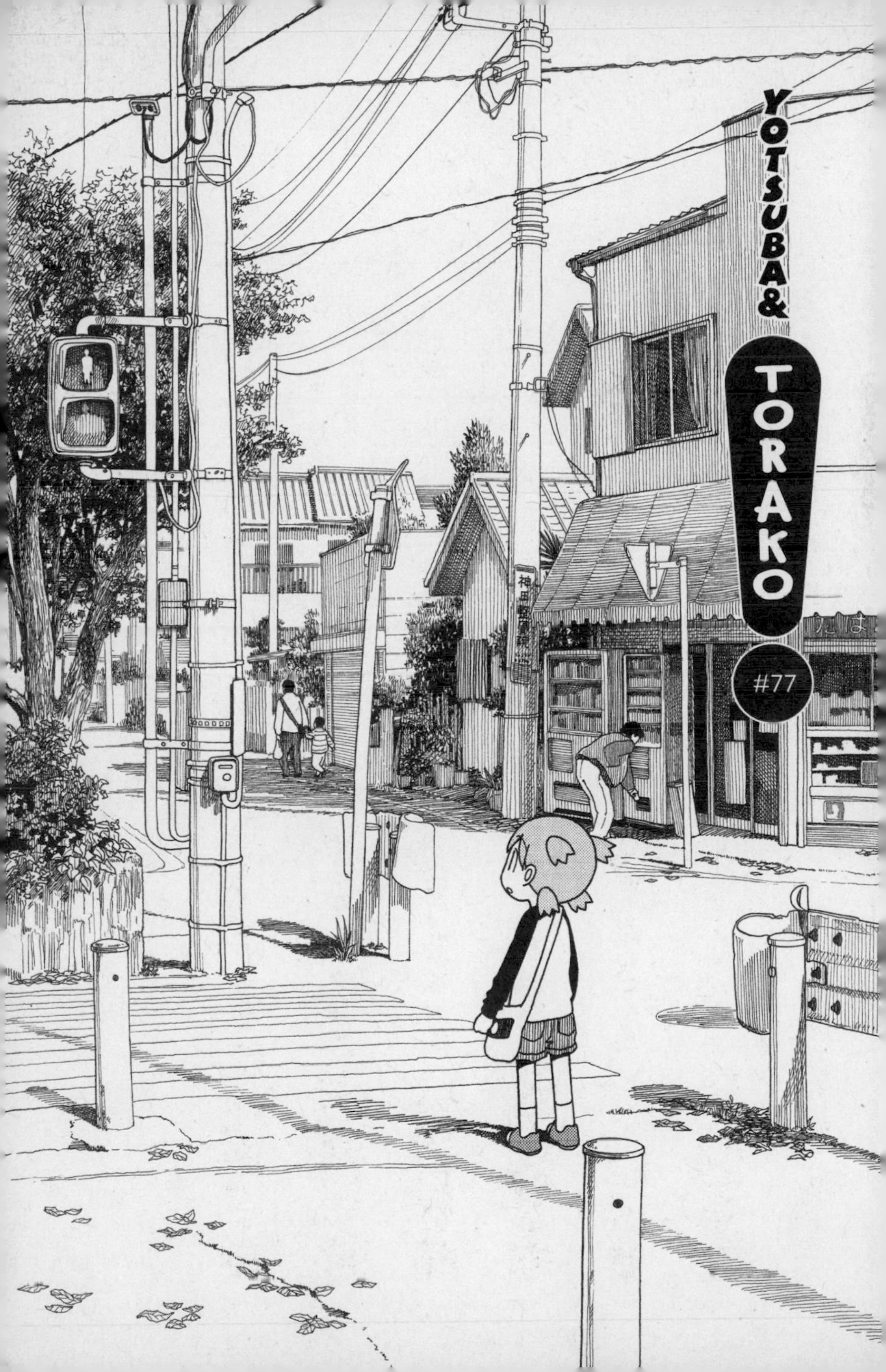
YOTSUBA&
TORAKO
#77

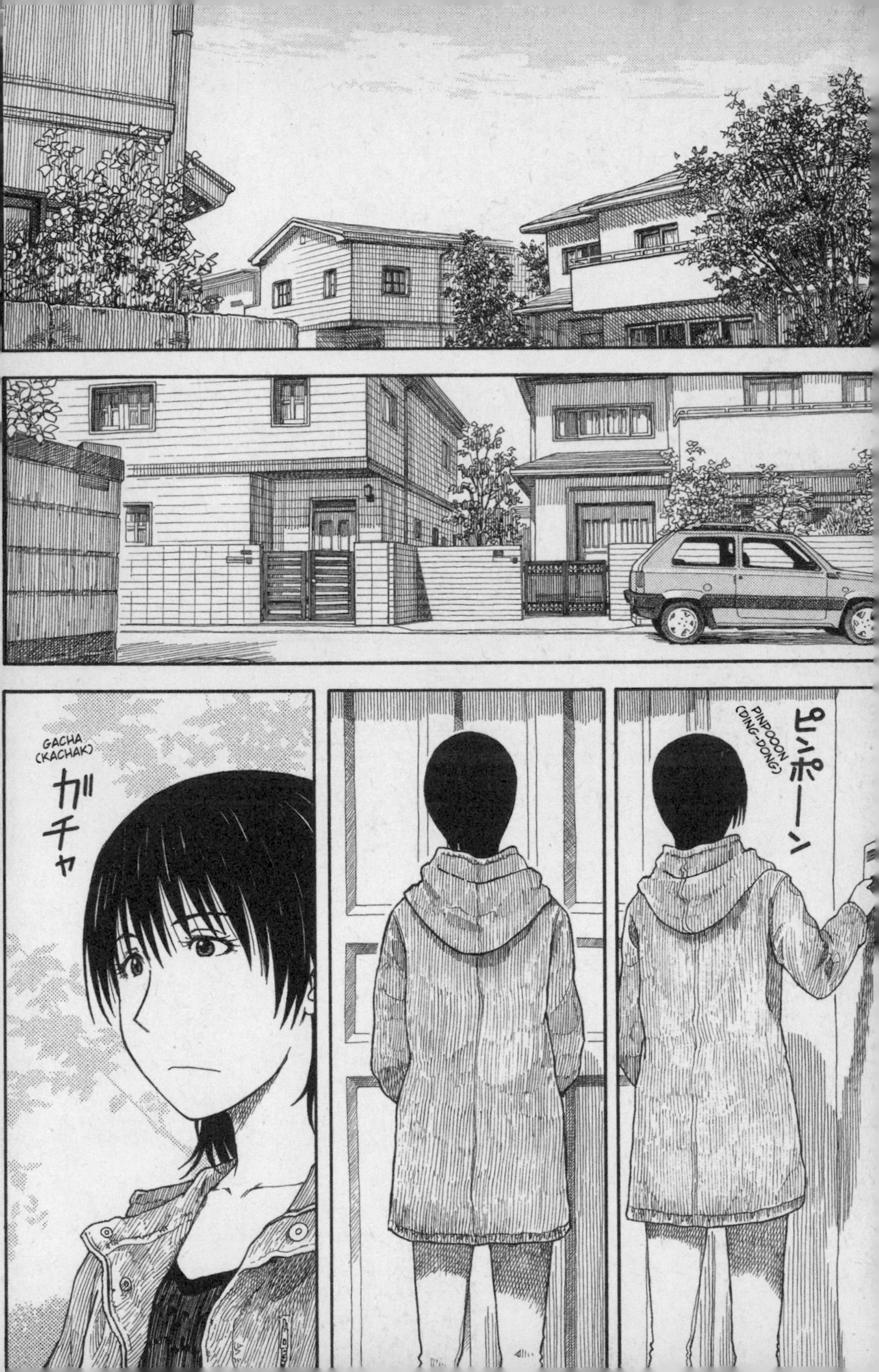
ピンポーン
PINPOOON (DING-DONG)
ガチャ
GACHA (KACHAK)

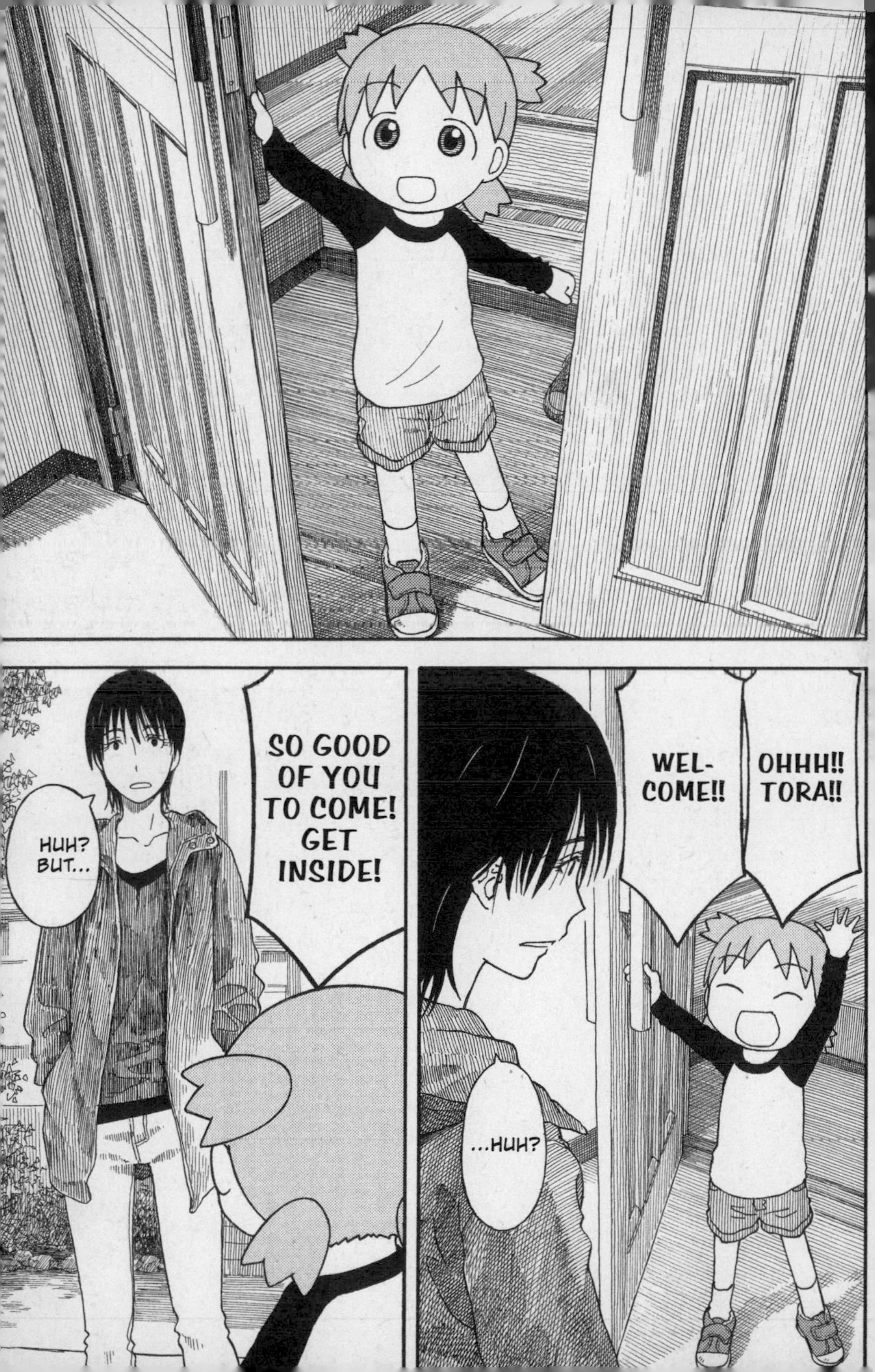
OHHH!! TORA!!
WEL-COME!!
...HUH?
SO GOOD OF YOU TO COME! GET INSIDE!
HUH? BUT...

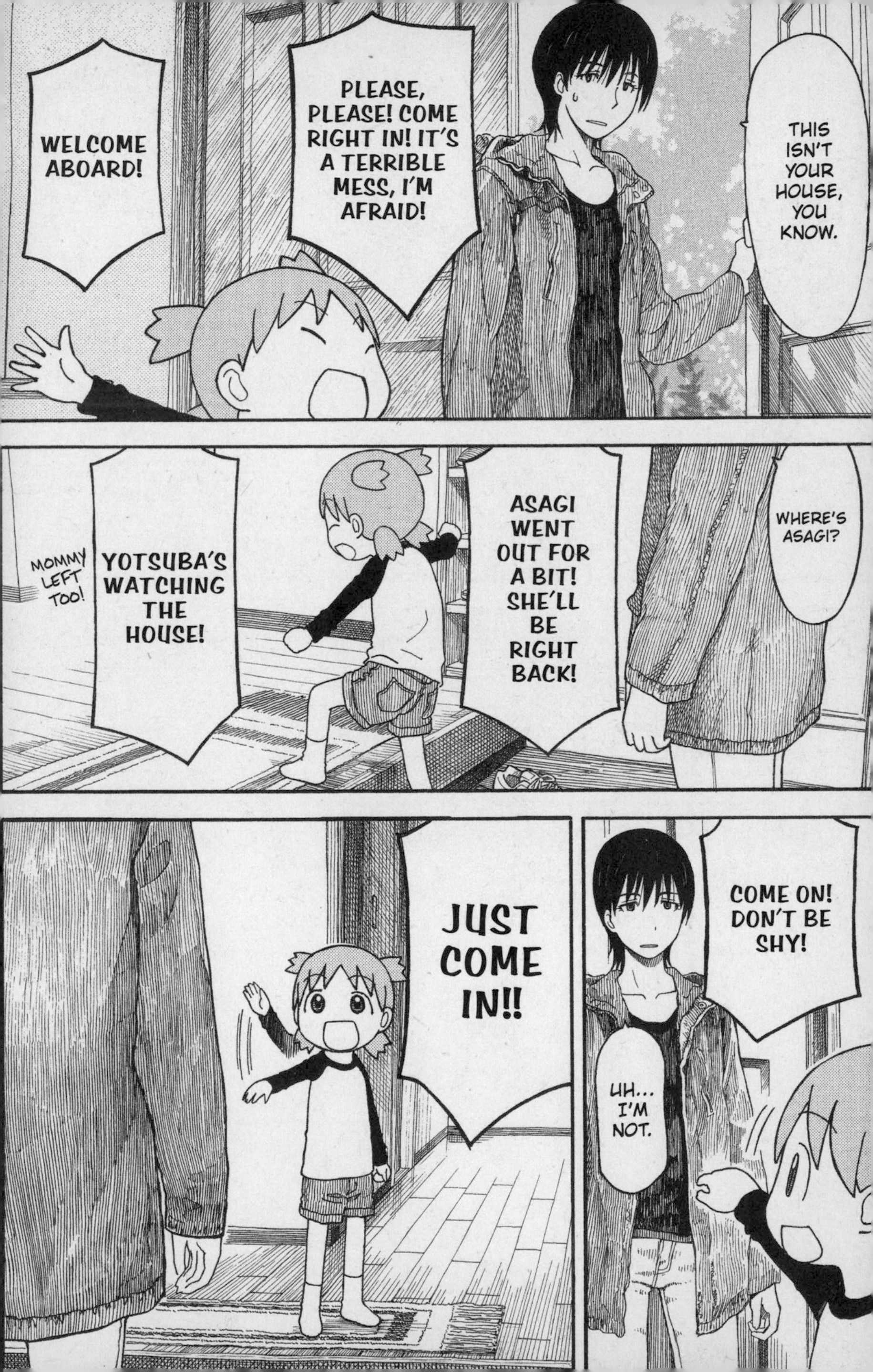
THIS ISN'T YOUR HOUSE, YOU KNOW.
PLEASE, PLEASE! COME RIGHT IN! IT'S A TERRIBLE MESS, I'M AFRAID!
WELCOME ABOARD!
WHERE'S ASAGI?
ASAGI WENT OUT FOR A BIT! SHE'LL BE RIGHT BACK!
YOTSUBA'S WATCHING THE HOUSE!
MOMMY LEFT TOO!
COME ON! DON'T BE SHY!
UH... I'M NOT.
JUST COME IN!!

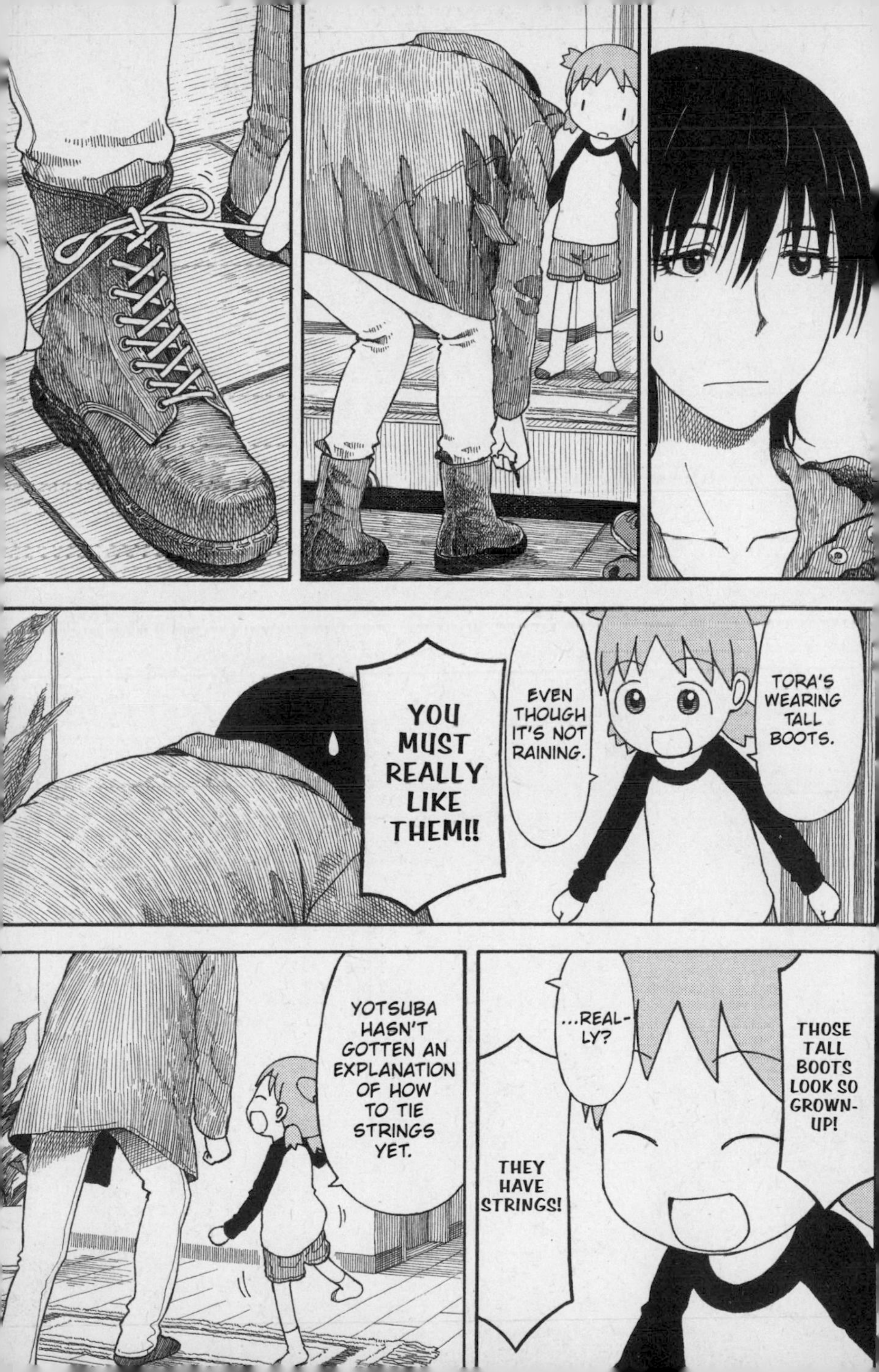
TORA'S WEARING TALL BOOTS.
EVEN THOUGH IT'S NOT RAINING.
YOU MUST REALLY LIKE THEM!!
THOSE TALL BOOTS LOOK SO GROWN-UP!
...REAL-LY?
THEY HAVE STRINGS!
YOTSUBA HASN'T GOTTEN AN EXPLANATION OF HOW TO TIE STRINGS YET.

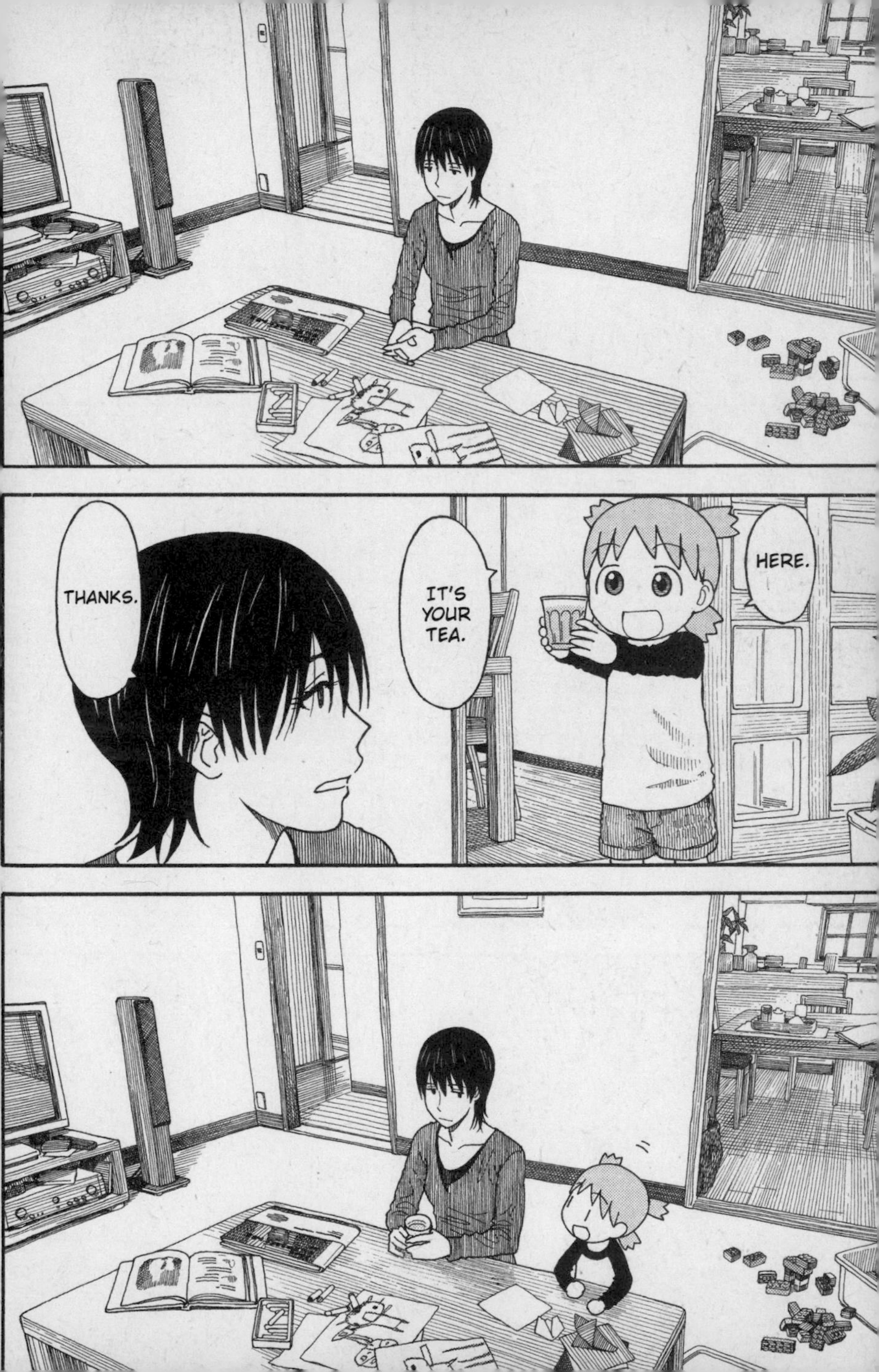
HERE.
IT'S YOUR TEA.
THANKS.

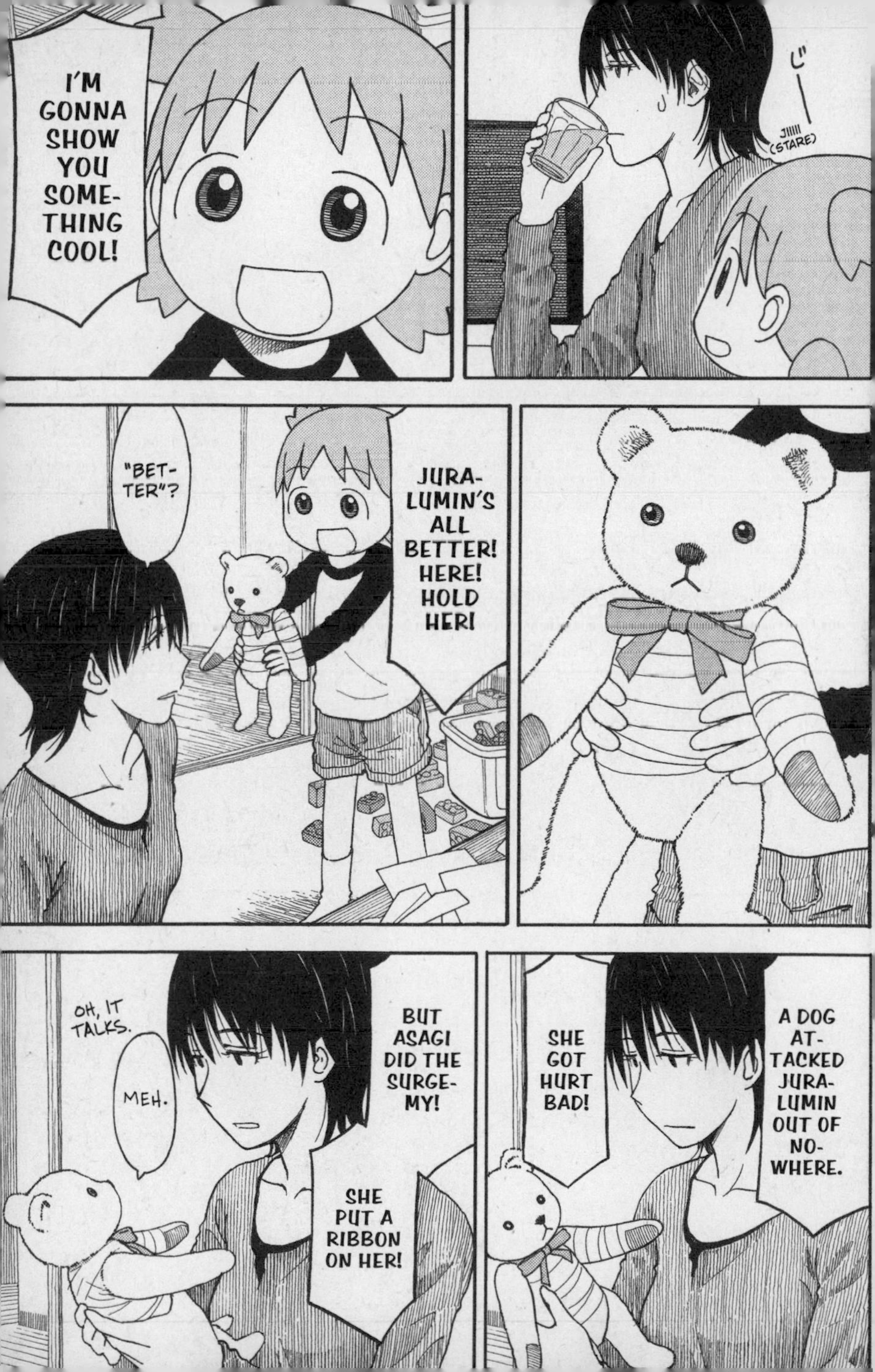
じー
JIIIII (STARE)
I'M GONNA SHOW YOU SOME-THING COOL!
JURA-LUMIN'S ALL BETTER! HERE! HOLD HER!
"BET-TER"?
A DOG AT-TACKED JURA-LUMIN OUT OF NO-WHERE.
SHE GOT HURT BAD!
BUT ASAGI DID THE SURGE-MY!
SHE PUT A RIBBON ON HER!
OH, IT TALKS.
MEH.

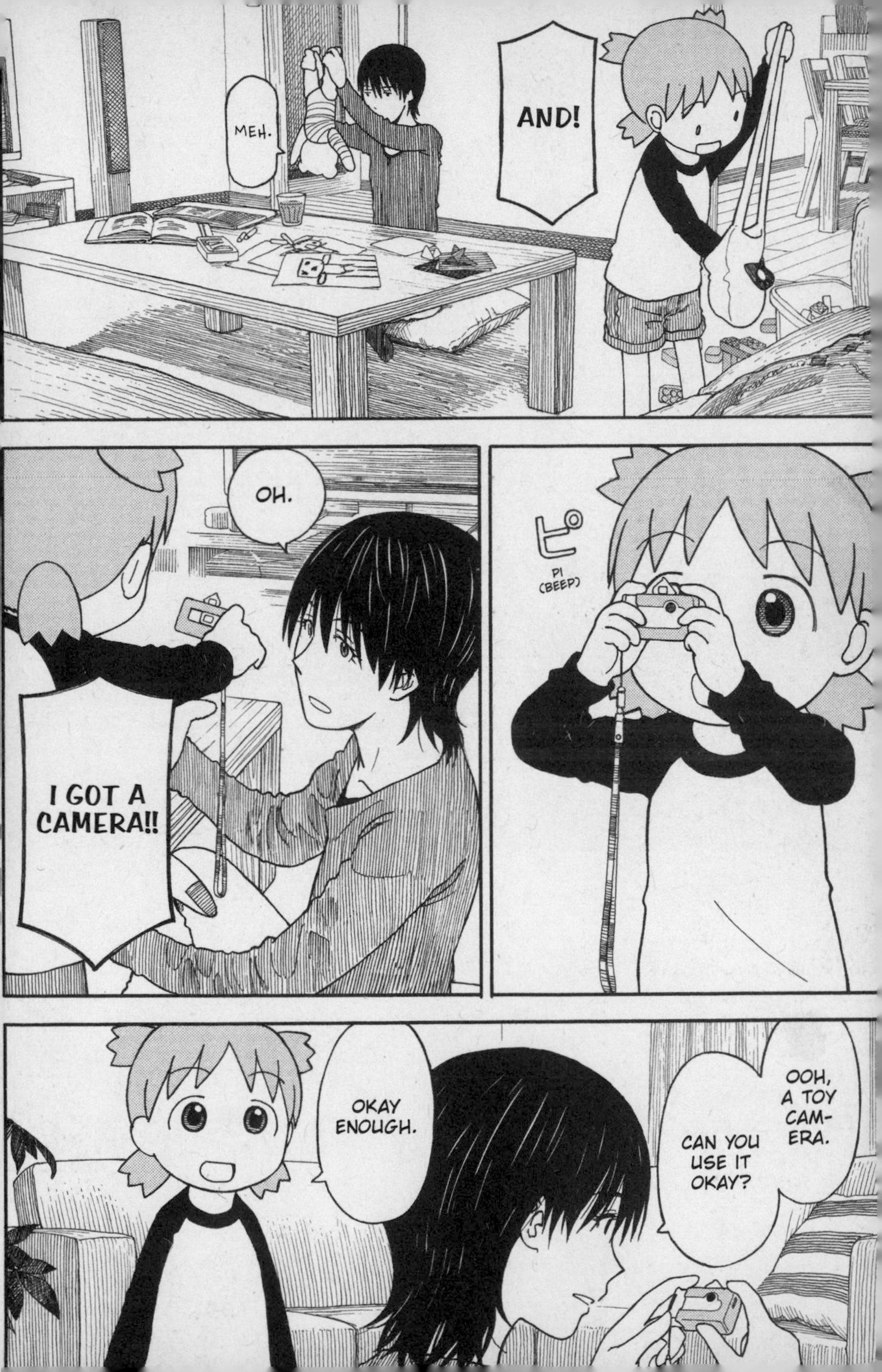
AND!
MEH.
ピ
PI
(BEEP)
OH.
I GOT A CAMERA!!
OOH, A TOY CAM-ERA.
CAN YOU USE IT OKAY?
OKAY ENOUGH.

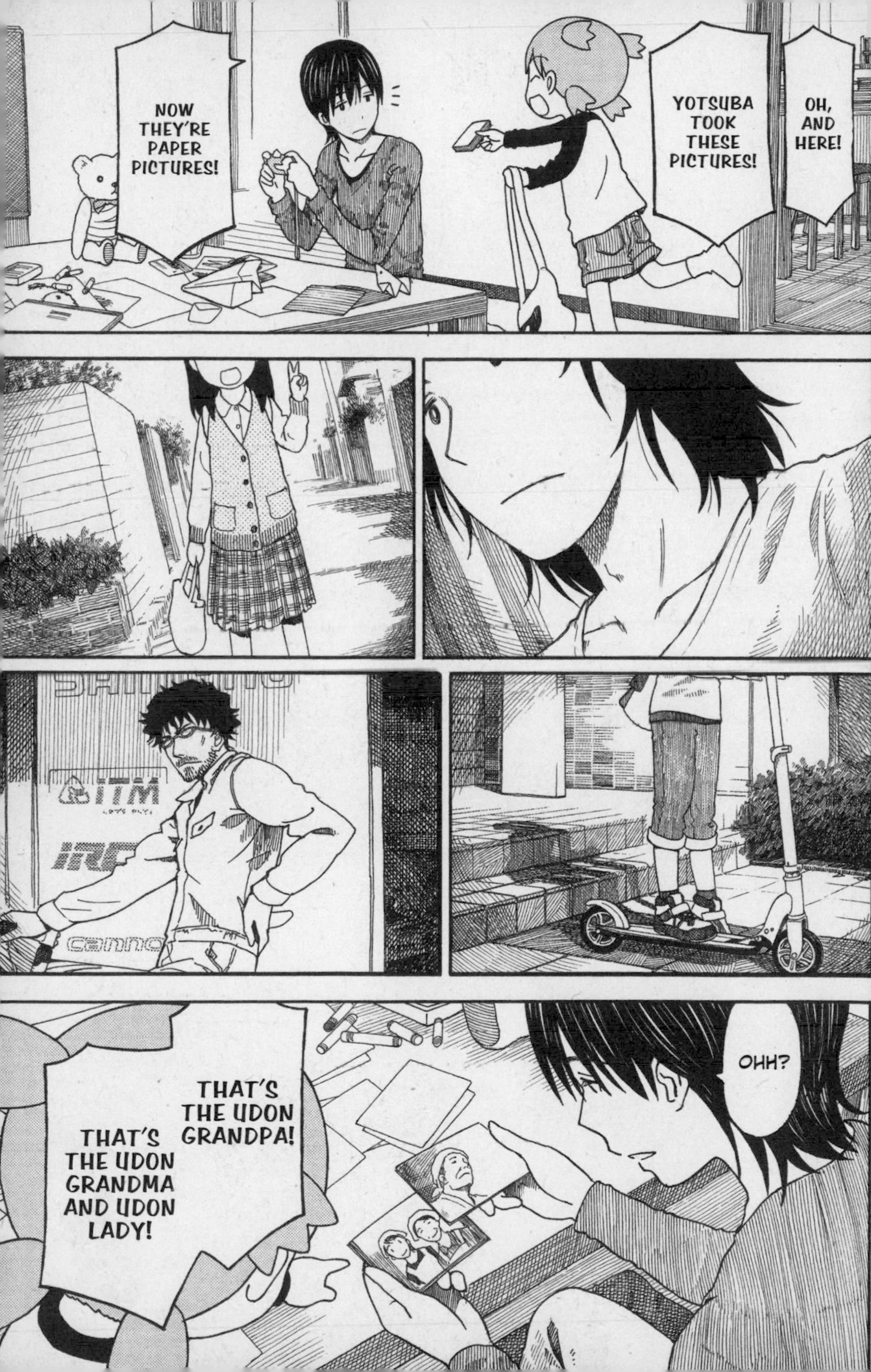
OH, AND HERE!
YOTSUBA TOOK THESE PICTURES!
NOW THEY'RE PAPER PICTURES!
OHH?
THAT'S THE UDON GRANDPA!
THAT'S THE UDON GRANDMA AND UDON LADY!

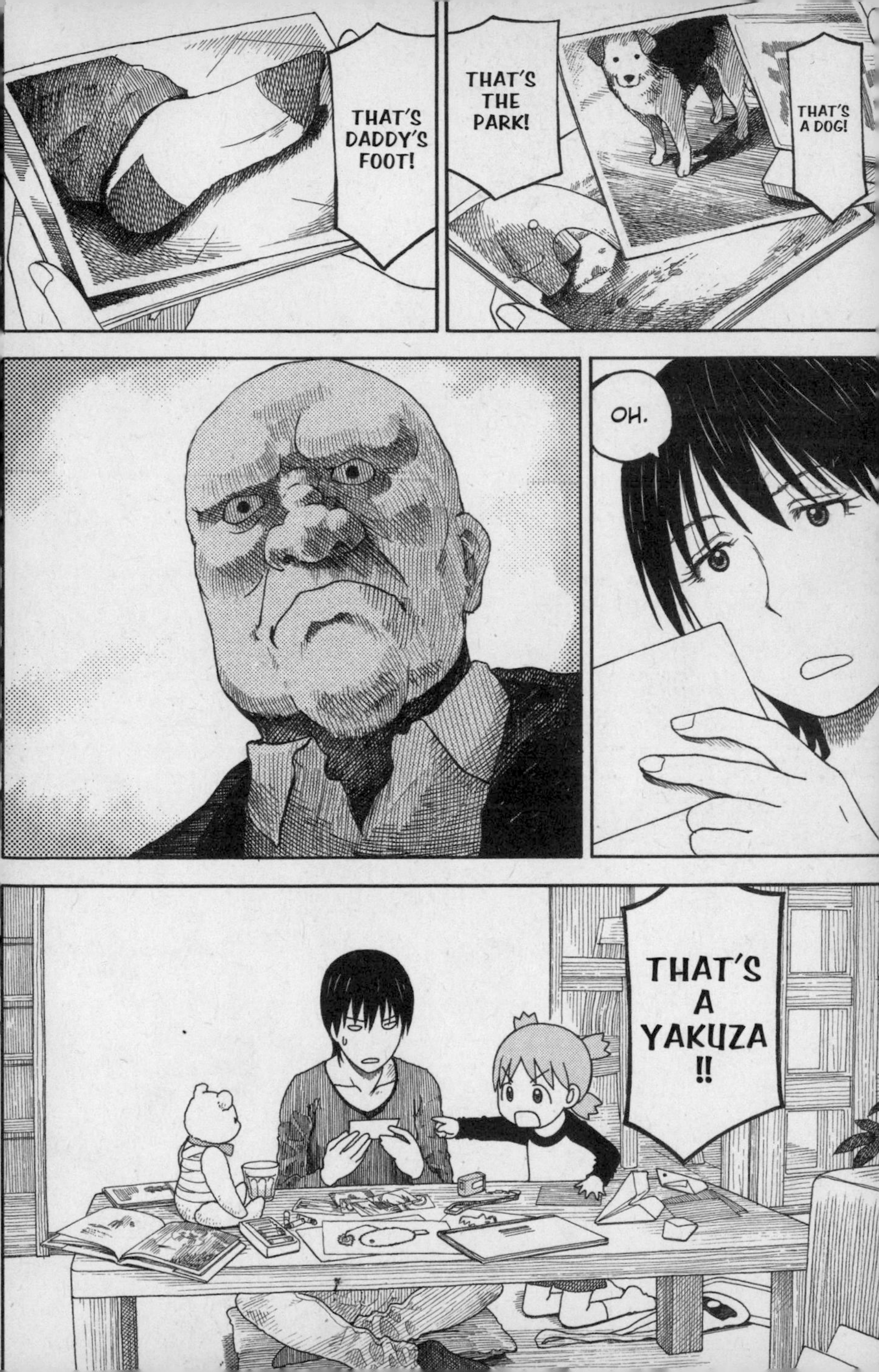
THAT'S A DOG!
THAT'S THE PARK!
THAT'S DADDY'S FOOT!
OH.
THAT'S A YAKUZA !!

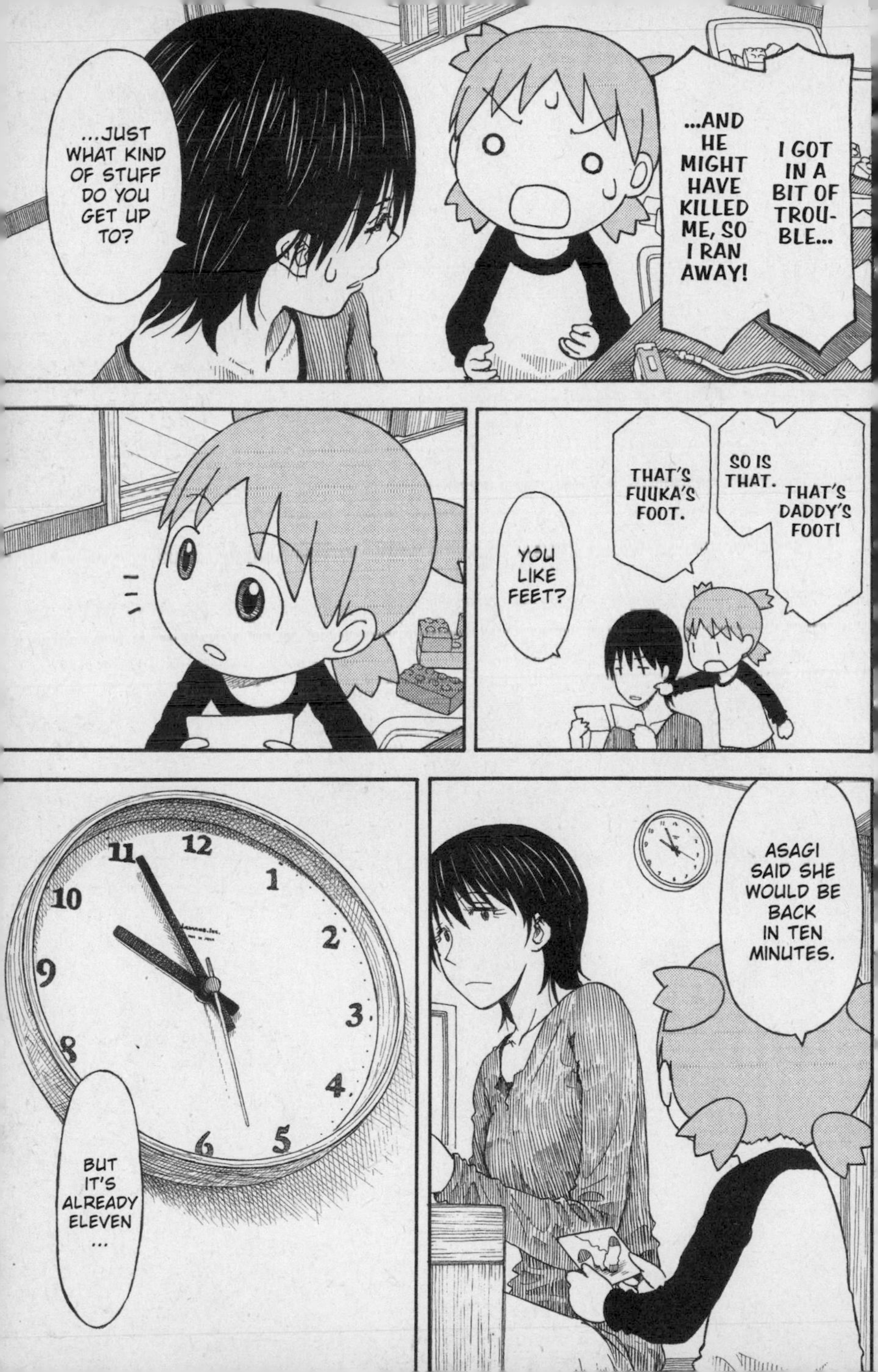
I GOT IN A BIT OF TROUBLE...
...AND HE MIGHT HAVE KILLED ME, SO I RAN AWAY!
...JUST WHAT KIND OF STUFF DO YOU GET UP TO?
THAT'S DADDY'S FOOT!
SO IS THAT.
THAT'S FUUKA'S FOOT.
YOU LIKE FEET?
ASAGI SAID SHE WOULD BE BACK IN TEN MINUTES.
BUT IT'S ALREADY ELEVEN ...

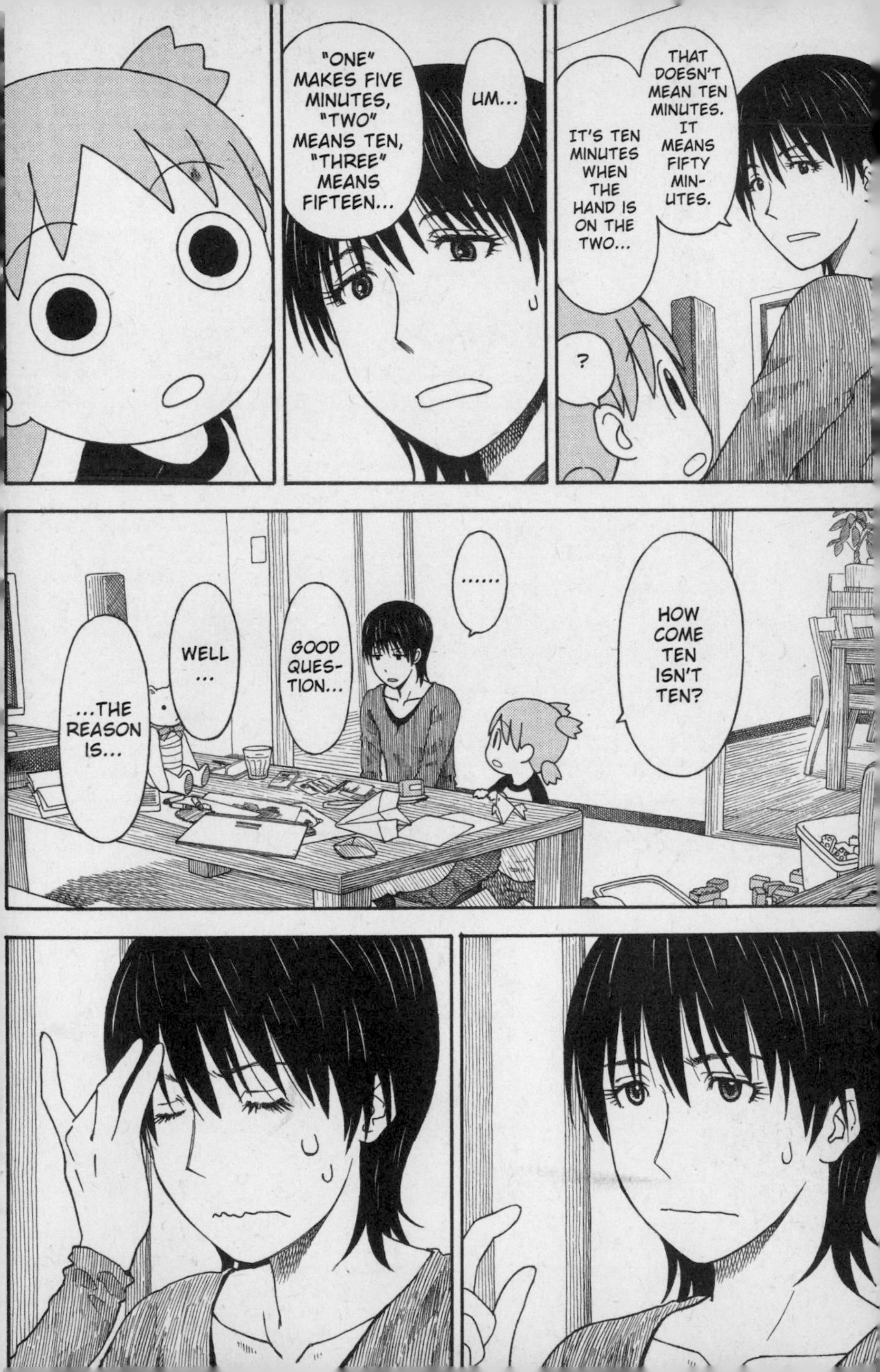
THAT DOESN'T MEAN TEN MINUTES. IT MEANS FIFTY MIN-UTES.
IT'S TEN MINUTES WHEN THE HAND IS ON THE TWO...
?
UM...
"ONE" MAKES FIVE MINUTES, "TWO" MEANS TEN, "THREE" MEANS FIFTEEN...
HOW COME TEN ISN'T TEN?
......
GOOD QUES-TION...
WELL ...
...THE REASON IS...

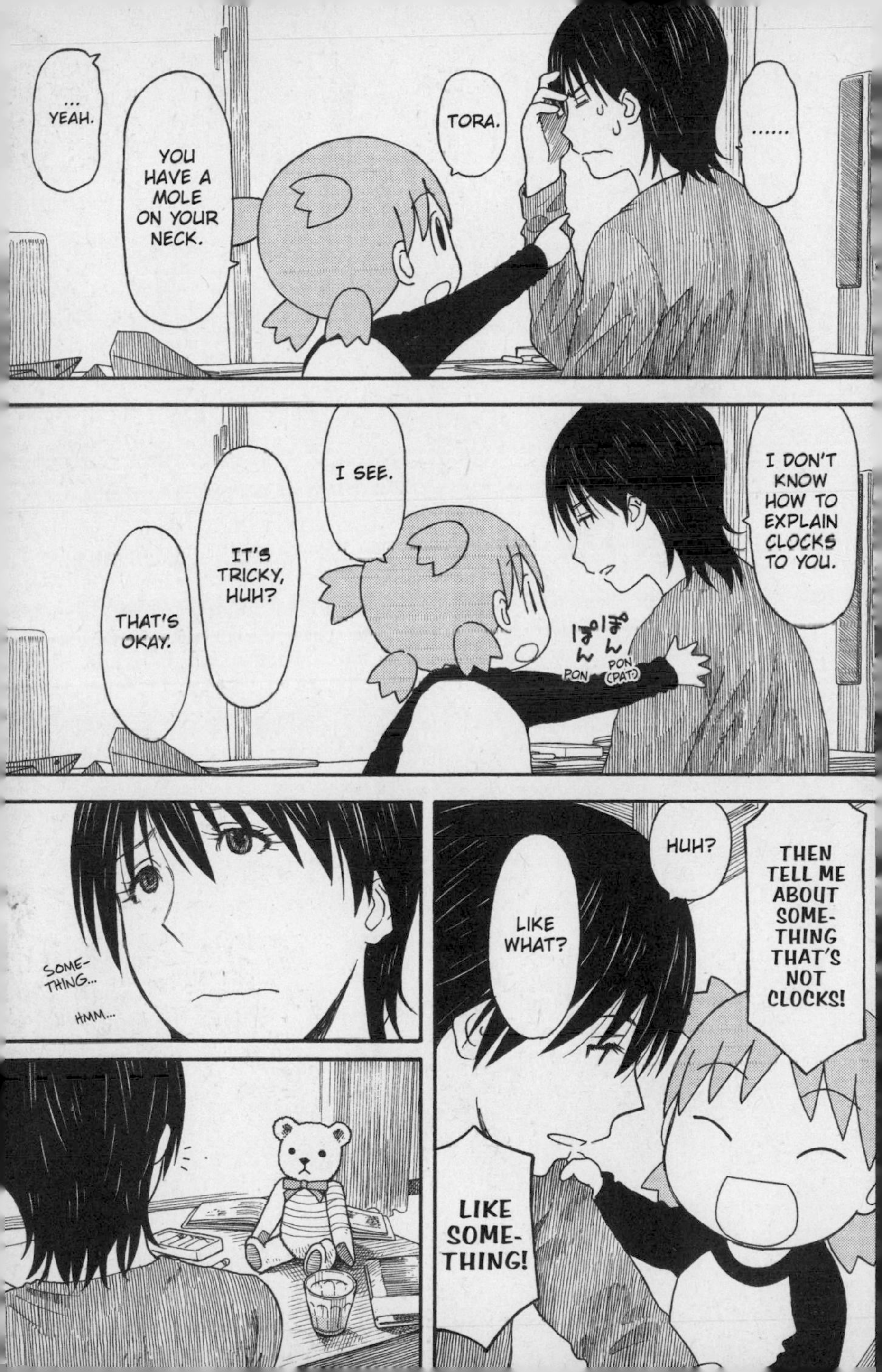
......
TORA.
YOU HAVE A MOLE ON YOUR NECK.
... YEAH.
I DON'T KNOW HOW TO EXPLAIN CLOCKS TO YOU.
ぽん ぽん
PON (PAT) PON
I SEE.
IT'S TRICKY, HUH?
THAT'S OKAY.
THEN TELL ME ABOUT SOME-THING THAT'S NOT CLOCKS!
HUH?
LIKE WHAT?
LIKE SOME-THING!
SOME-THING...
HMM...

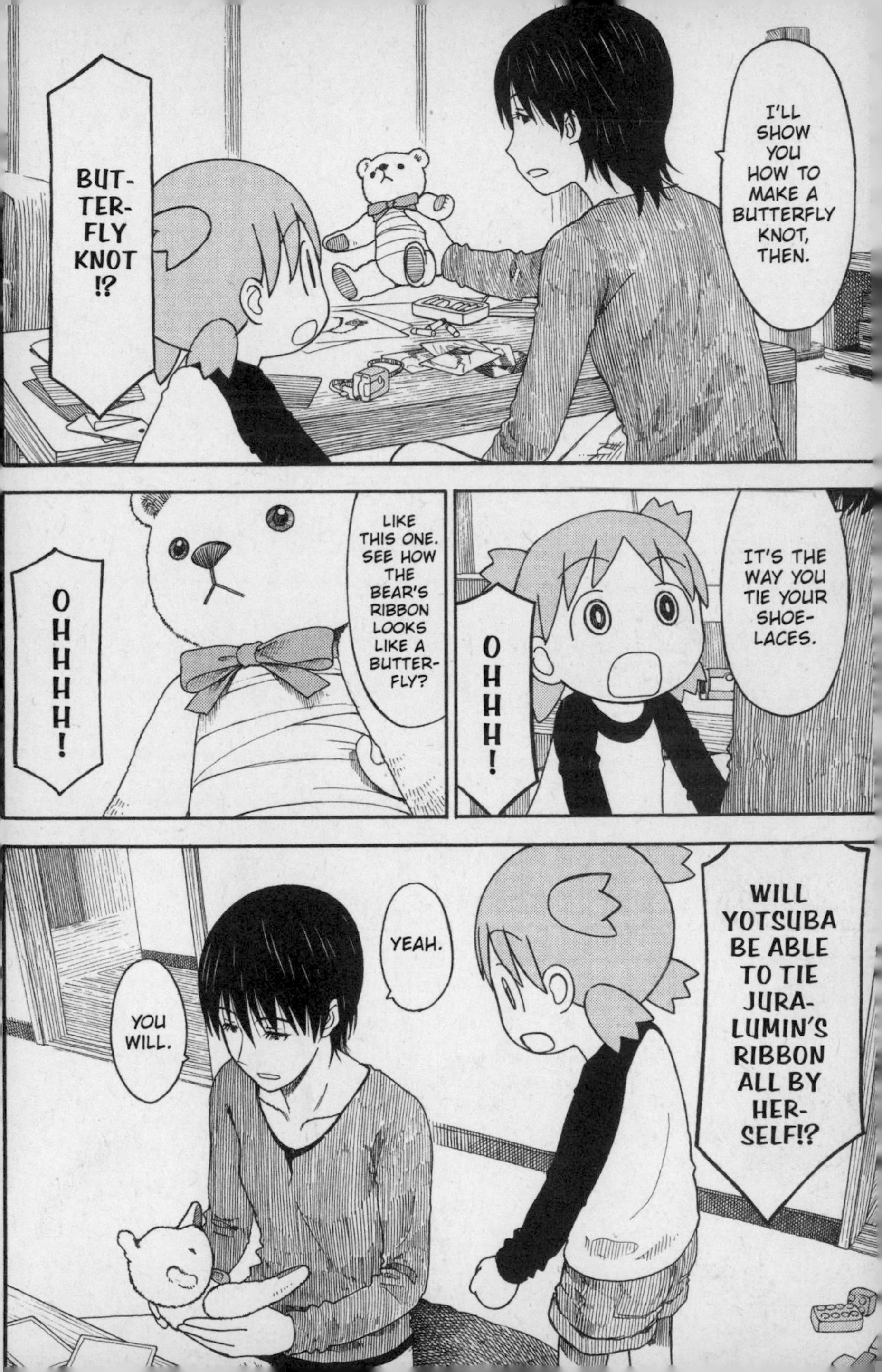
I'LL SHOW YOU HOW TO MAKE A BUTTERFLY KNOT, THEN.
BUTTERFLY KNOT!?
IT'S THE WAY YOU TIE YOUR SHOELACES.
OHHH!
LIKE THIS ONE. SEE HOW THE BEAR'S RIBBON LOOKS LIKE A BUTTERFLY?
OHHHH!
WILL YOTSUBA BE ABLE TO TIE JURALUMIN'S RIBBON ALL BY HERSELF!?
YEAH.
YOU WILL.

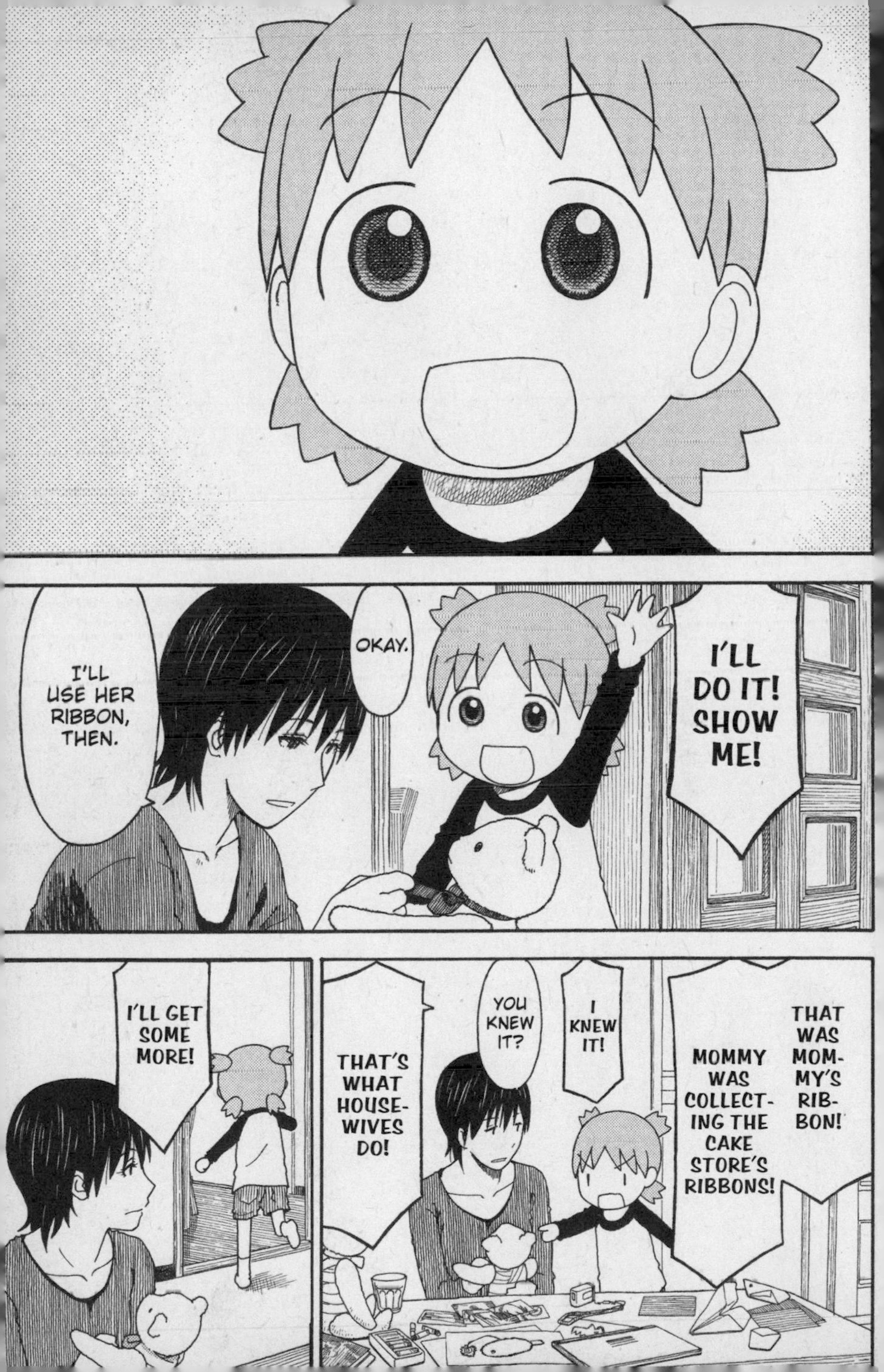
I'LL DO IT! SHOW ME!
OKAY.
I'LL USE HER RIBBON, THEN.
THAT WAS MOMMY'S RIBBON!
MOMMY WAS COLLECTING THE CAKE STORE'S RIBBONS!
I KNEW IT!
YOU KNEW IT?
THAT'S WHAT HOUSEWIVES DO!
I'LL GET SOME MORE!

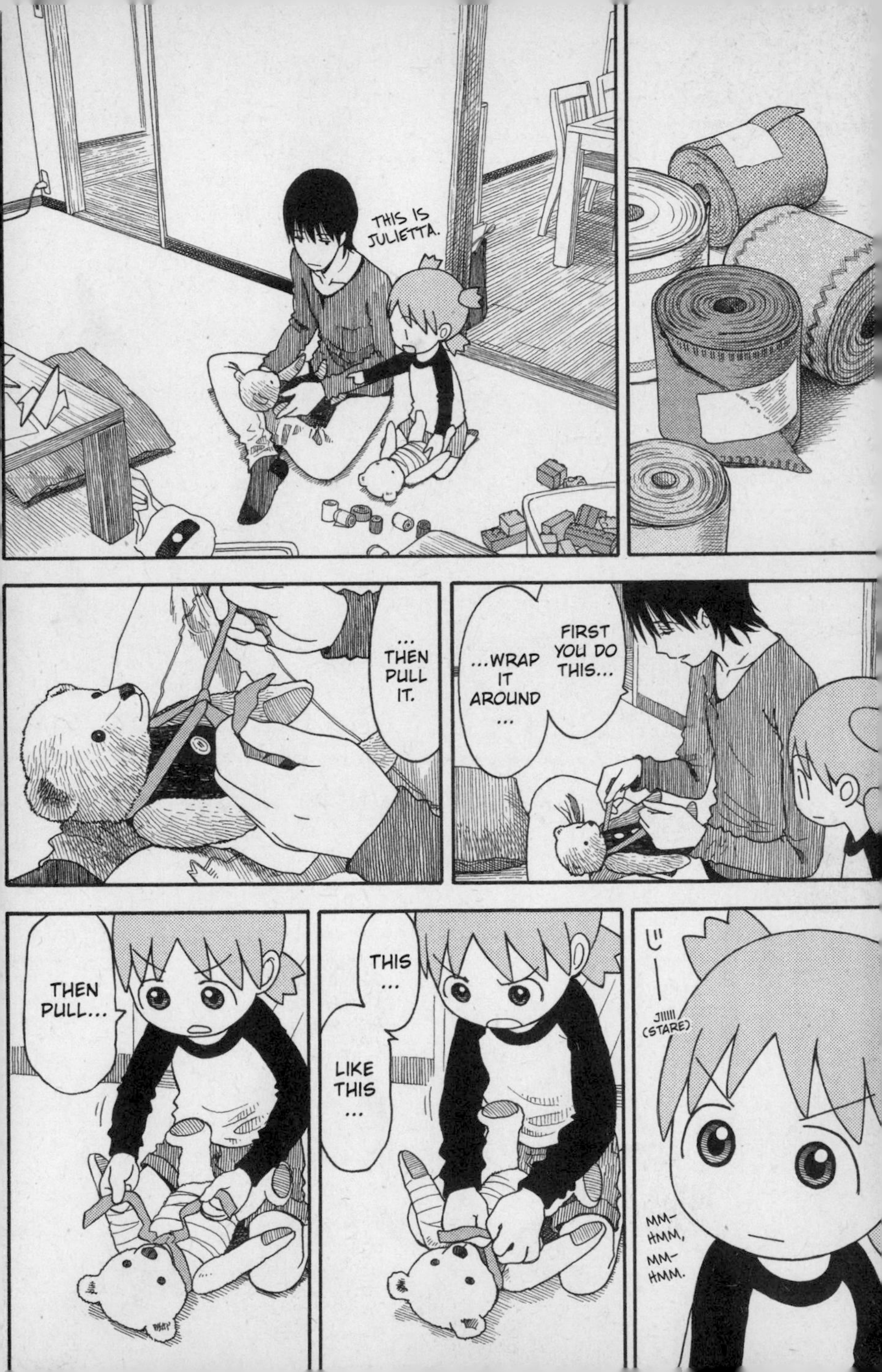
THIS IS JULIETTA.
FIRST YOU DO THIS...
...WRAP IT AROUND ...
... THEN PULL IT.
じー
JIIIII (STARE)
MM-HMM, MM-HMM.
THIS ...
LIKE THIS ...
THEN PULL...

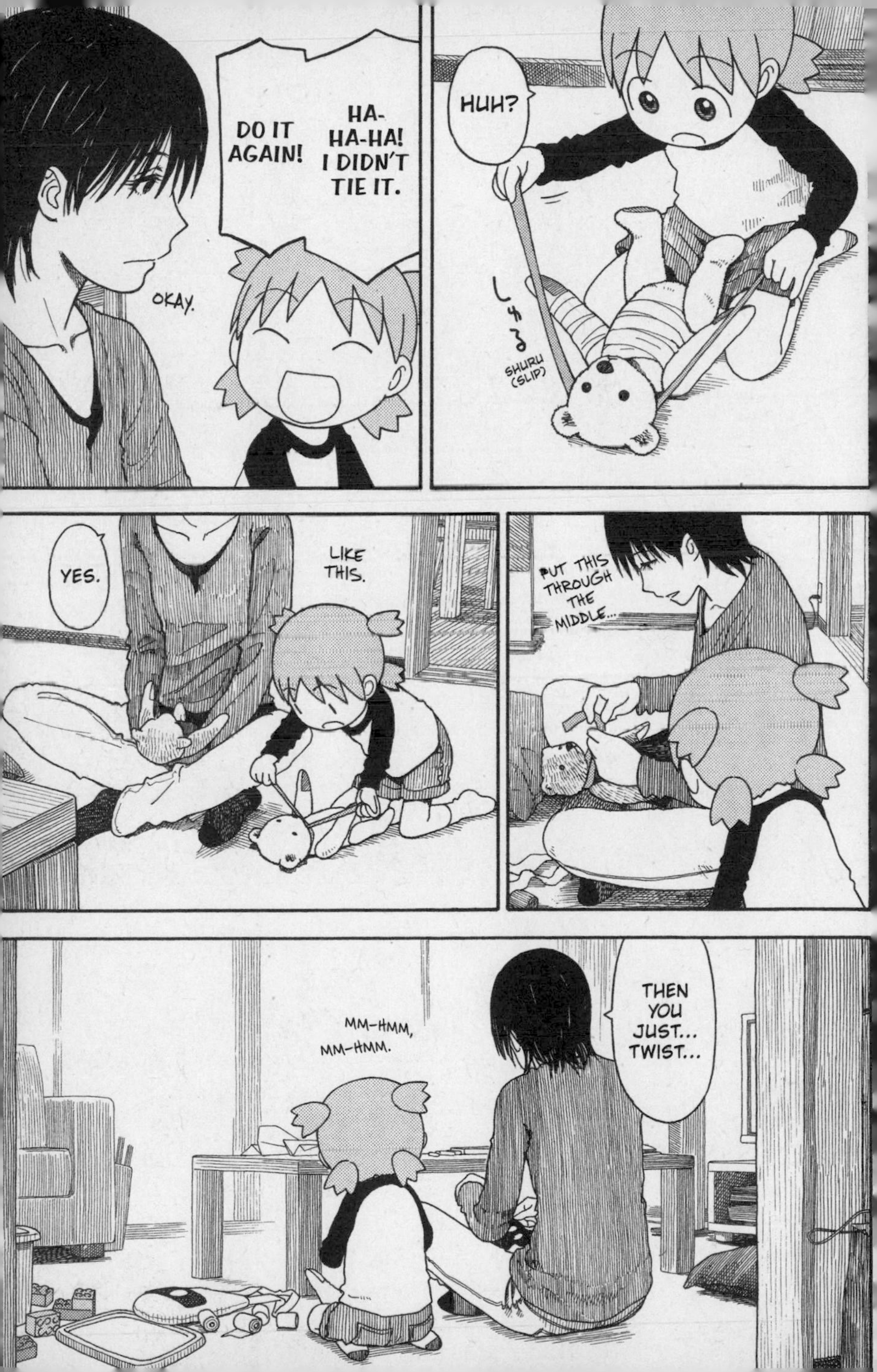
HUH?
しゅる
SHURU (SLIP)
HA-HA-HA! I DIDN'T TIE IT.
DO IT AGAIN!
OKAY.
PUT THIS THROUGH THE MIDDLE...
LIKE THIS.
YES.
THEN YOU JUST... TWIST...
MM-HMM, MM-HMM.

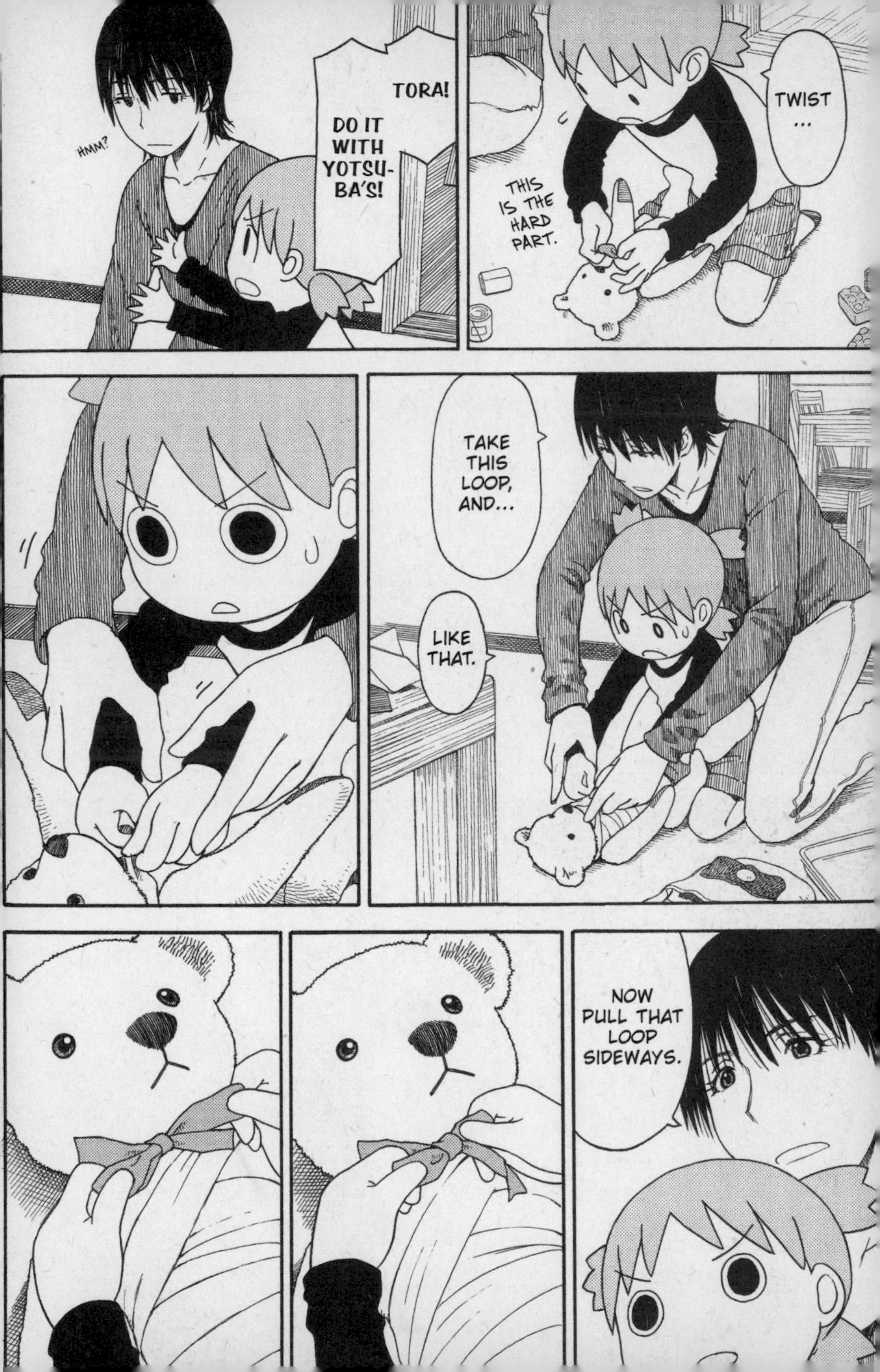
TWIST ...
THIS IS THE HARD PART.
TORA!
DO IT WITH YOTSU-BA'S!
HMM?
TAKE THIS LOOP, AND...
LIKE THAT.
NOW PULL THAT LOOP SIDEWAYS.

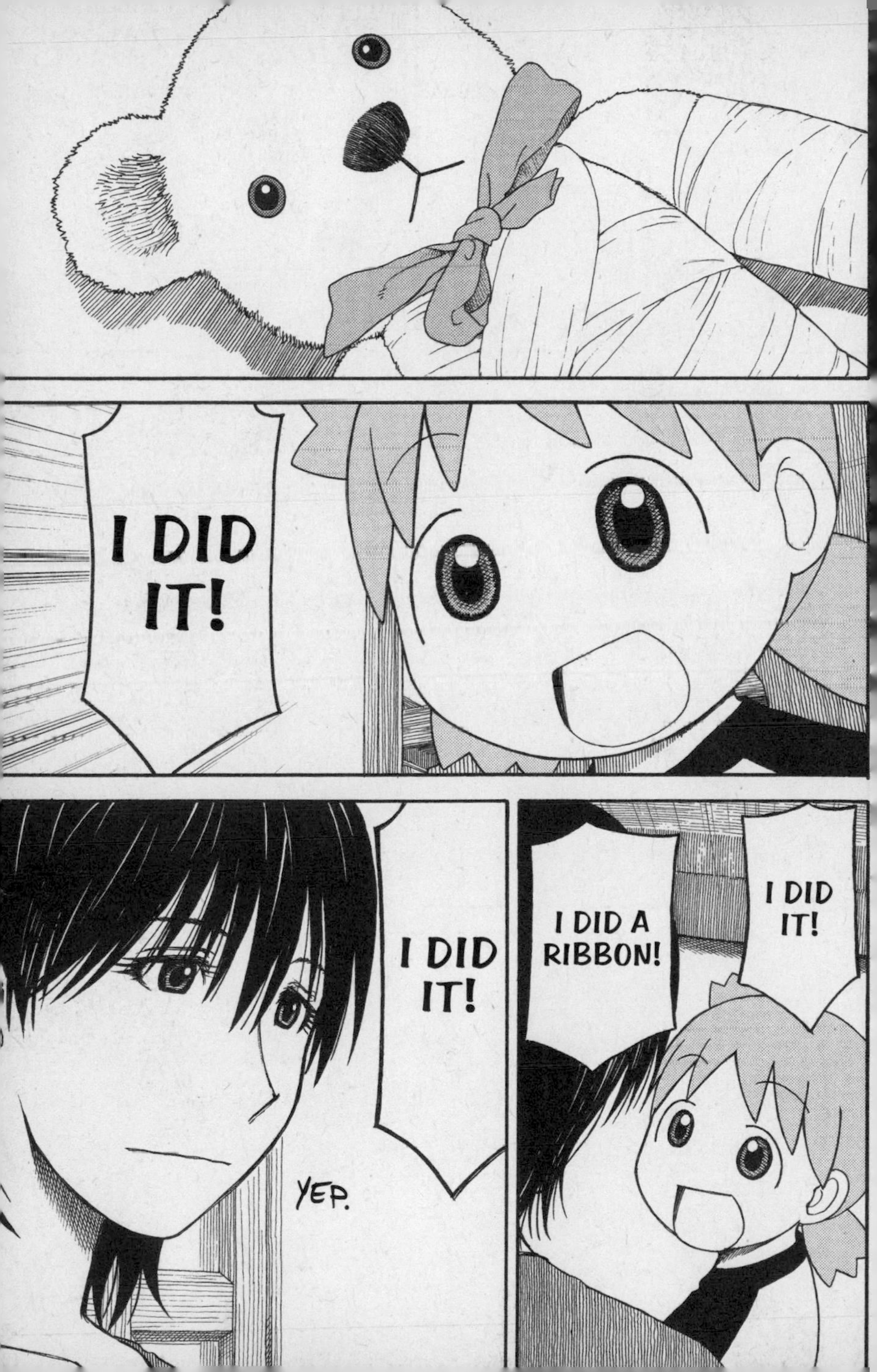
I DID IT!
I DID IT!
I DID A RIBBON!
I DID IT!
YEP.

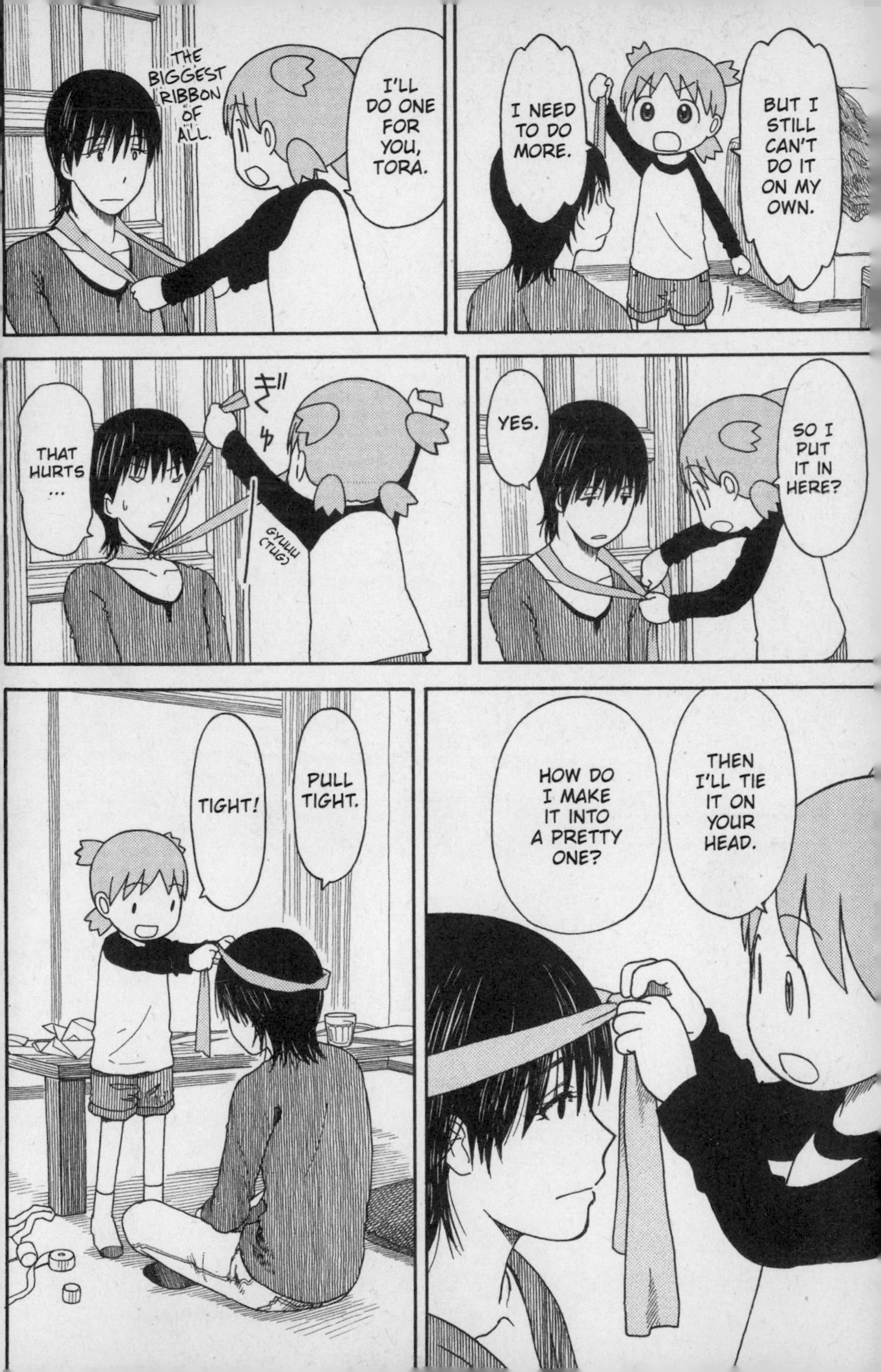
BUT I STILL CAN'T DO IT ON MY OWN.
I NEED TO DO MORE.
I'LL DO ONE FOR YOU, TORA.
THE BIGGEST RIBBON OF ALL.
SO I PUT IT IN HERE?
YES.
ぎゅ
GYUUU (TUG)
THAT HURTS...
THEN I'LL TIE IT ON YOUR HEAD.
HOW DO I MAKE IT INTO A PRETTY ONE?
PULL TIGHT.
TIGHT!

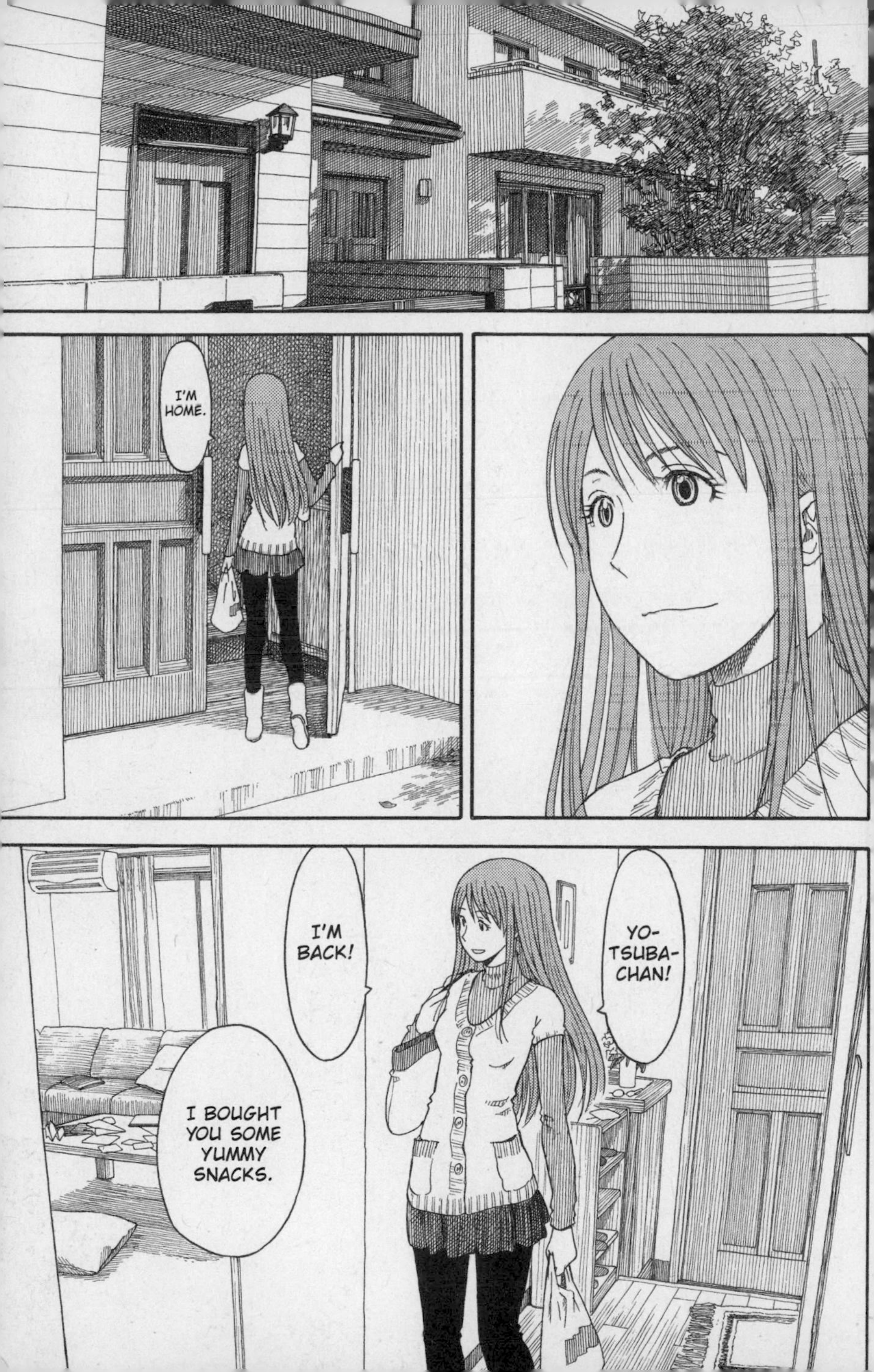
I'M HOME.
YO-TSUBA-CHAN!
I'M BACK!
I BOUGHT YOU SOME YUMMY SNACKS.

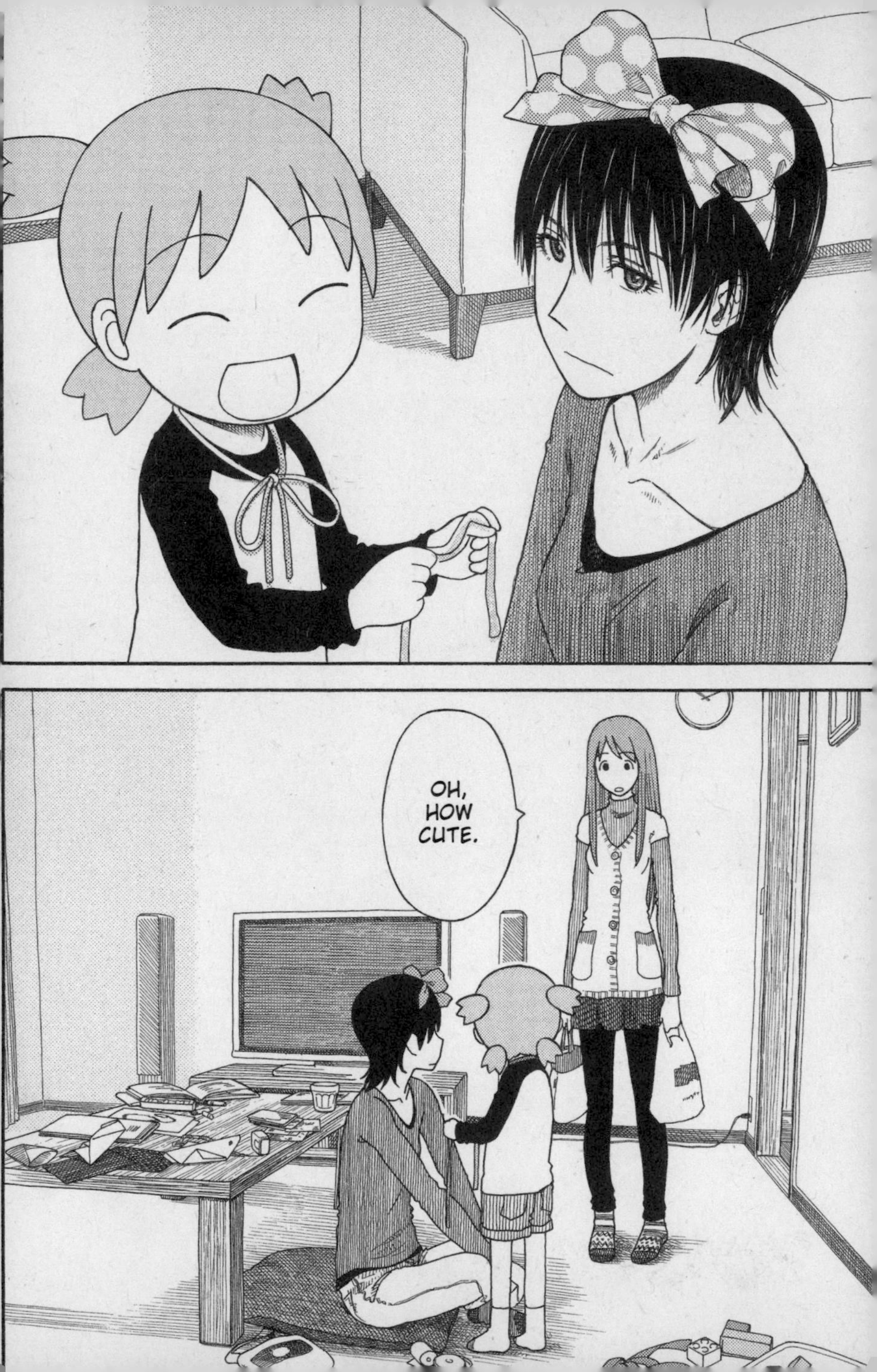
OH, HOW CUTE.

**YOTSUBA&!**

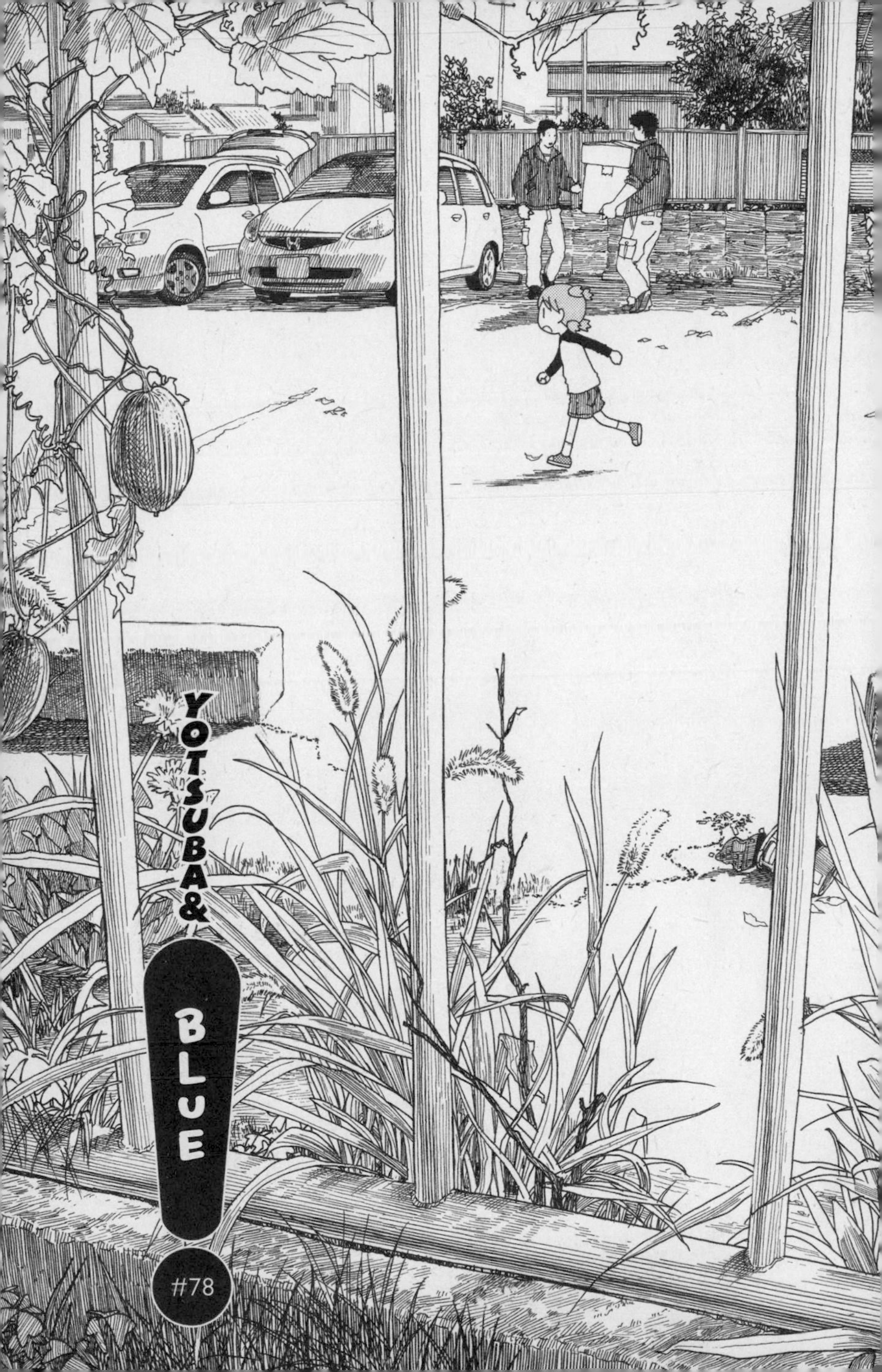
YOTSUBA&
BLUE
#78

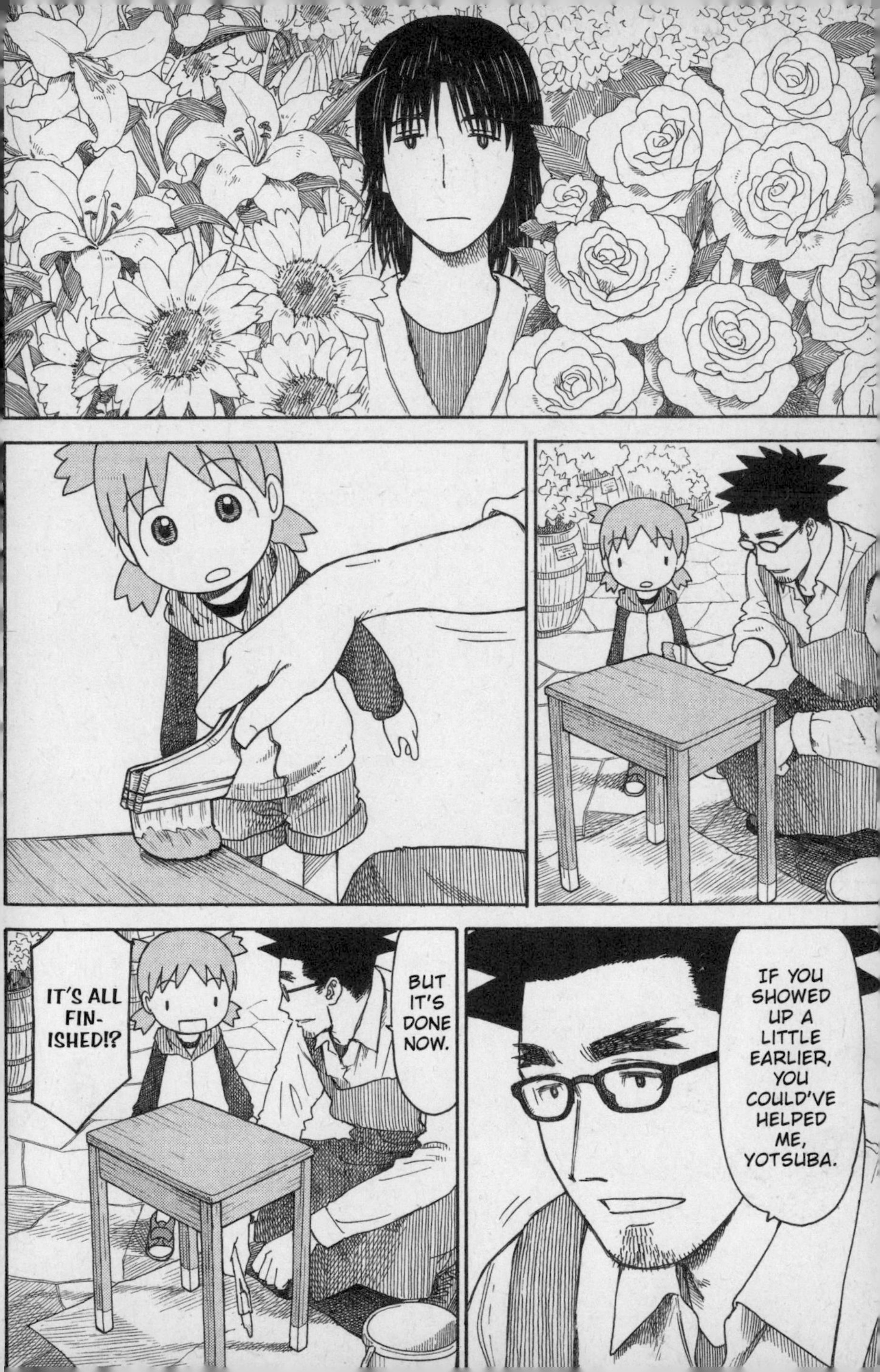
IF YOU SHOWED UP A LITTLE EARLIER, YOU COULD'VE HELPED ME, YOTSUBA.
BUT IT'S DONE NOW.
IT'S ALL FIN-ISHED!?

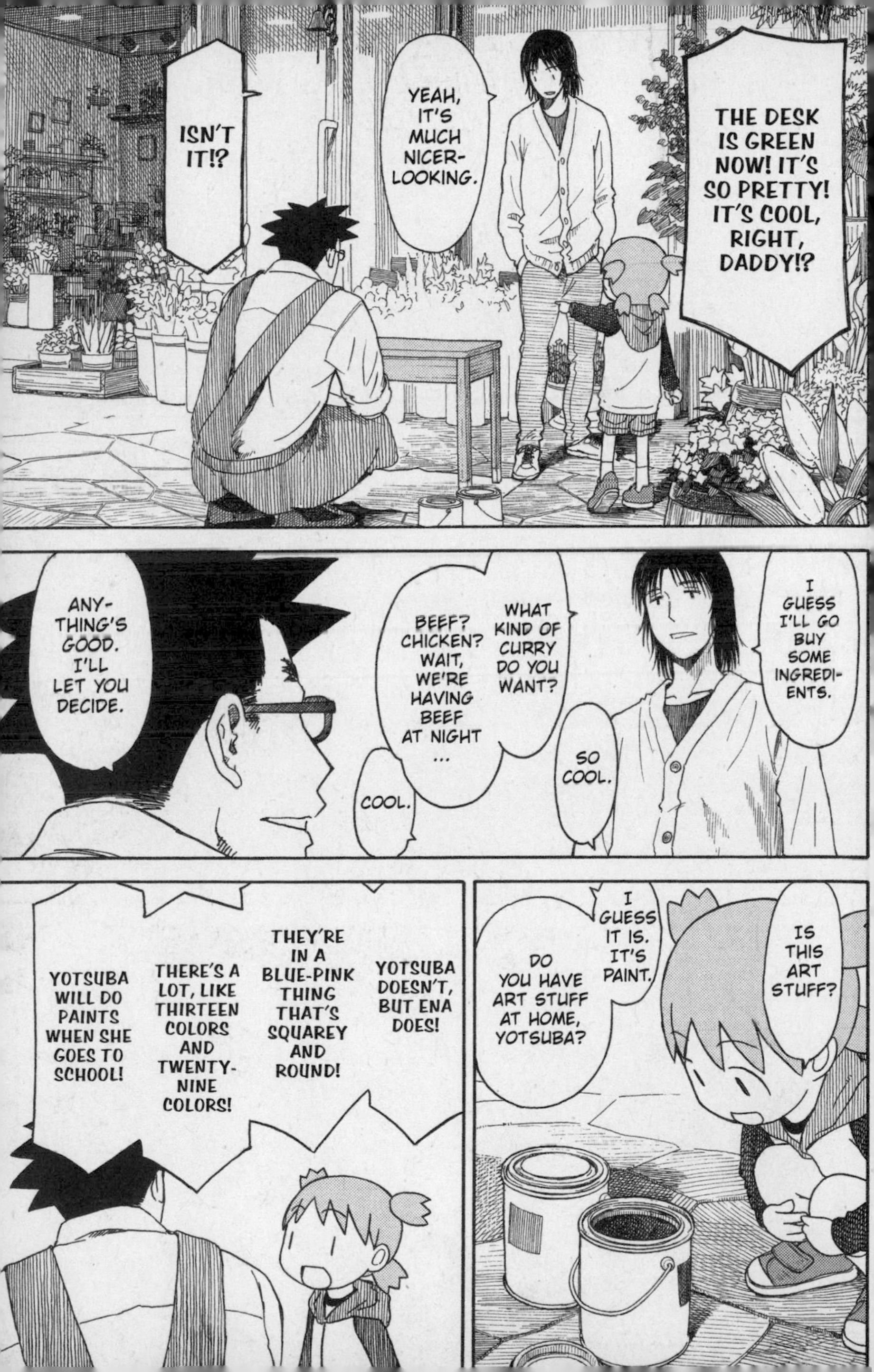
THE DESK IS GREEN NOW! IT'S SO PRETTY! IT'S COOL, RIGHT, DADDY!?
YEAH, IT'S MUCH NICER-LOOKING.
ISN'T IT!?
I GUESS I'LL GO BUY SOME INGREDIENTS.
SO COOL.
WHAT KIND OF CURRY DO YOU WANT?
BEEF? CHICKEN? WAIT, WE'RE HAVING BEEF AT NIGHT ...
COOL.
ANYTHING'S GOOD. I'LL LET YOU DECIDE.
IS THIS ART STUFF?
I GUESS IT IS. IT'S PAINT.
DO YOU HAVE ART STUFF AT HOME, YOTSUBA?
YOTSUBA DOESN'T, BUT ENA DOES!
THEY'RE IN A BLUE-PINK THING THAT'S SQUAREY AND ROUND!
THERE'S A LOT, LIKE THIRTEEN COLORS AND TWENTY-NINE COLORS!
YOTSUBA WILL DO PAINTS WHEN SHE GOES TO SCHOOL!

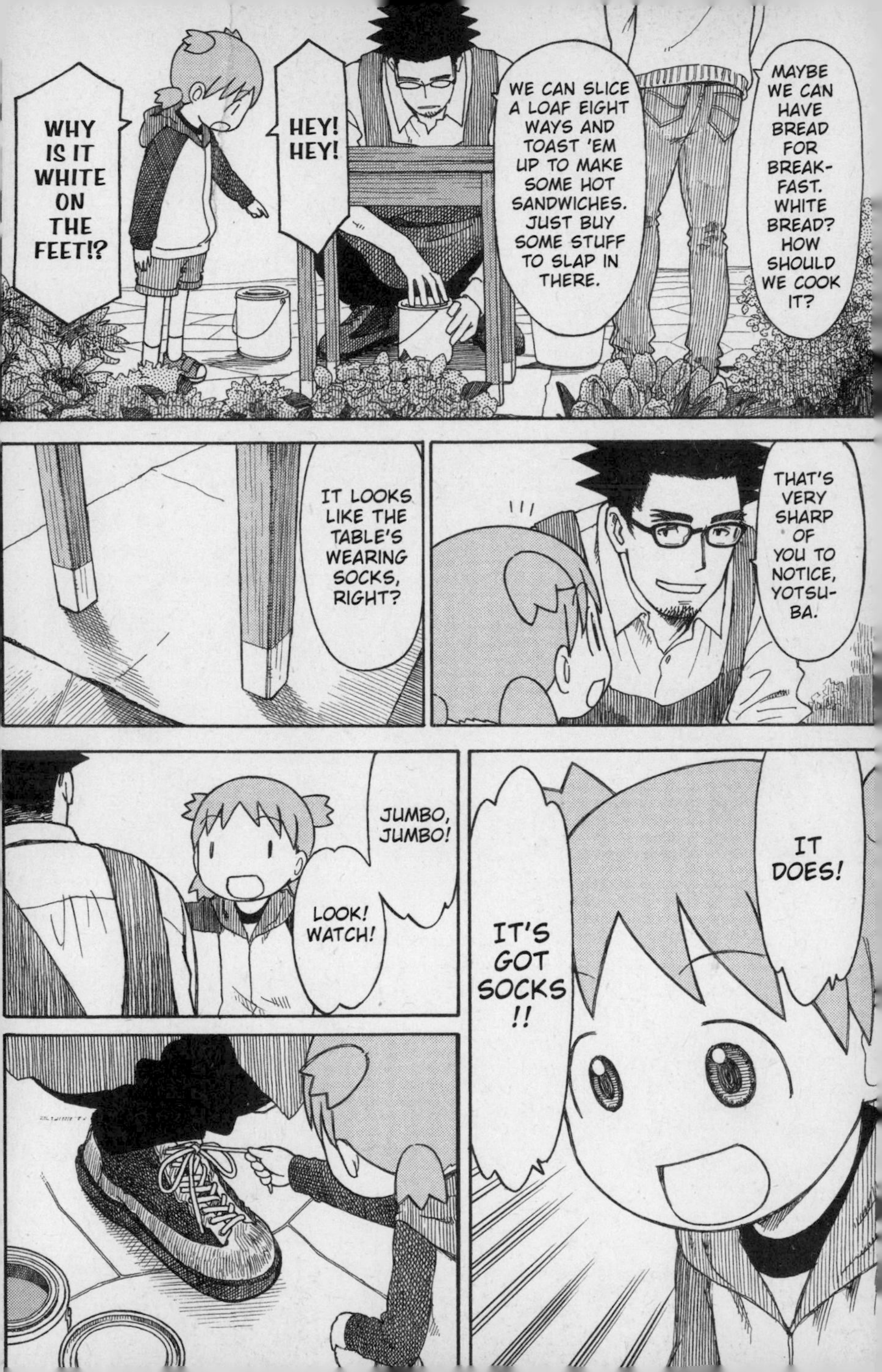
MAYBE WE CAN HAVE BREAD FOR BREAK-FAST. WHITE BREAD? HOW SHOULD WE COOK IT?
WE CAN SLICE A LOAF EIGHT WAYS AND TOAST 'EM UP TO MAKE SOME HOT SANDWICHES. JUST BUY SOME STUFF TO SLAP IN THERE.
HEY! HEY!
WHY IS IT WHITE ON THE FEET!?
THAT'S VERY SHARP OF YOU TO NOTICE, YOTSU-BA.
IT LOOKS LIKE THE TABLE'S WEARING SOCKS, RIGHT?
IT DOES!
IT'S GOT SOCKS!!
JUMBO, JUMBO!
LOOK! WATCH!

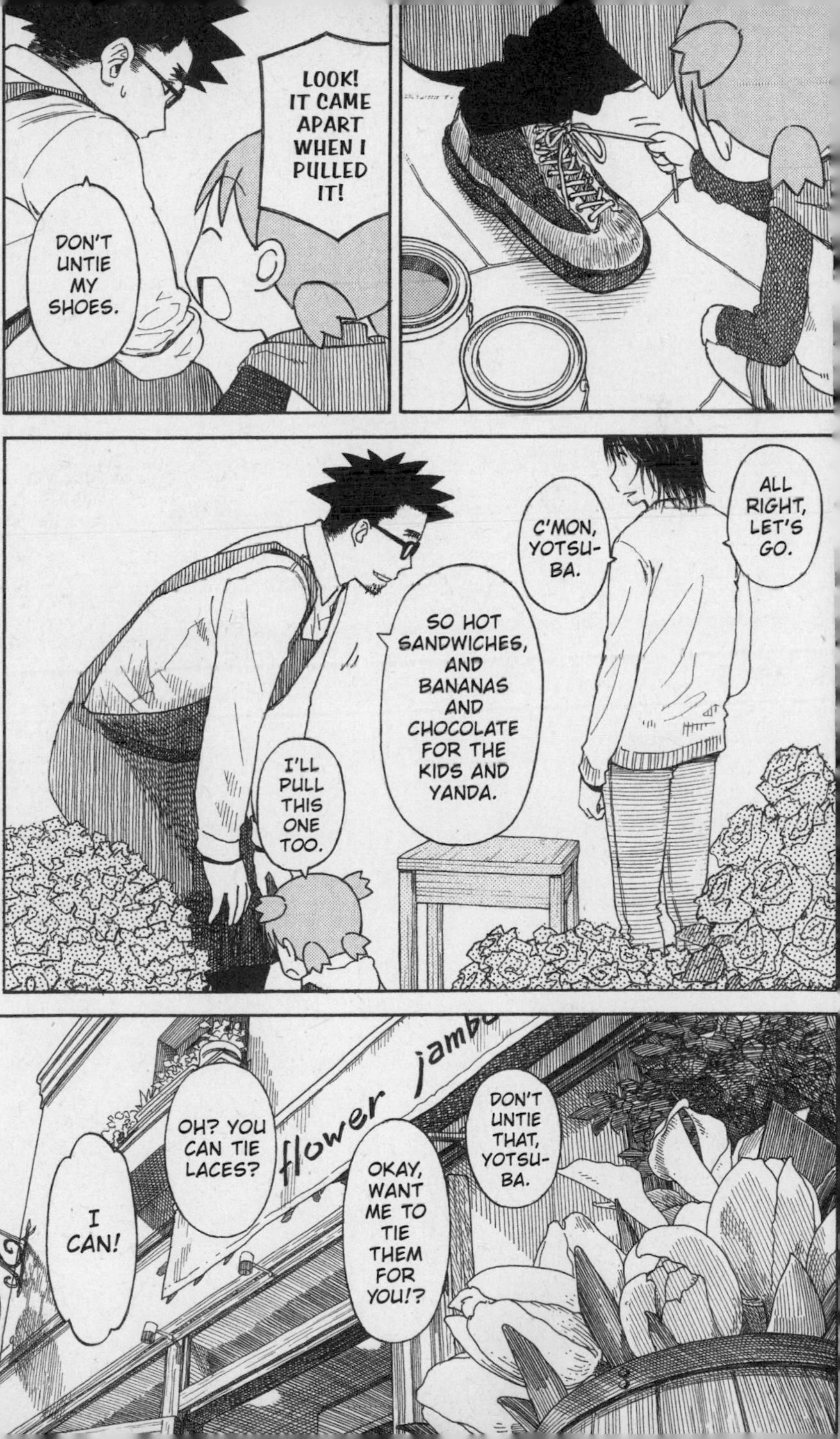
LOOK! IT CAME APART WHEN I PULLED IT!
DON'T UNTIE MY SHOES.
ALL RIGHT, LET'S GO.
C'MON, YOTSU-BA.
SO HOT SANDWICHES, AND BANANAS AND CHOCOLATE FOR THE KIDS AND YANDA.
I'LL PULL THIS ONE TOO.
DON'T UNTIE THAT, YOTSU-BA.
OKAY, WANT ME TO TIE THEM FOR YOU!?
OH? YOU CAN TIE LACES?
I CAN!
flower jambo

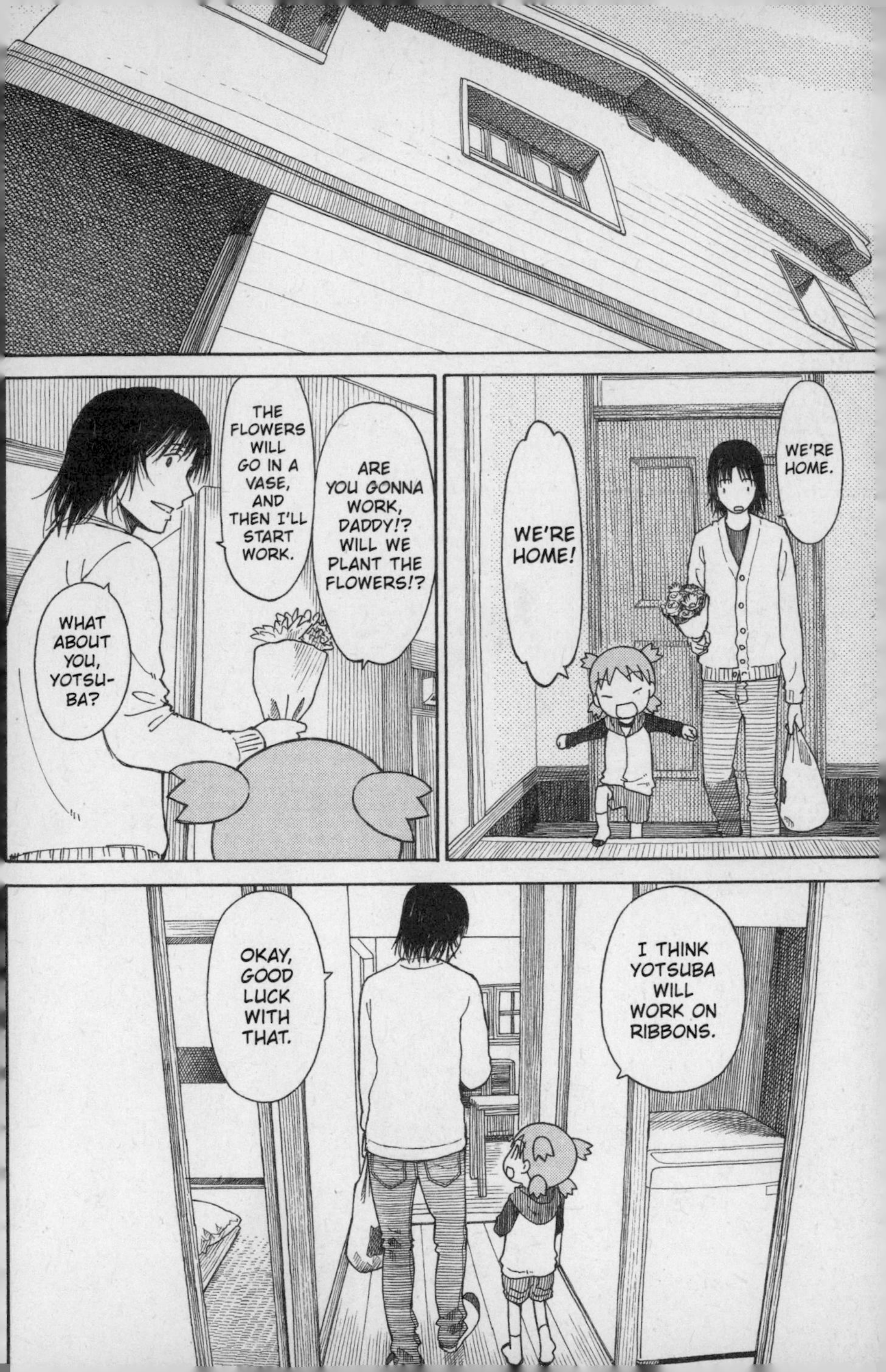
WE'RE HOME.
WE'RE HOME!
ARE YOU GONNA WORK, DADDY!? WILL WE PLANT THE FLOWERS!?
THE FLOWERS WILL GO IN A VASE, AND THEN I'LL START WORK.
WHAT ABOUT YOU, YOTSUBA?
I THINK YOTSUBA WILL WORK ON RIBBONS.
OKAY, GOOD LUCK WITH THAT.

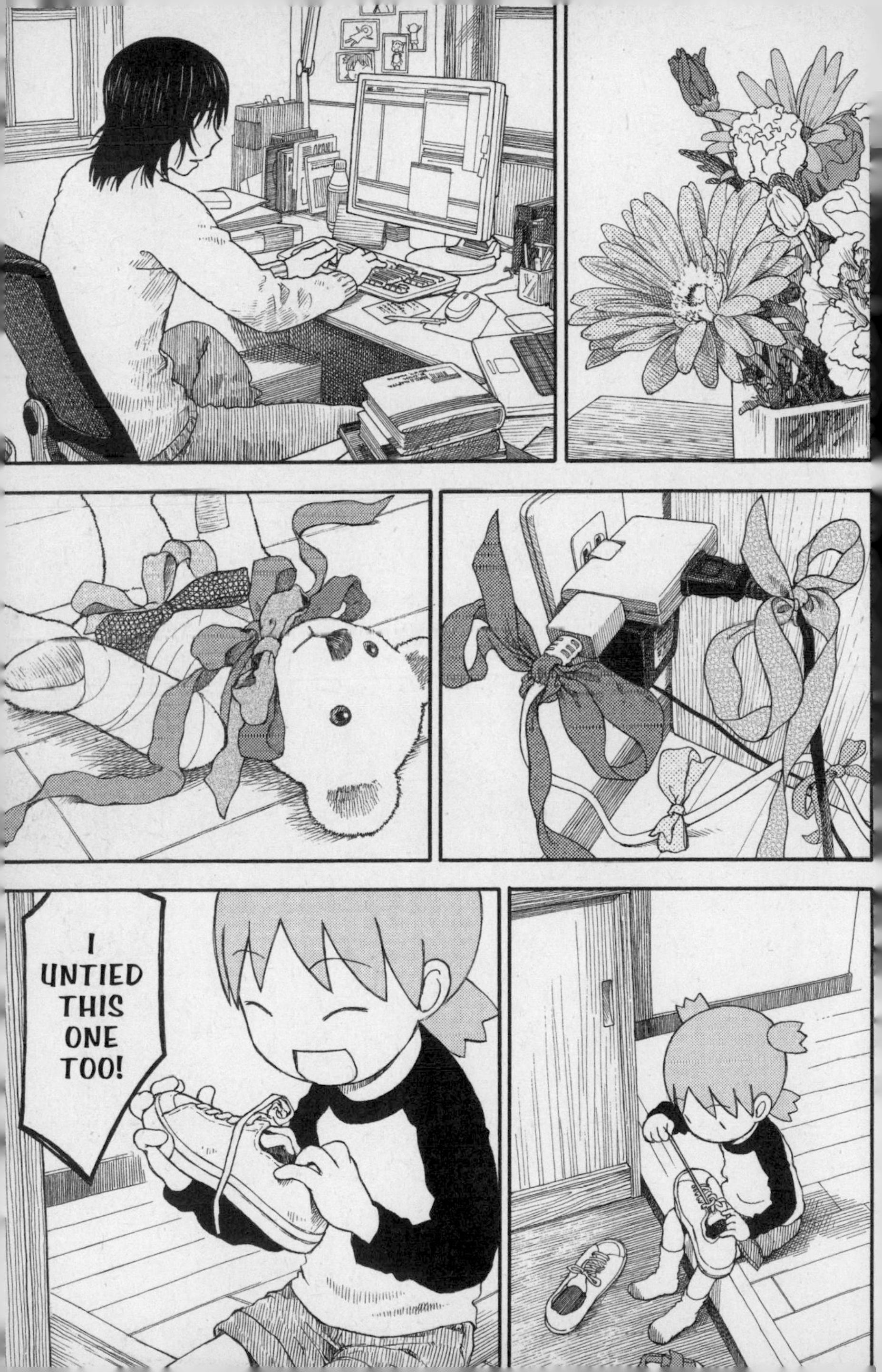
I UNTIED THIS ONE TOO!

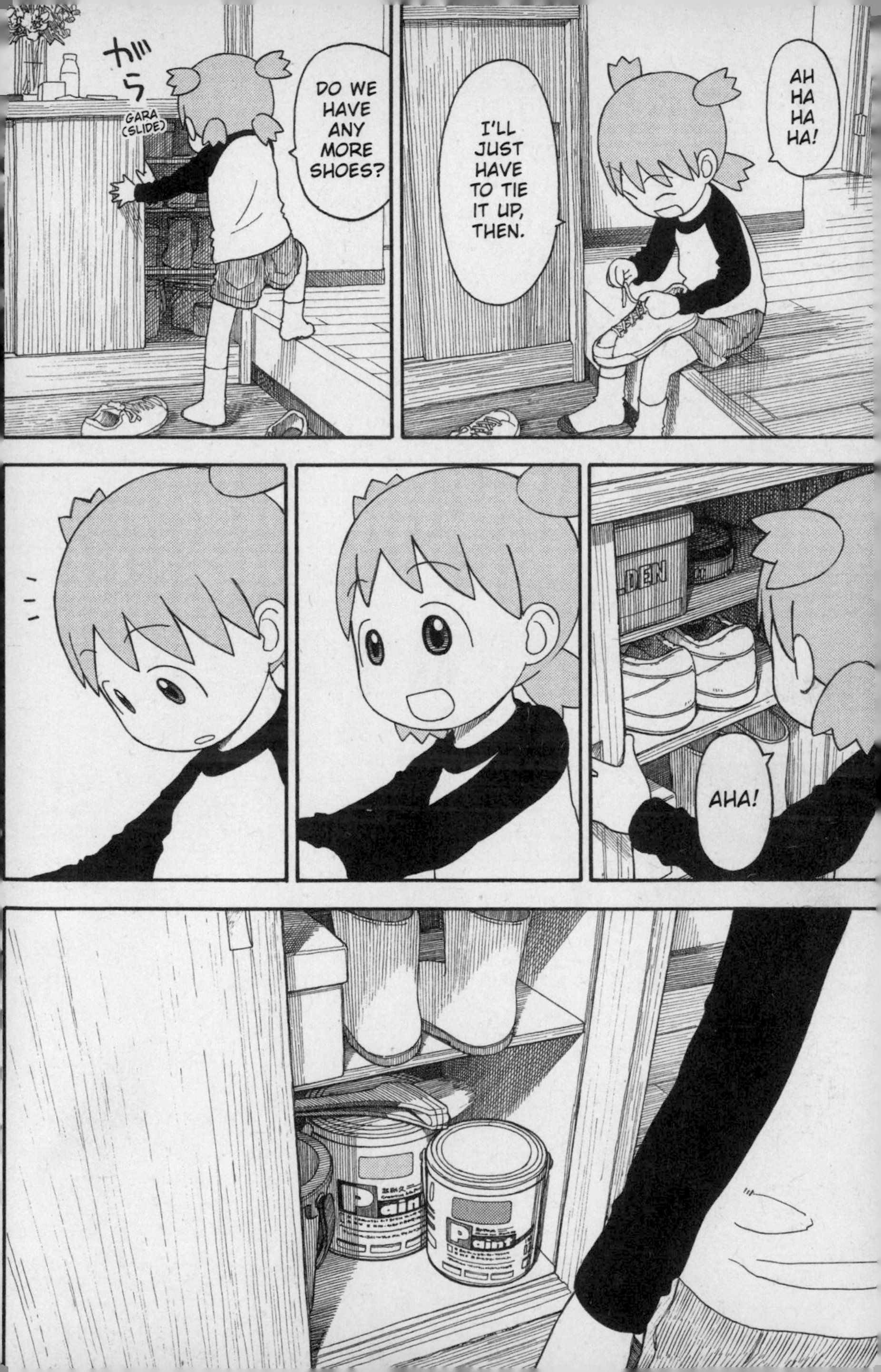
AH HA HA HA!
I'LL JUST HAVE TO TIE IT UP, THEN.
DO WE HAVE ANY MORE SHOES?
がら
GARA (SLIDE)
AHA!

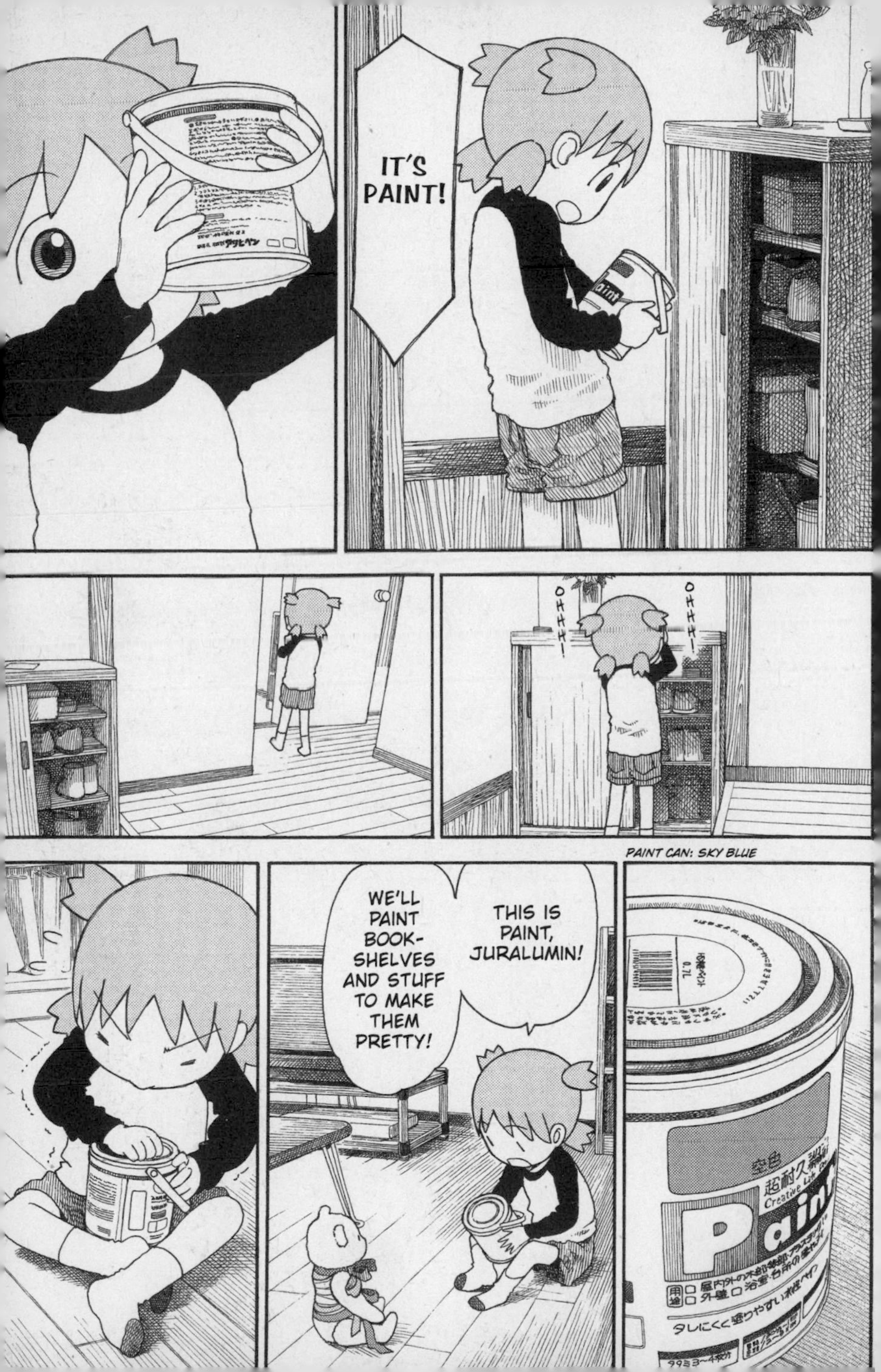
IT'S PAINT!
OHHH!
OHHH!
PAINT CAN: SKY BLUE
空色
Paint
THIS IS PAINT, JURALUMIN!
WE'LL PAINT BOOK-SHELVES AND STUFF TO MAKE THEM PRETTY!

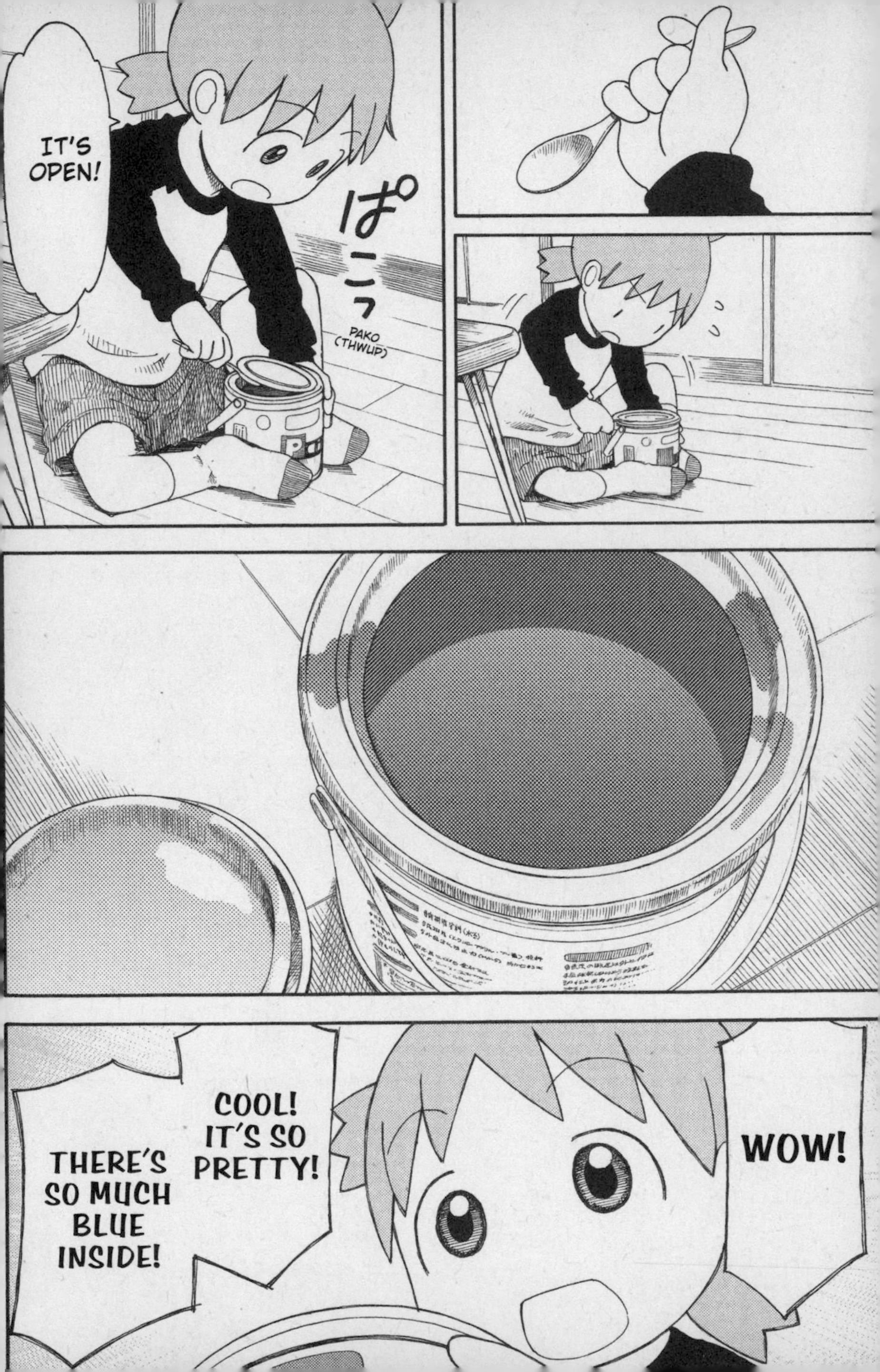
ぱこっ
PAKO (THWUP)
IT'S OPEN!
WOW!
COOL! IT'S SO PRETTY!
THERE'S SO MUCH BLUE INSIDE!

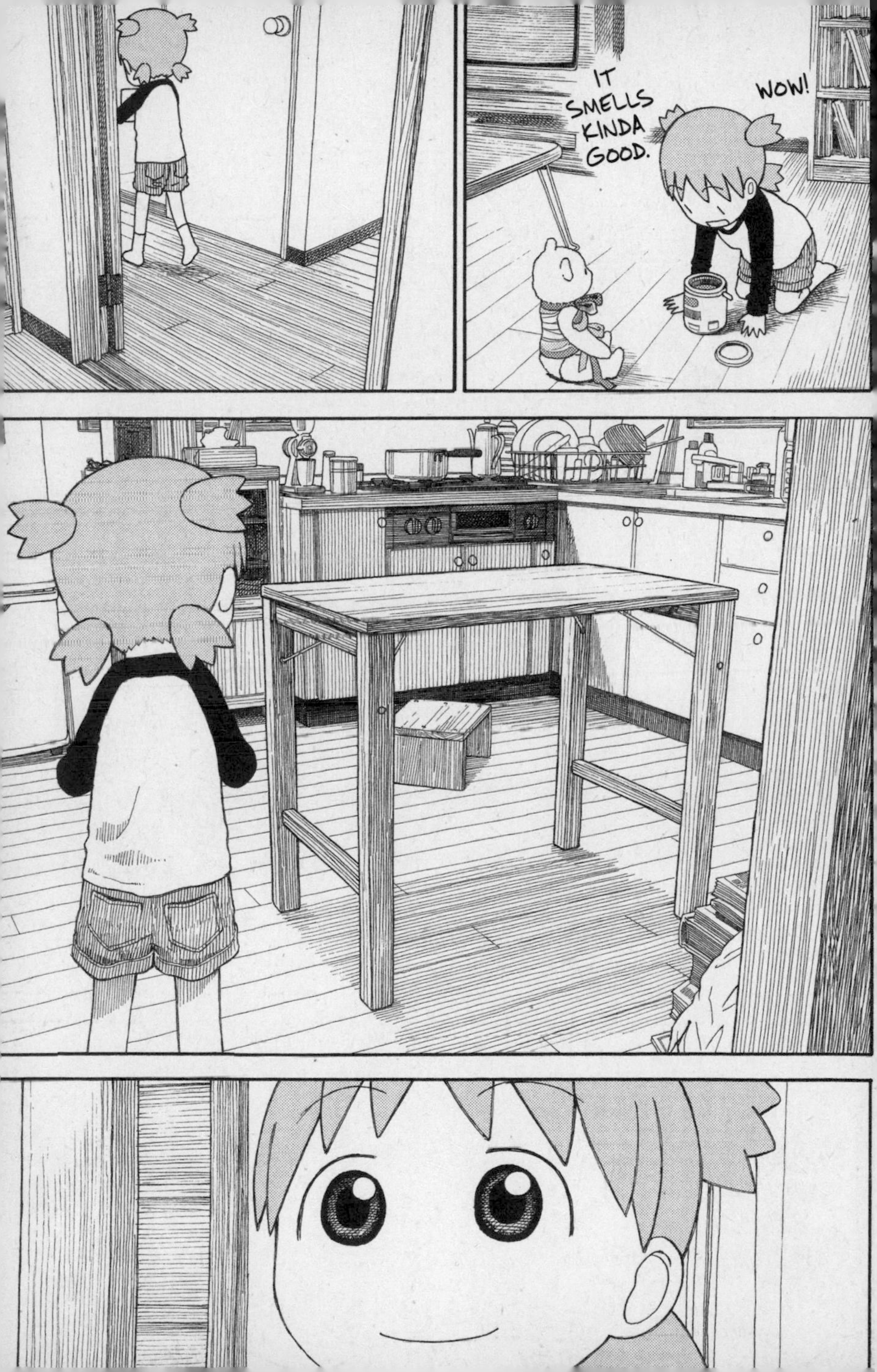
WOW!
IT SMELLS KINDA GOOD.

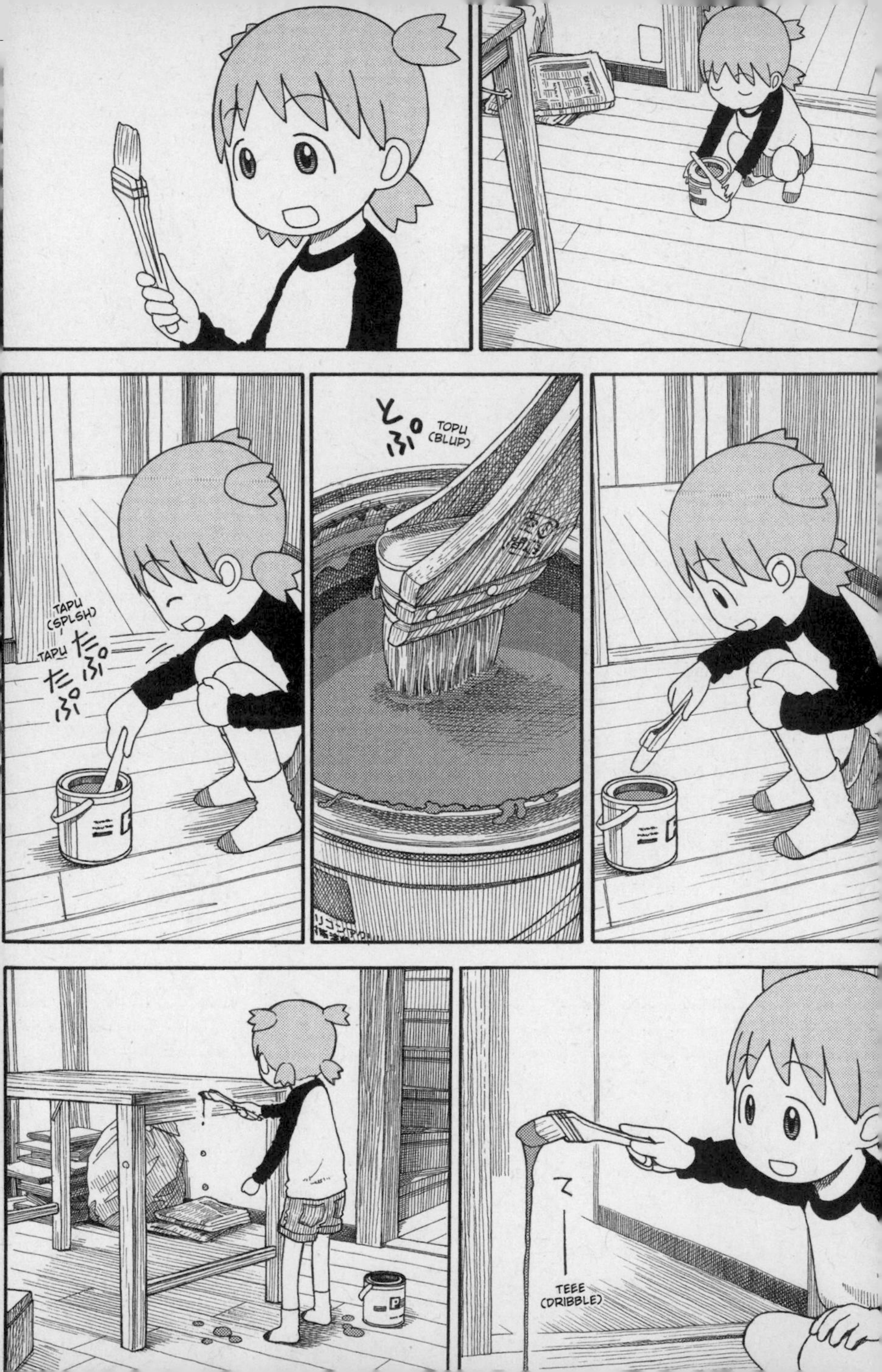
とぷ
TOPU (BLUP)
たぷ たぷ
TAPU (SPLSH) TAPU
てー
TEEE (DRIBBLE)

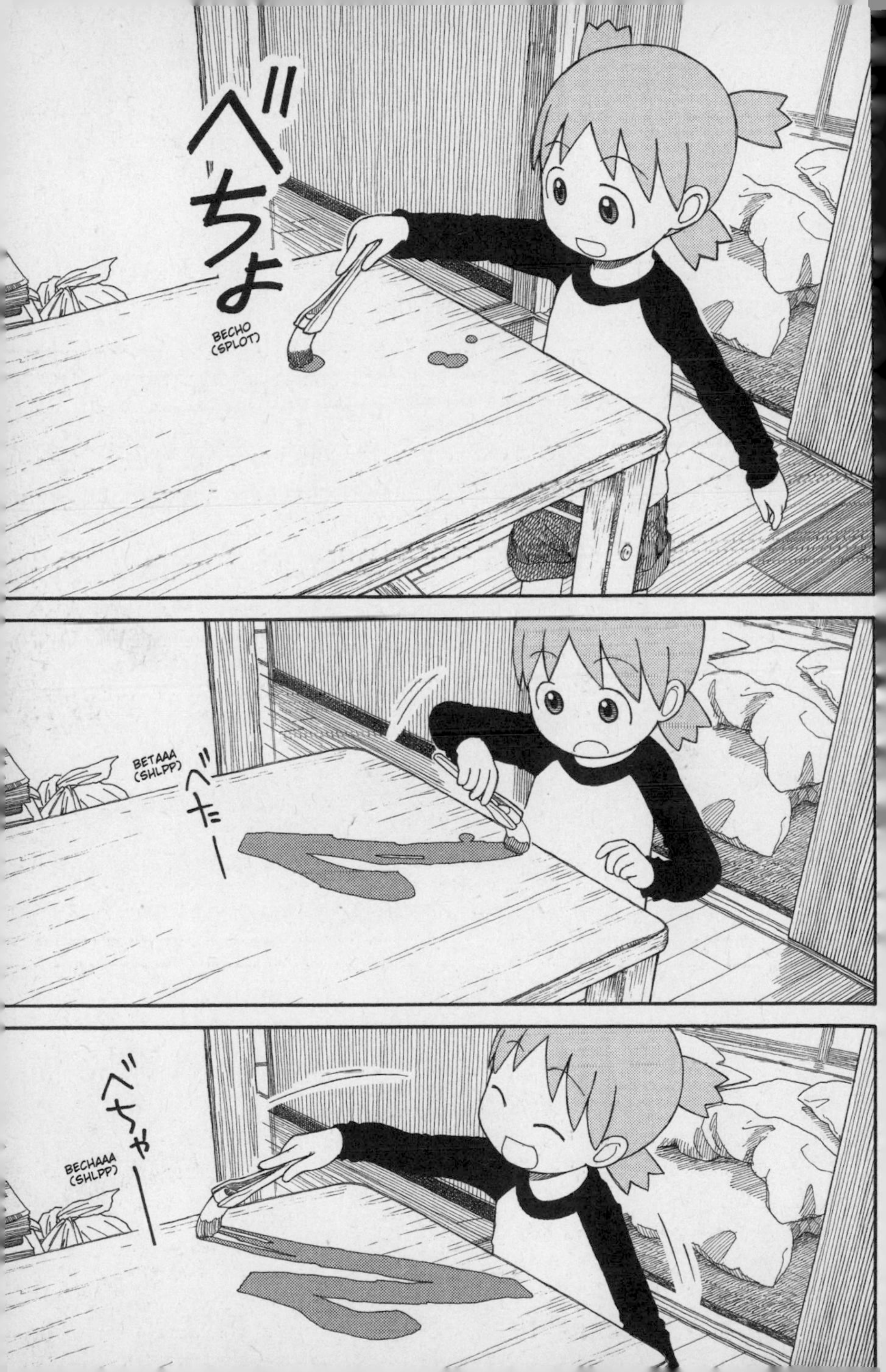
べちょ
BECHO (SPLOT)
べたー
BETAAA (SHLPP)
べちゃー
BECHAAA (SHLPP)

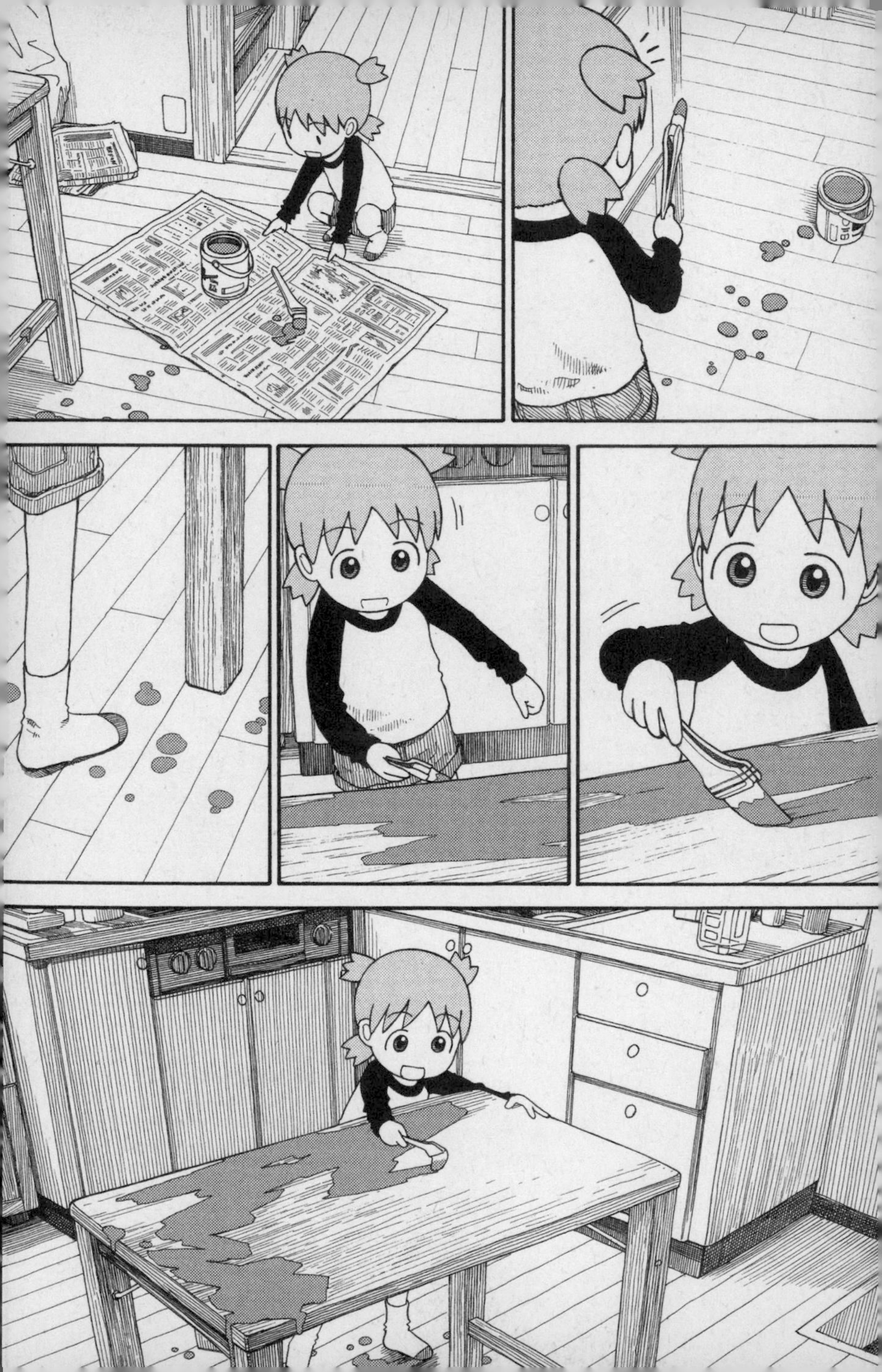

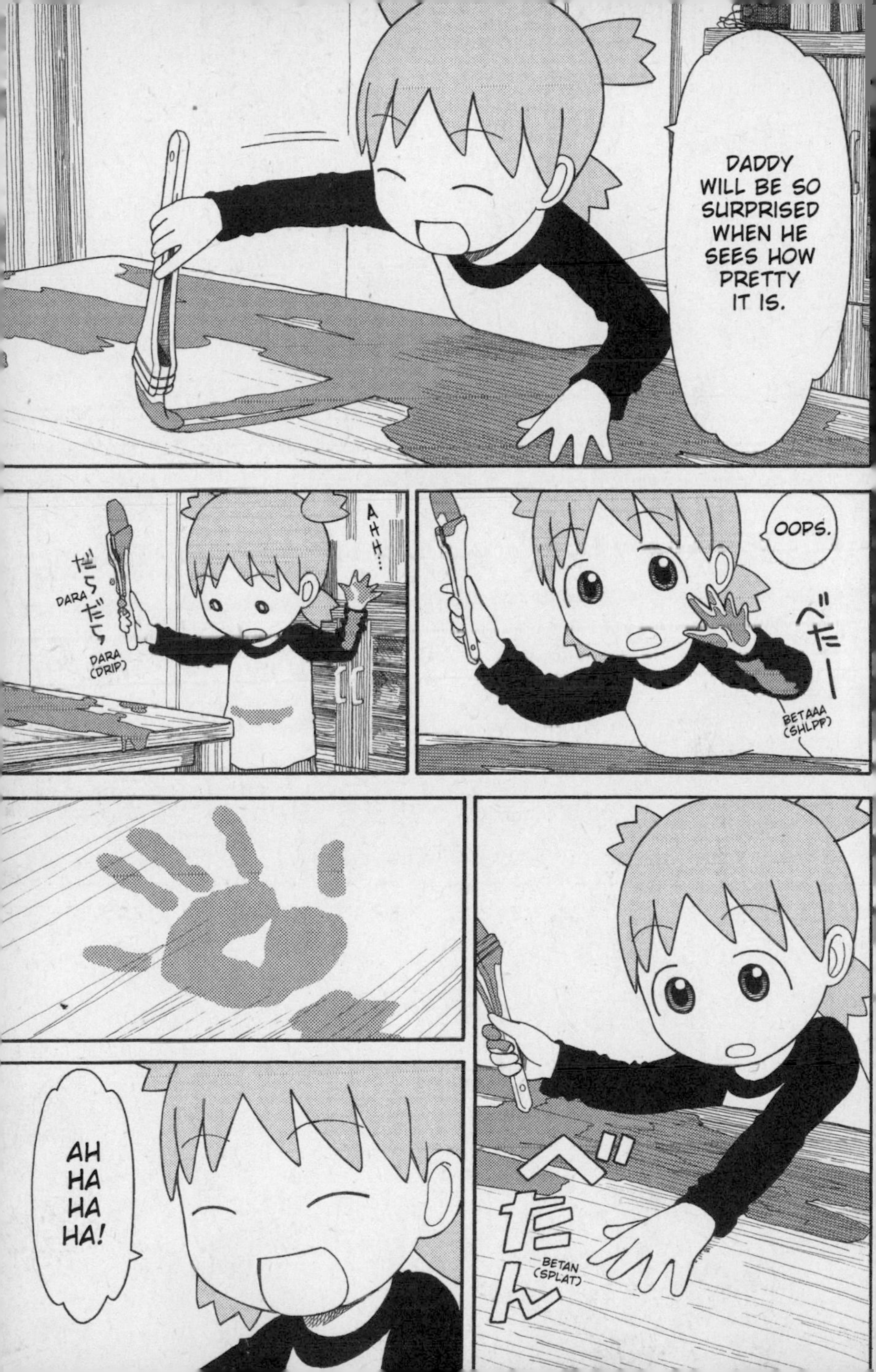
DADDY WILL BE SO SURPRISED WHEN HE SEES HOW PRETTY IT IS.
OOPS.
べたー
BETAAA (SHLPP)
AHH...
だらだら
DARA DARA (DRIP)
べたん
BETAN (SPLAT)
AH HA HA HA!

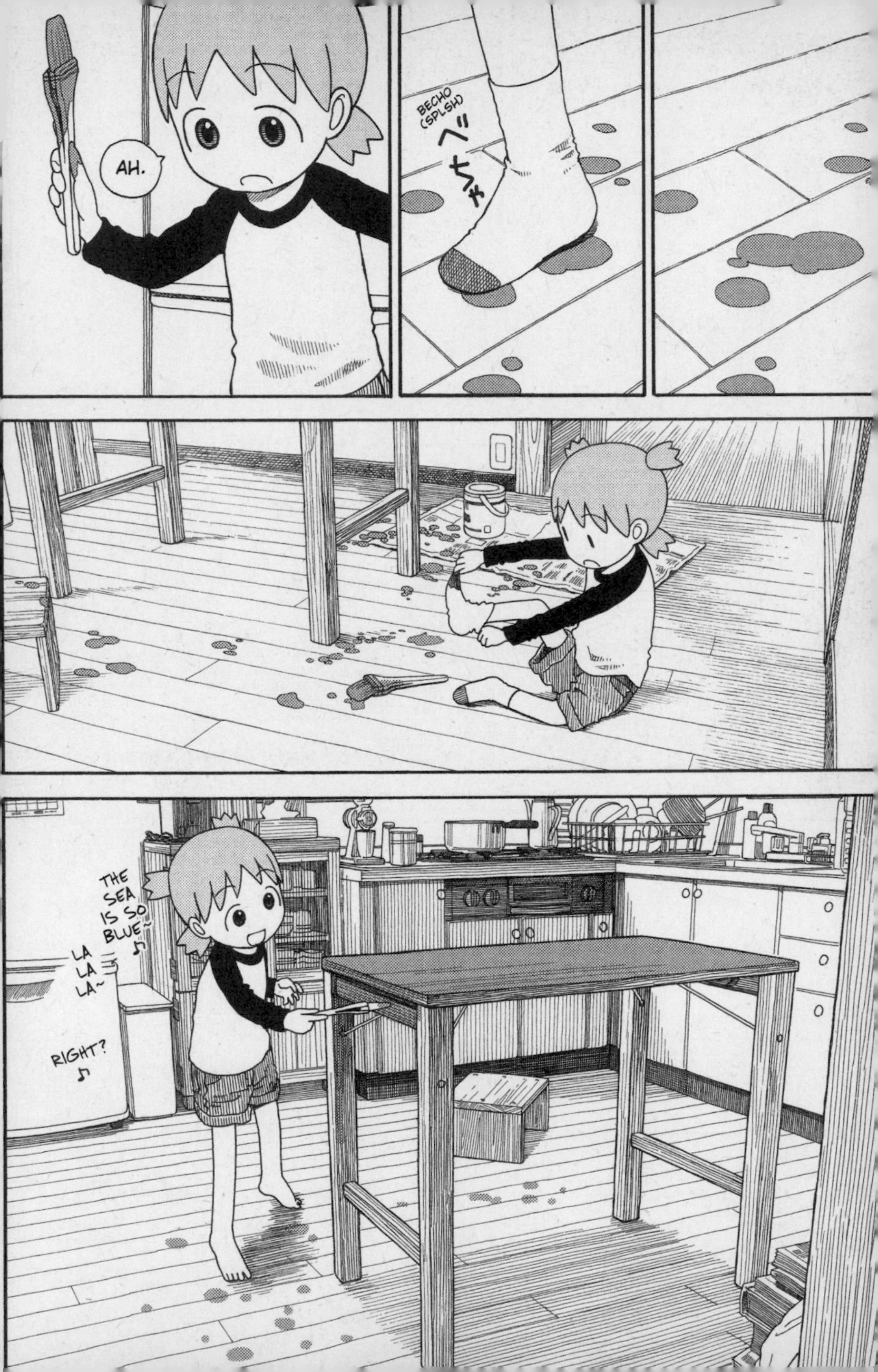
BECHO (SPLSH)
べちゃ
AH.
THE SEA IS SO BLUE~ ♪
LA LA LA~
RIGHT? ♪

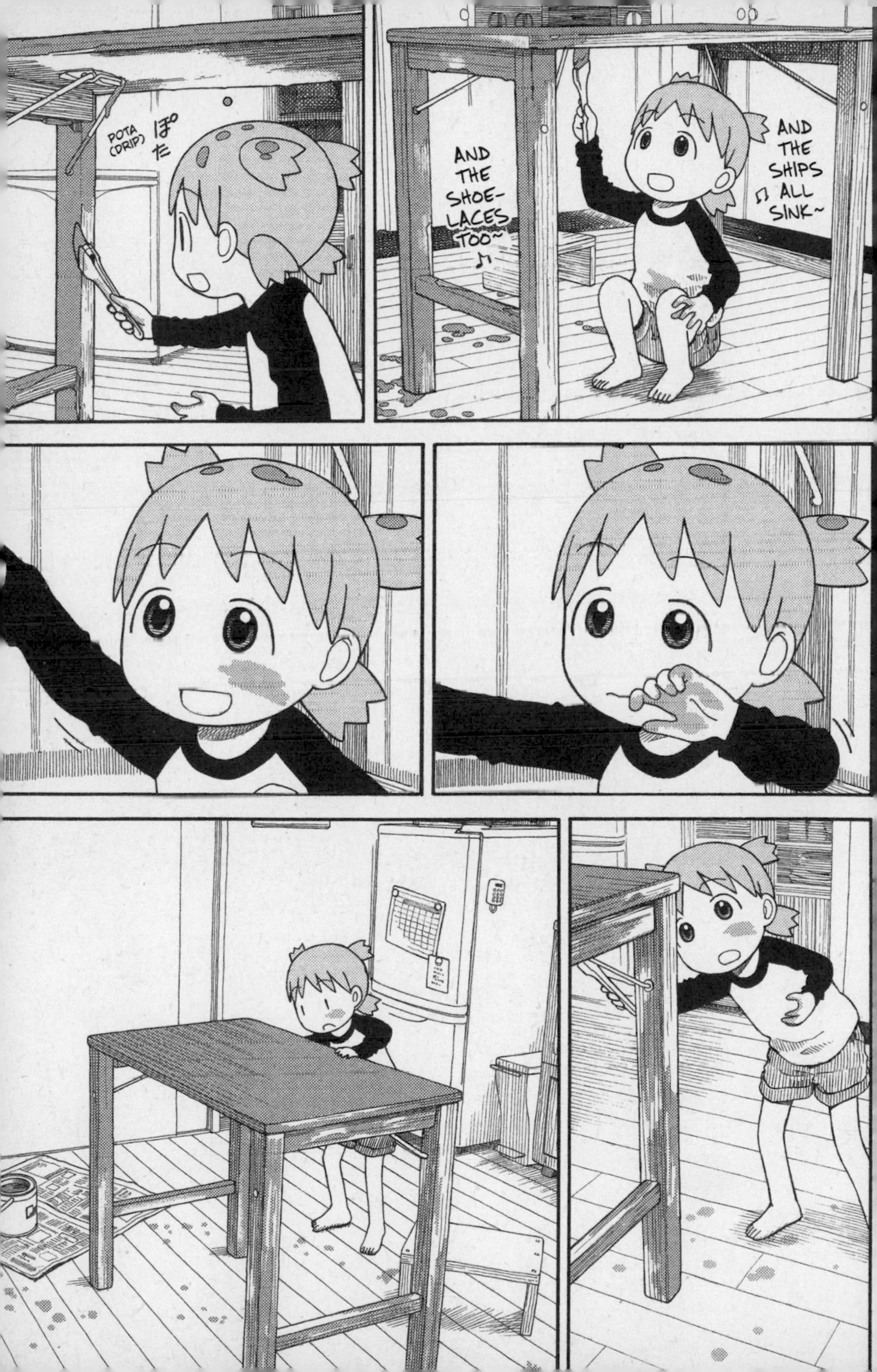
AND THE SHIPS ALL SINK~ ♫
AND THE SHOE-LACES TOO~ ♪
POTA (DRIP) ぽた

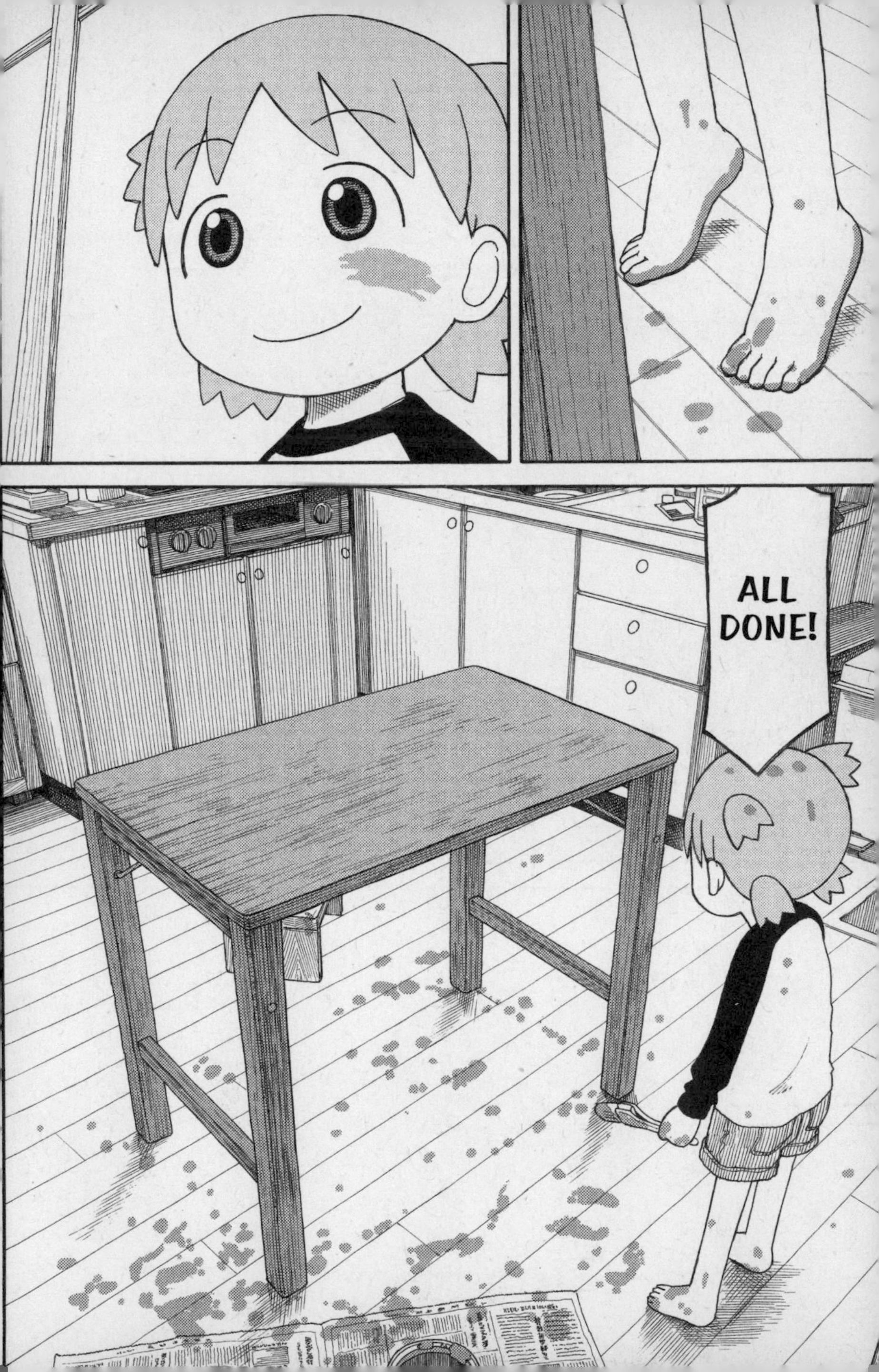
ALL DONE!

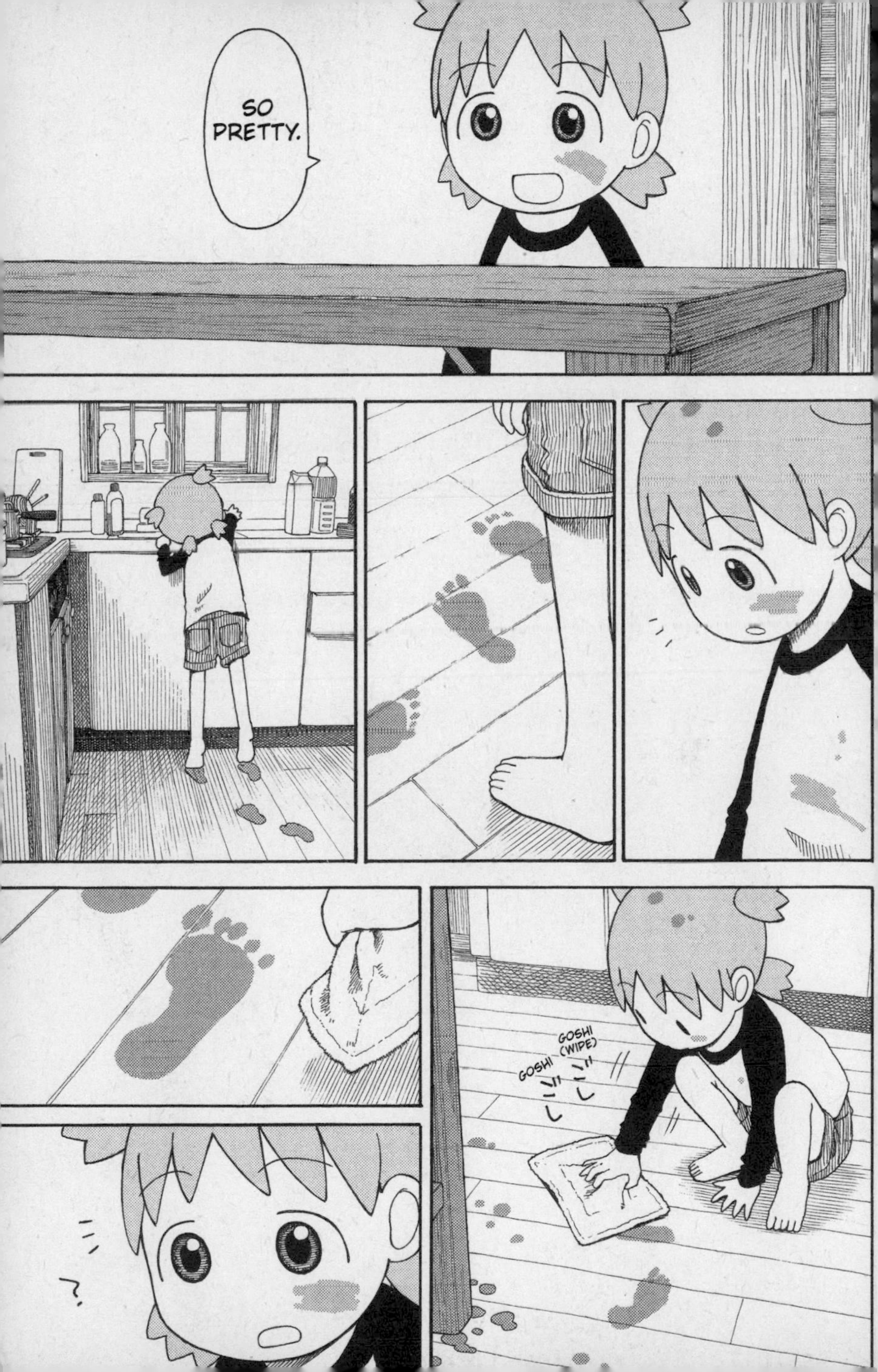
SO PRETTY.
GOSHI (WIPE)
GOSHI

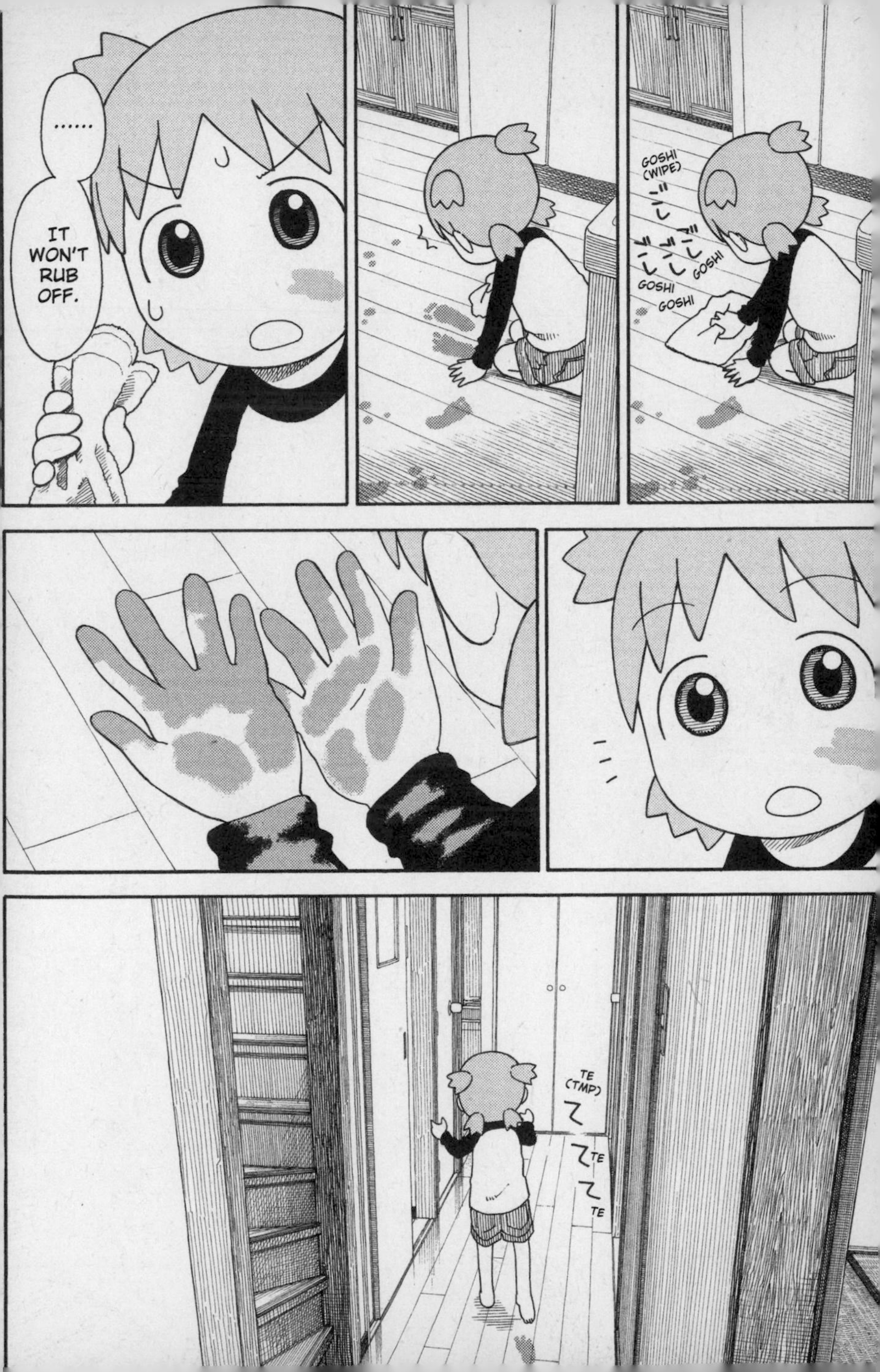
GOSHI (WIPE)
GOSHI
GOSHI
GOSHI
......
IT WON'T RUB OFF.
TE (TMP)
TE
TE

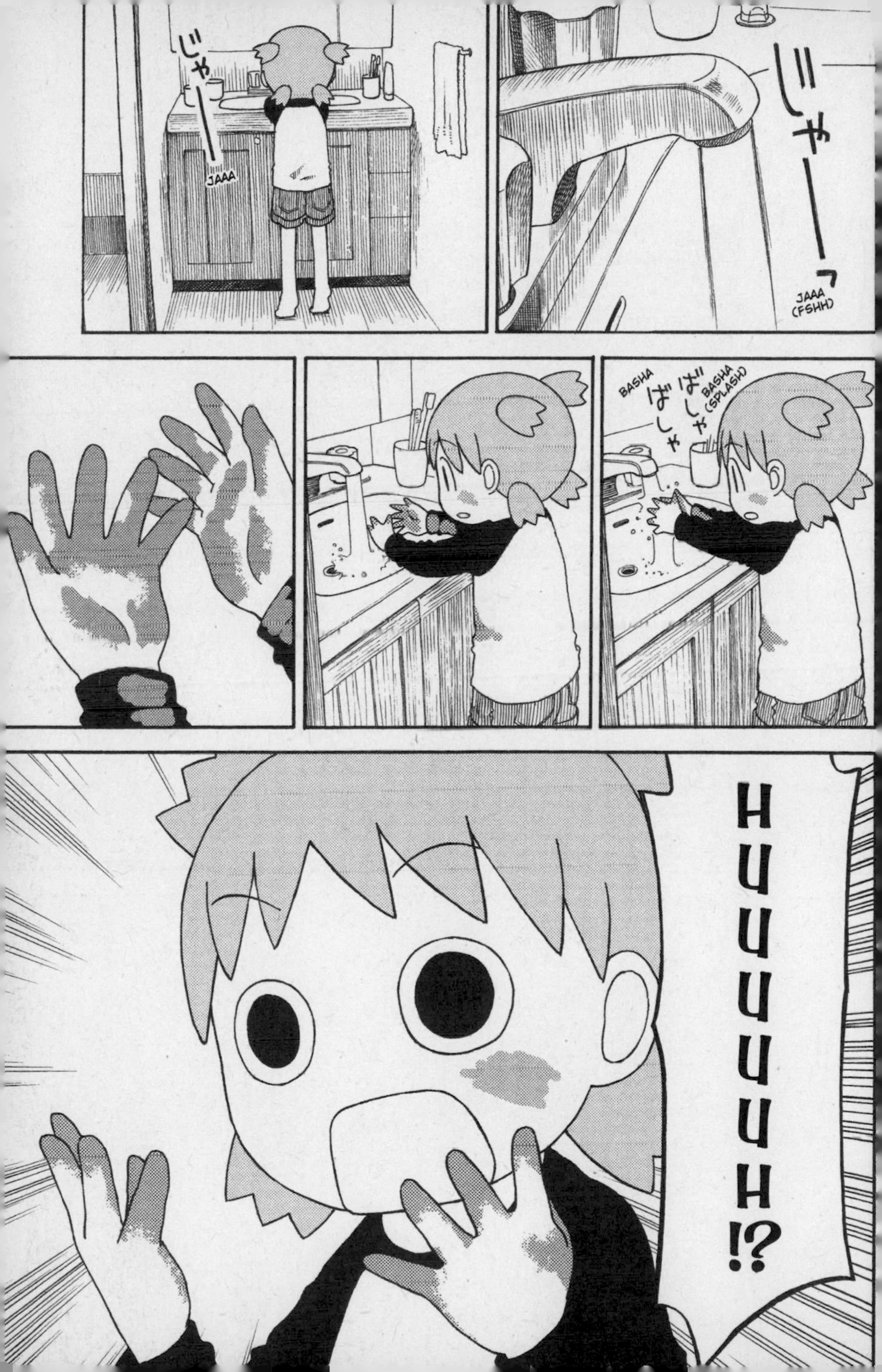
ジャー
JAAA (FSHH)
じゃー
JAAA
ばしゃ
BASHA (SPLASH)
ばしゃ
BASHA
HUUUUUH!?

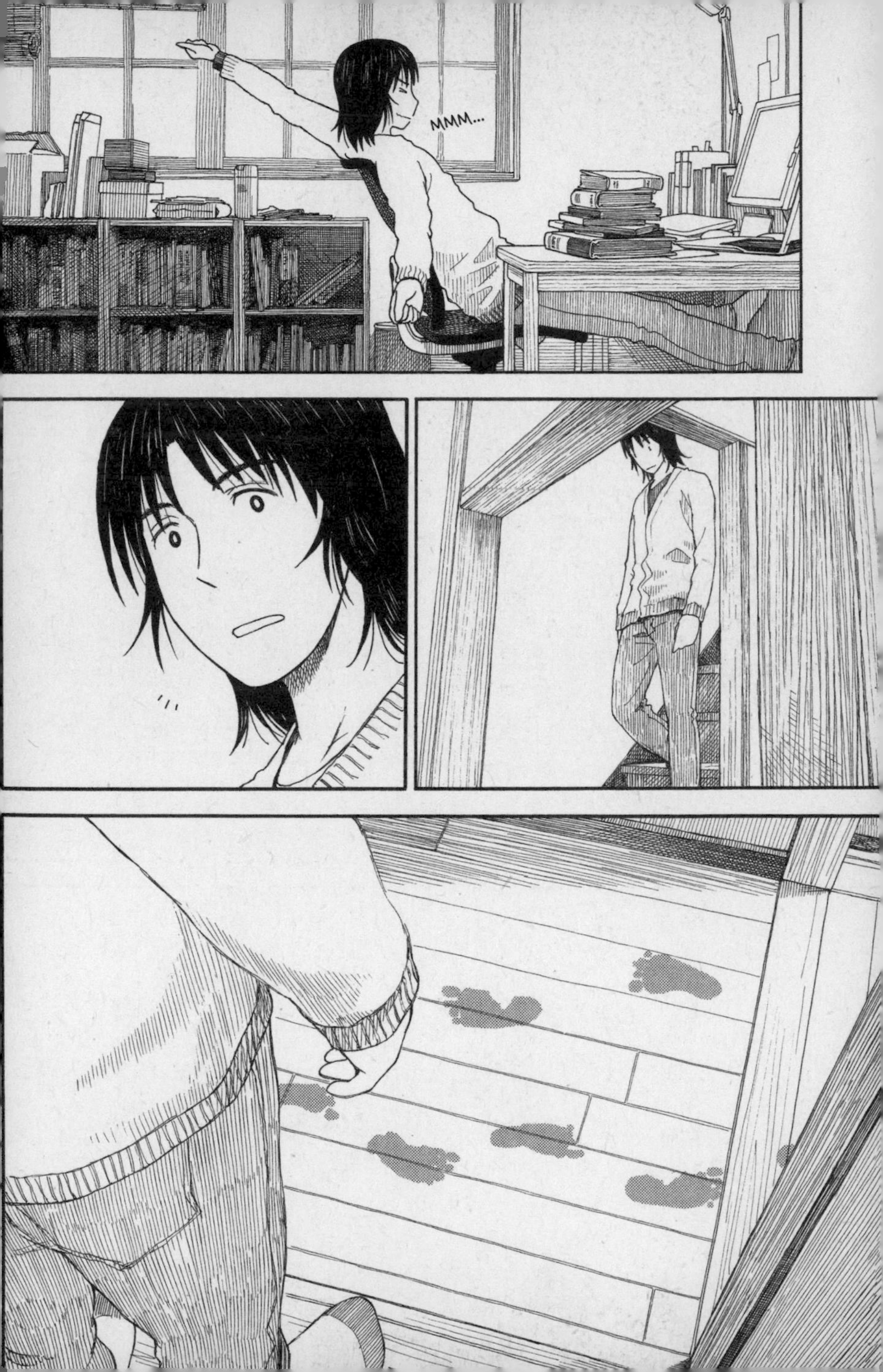
MMM...

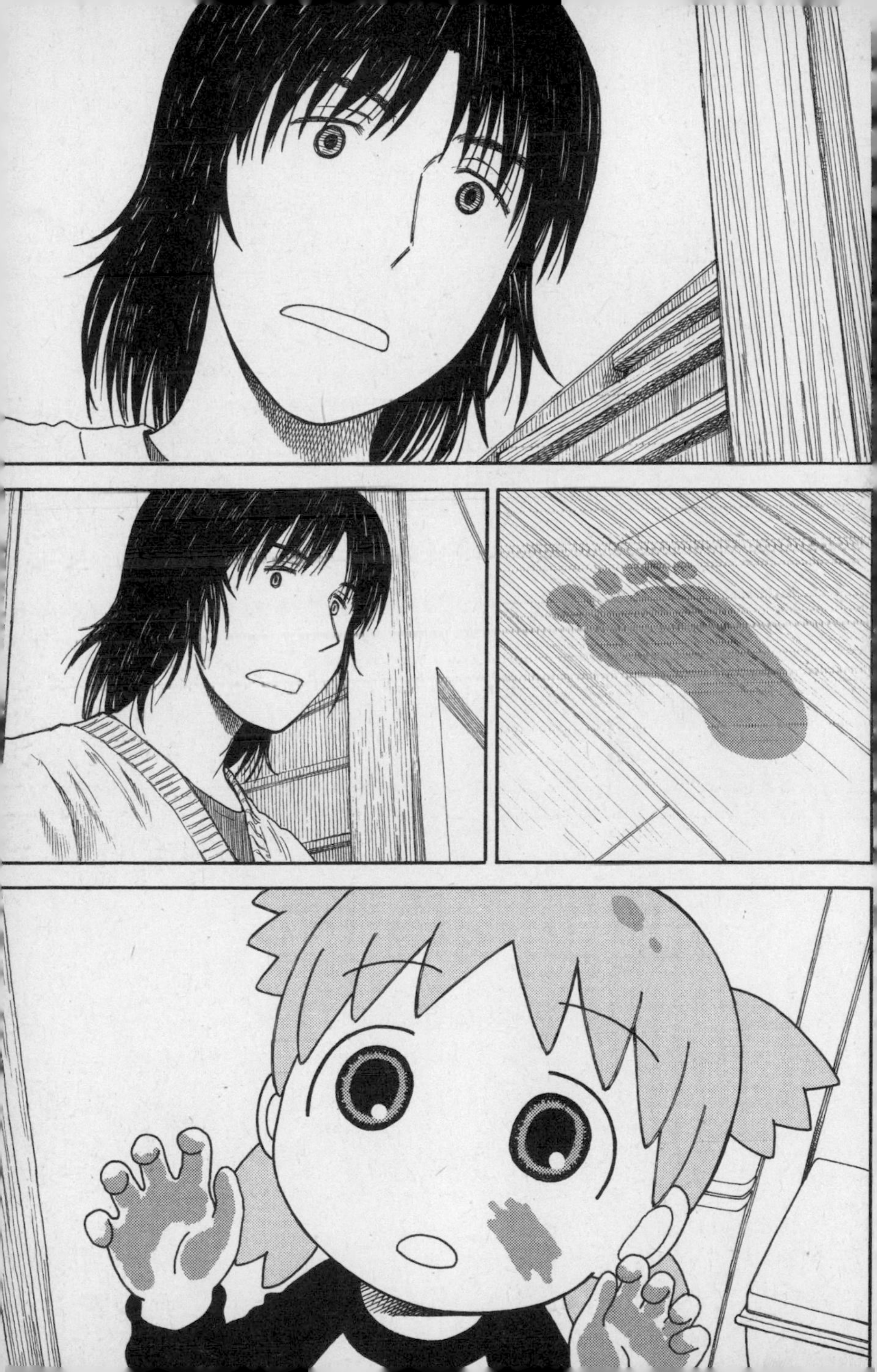

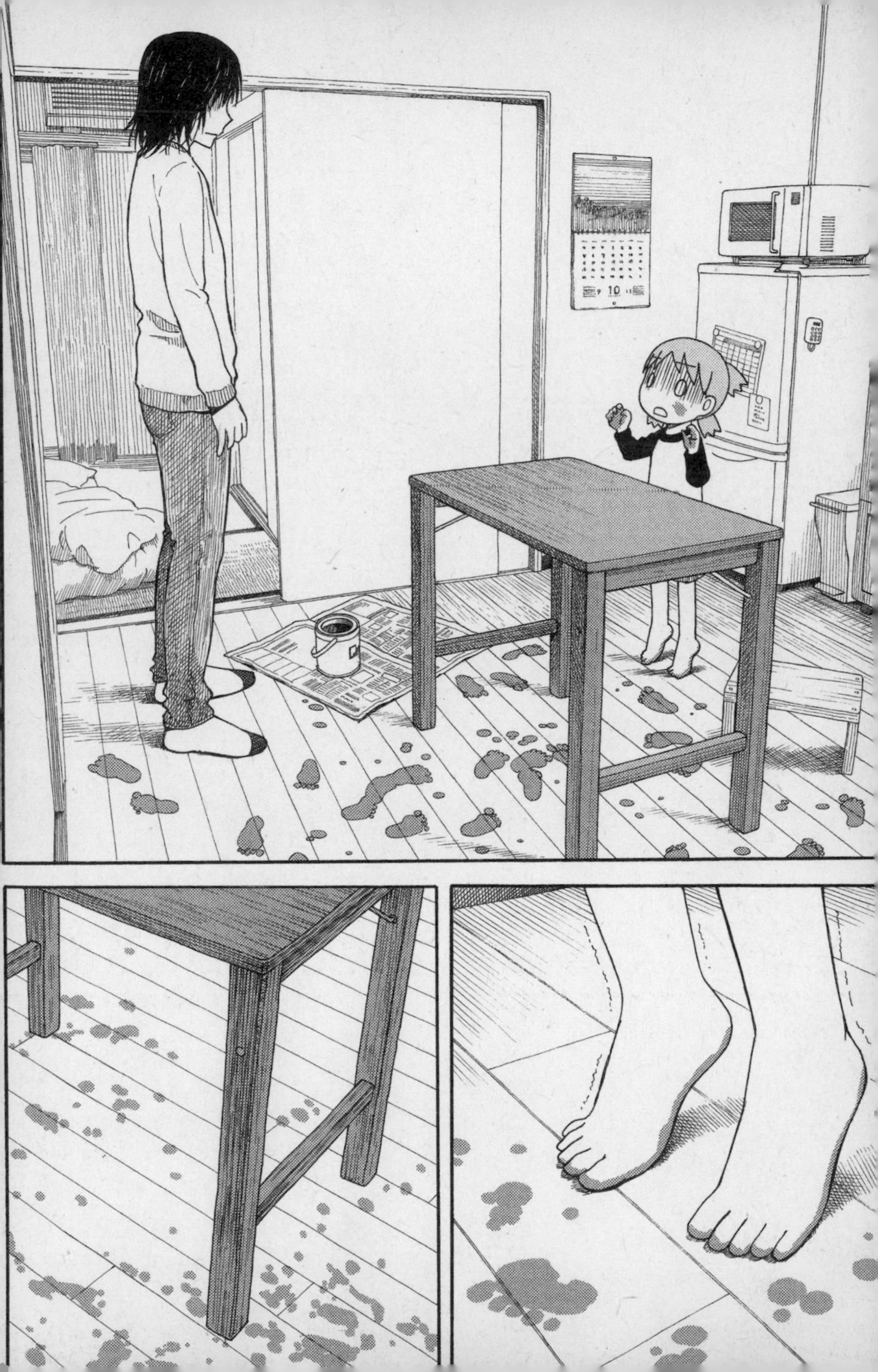

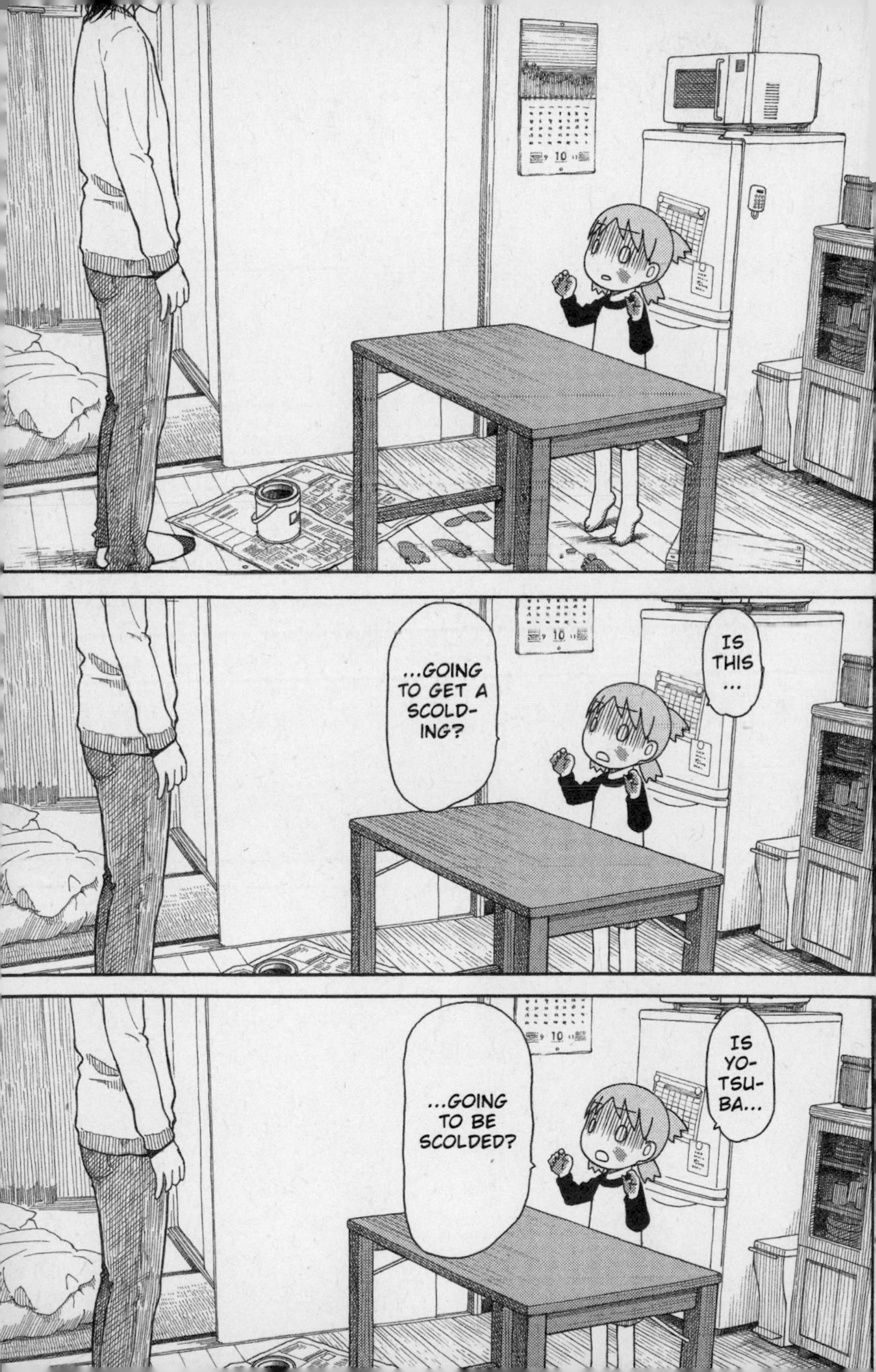
IS THIS...
...GOING TO GET A SCOLDING?
IS YOTSUBA...
...GOING TO BE SCOLDED?

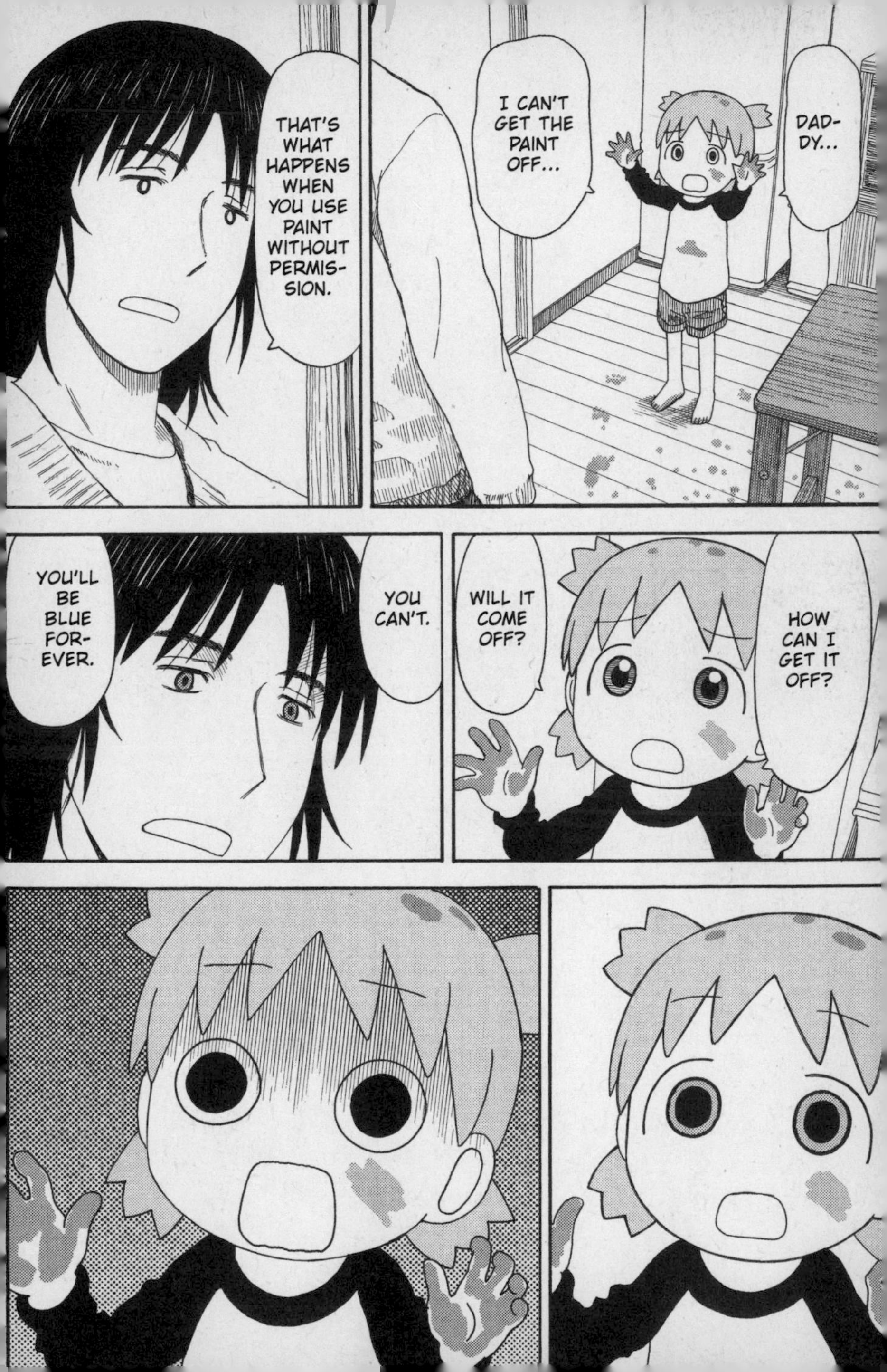
DAD-
DY...
I CAN'T GET THE PAINT OFF...
THAT'S WHAT HAPPENS WHEN YOU USE PAINT WITHOUT PERMIS-
SION.
HOW CAN I GET IT OFF?
WILL IT COME OFF?
YOU CAN'T.
YOU'LL BE BLUE FOR-
EVER.

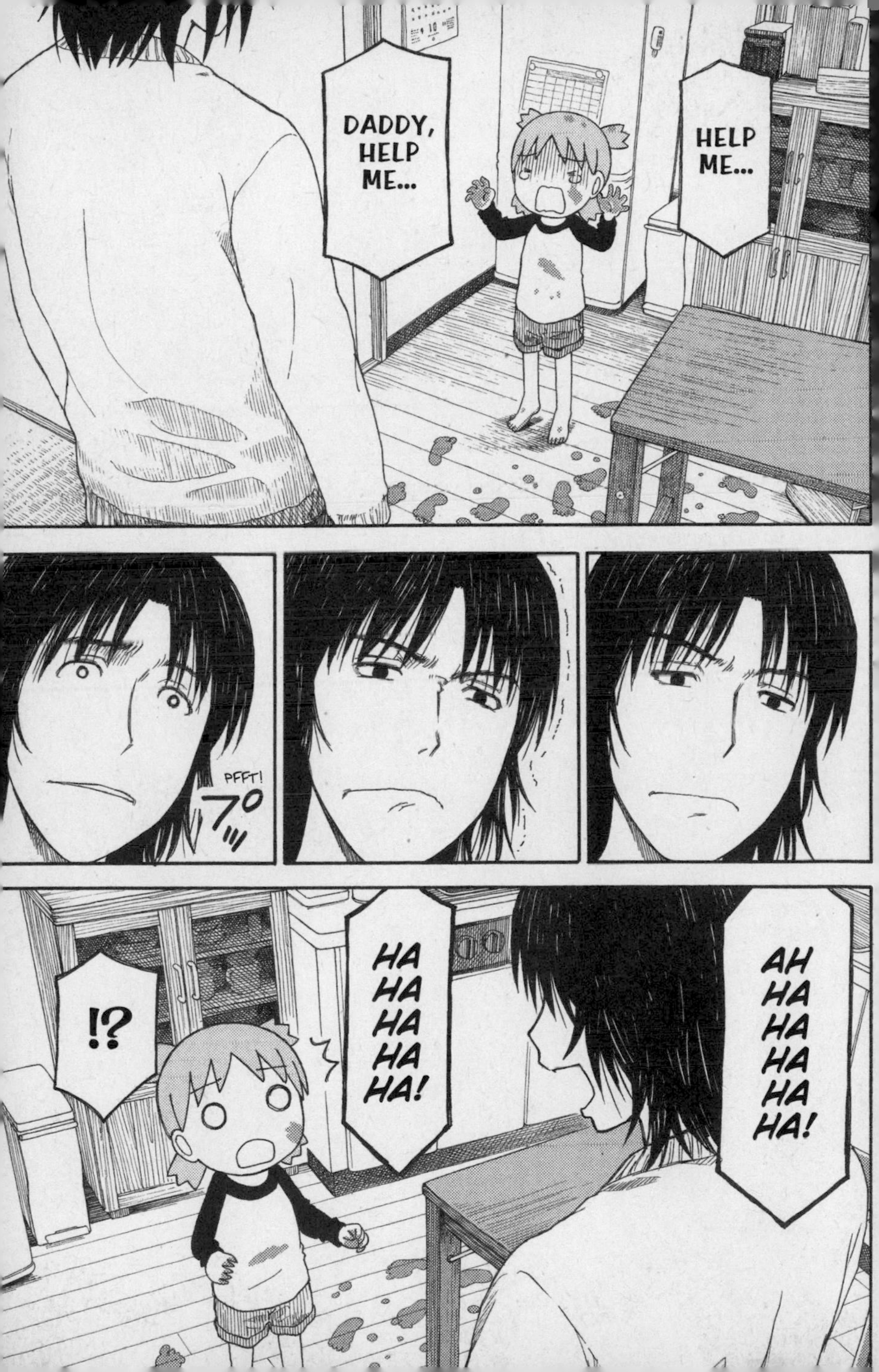
HELP ME...
DADDY, HELP ME...
PFFT!
AH HA HA HA HA HA HA!
HA HA HA HA HA!
!?

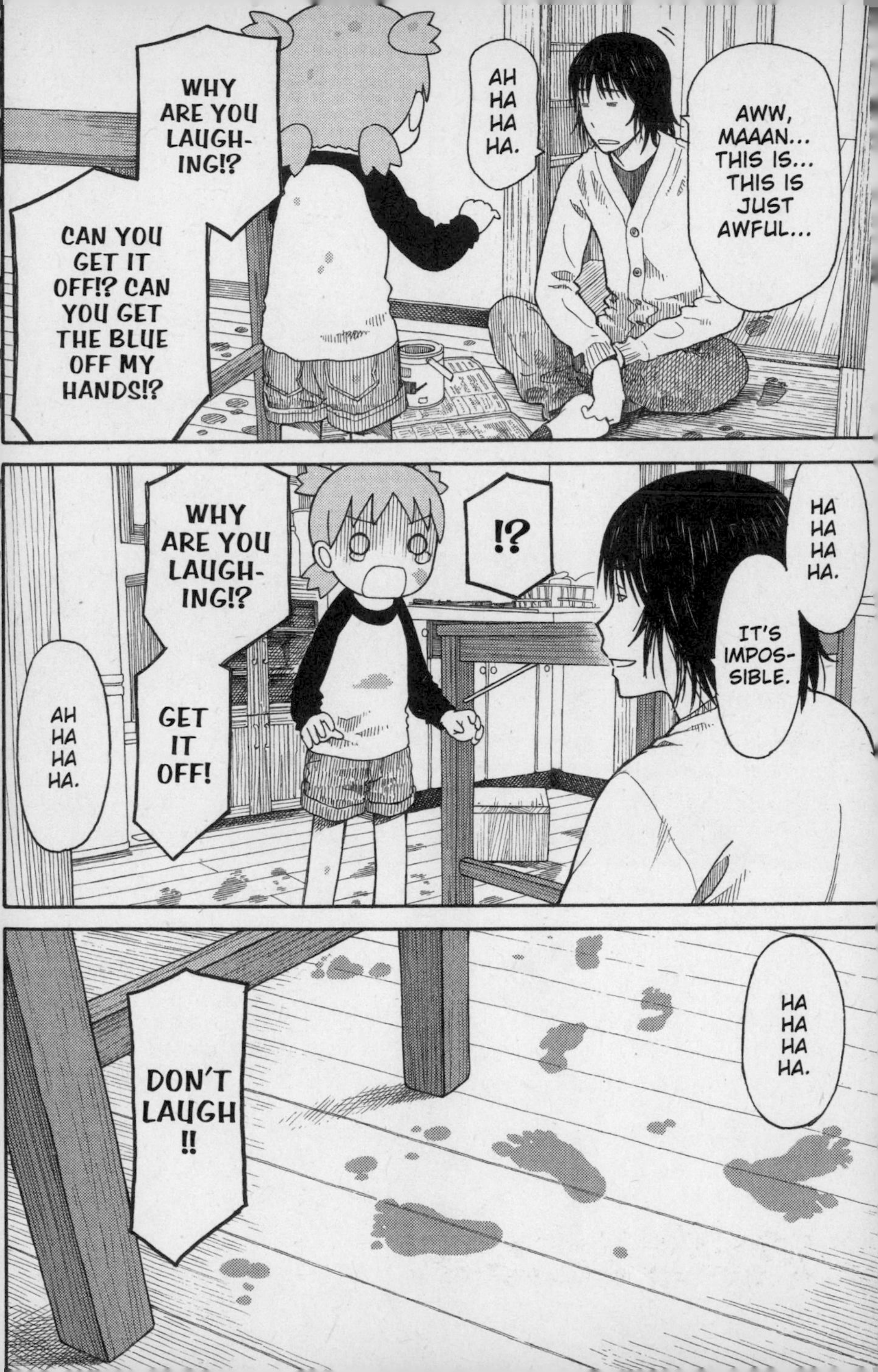
AWW, MAAAN... THIS IS... THIS IS JUST AWFUL...
AH HA HA HA.
WHY ARE YOU LAUGHING!?
CAN YOU GET IT OFF!? CAN YOU GET THE BLUE OFF MY HANDS!?
HA HA HA HA.
IT'S IMPOSSIBLE.
!?
WHY ARE YOU LAUGHING!?
GET IT OFF!
AH HA HA HA.
HA HA HA HA.
DON'T LAUGH!!

YOTSUBA&!

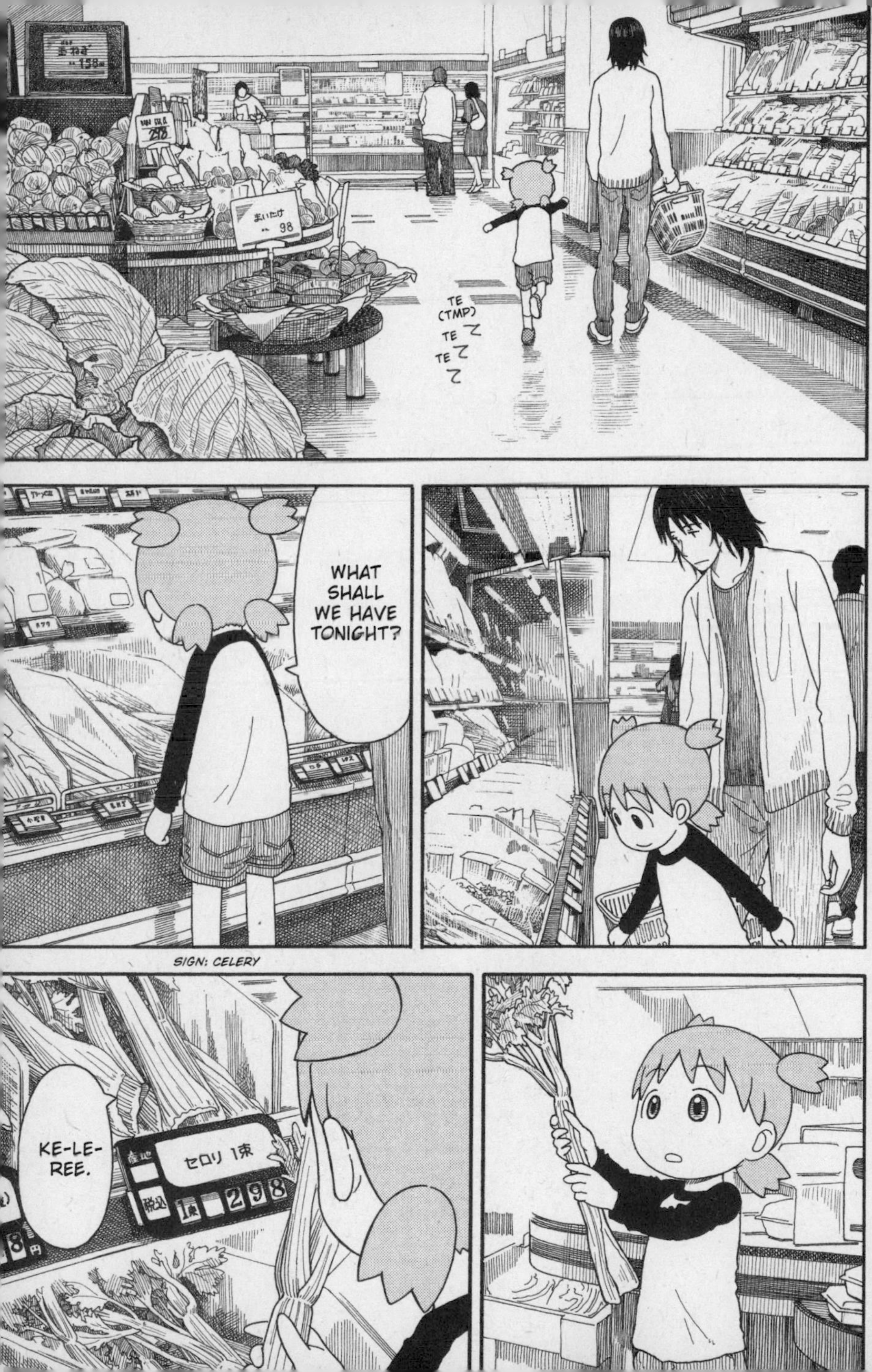
まいたけ 98
TE (TMP)
TE
TE
WHAT SHALL WE HAVE TONIGHT?
SIGN: CELERY
KE-LE-REE.
セロリ 1束
税込 1束 298

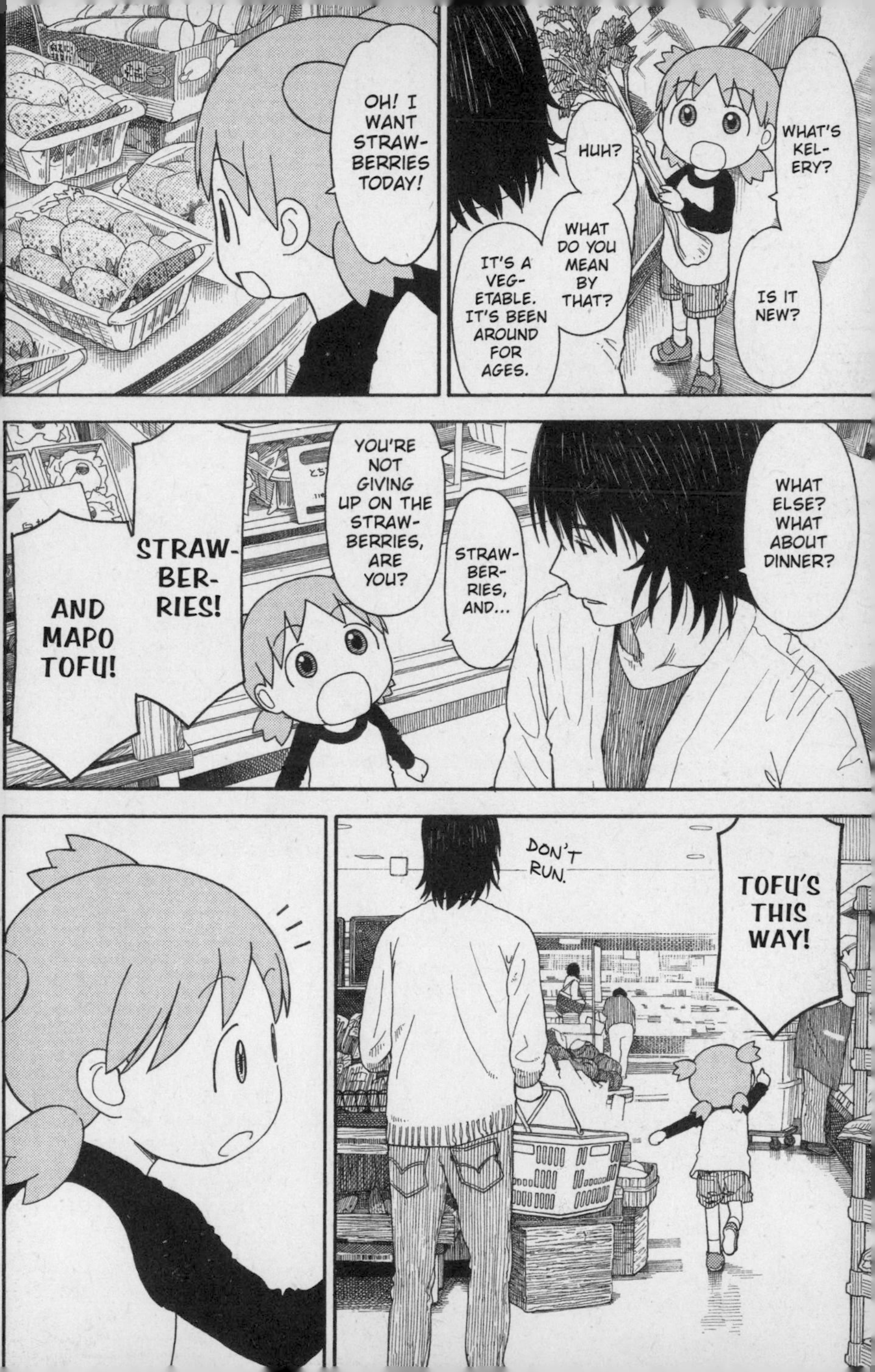
WHAT'S KEL-ERY?
IS IT NEW?
HUH?
WHAT DO YOU MEAN BY THAT?
IT'S A VEG-ETABLE. IT'S BEEN AROUND FOR AGES.
OH! I WANT STRAW-BERRIES TODAY!
WHAT ELSE? WHAT ABOUT DINNER?
STRAW-BER-RIES, AND...
YOU'RE NOT GIVING UP ON THE STRAW-BERRIES, ARE YOU?
STRAW-BER-RIES!
AND MAPO TOFU!
TOFU'S THIS WAY!
DON'T RUN.

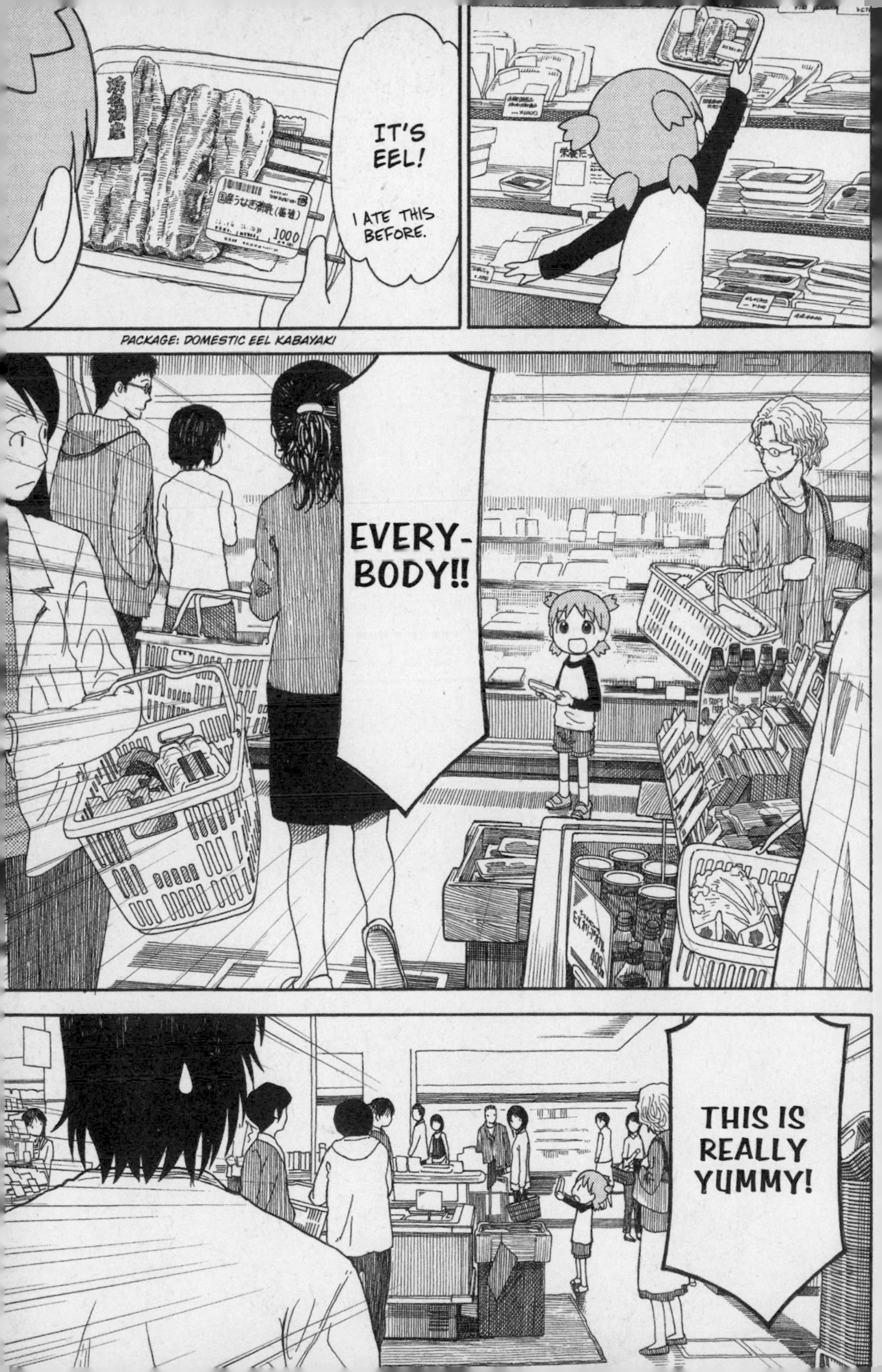
浜名湖産
IT'S EEL!
I ATE THIS BEFORE.
PACKAGE: DOMESTIC EEL KABAYAKI
EVERY-BODY!!
THIS IS REALLY YUMMY!

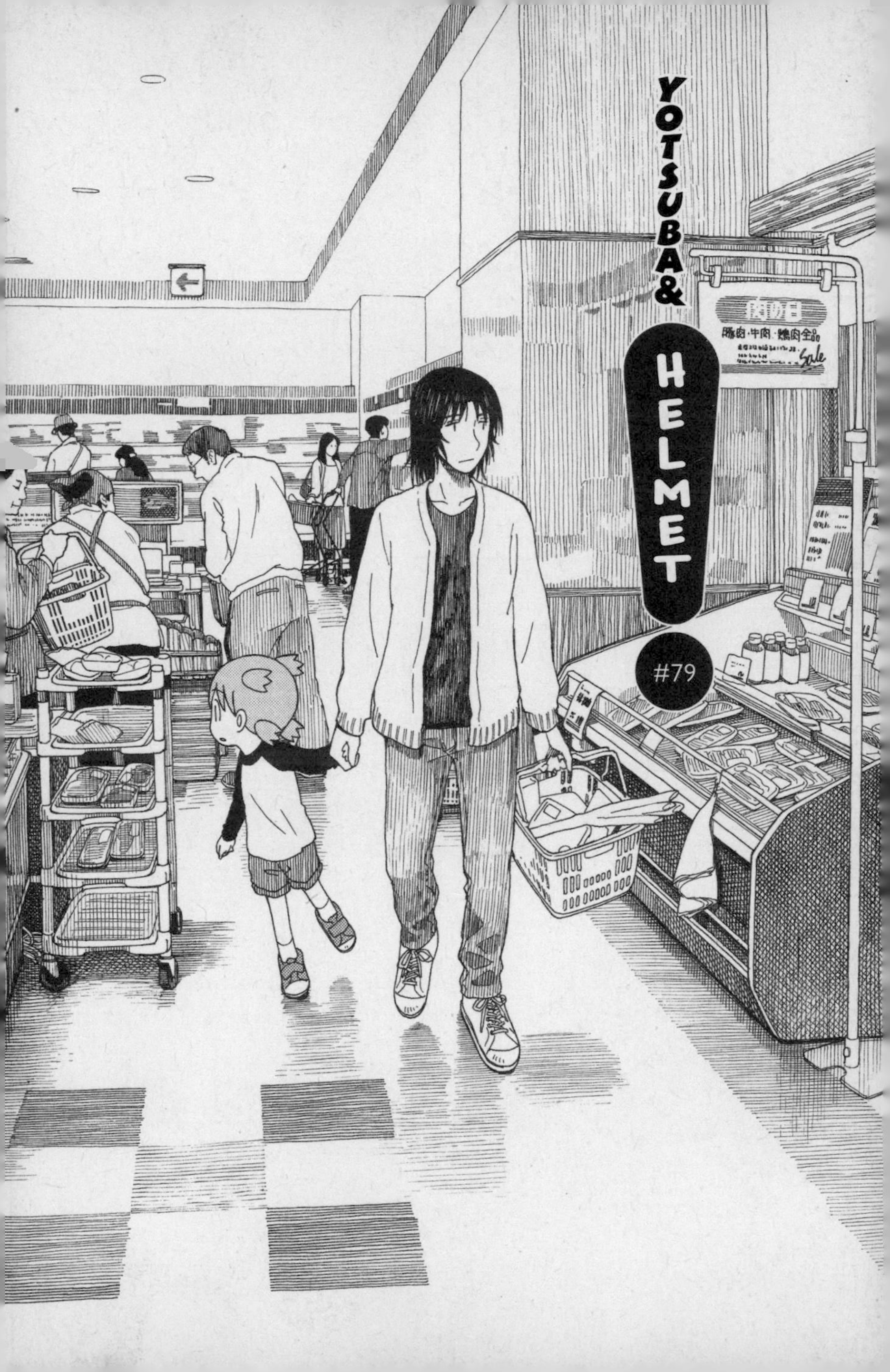
YOTSUBA&
HELMET
#79
豚肉・牛肉・鶏肉全品
Sale

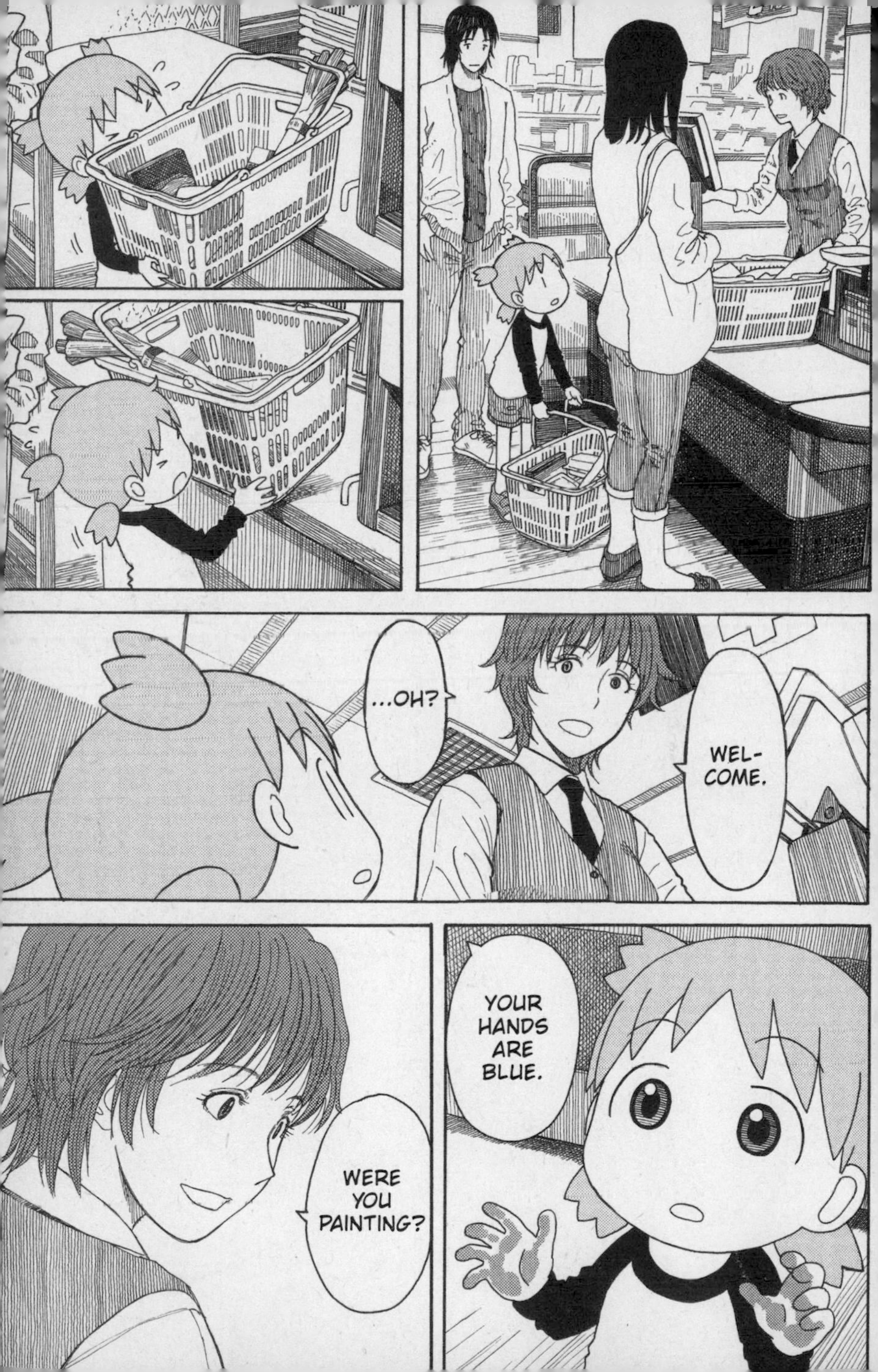
WEL-
COME.
...OH?
YOUR HANDS ARE BLUE.
WERE YOU PAINTING?

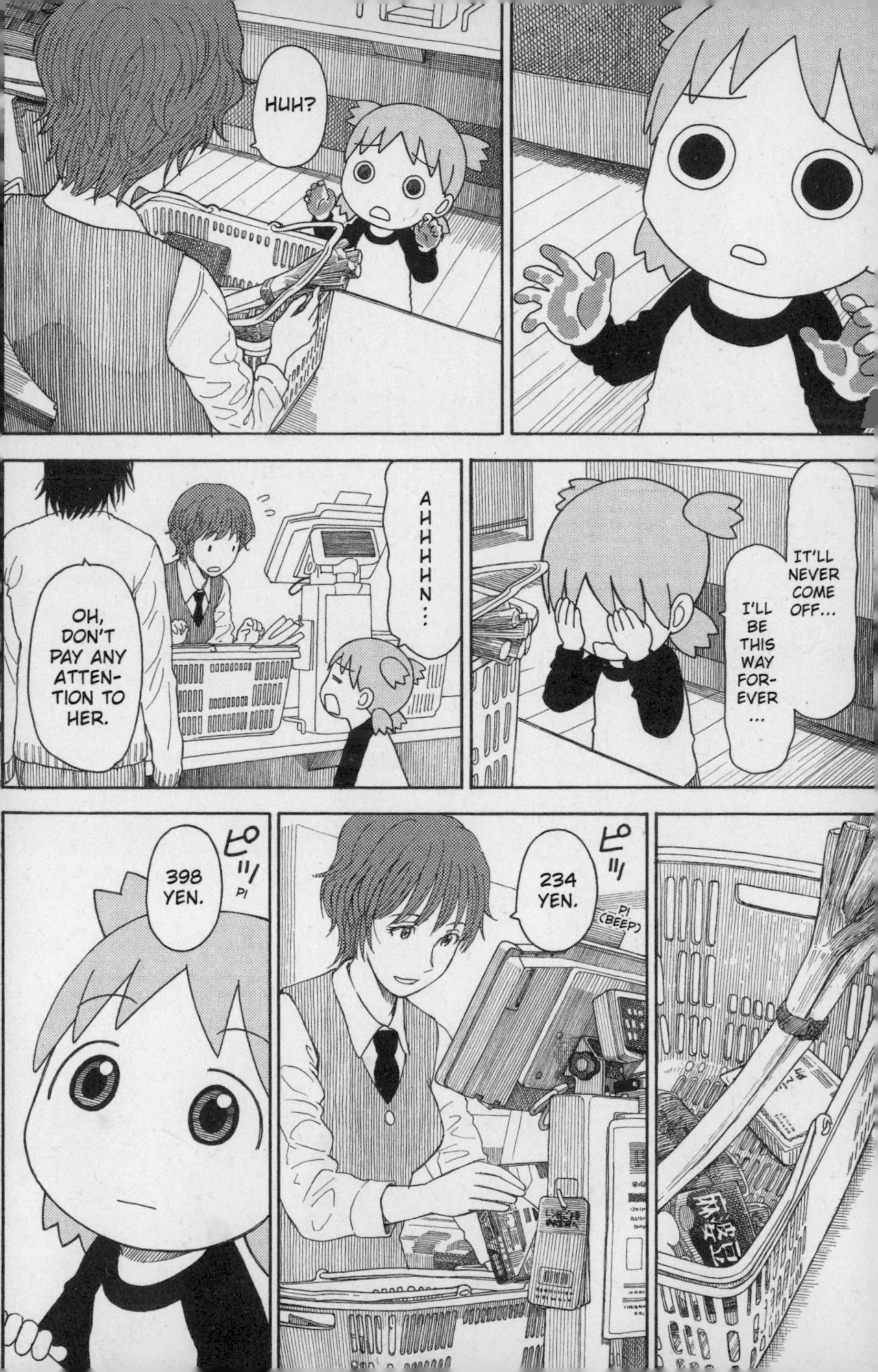
HUH?
IT'LL NEVER COME OFF...
I'LL BE THIS WAY FOR-EVER...
AHHHHHN...
OH, DON'T PAY ANY ATTEN-TION TO HER.
ピッ
234 YEN.
PI (BEEP)
ピッ
398 YEN.
PI

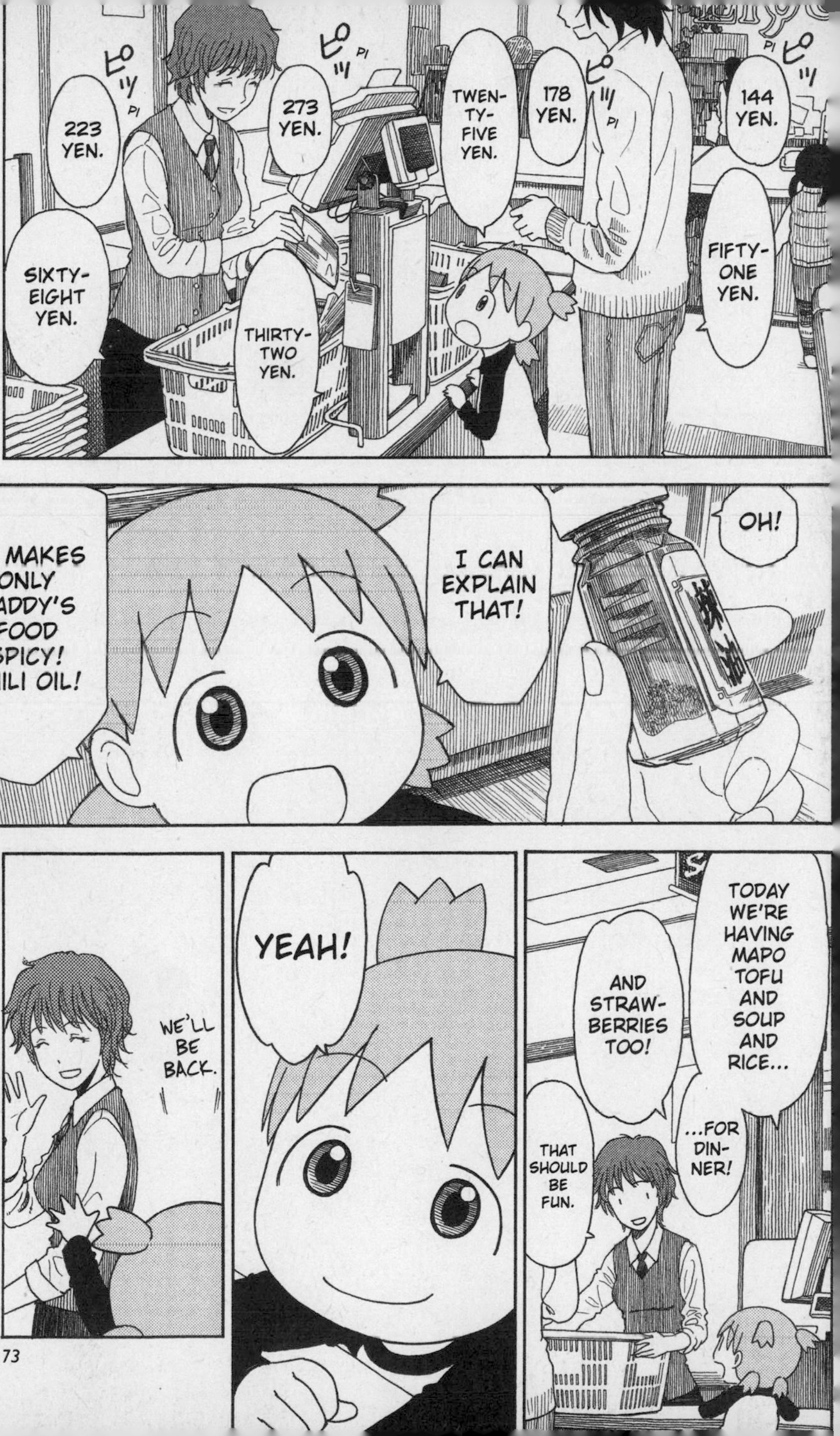
ピッ PI
144 YEN.
ピッ PI
178 YEN.
TWENTY-FIVE YEN.
ピッ PI
273 YEN.
ピッ PI
223 YEN.
FIFTY-ONE YEN.
THIRTY-TWO YEN.
SIXTY-EIGHT YEN.
OH!
I CAN EXPLAIN THAT!
IT MAKES ONLY DADDY'S FOOD SPICY! CHILI OIL!
TODAY WE'RE HAVING MAPO TOFU AND SOUP AND RICE...
AND STRAWBERRIES TOO!
...FOR DINNER!
THAT SHOULD BE FUN.
YEAH!
WE'LL BE BACK.

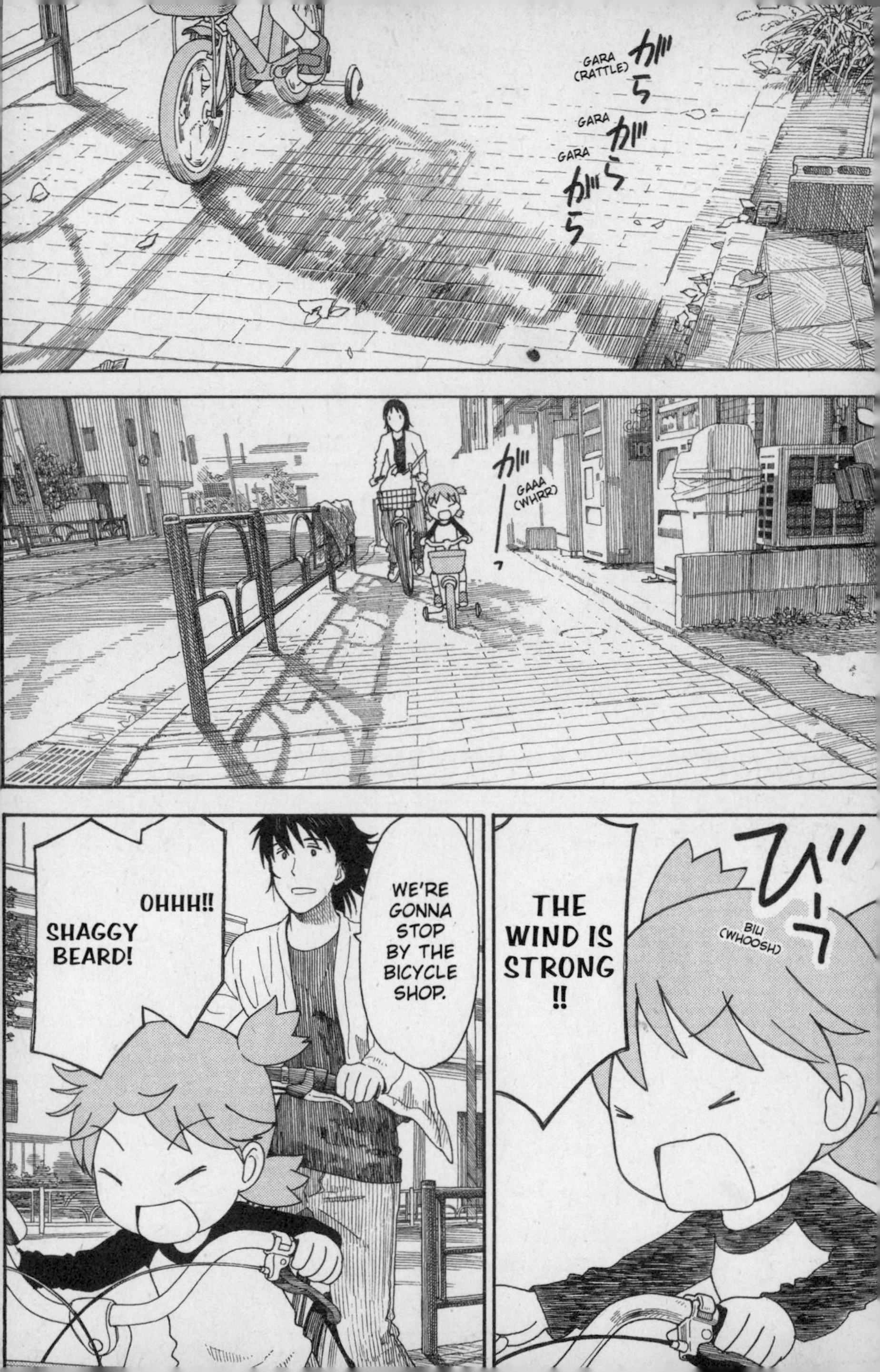
がら
GARA (RATTLE)
がら
GARA
がら
GARA
があ
GAAA (WHRR)
びゅ
BIU (WHOOSH)
THE WIND IS STRONG !!
WE'RE GONNA STOP BY THE BICYCLE SHOP.
OHHH!! SHAGGY BEARD!

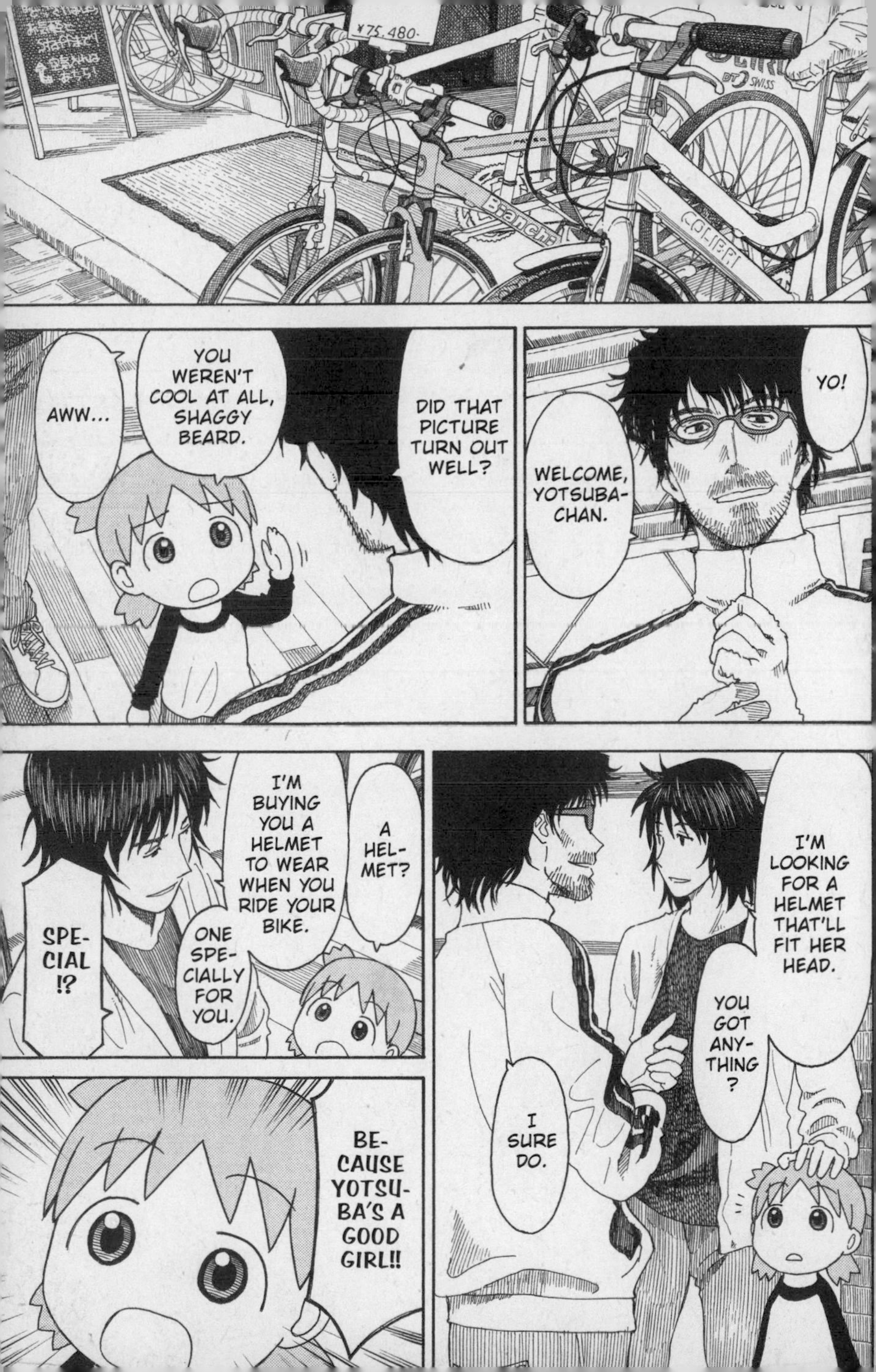
¥75,480-
YO!
WELCOME, YOTSUBA-CHAN.
DID THAT PICTURE TURN OUT WELL?
YOU WEREN'T COOL AT ALL, SHAGGY BEARD.
AWW...
I'M LOOKING FOR A HELMET THAT'LL FIT HER HEAD.
YOU GOT ANYTHING?
I SURE DO.
A HELMET?
I'M BUYING YOU A HELMET TO WEAR WHEN YOU RIDE YOUR BIKE.
ONE SPECIALLY FOR YOU.
SPECIAL!?
BECAUSE YOTSUBA'S A GOOD GIRL!!

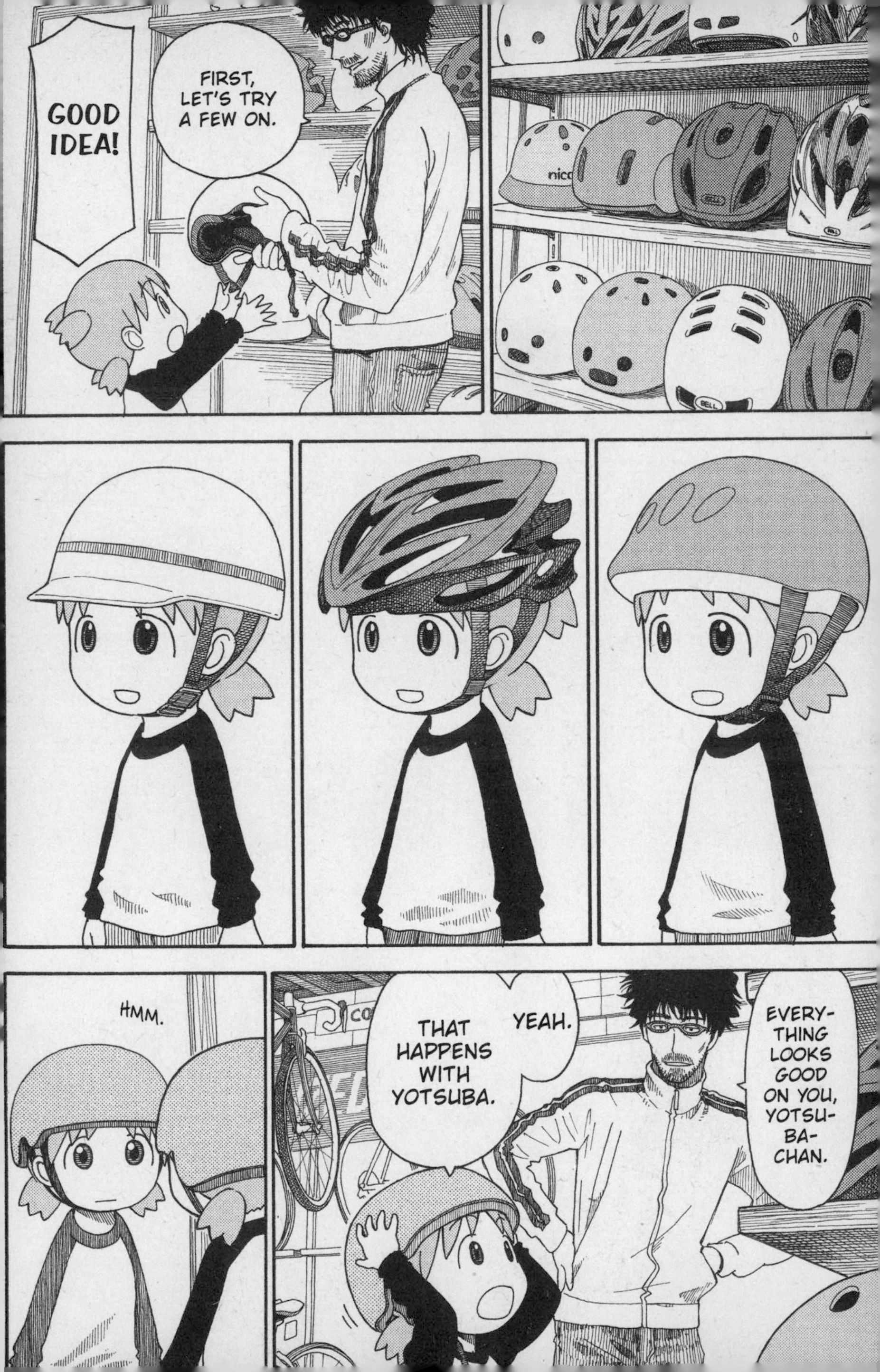
FIRST, LET'S TRY A FEW ON.
GOOD IDEA!
EVERYTHING LOOKS GOOD ON YOU, YOTSUBA-CHAN.
YEAH. THAT HAPPENS WITH YOTSUBA.
HMM.

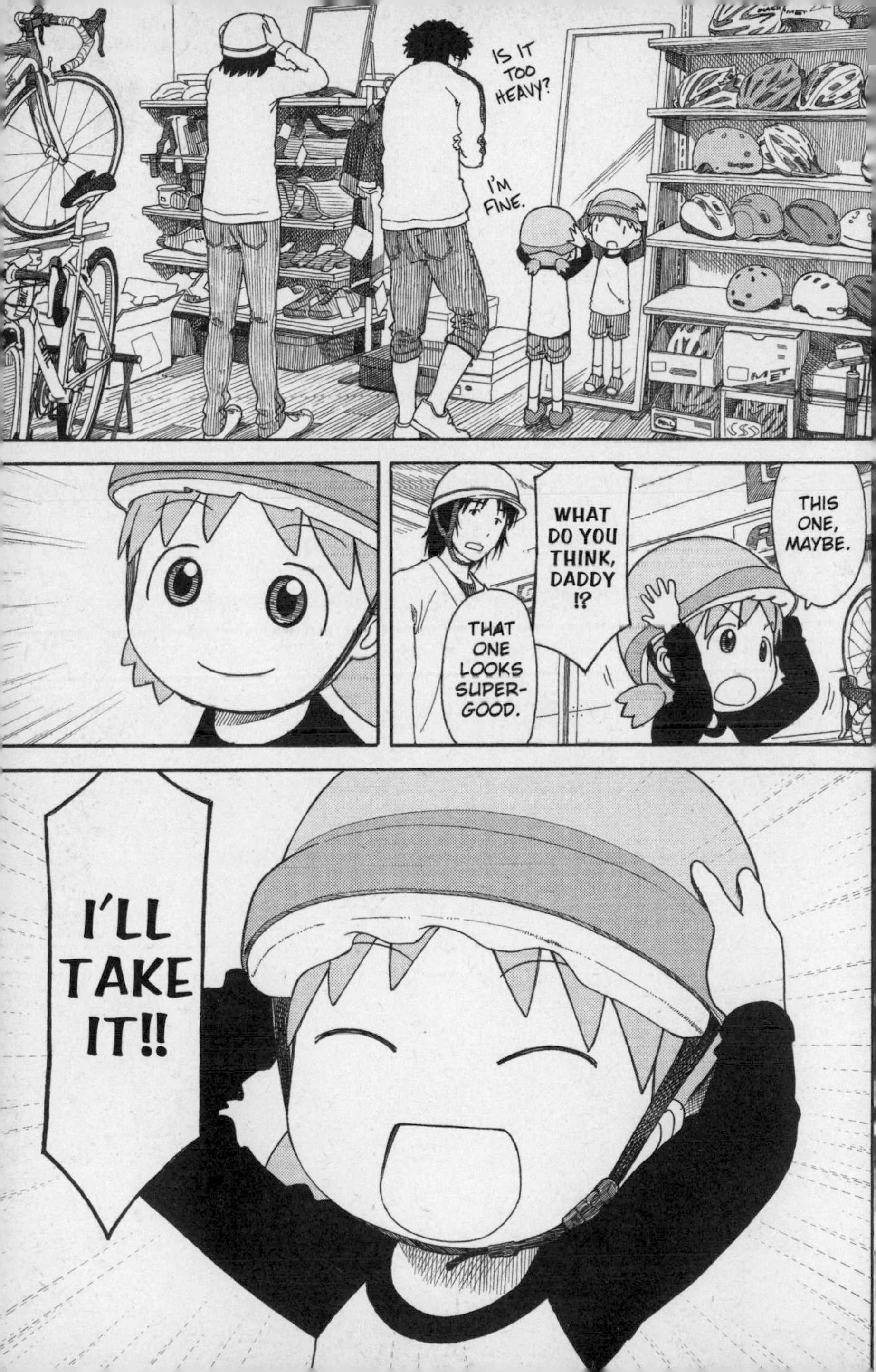
IS IT TOO HEAVY?
I'M FINE.
THIS ONE, MAYBE.
WHAT DO YOU THINK, DADDY!?
THAT ONE LOOKS SUPER-GOOD.
I'LL TAKE IT!!

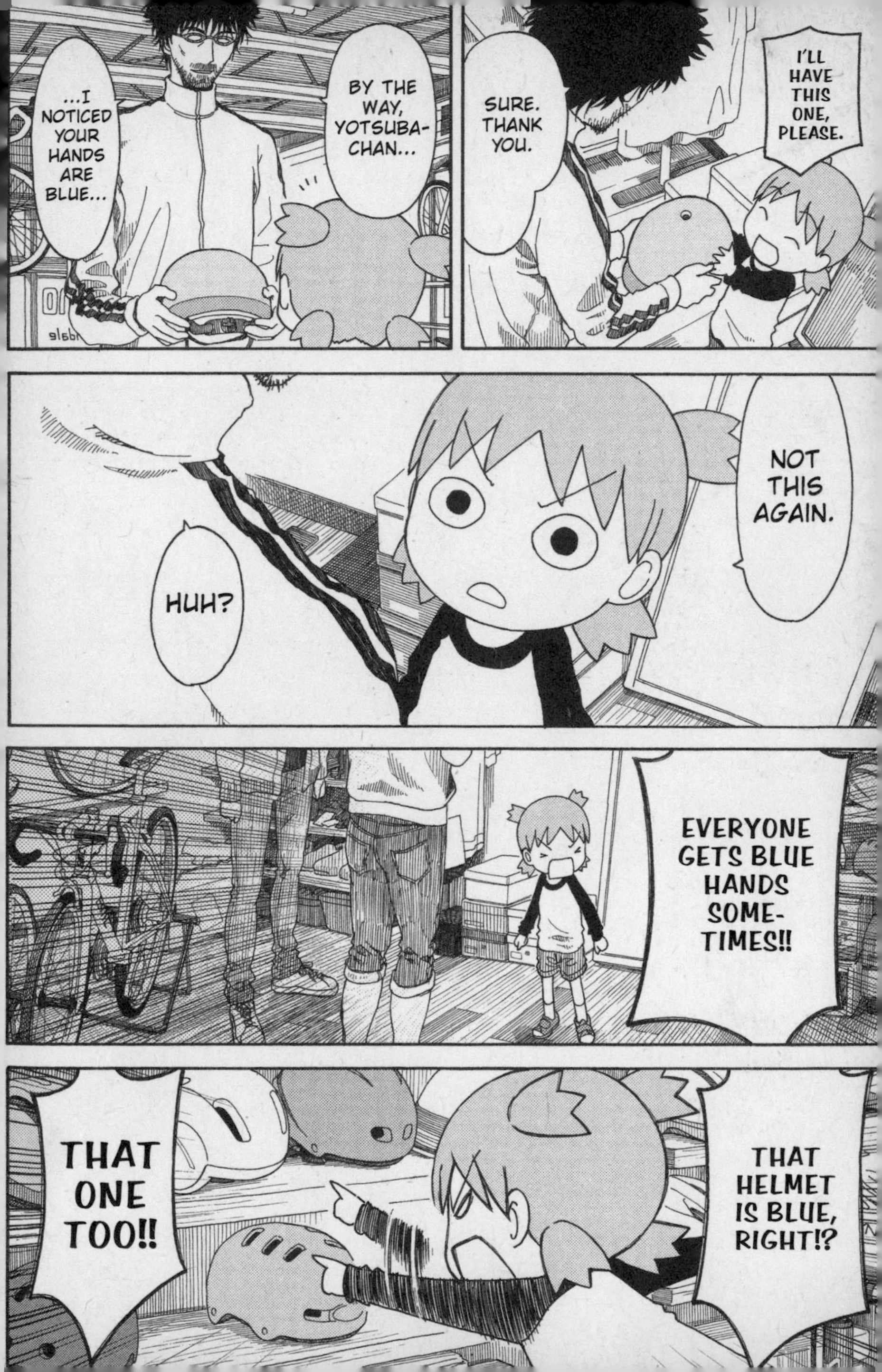
I'LL HAVE THIS ONE, PLEASE.
SURE. THANK YOU.
BY THE WAY, YOTSUBA-CHAN...
...I NOTICED YOUR HANDS ARE BLUE...
NOT THIS AGAIN.
HUH?
EVERYONE GETS BLUE HANDS SOME-TIMES!!
THAT HELMET IS BLUE, RIGHT!?
THAT ONE TOO!!

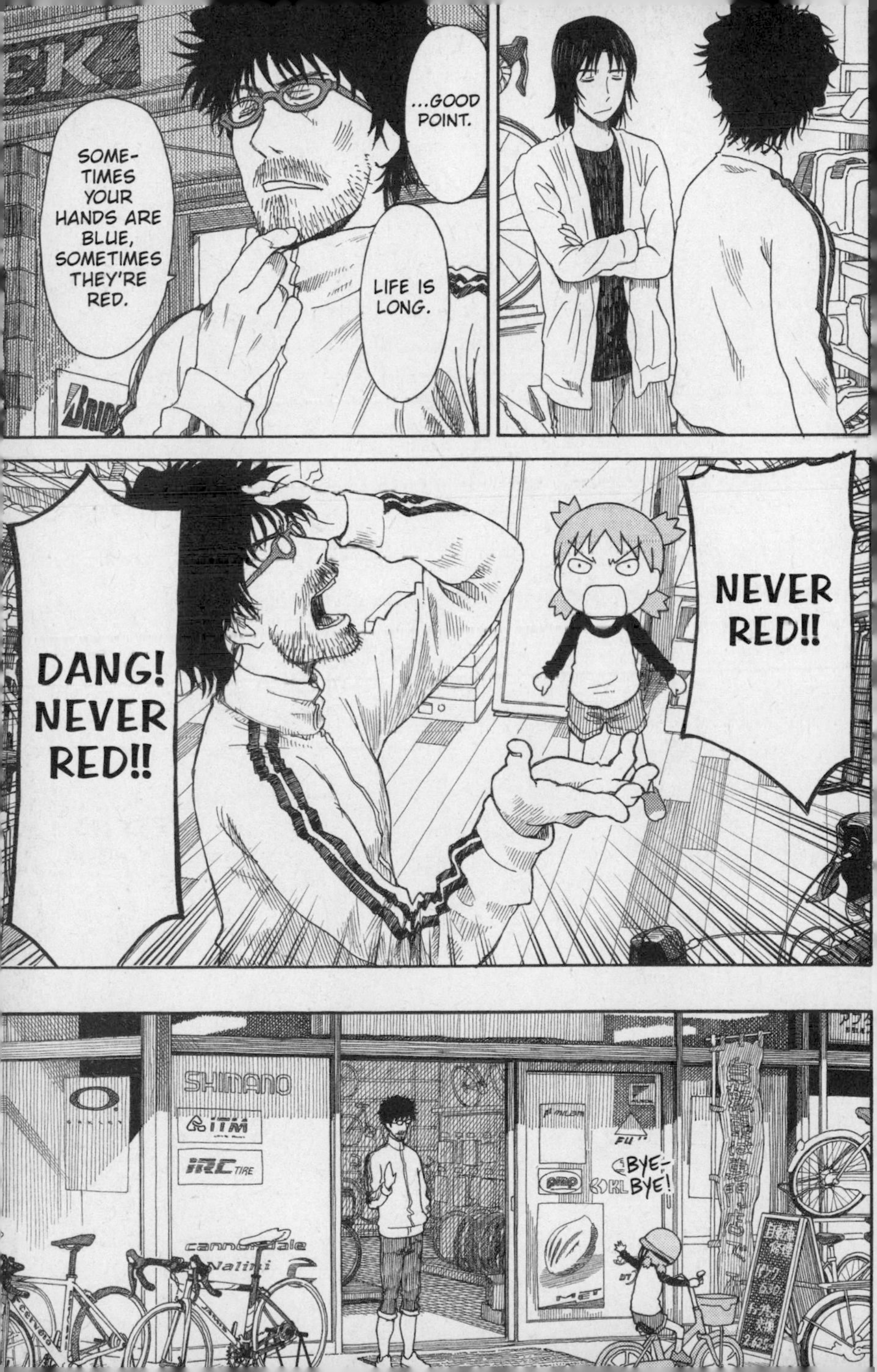

...GOOD POINT.
LIFE IS LONG.
SOME-TIMES YOUR HANDS ARE BLUE, SOMETIMES THEY'RE RED.
NEVER RED!!
DANG! NEVER RED!!
BYE-BYE!
SHIMANO
ITM
IRC TIRE
cannondale
Nalini

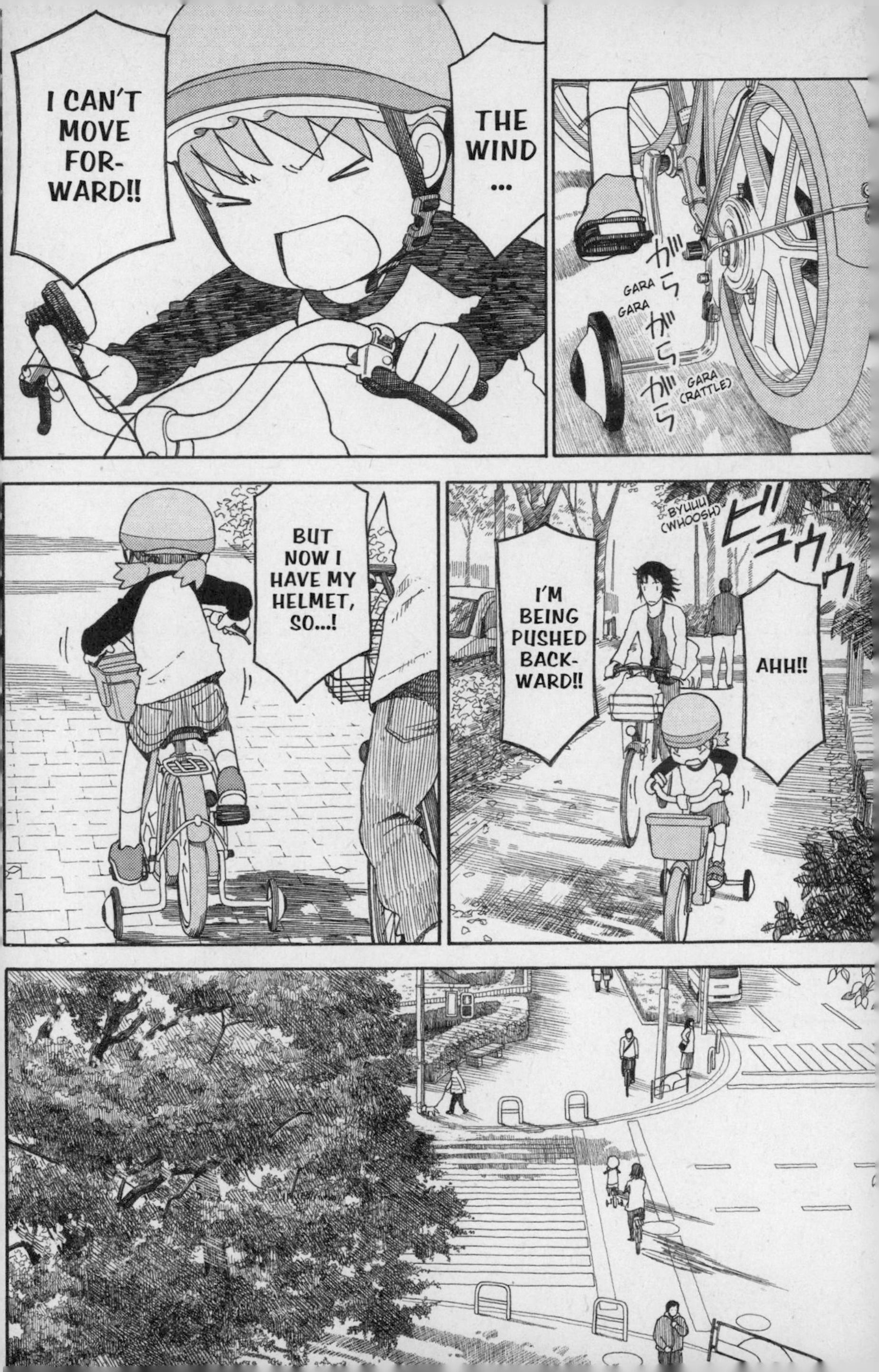
がらがらがら
GARA GARA GARA (RATTLE)
THE WIND...
I CAN'T MOVE FOR-WARD!!
ビュウウ
BYUUU (WHOOSH)
AHH!!
I'M BEING PUSHED BACK-WARD!!
BUT NOW I HAVE MY HELMET, SO...!

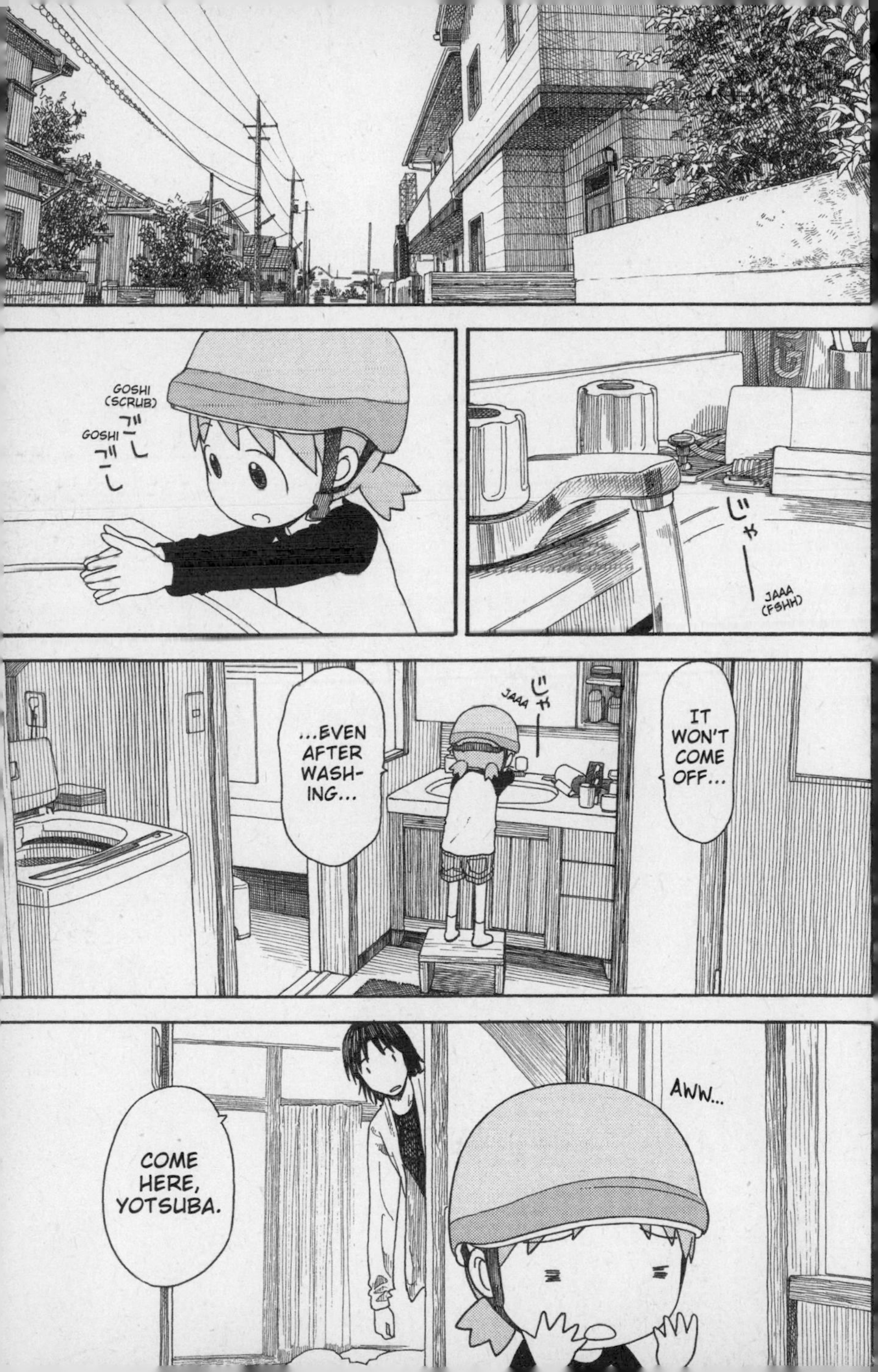
じゃー
JAAA (FSHH)
ごし ごし
GOSHI (SCRUB)
GOSHI
IT WON'T COME OFF...
じゃー
JAAA
...EVEN AFTER WASH-ING...
AWW...
COME HERE, YOTSUBA.

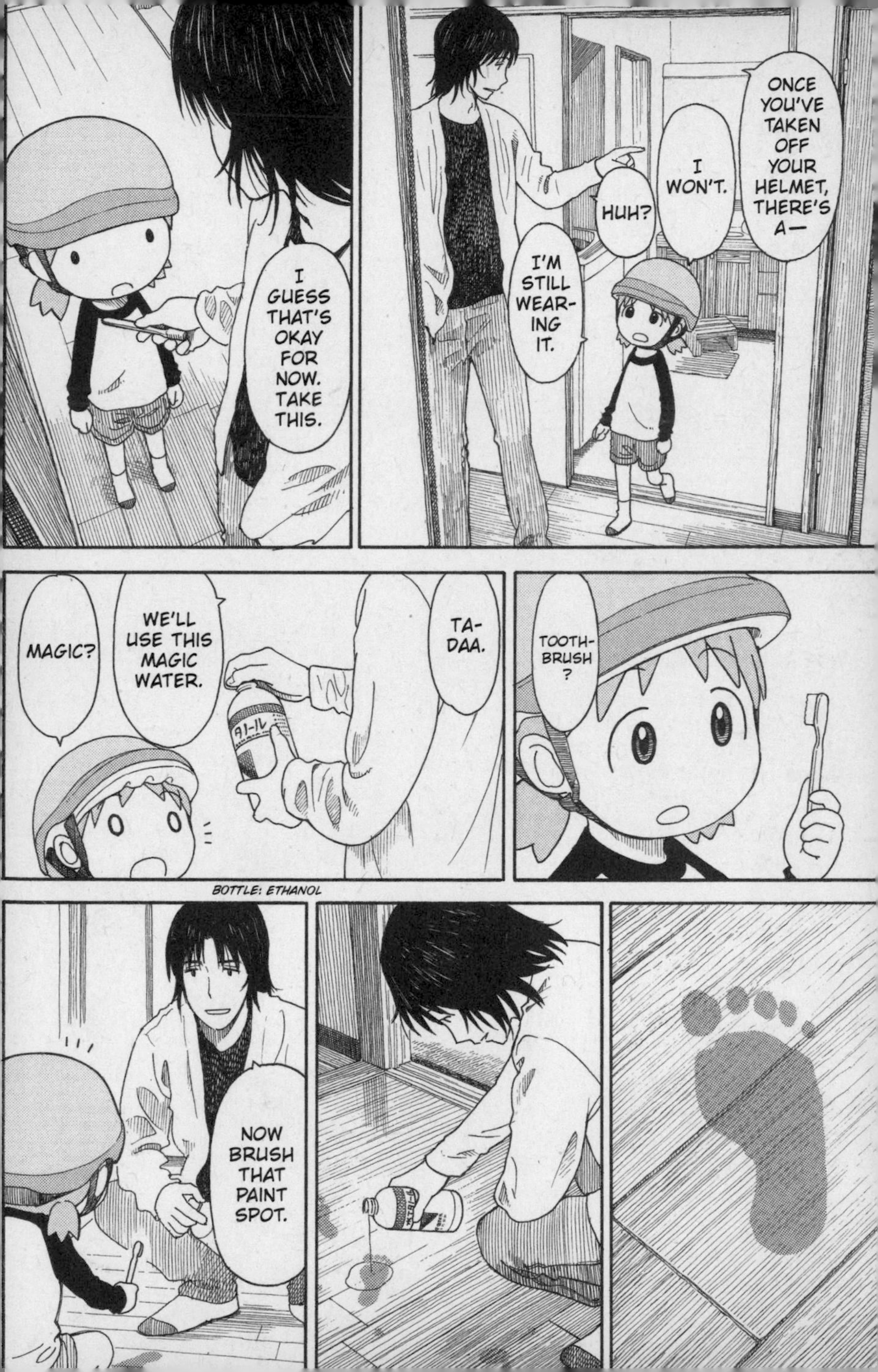
ONCE YOU'VE TAKEN OFF YOUR HELMET, THERE'S A—
I WON'T.
HUH?
I'M STILL WEARING IT.
I GUESS THAT'S OKAY FOR NOW. TAKE THIS.
TOOTHBRUSH?
TA-DAA.
WE'LL USE THIS MAGIC WATER.
MAGIC?
BOTTLE: ETHANOL
NOW BRUSH THAT PAINT SPOT.

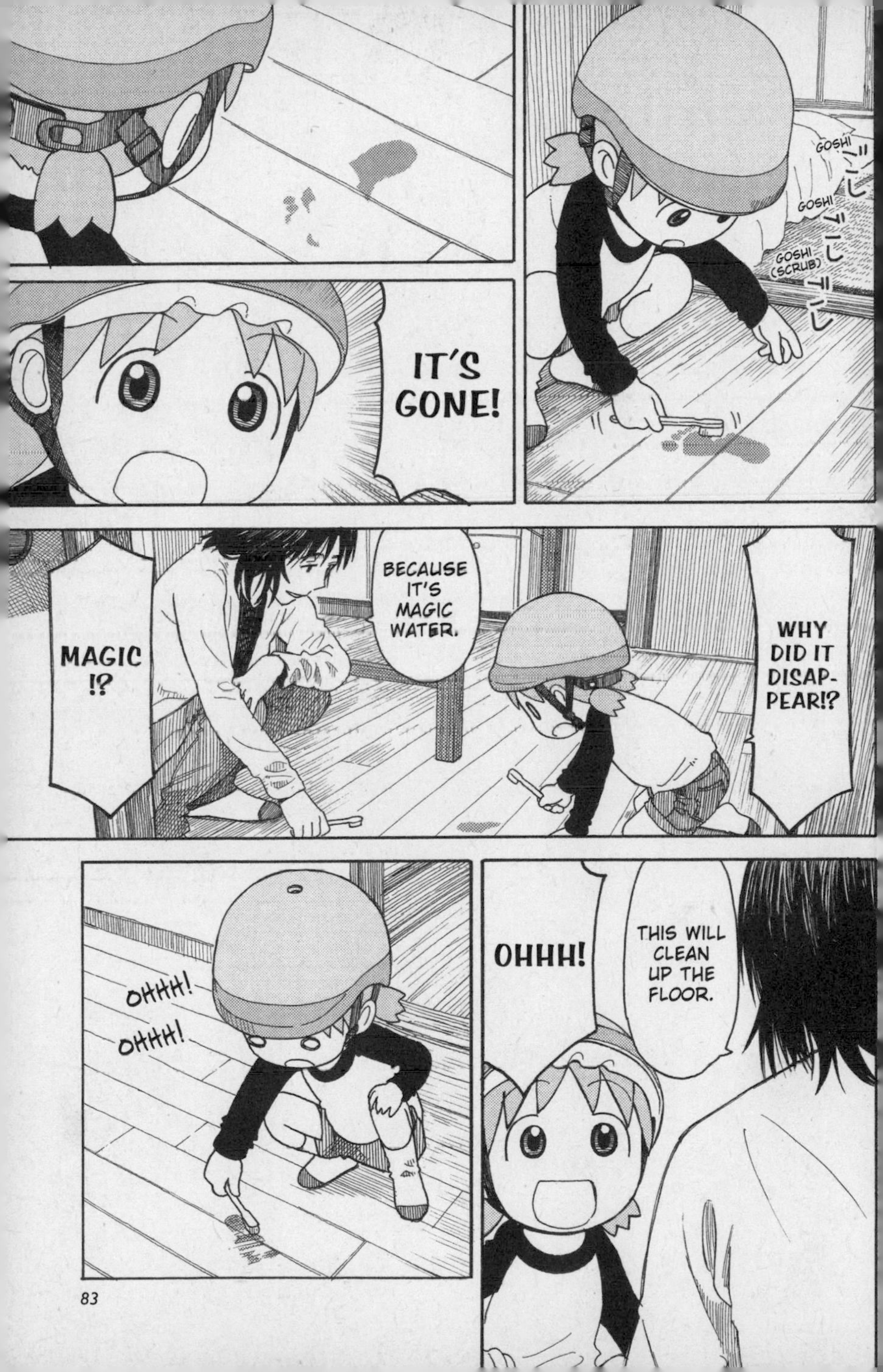
GOSHI
GOSHI
GOSHI (SCRUB)
IT'S GONE!
WHY DID IT DISAP-PEAR!?
BECAUSE IT'S MAGIC WATER.
MAGIC!?
THIS WILL CLEAN UP THE FLOOR.
OHHHH!
OHHH!
OHHH!

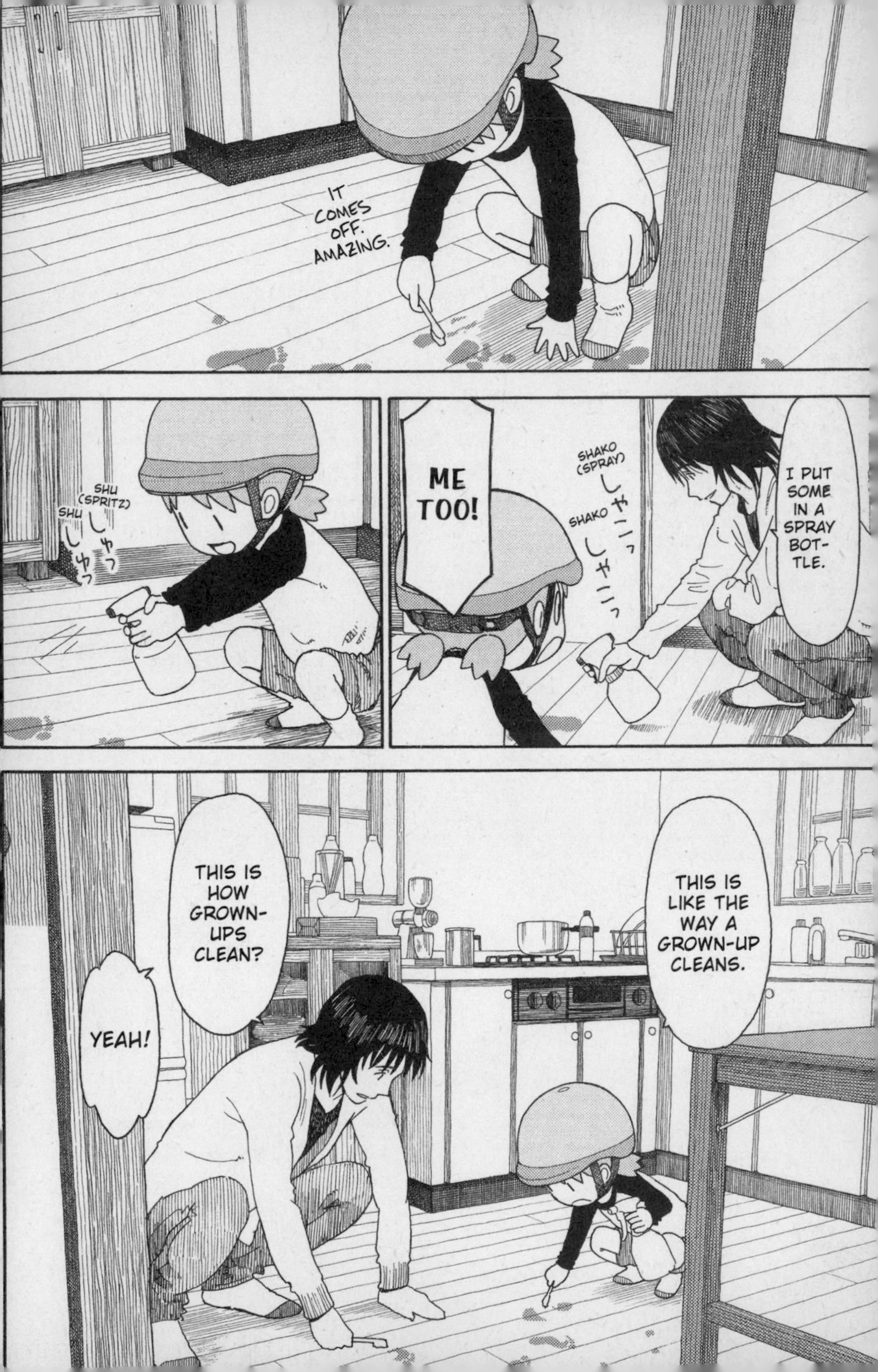
IT COMES OFF. AMAZING.
I PUT SOME IN A SPRAY BOTTLE.
SHAKO (SPRAY) しゃこっ
SHAKO しゃこっ
ME TOO!
SHU (SPRITZ) しゅっ
SHU しゅっ
THIS IS LIKE THE WAY A GROWN-UP CLEANS.
THIS IS HOW GROWN-UPS CLEAN?
YEAH!

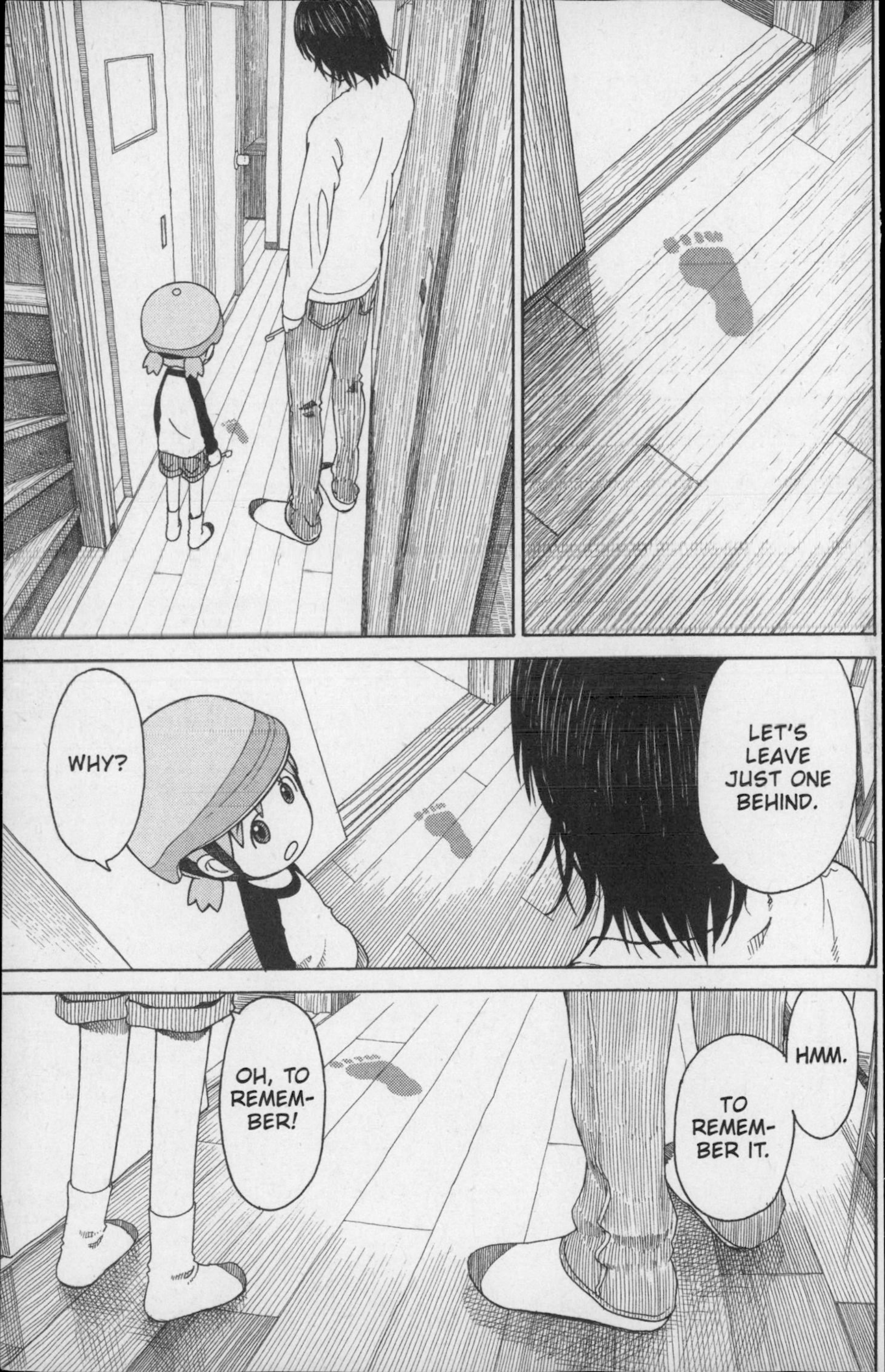
LET'S LEAVE JUST ONE BEHIND.
WHY?
HMM.
TO REMEMBER IT.
OH, TO REMEMBER!

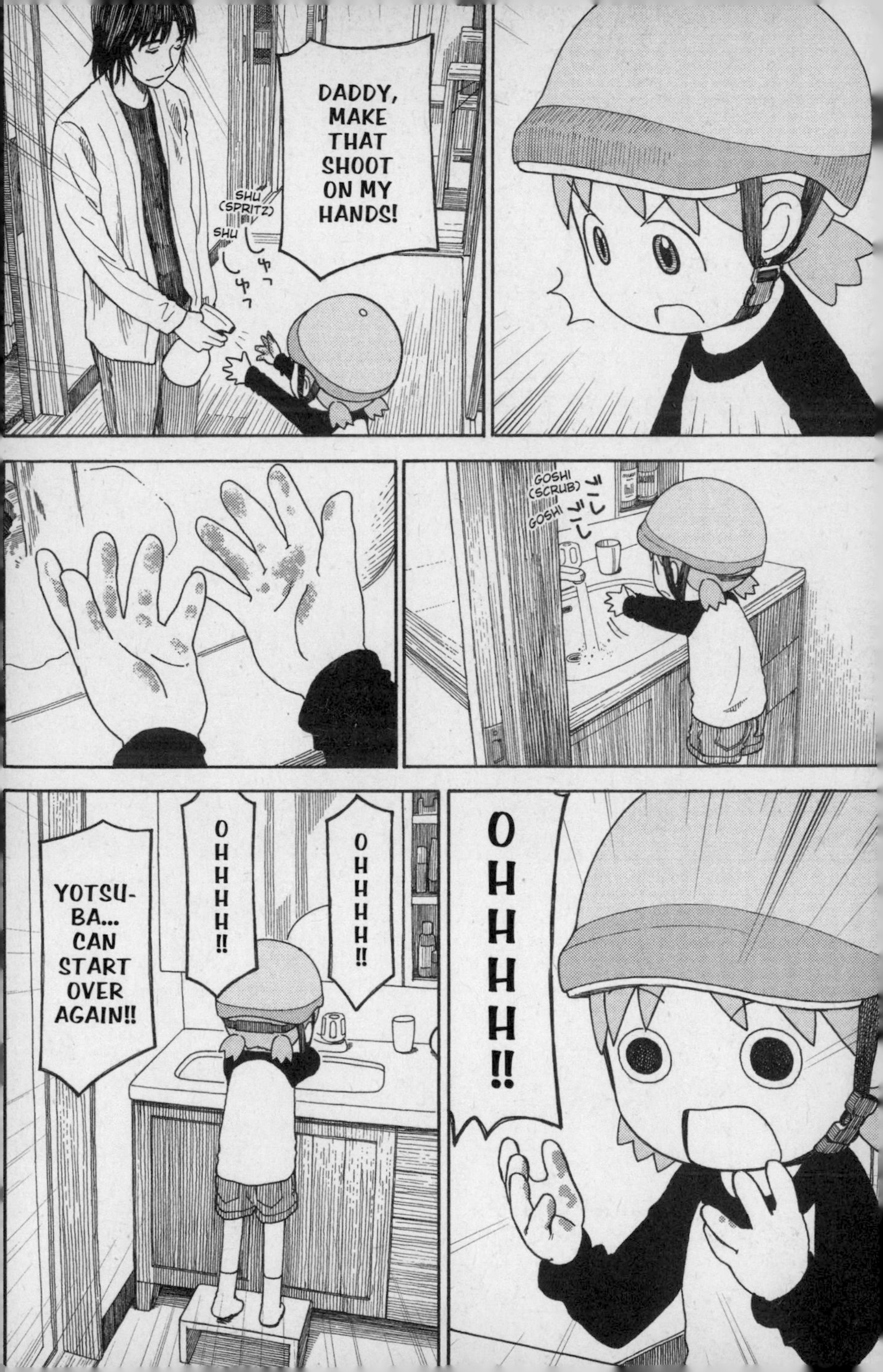
DADDY, MAKE THAT SHOOT ON MY HANDS!
SHU (SPRITZ)
SHU
GOSHI (SCRUB)
GOSHI
OHHHH!!
OHHHHH!!
OHHHHH!!
YOTSUBA... CAN START OVER AGAIN!!

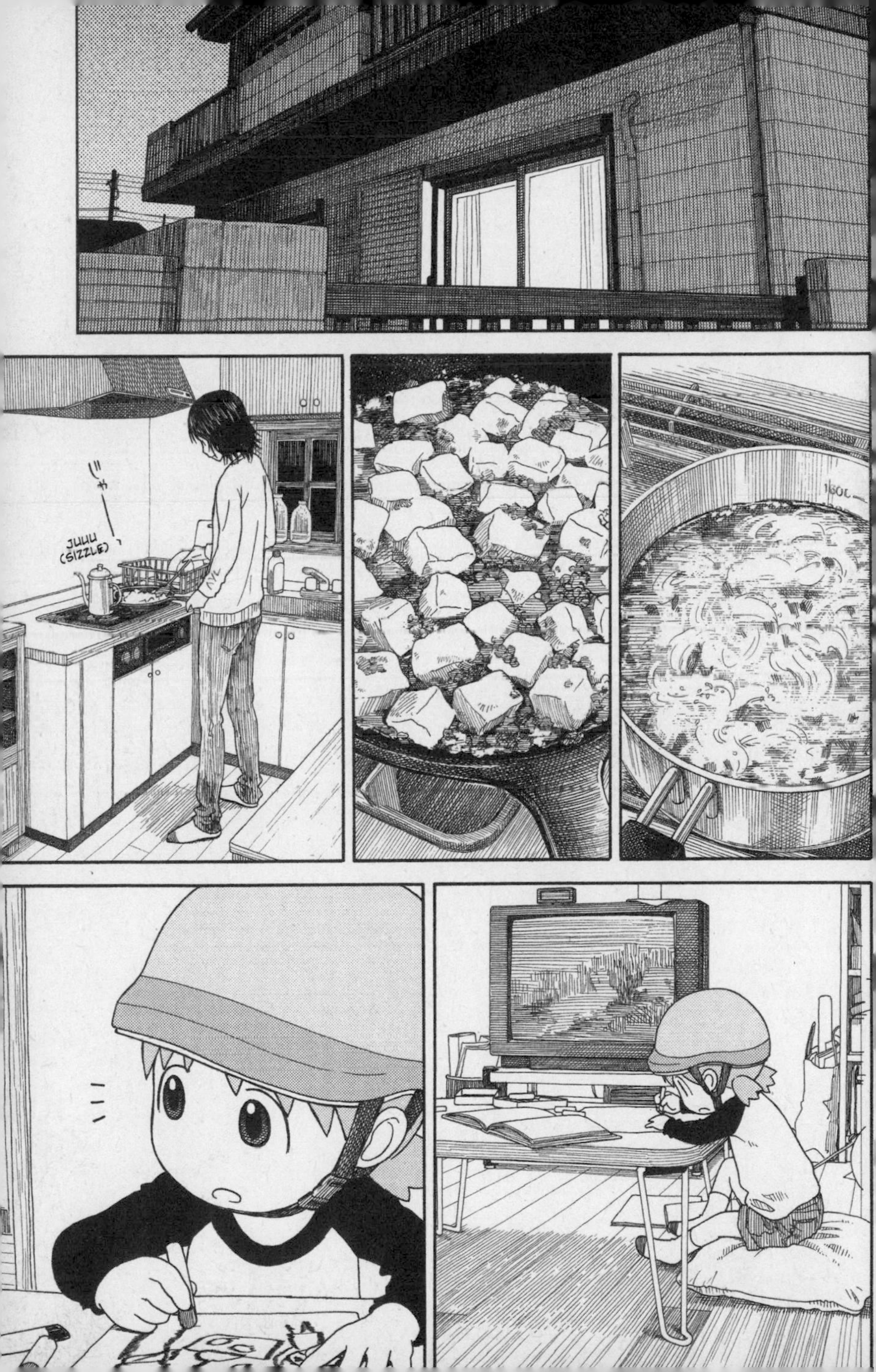
じゃー
JUUU (SIZZLE)

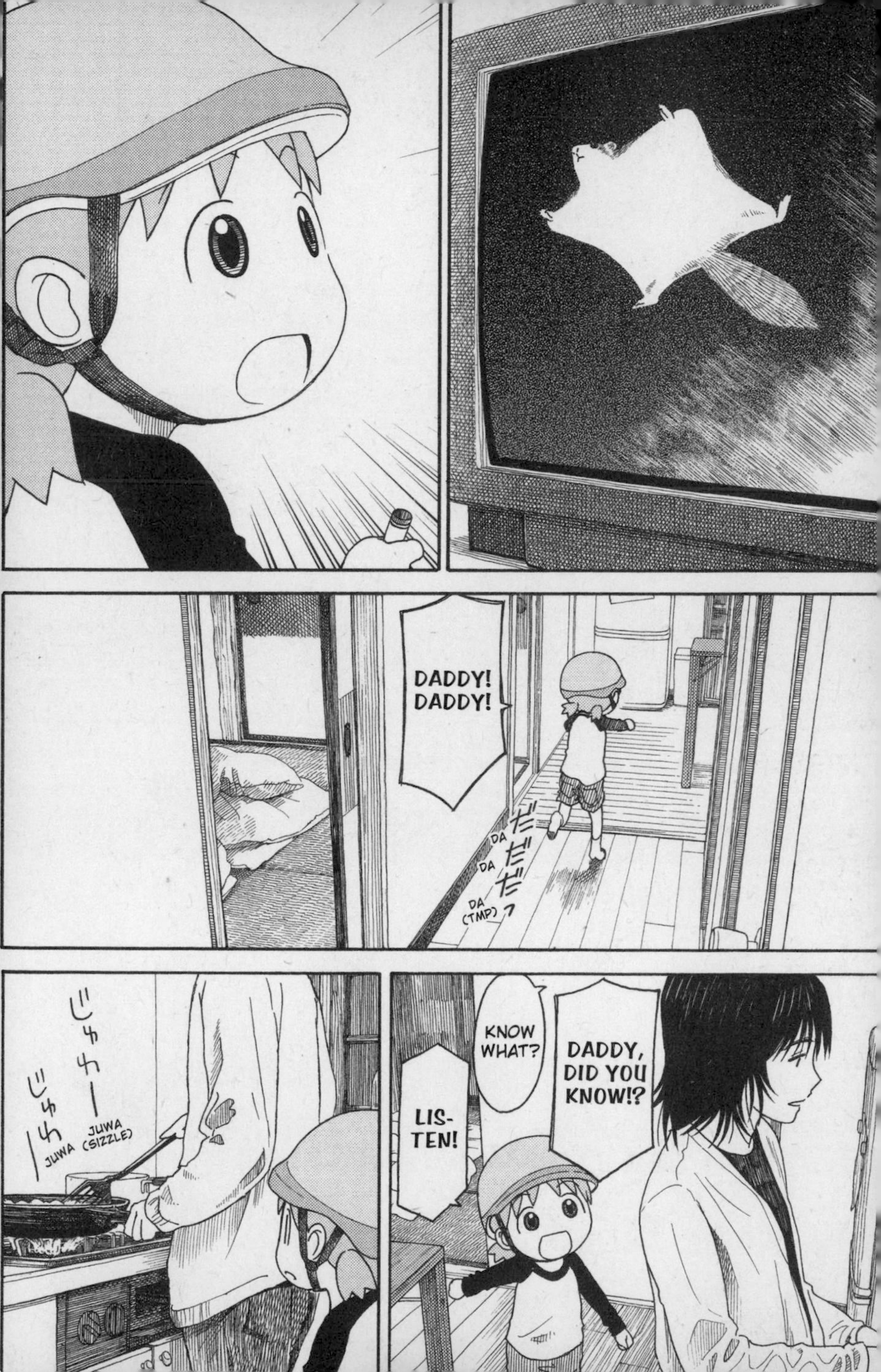
DADDY! DADDY!
だだだっ
DA DA DA (TMP)
DADDY, DID YOU KNOW!?
KNOW WHAT?
LIS-TEN!
じゅわー
じゅわー
JUWA (SIZZLE)
JUWA

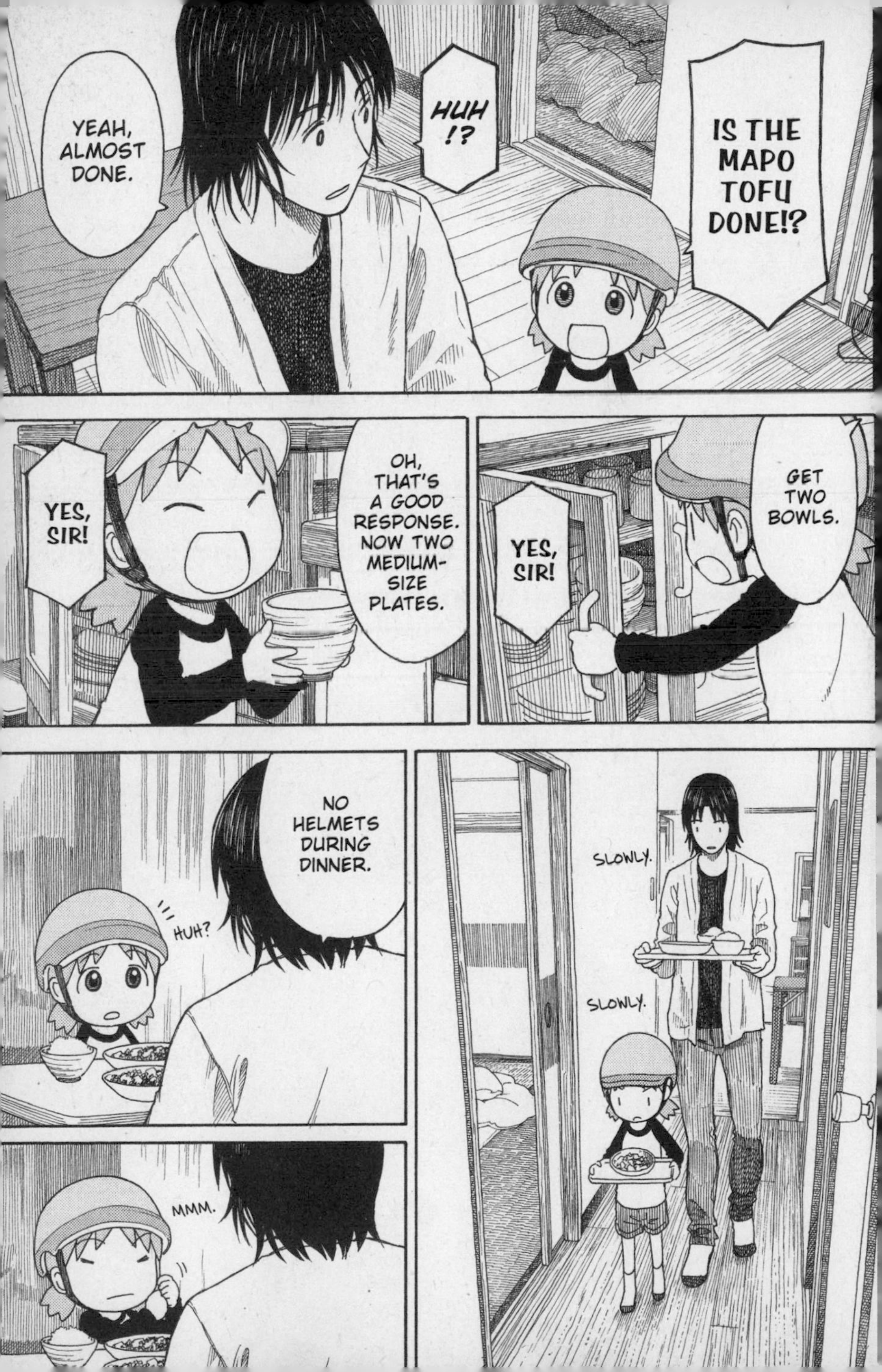
IS THE MAPO TOFU DONE!?
HUH!?
YEAH, ALMOST DONE.
GET TWO BOWLS.
YES, SIR!
OH, THAT'S A GOOD RESPONSE. NOW TWO MEDIUM-SIZE PLATES.
YES, SIR!
SLOWLY.
SLOWLY.
NO HELMETS DURING DINNER.
HUH?
MMM.

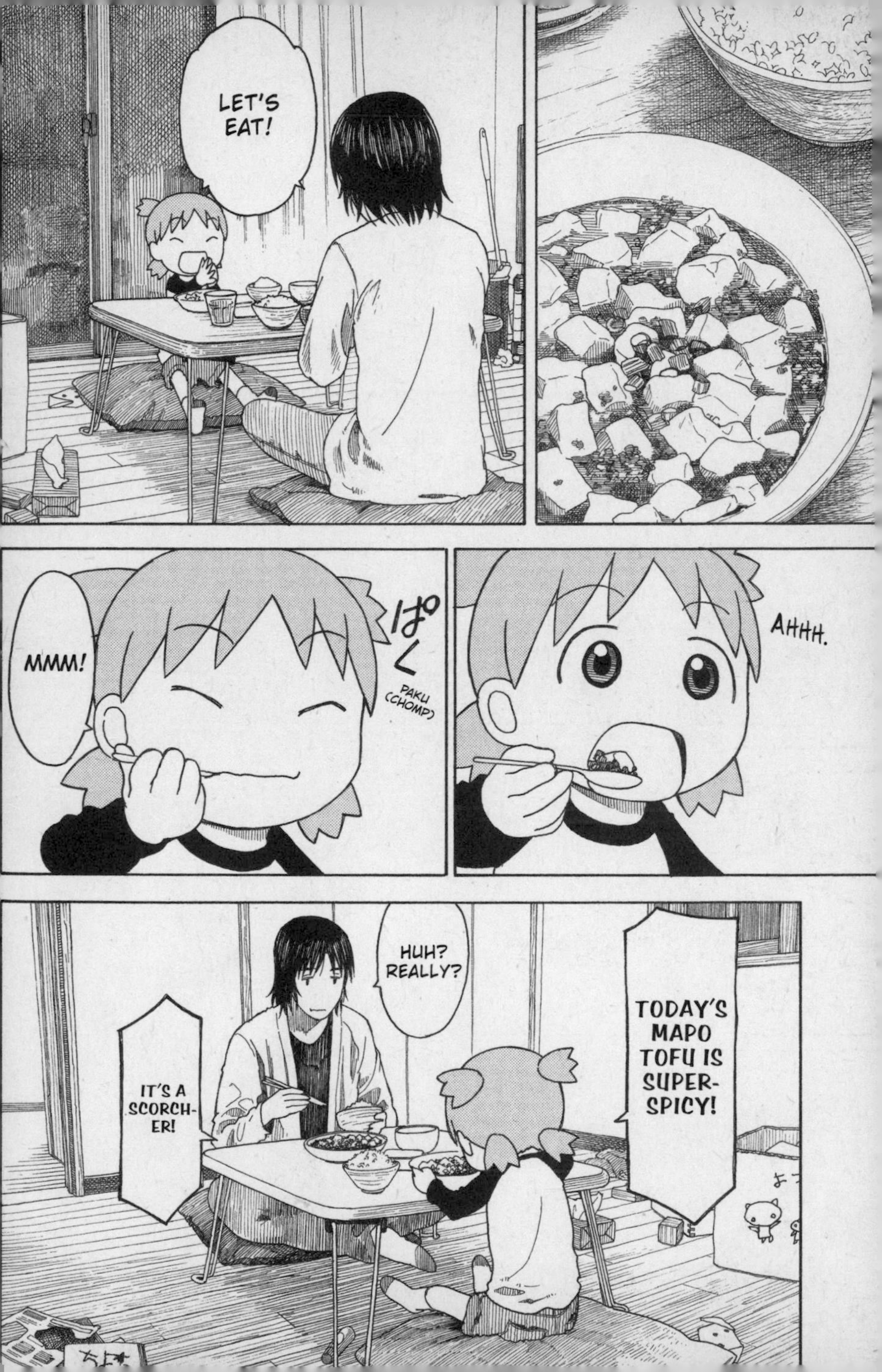
LET'S EAT!
AHHH.
MMM!
ぱく
PAKU (CHOMP)
TODAY'S MAPO TOFU IS SUPER-SPICY!
HUH? REALLY?
IT'S A SCORCH-ER!

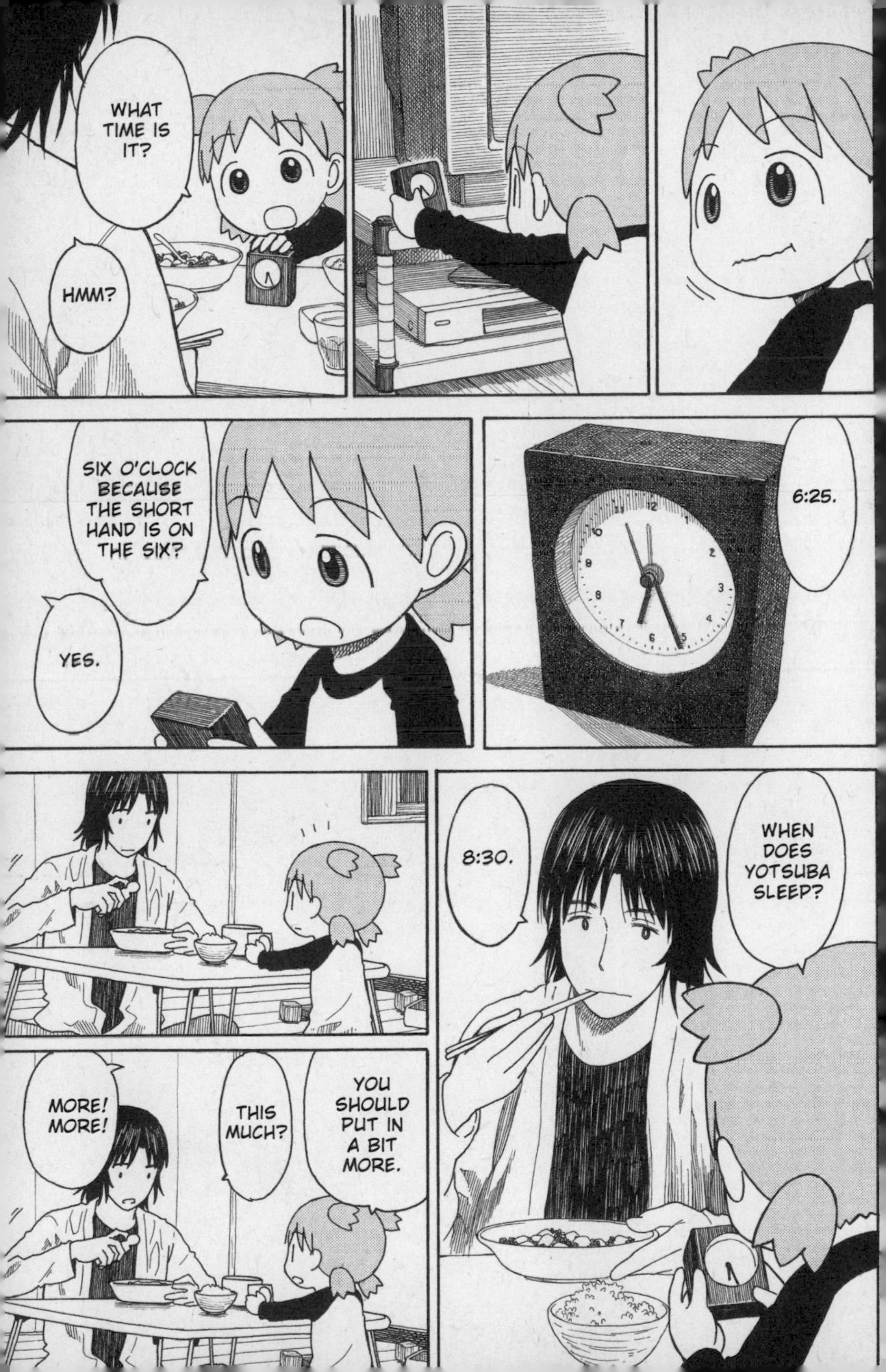
WHAT TIME IS IT?
HMM?
6:25.
SIX O'CLOCK BECAUSE THE SHORT HAND IS ON THE SIX?
YES.
WHEN DOES YOTSUBA SLEEP?
8:30.
YOU SHOULD PUT IN A BIT MORE.
THIS MUCH?
MORE! MORE!

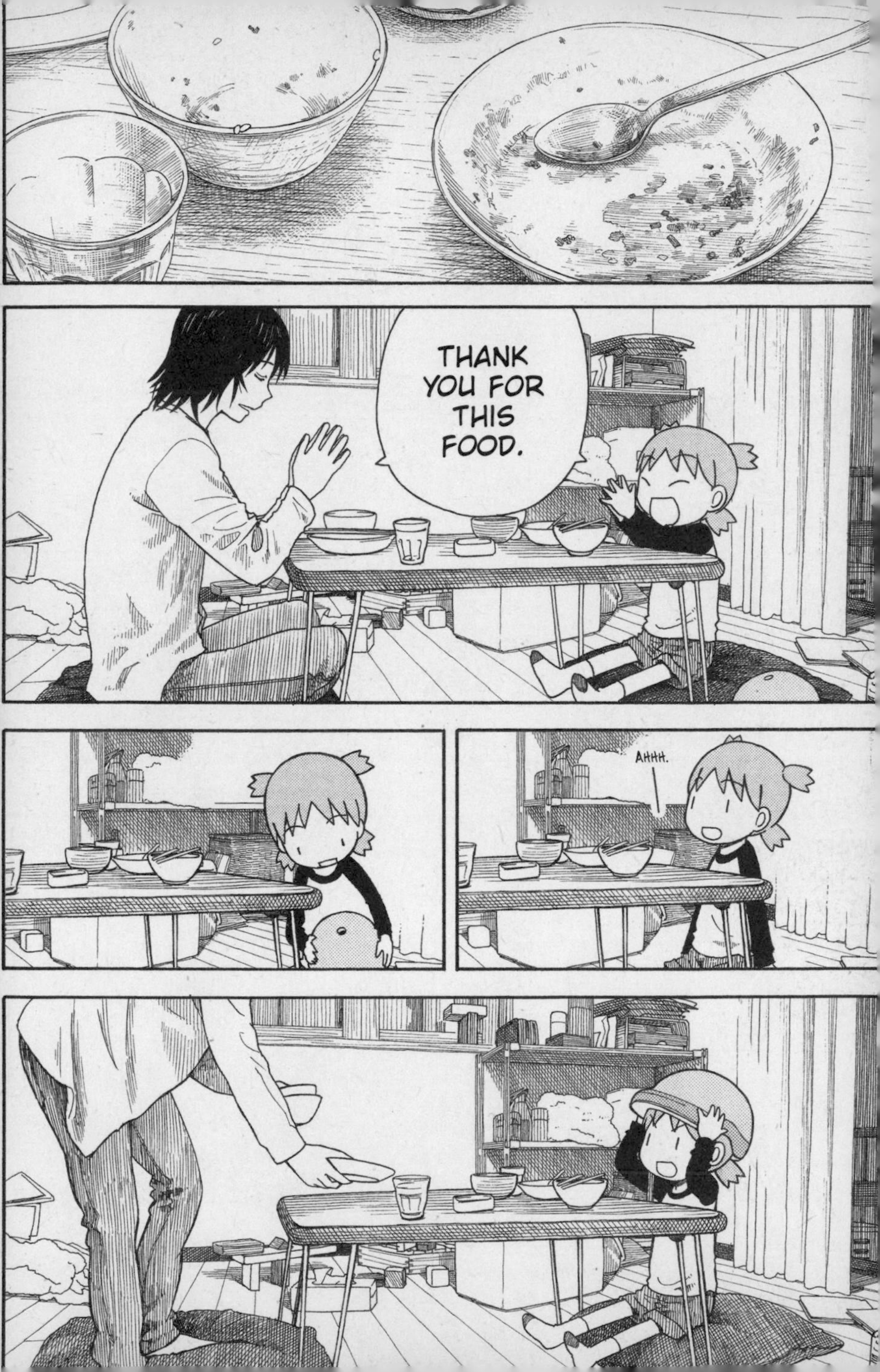
THANK YOU FOR THIS FOOD.
AHHH.

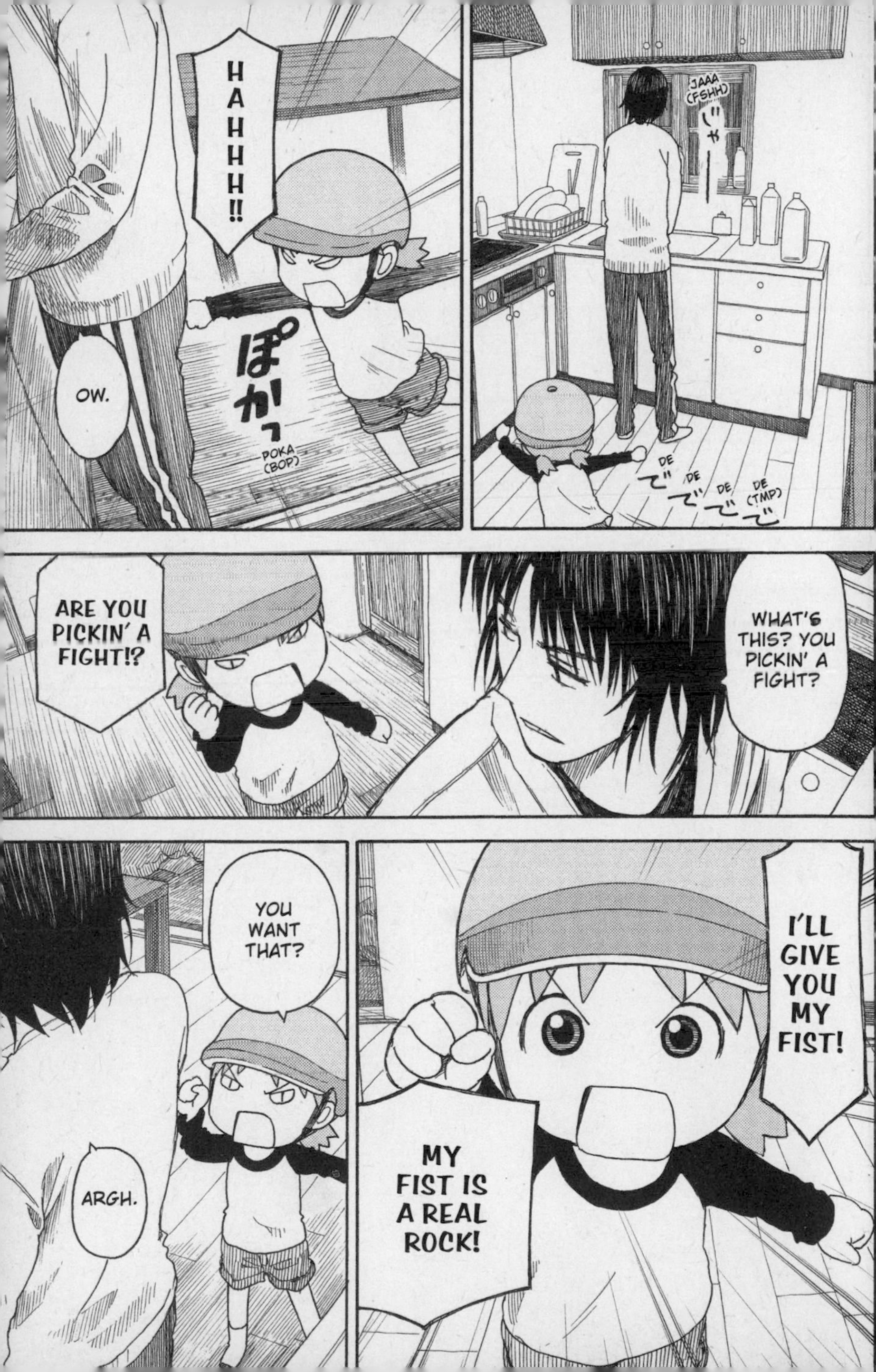
JAAA (FSHH)
じゃー
DE DE DE DE (TMP)
でででで
HAHHHH!!
ぽかっ
POKA (BOP)
OW.
WHAT'S THIS? YOU PICKIN' A FIGHT?
ARE YOU PICKIN' A FIGHT!?
I'LL GIVE YOU MY FIST!
MY FIST IS A REAL ROCK!
YOU WANT THAT?
ARGH.

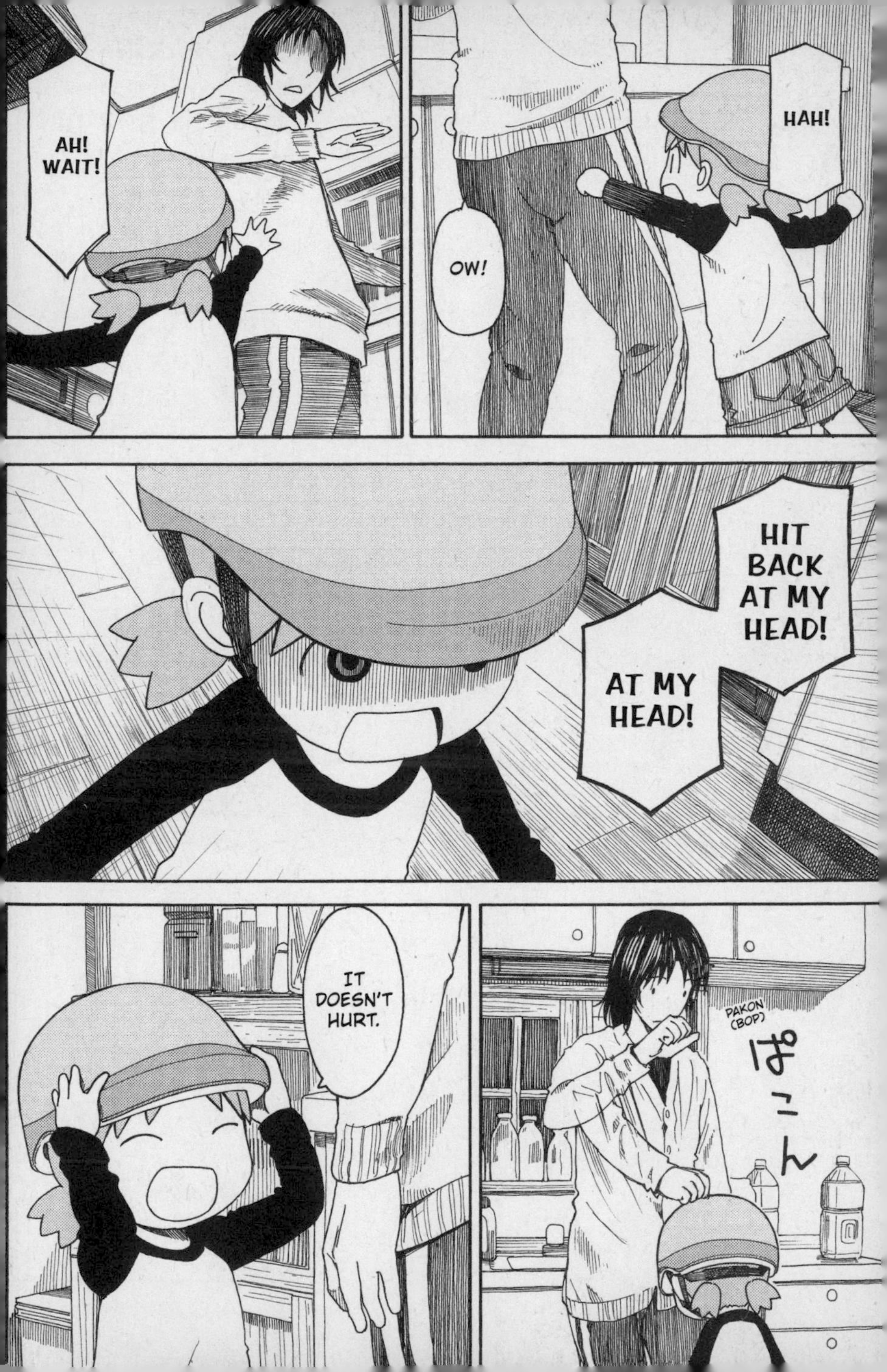
HAH!
OW!
AH! WAIT!
HIT BACK AT MY HEAD!
AT MY HEAD!
PAKON (BOP)
ぱこん
IT DOESN'T HURT.

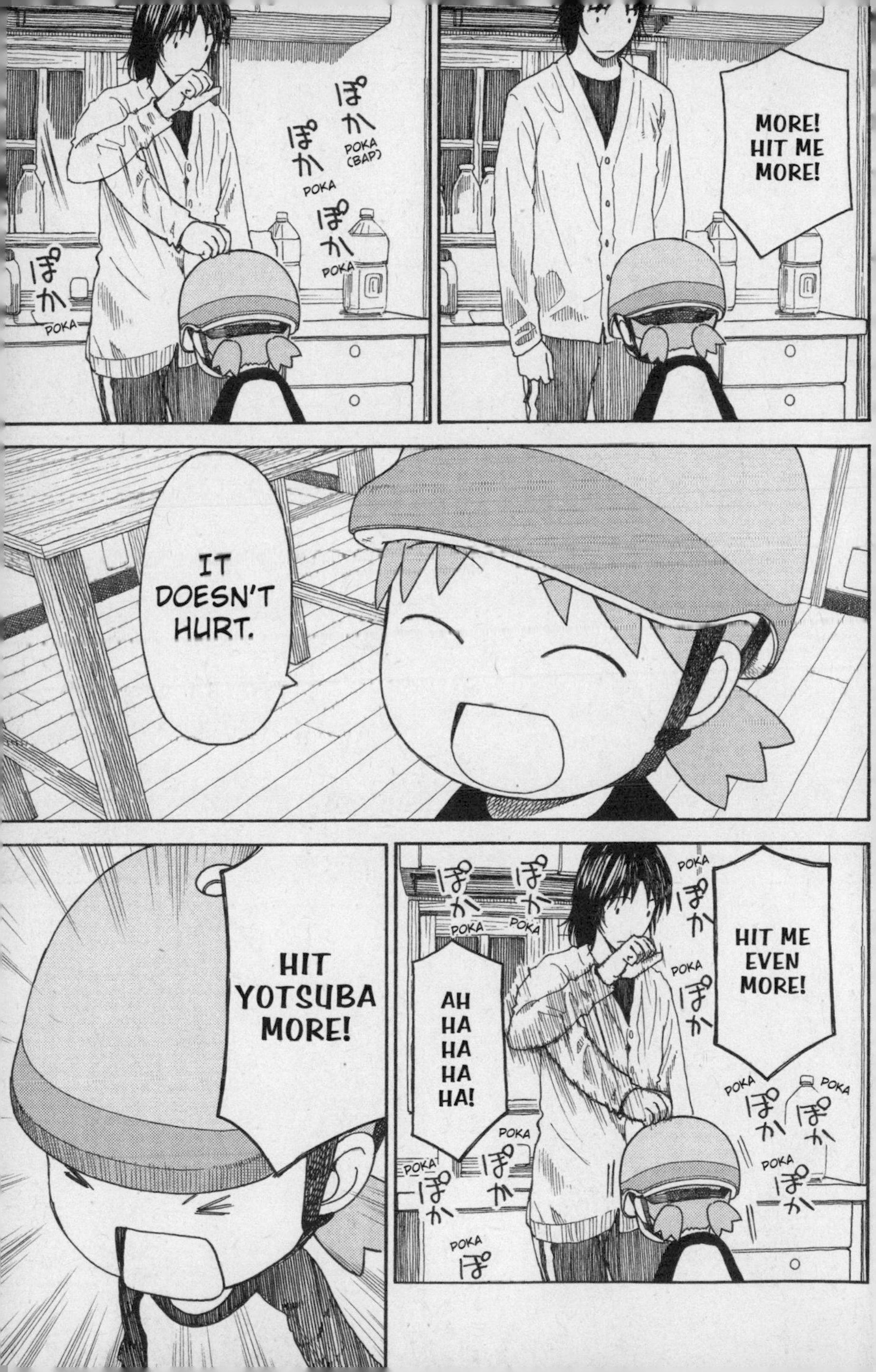
MORE! HIT ME MORE!
ぽか
POKA (BAP)
ぽか
POKA
ぽか
POKA
ぽか
POKA
IT DOESN'T HURT.
HIT ME EVEN MORE!
POKA
ぽか
POKA
ぽか
POKA
ぽか
POKA
ぽか
POKA
ぽか
POKA
ぽか
AH HA HA HA HA!
POKA
ぽか
POKA
ぽか
POKA
ぽか
POKA
ぽ
HIT YOTSUBA MORE!

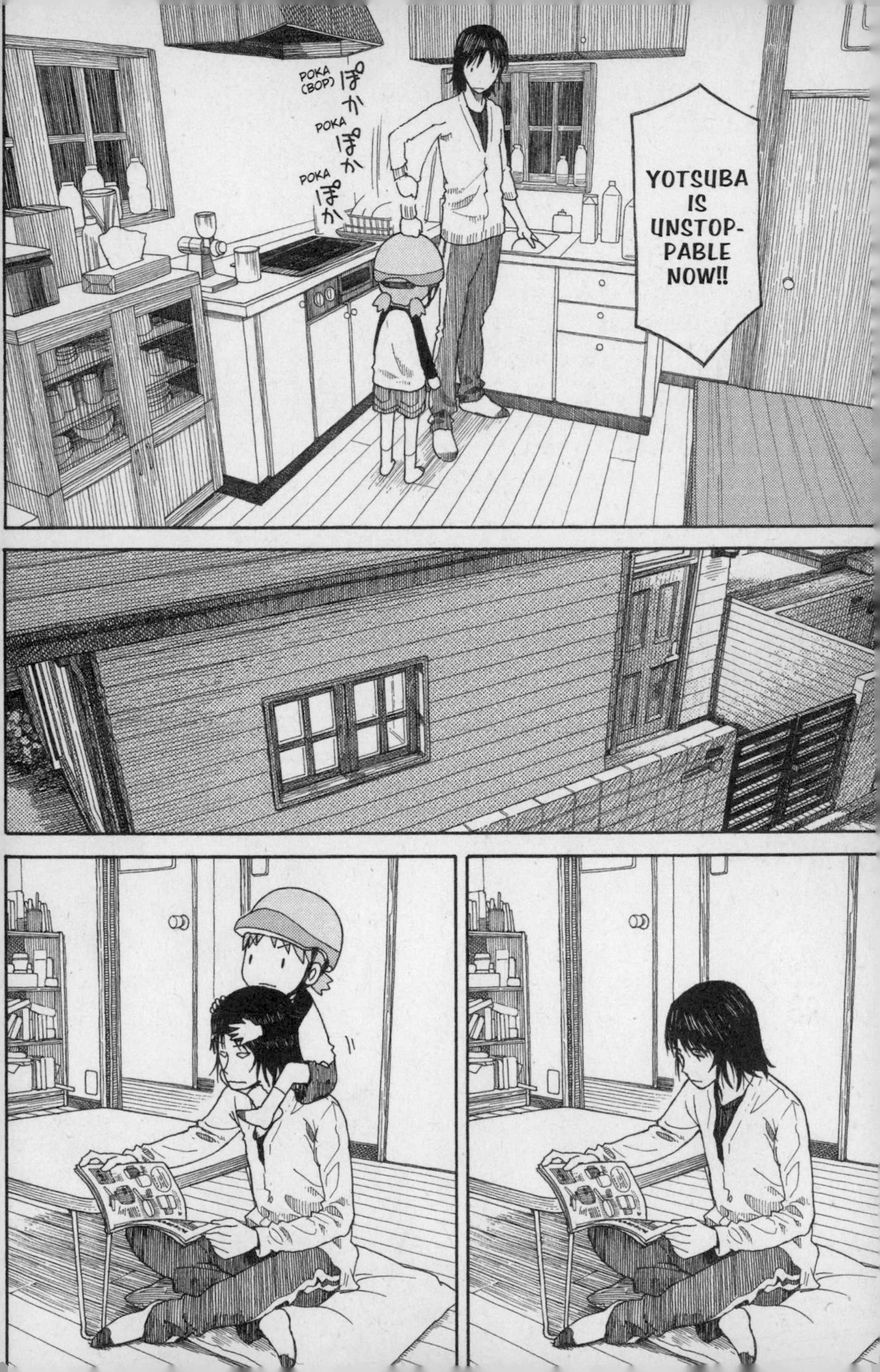
YOTSUBA IS UNSTOP-PABLE NOW!!
POKA (BOP) ぽか
POKA ぽか
POKA ぽか

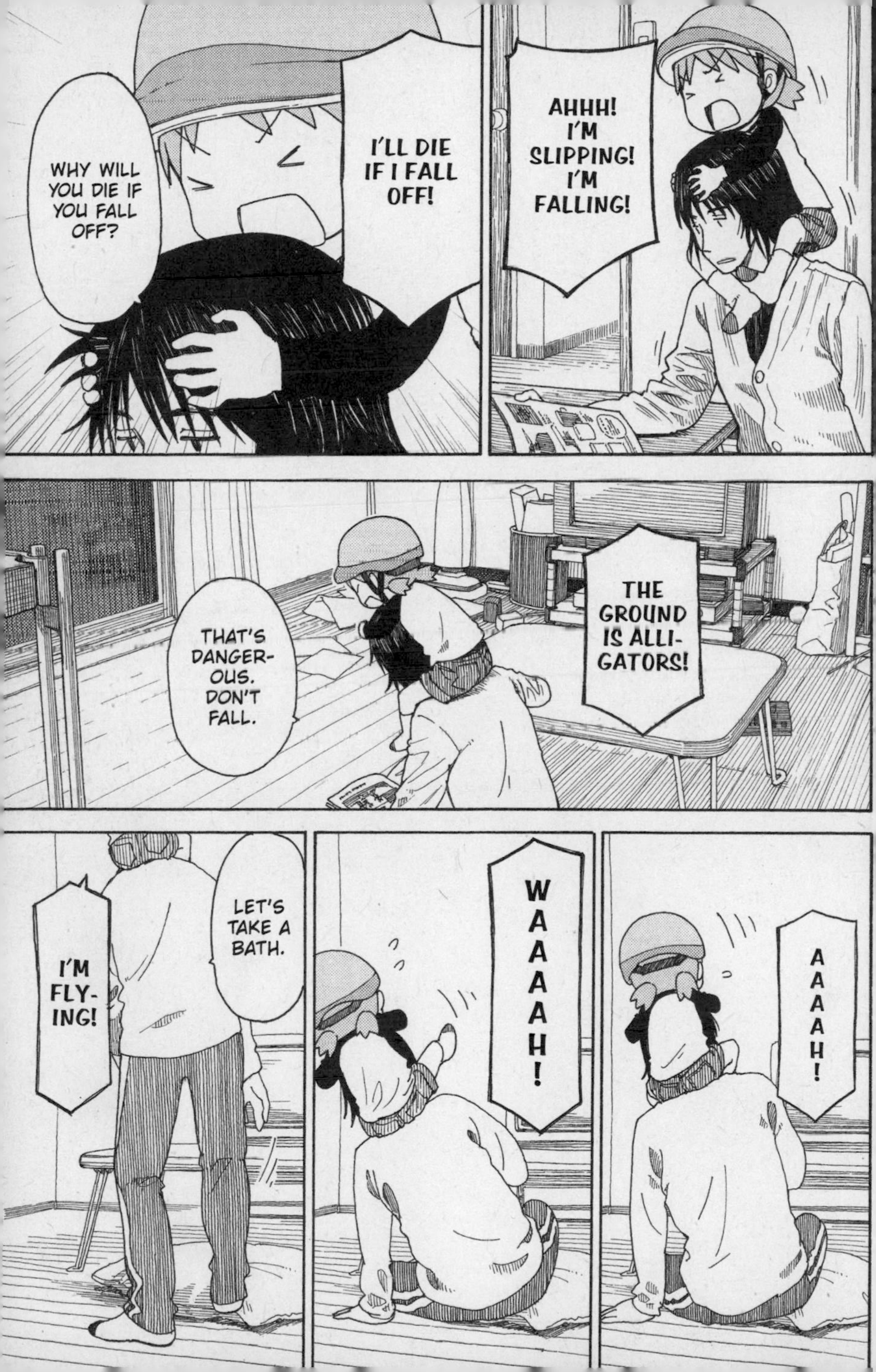
AHHH! I'M SLIPPING! I'M FALLING!
I'LL DIE IF I FALL OFF!
WHY WILL YOU DIE IF YOU FALL OFF?
THE GROUND IS ALLI-GATORS!
THAT'S DANGER-OUS. DON'T FALL.
AAAAAH!
WAAAAAH!
LET'S TAKE A BATH.
I'M FLY-ING!

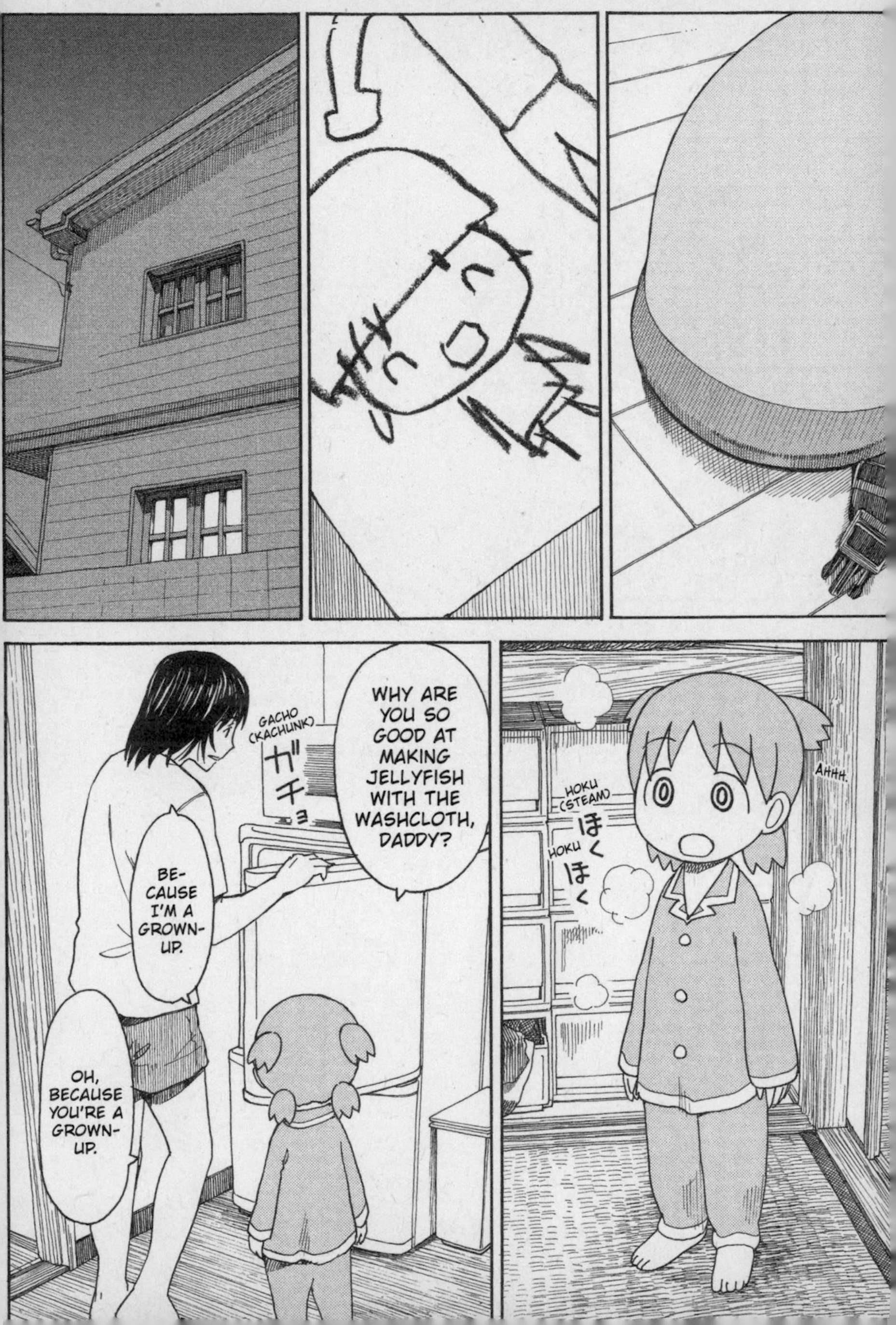
AHHH.
HOKU (STEAM) ほく
HOKU ほく
WHY ARE YOU SO GOOD AT MAKING JELLYFISH WITH THE WASHCLOTH, DADDY?
GACHO (KACHUNK) ガチョ
BE-CAUSE I'M A GROWN-UP.
OH, BECAUSE YOU'RE A GROWN-UP.

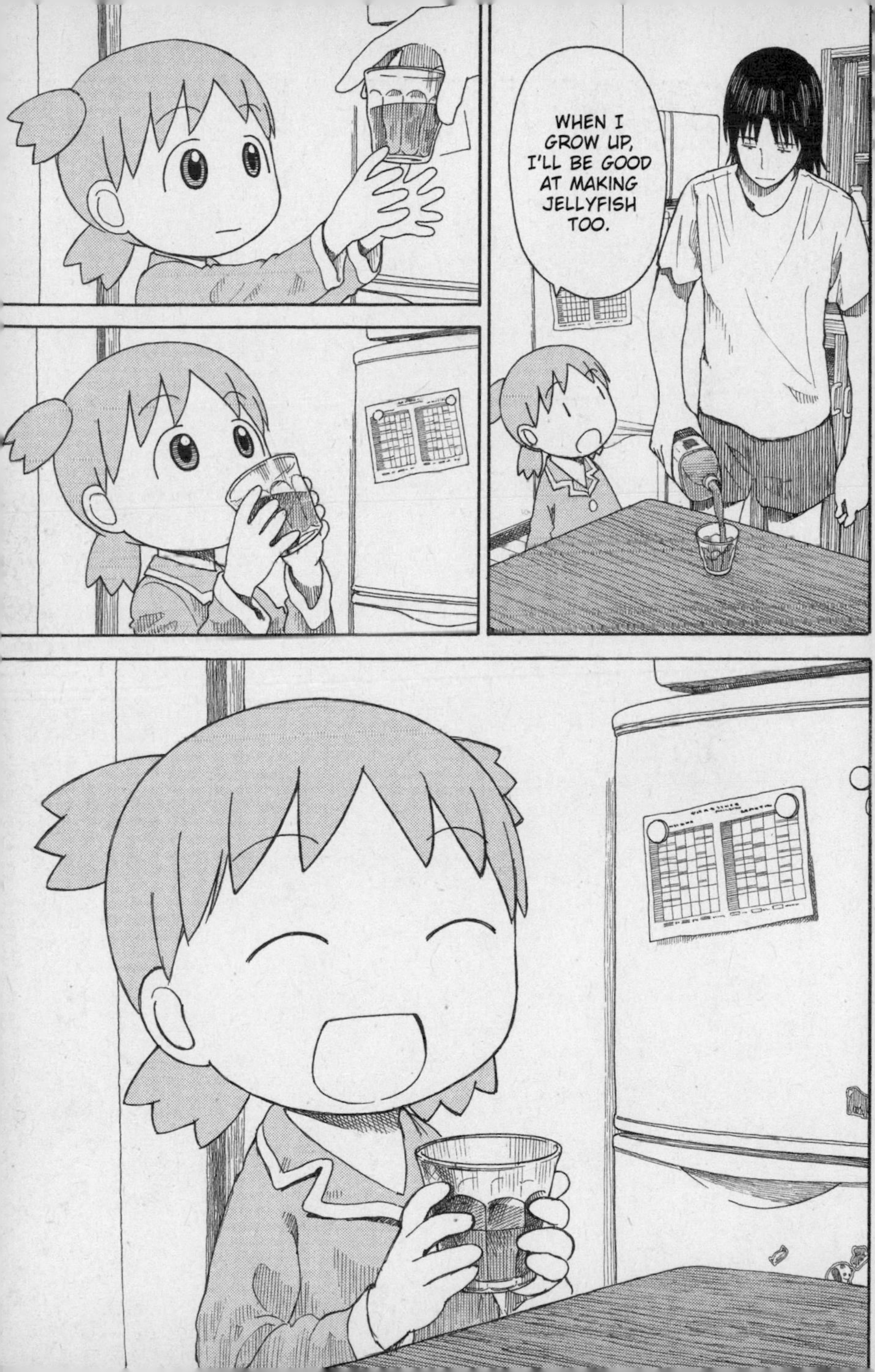
WHEN I GROW UP, I'LL BE GOOD AT MAKING JELLYFISH TOO.

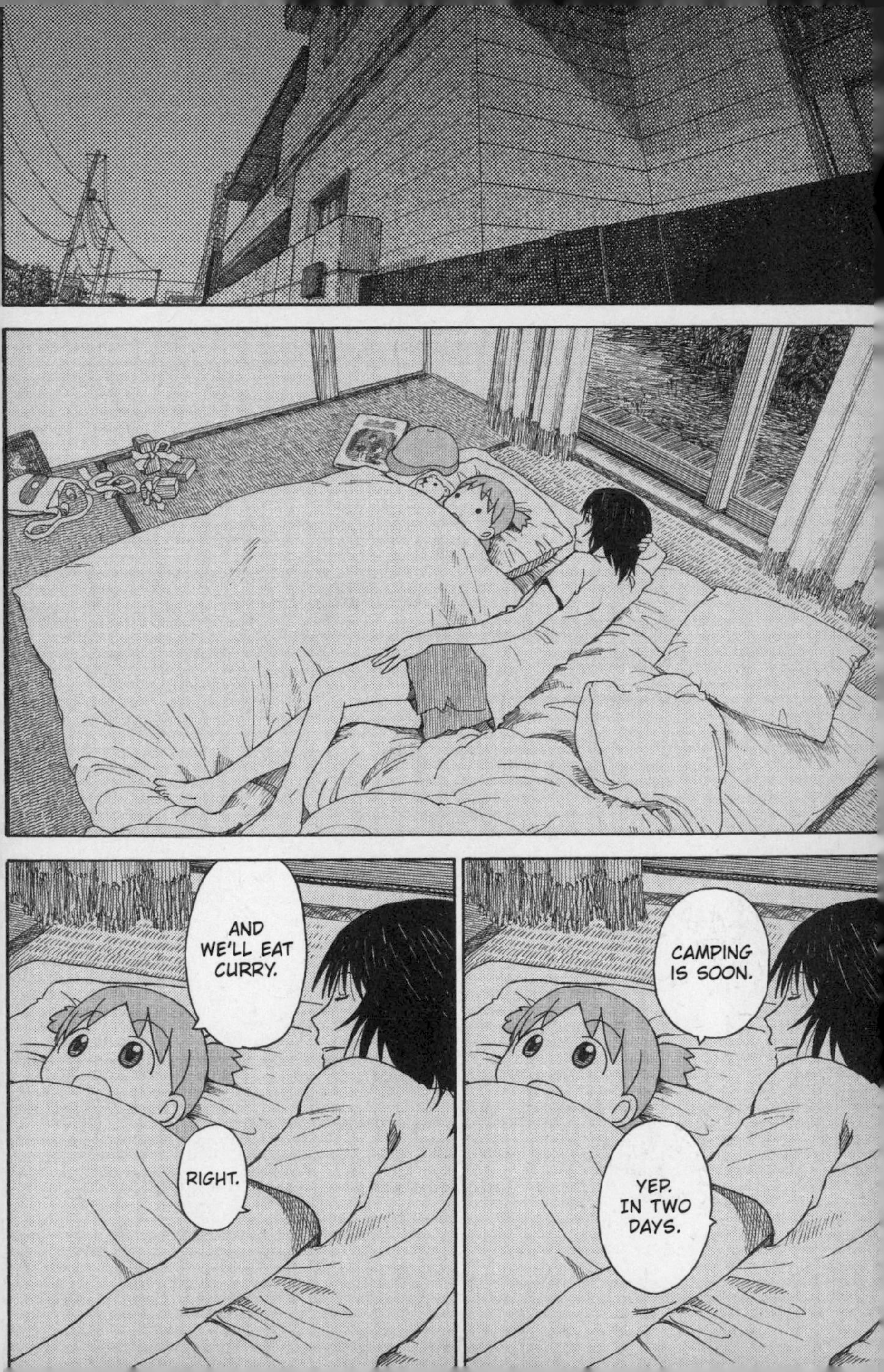
CAMPING IS SOON.
YEP. IN TWO DAYS.
AND WE'LL EAT CURRY.
RIGHT.

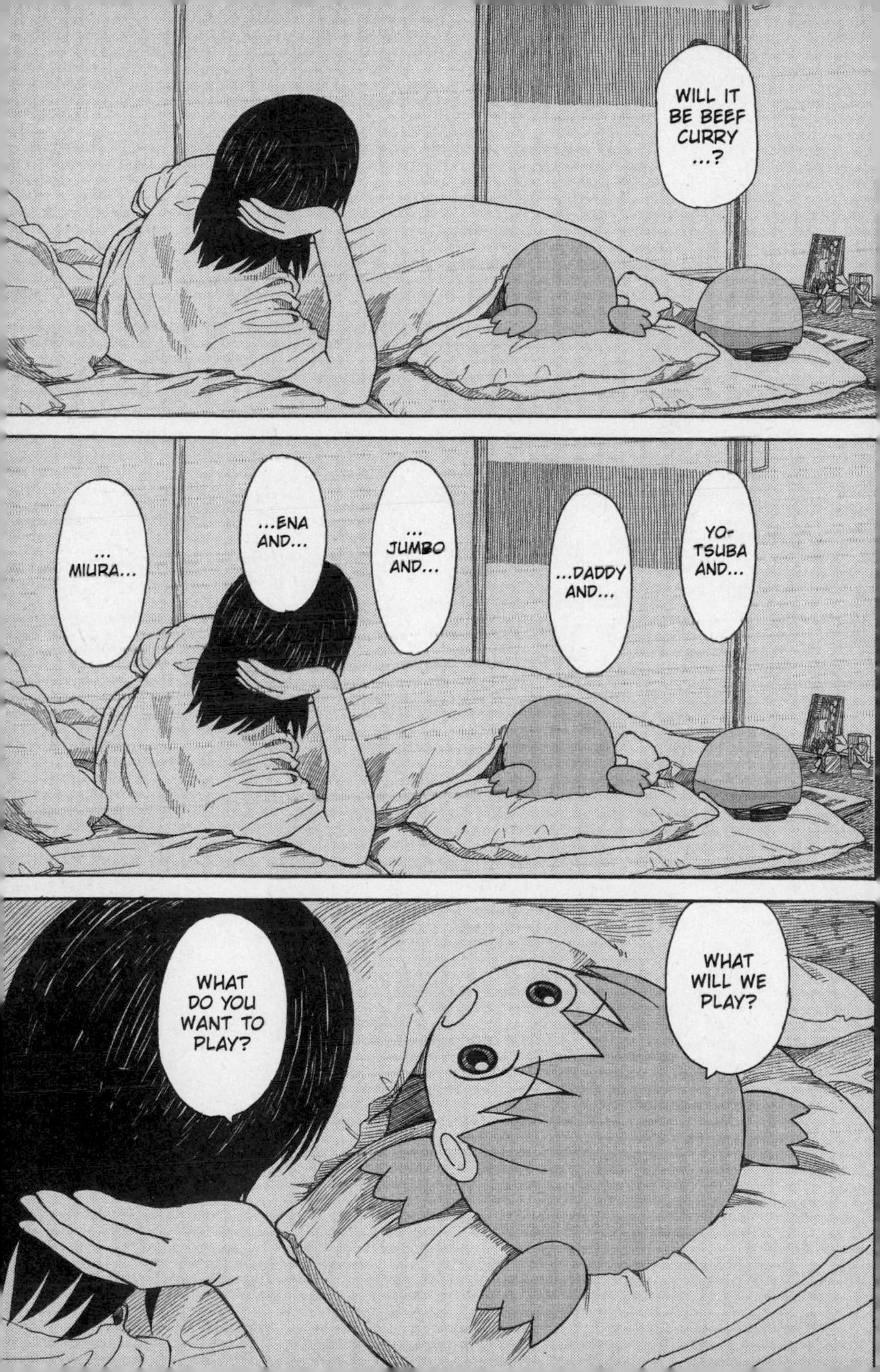
WILL IT BE BEEF CURRY ...?
YO-TSUBA AND...
...DADDY AND...
... JUMBO AND...
...ENA AND...
... MIURA...
WHAT WILL WE PLAY?
WHAT DO YOU WANT TO PLAY?

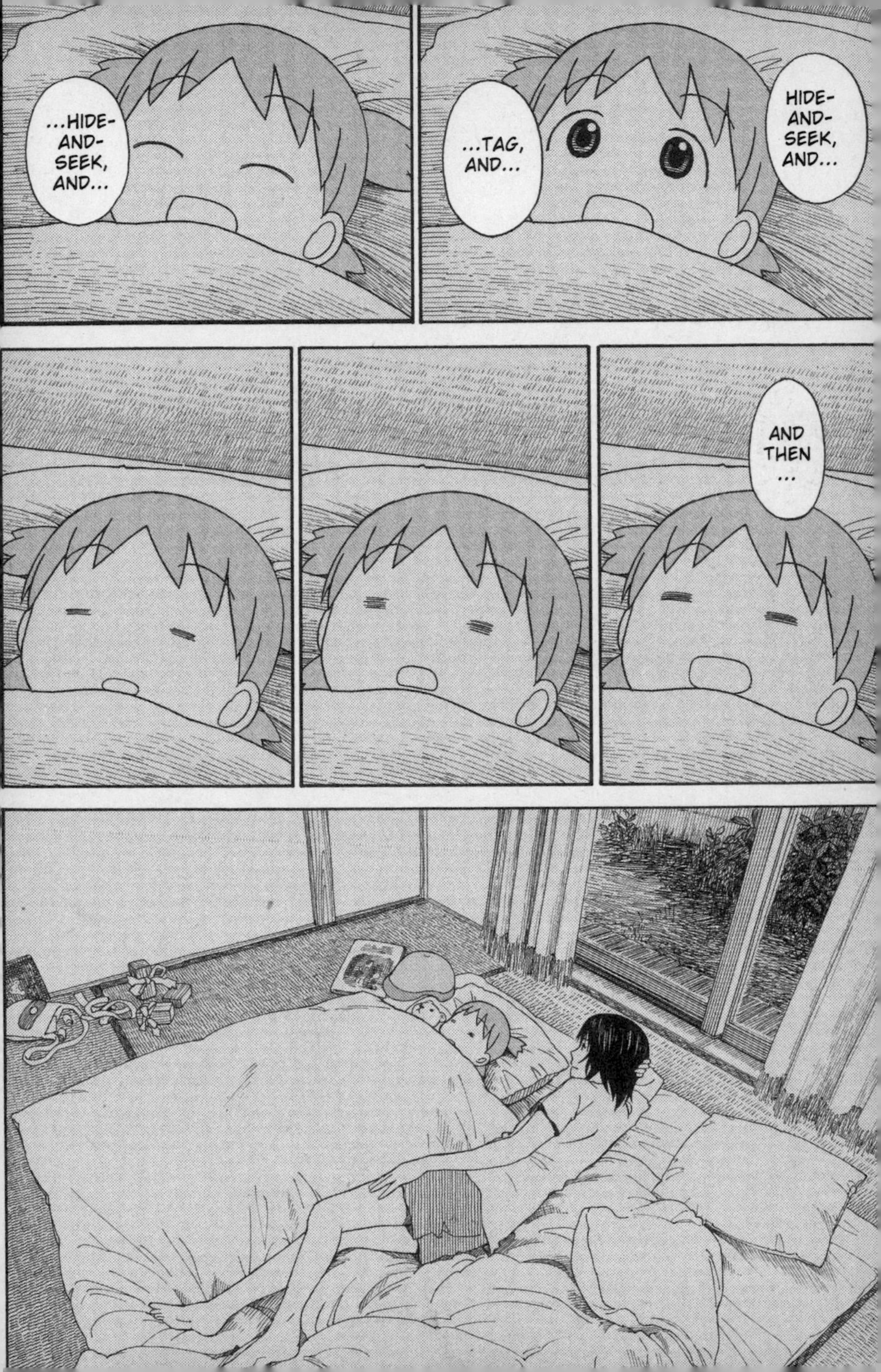
HIDE-AND-SEEK, AND...
...TAG, AND...
...HIDE-AND-SEEK, AND...
AND THEN ...

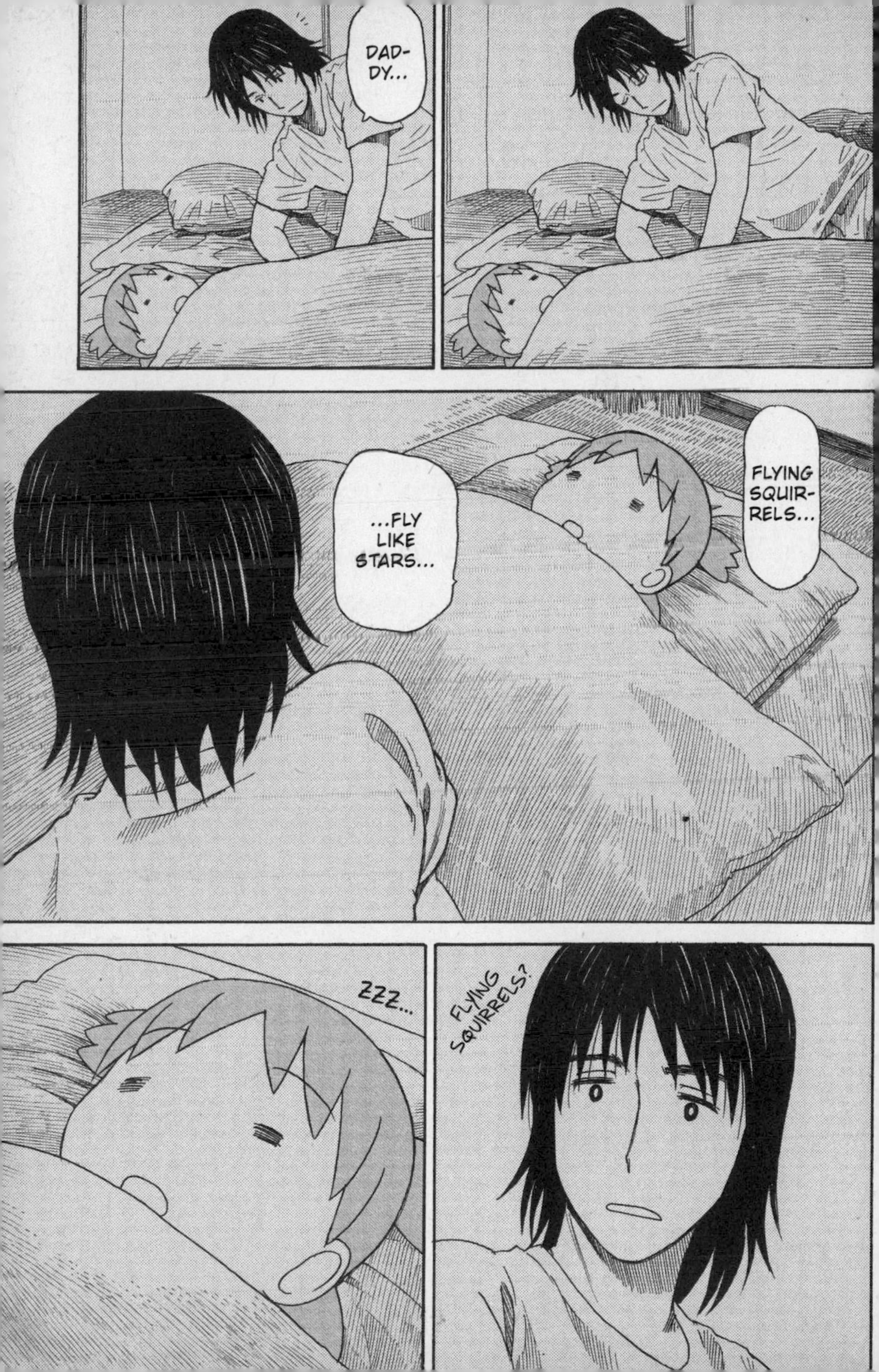
DAD-DY...
FLYING SQUIR-RELS...
...FLY LIKE STARS...
FLYING SQUIRRELS?
ZZZ...

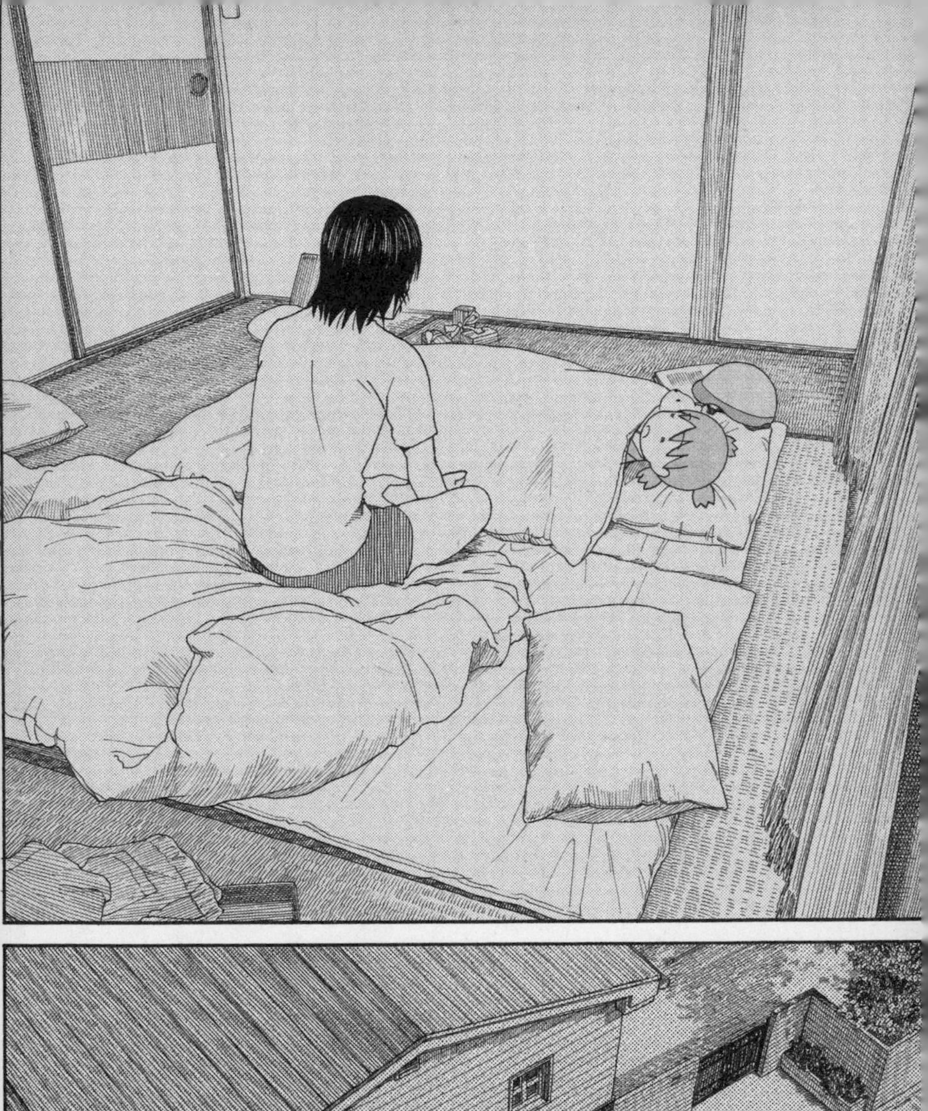
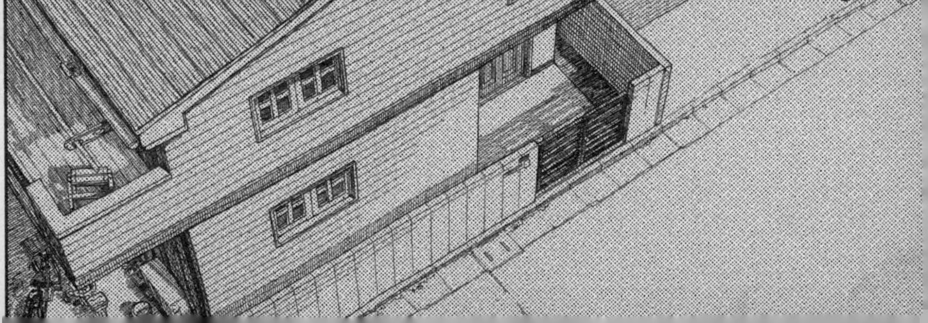

YOTSUBA&!

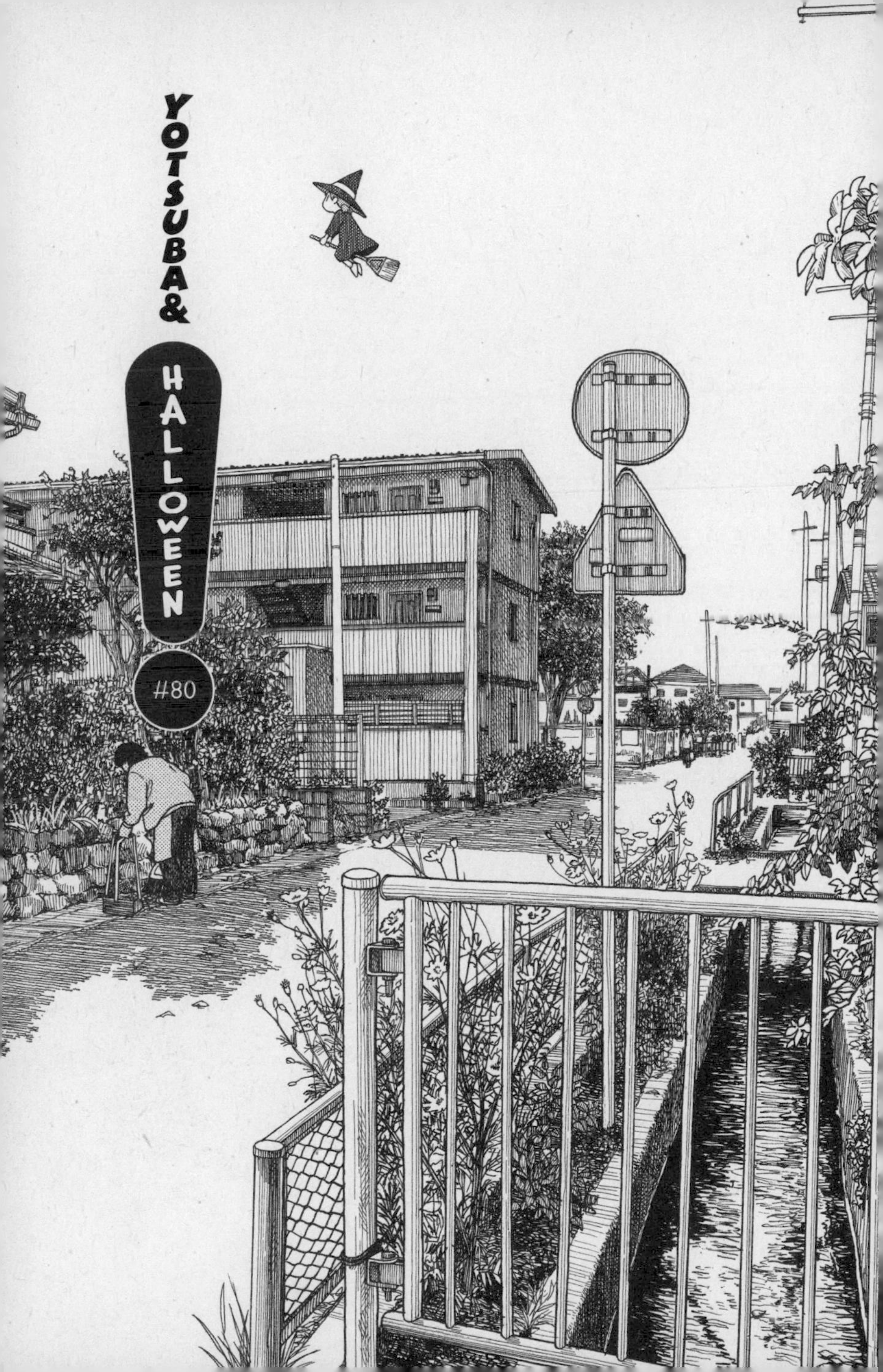
YOTSUBA&
HALLOWEEN
#80

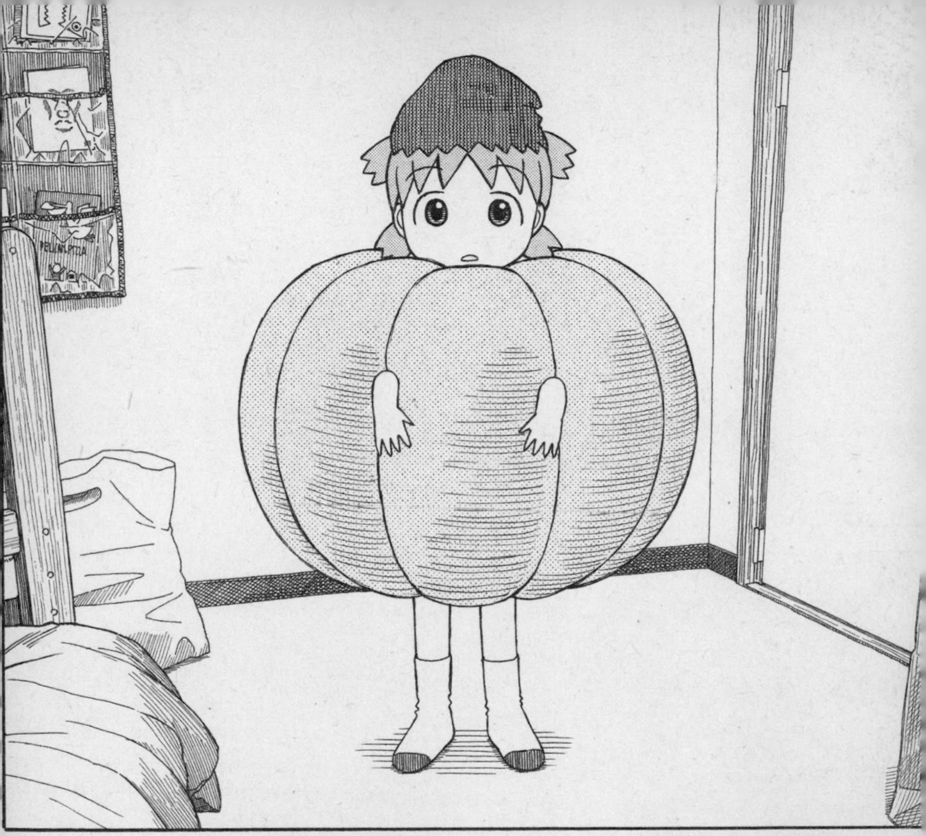

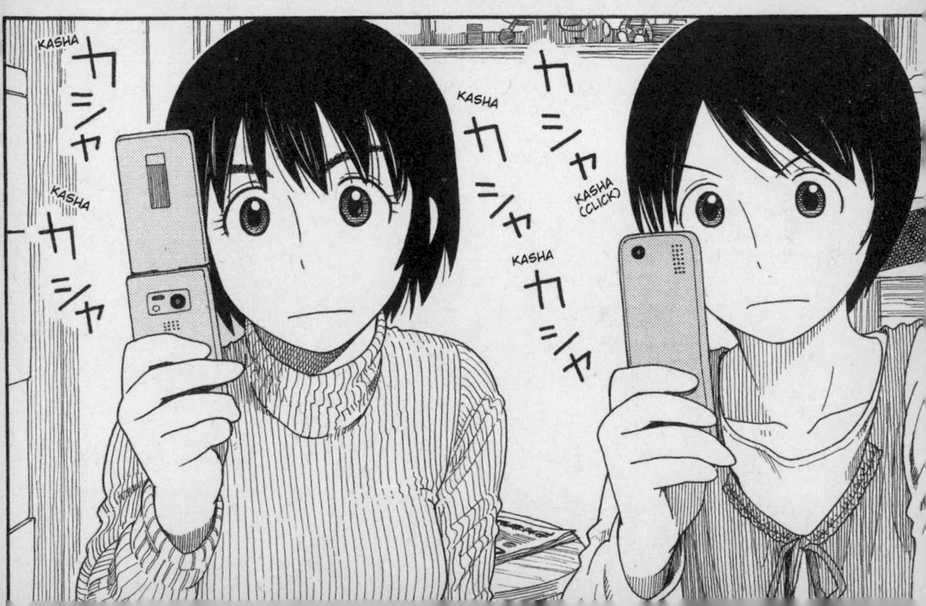

カシャ KASHA (CLICK)
カシャ KASHA
カシャ KASHA
カシャ KASHA
カシャ KASHA

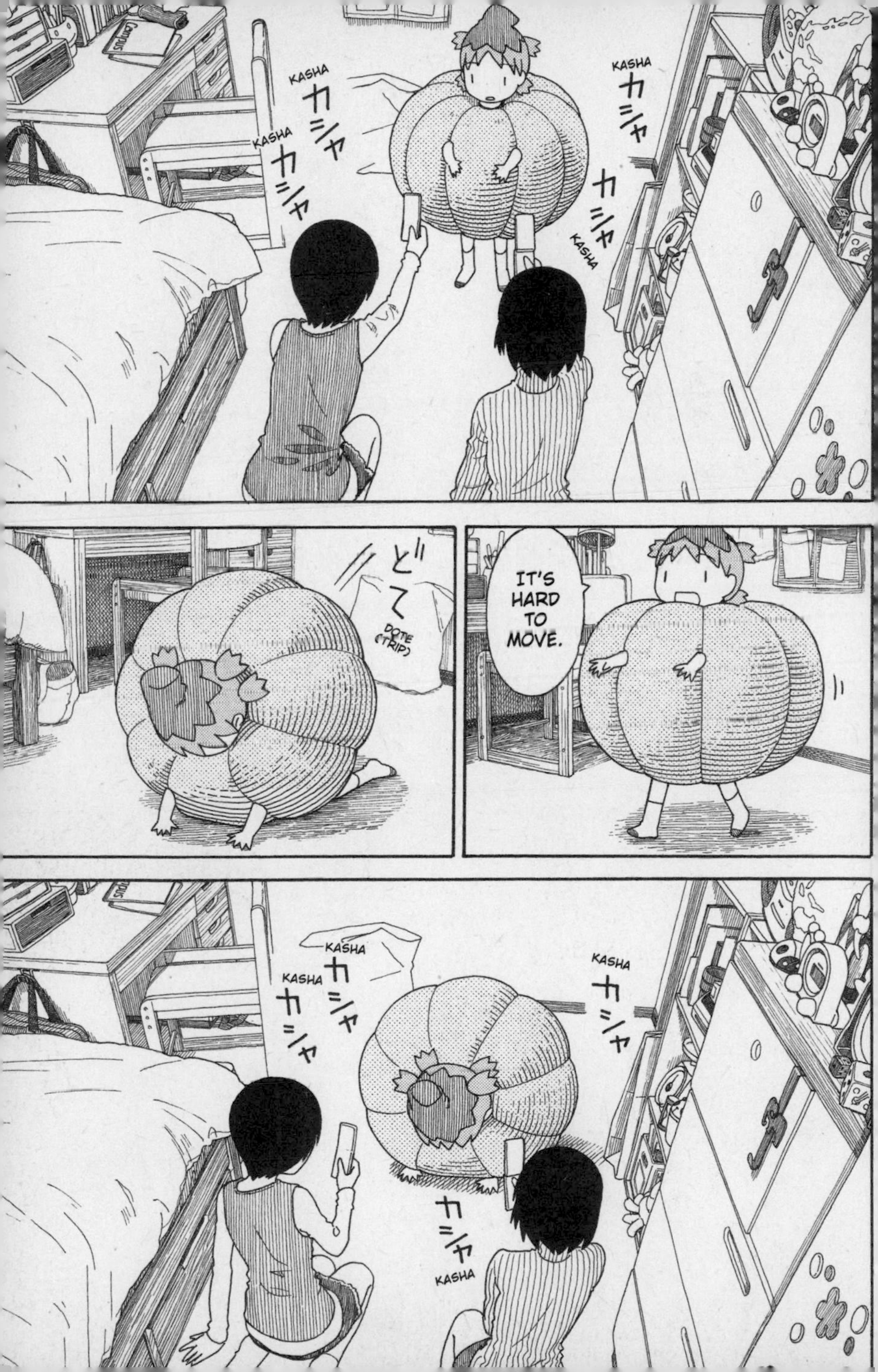
KASHA
カシャ
カシャ
KASHA
KASHA
カシャ
KASHA
カシャ
IT'S HARD TO MOVE.
どて
DOTE (TRIP)
KASHA
カシャ
KASHA
カシャ
KASHA
カシャ
カシャ
KASHA

THE PUMPKINI-ZATION OF YOTSUBA-CHAN WAS A SUCCESS!
YES, DOCTOR!
I CAN'T STAND UP...
GORON (ROLL)
ごろん

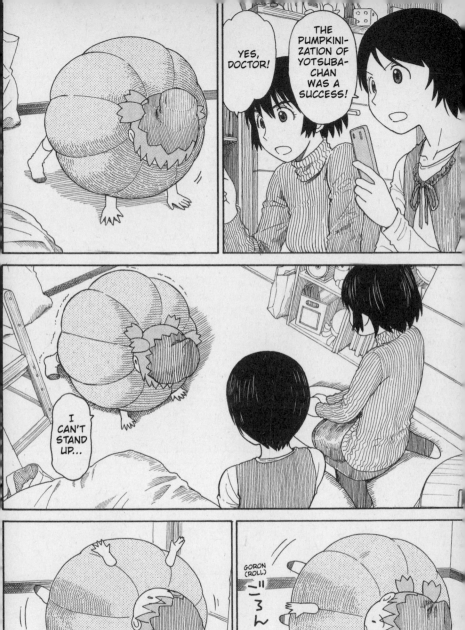

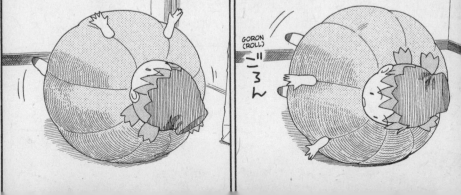

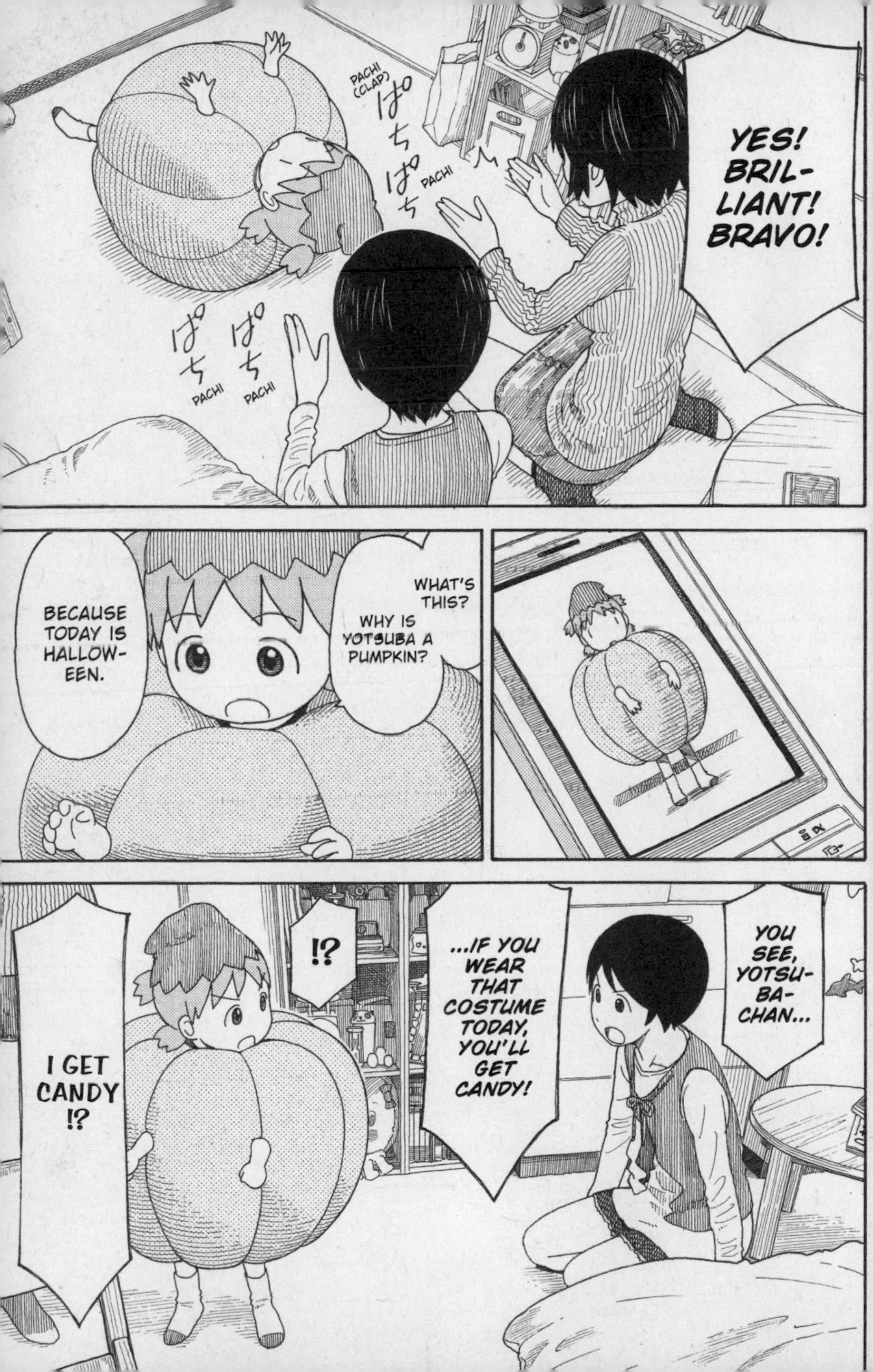
YES! BRIL-LIANT! BRAVO!
ぱち PACHI (CLAP)
ぱち PACHI
ぱち PACHI
ぱち PACHI
WHAT'S THIS? WHY IS YOTSUBA A PUMPKIN?
BECAUSE TODAY IS HALLOW-EEN.
YOU SEE, YOTSU-BA-CHAN...
...IF YOU WEAR THAT COSTUME TODAY, YOU'LL GET CANDY!
!?
I GET CANDY !?

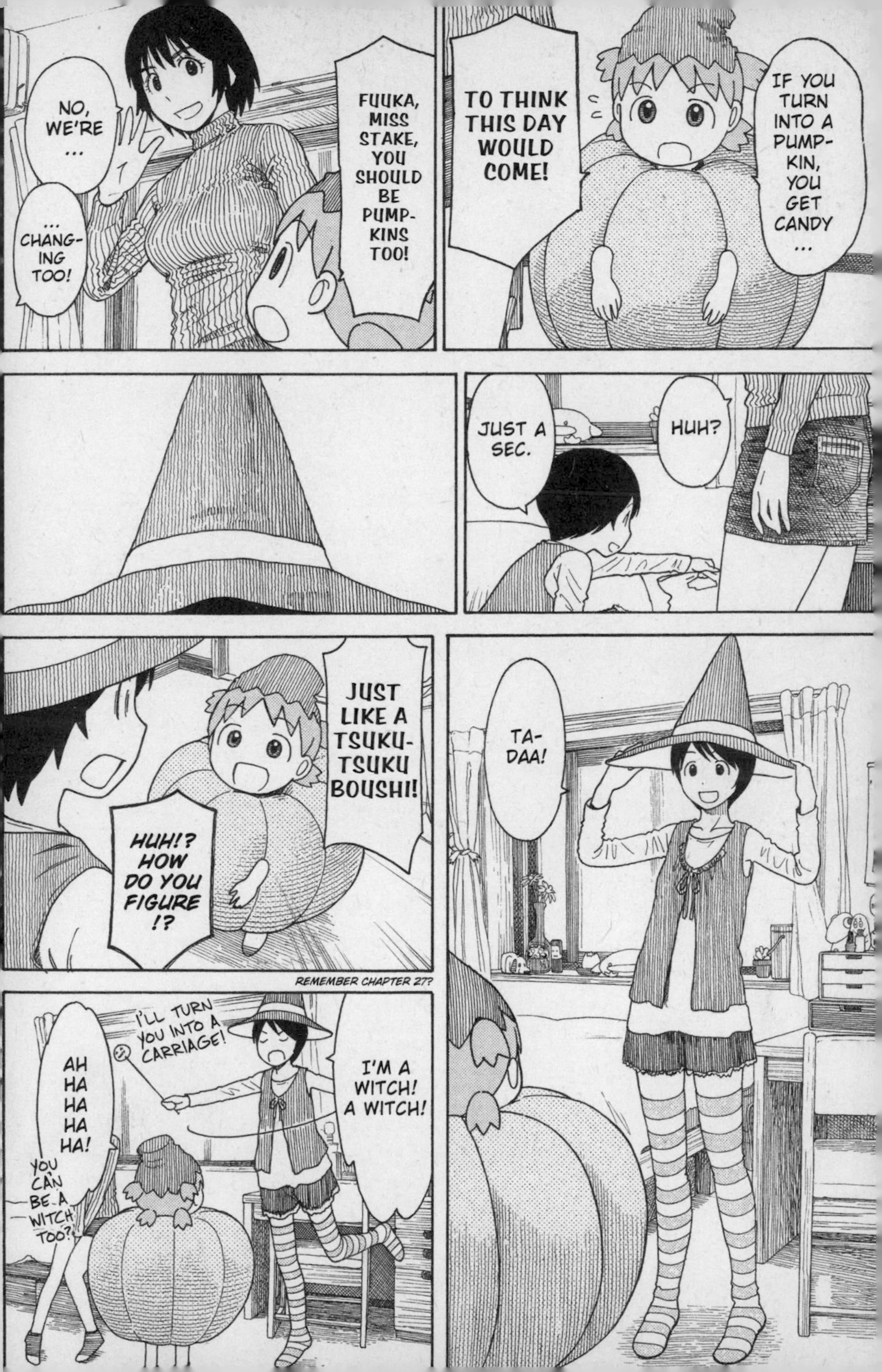
IF YOU TURN INTO A PUMP-KIN, YOU GET CANDY ...
TO THINK THIS DAY WOULD COME!
FUUKA, MISS STAKE, YOU SHOULD BE PUMP-KINS TOO!
NO, WE'RE ...
... CHANG-ING TOO!
HUH?
JUST A SEC.
TA-DAA!
JUST LIKE A TSUKU-TSUKU BOUSHI!
HUH!? HOW DO YOU FIGURE !?
REMEMBER CHAPTER 27?
I'M A WITCH! A WITCH!
I'LL TURN YOU INTO A CARRIAGE!
AH HA HA HA HA!
YOU CAN BE A WITCH TOO?

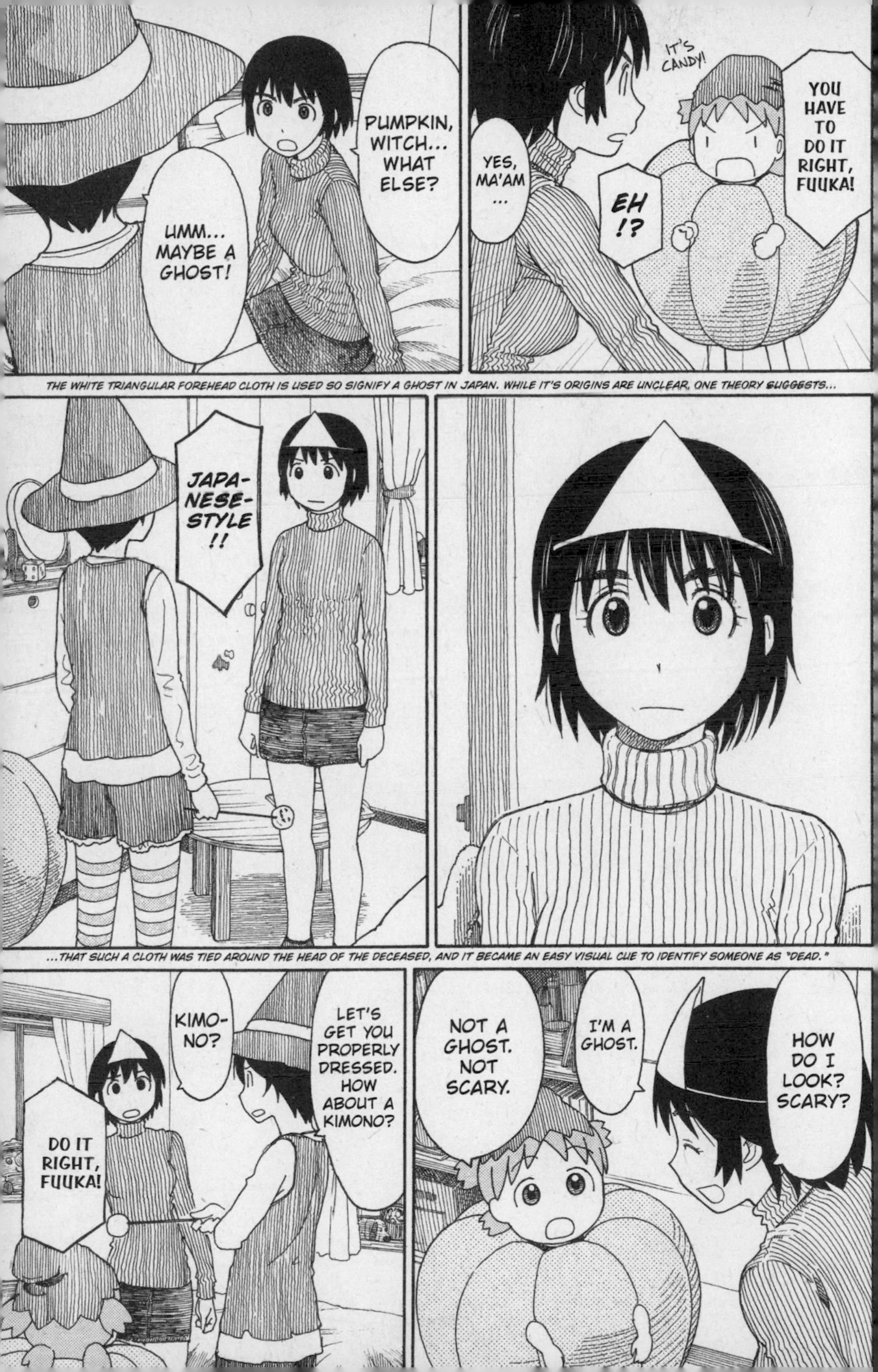
IT'S CANDY!
YOU HAVE TO DO IT RIGHT, FUUKA!
EH!?
YES, MA'AM...
PUMPKIN, WITCH... WHAT ELSE?
UMM... MAYBE A GHOST!
THE WHITE TRIANGULAR FOREHEAD CLOTH IS USED SO SIGNIFY A GHOST IN JAPAN. WHILE IT'S ORIGINS ARE UNCLEAR, ONE THEORY SUGGESTS...
JAPA-NESE-STYLE!!
...THAT SUCH A CLOTH WAS TIED AROUND THE HEAD OF THE DECEASED, AND IT BECAME AN EASY VISUAL CUE TO IDENTIFY SOMEONE AS "DEAD."
HOW DO I LOOK? SCARY?
I'M A GHOST.
NOT A GHOST. NOT SCARY.
LET'S GET YOU PROPERLY DRESSED. HOW ABOUT A KIMONO?
KIMO-NO?
DO IT RIGHT, FUUKA!

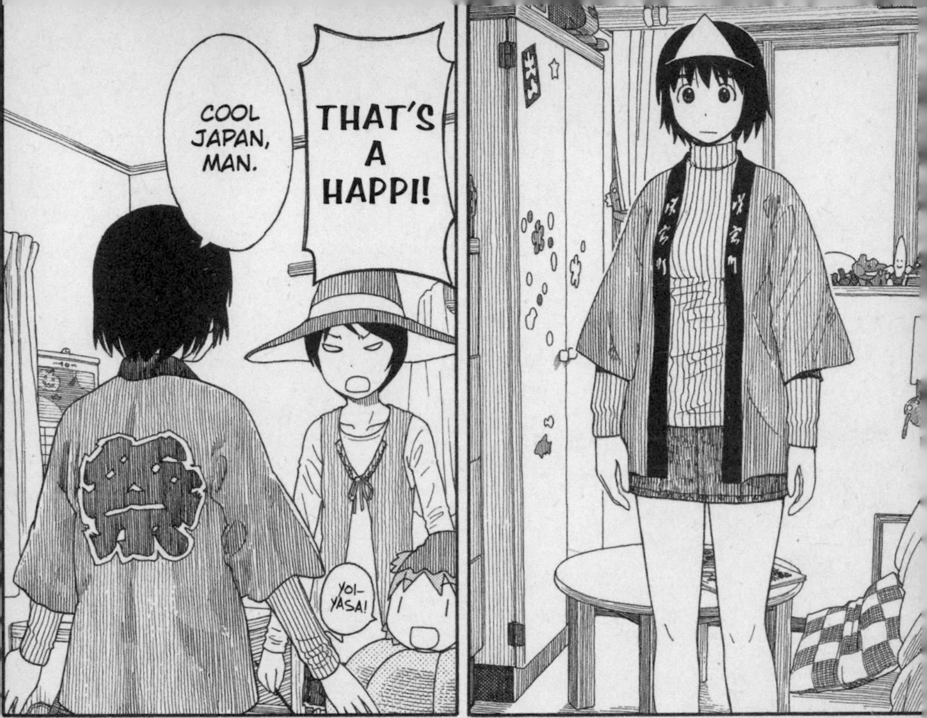
THAT'S A HAPPI!
COOL JAPAN, MAN.
YOI-YASA!

A HAPPI IS A SHORT-SLEEVED TRADITIONAL COAT. NOWADAYS, HAPPI ARE ONLY WORN TO FESTIVALS, USUALLY BY THOSE PARTICIPATING IN CEREMONIES.

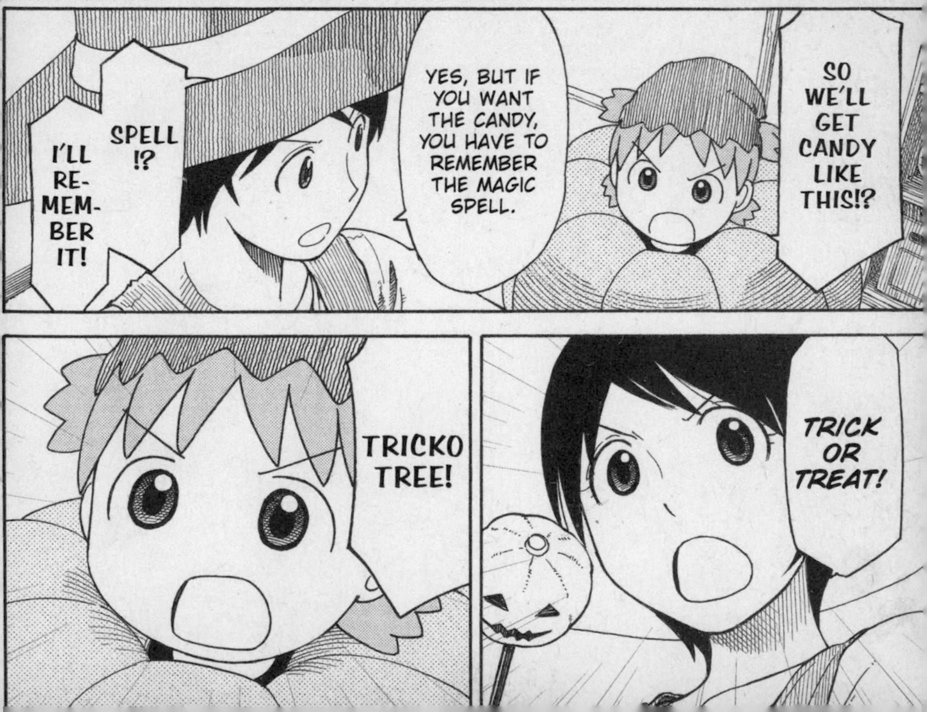
SO WE'LL GET CANDY LIKE THIS!?
YES, BUT IF YOU WANT THE CANDY, YOU HAVE TO REMEMBER THE MAGIC SPELL.
SPELL !?
I'LL RE-MEM-BER IT!
TRICK OR TREAT!
TRICKO TREE!

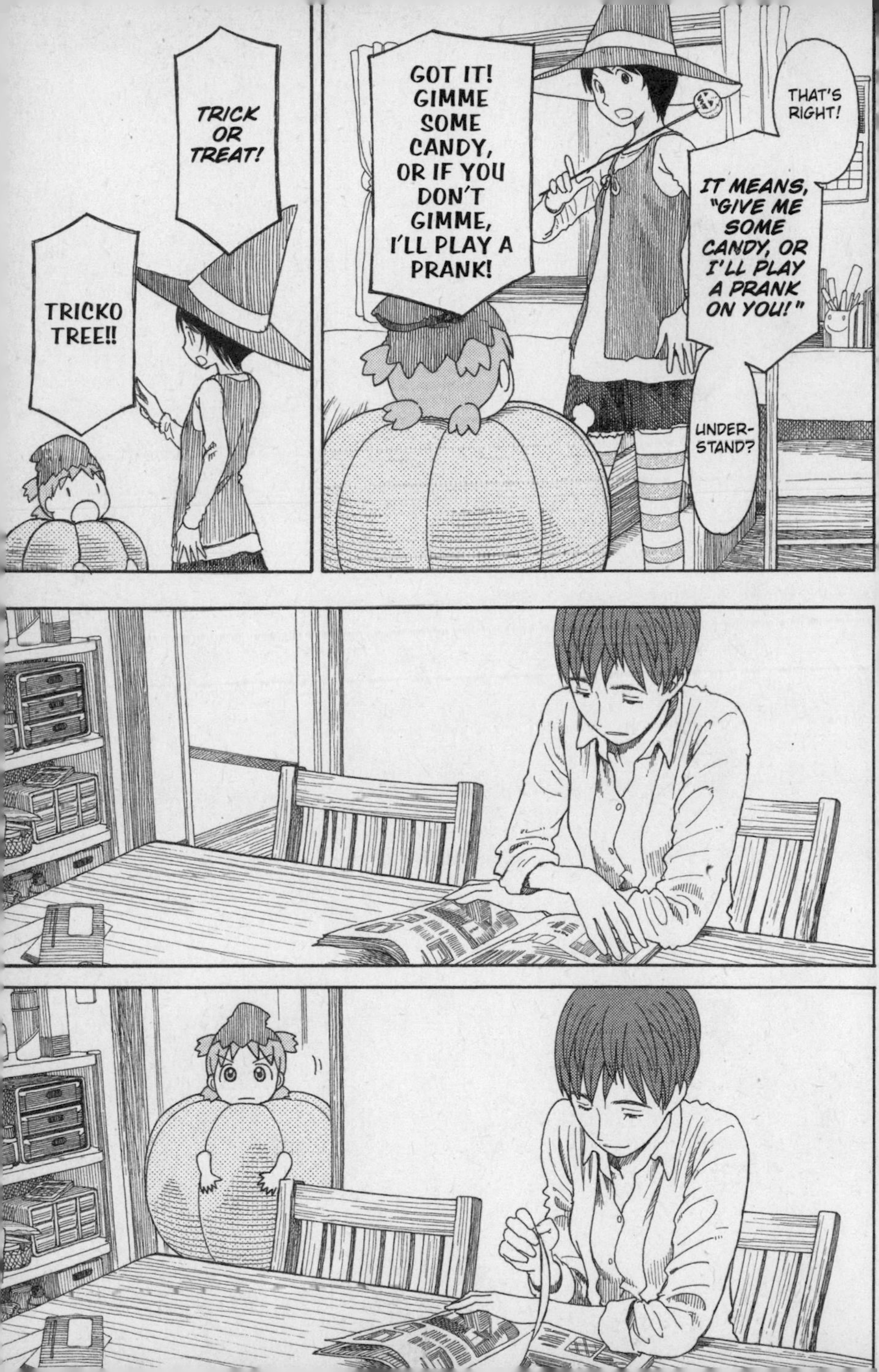
THAT'S RIGHT!
IT MEANS, "GIVE ME SOME CANDY, OR I'LL PLAY A PRANK ON YOU!"
UNDER-STAND?
GOT IT! GIMME SOME CANDY, OR IF YOU DON'T GIMME, I'LL PLAY A PRANK!
TRICK OR TREAT!
TRICKO TREE!!

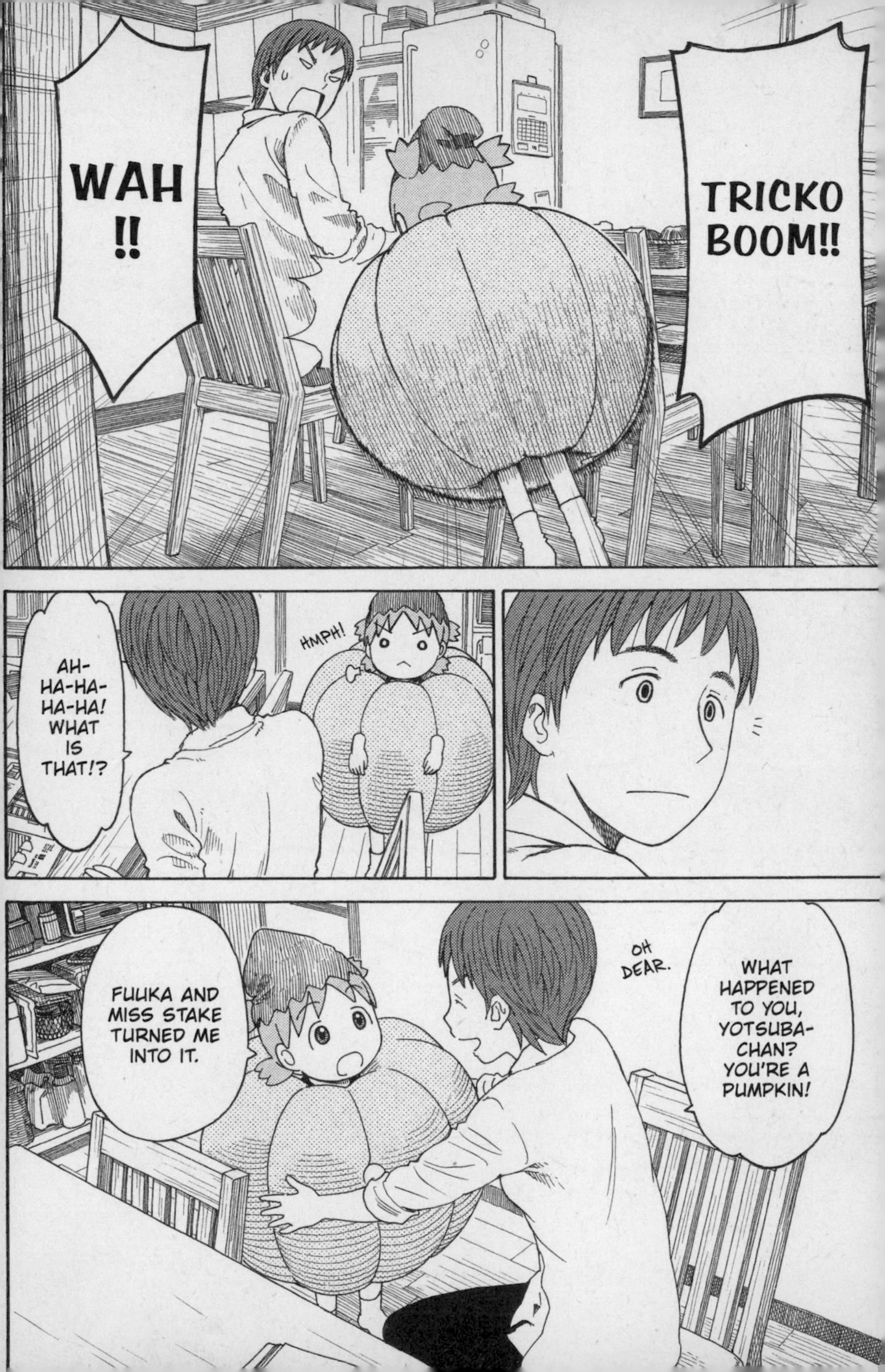
TRICKO BOOM!!
WAH !!
AH-HA-HA-HA-HA! WHAT IS THAT!?
HMPH!
WHAT HAPPENED TO YOU, YOTSUBA-CHAN? YOU'RE A PUMPKIN!
OH DEAR.
FUUKA AND MISS STAKE TURNED ME INTO IT.

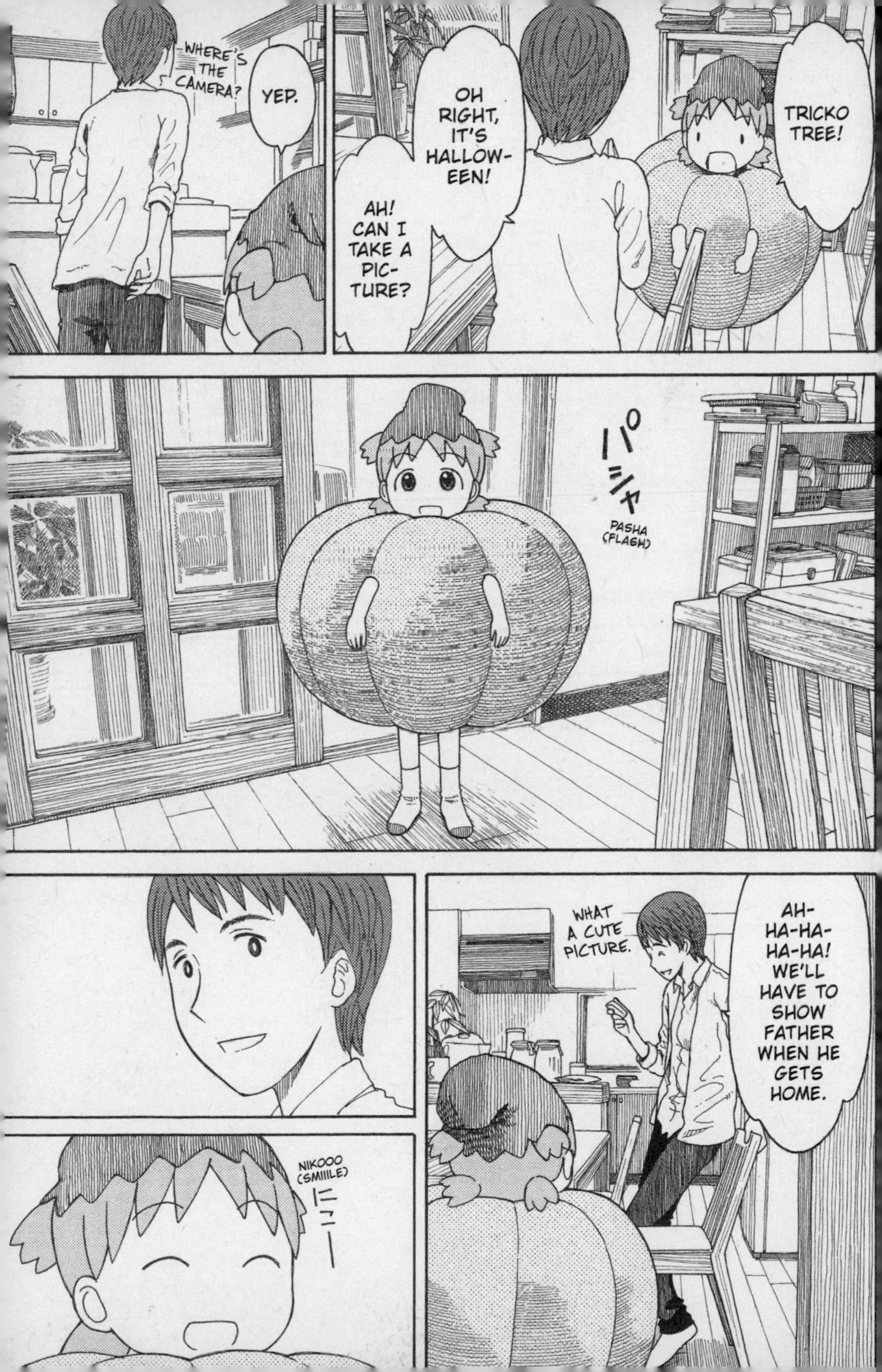
TRICKO TREE!
OH RIGHT, IT'S HALLOW-EEN!
AH! CAN I TAKE A PIC-TURE?
YEP.
WHERE'S THE CAMERA?
パシャ
PASHA (FLASH)
AH-HA-HA-HA-HA! WE'LL HAVE TO SHOW FATHER WHEN HE GETS HOME.
WHAT A CUTE PICTURE.
ニコー
NIKOOO (SMIIILE)

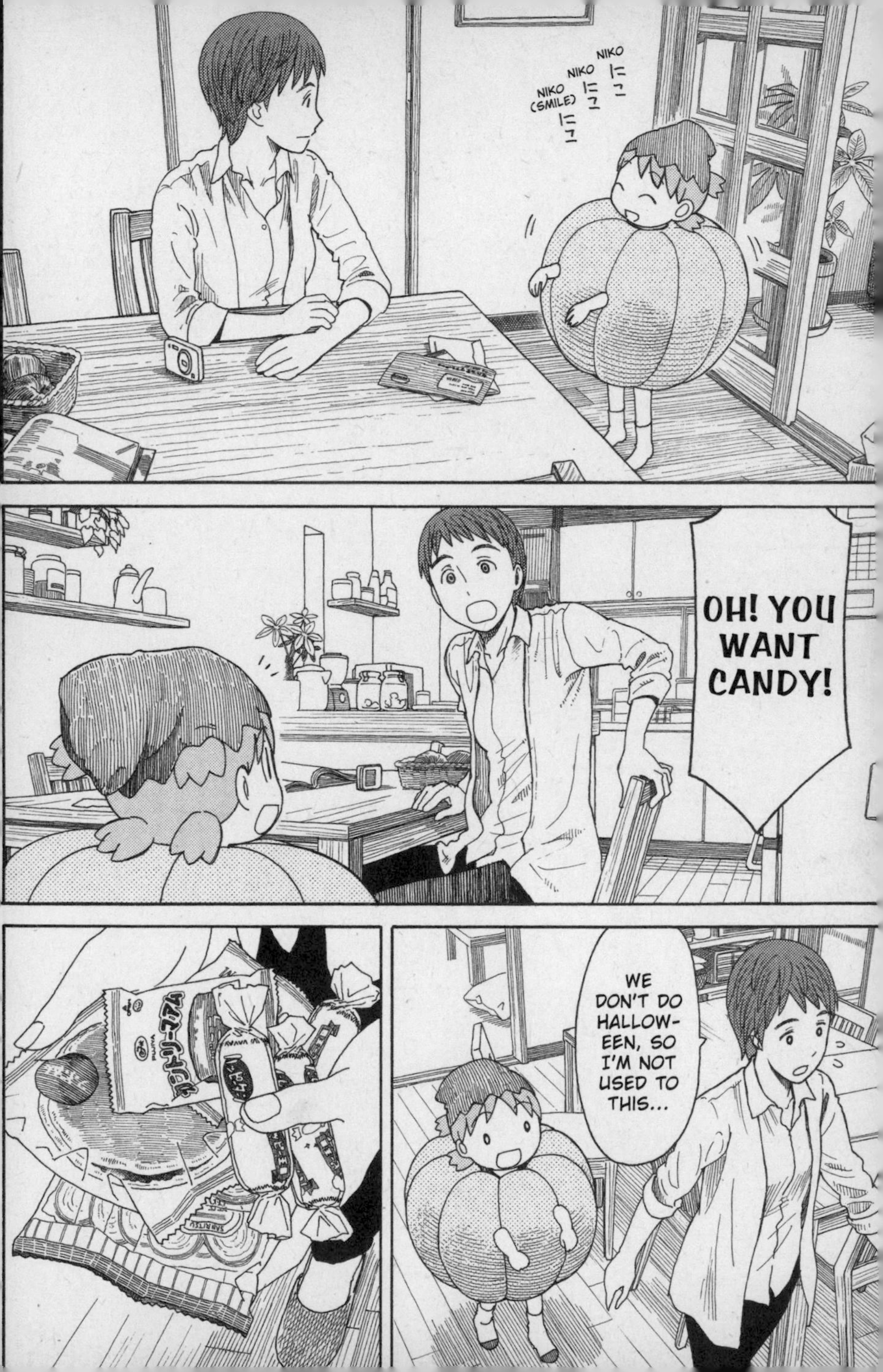
にこ
NIKO
にこ
NIKO
にこ
NIKO (SMILE)
OH! YOU WANT CANDY!
WE DON'T DO HALLOW-EEN, SO I'M NOT USED TO THIS...

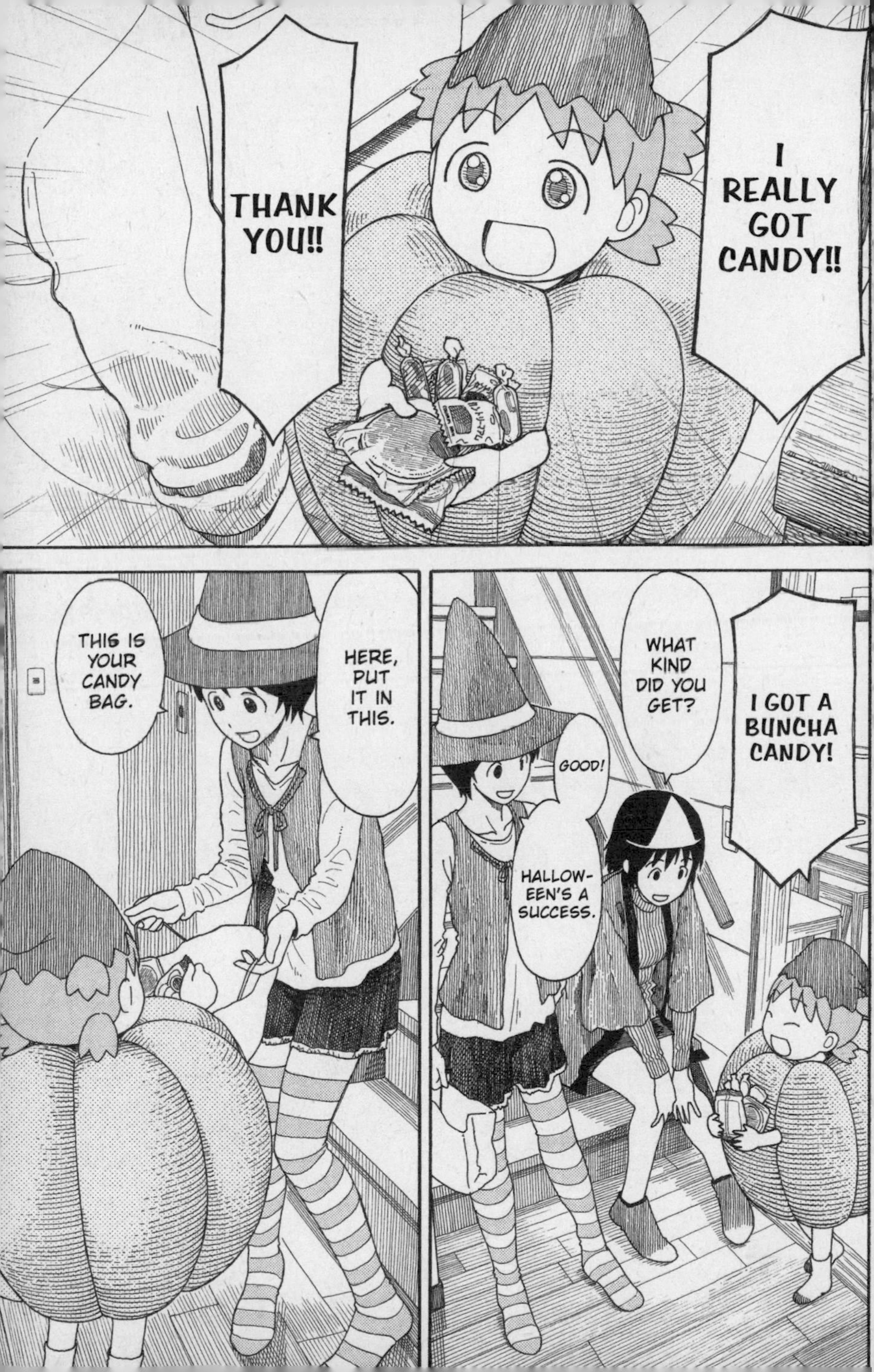
I REALLY GOT CANDY!!
THANK YOU!!
I GOT A BUNCHA CANDY!
WHAT KIND DID YOU GET?
GOOD!
HALLOW-EEN'S A SUCCESS.
HERE, PUT IT IN THIS.
THIS IS YOUR CANDY BAG.

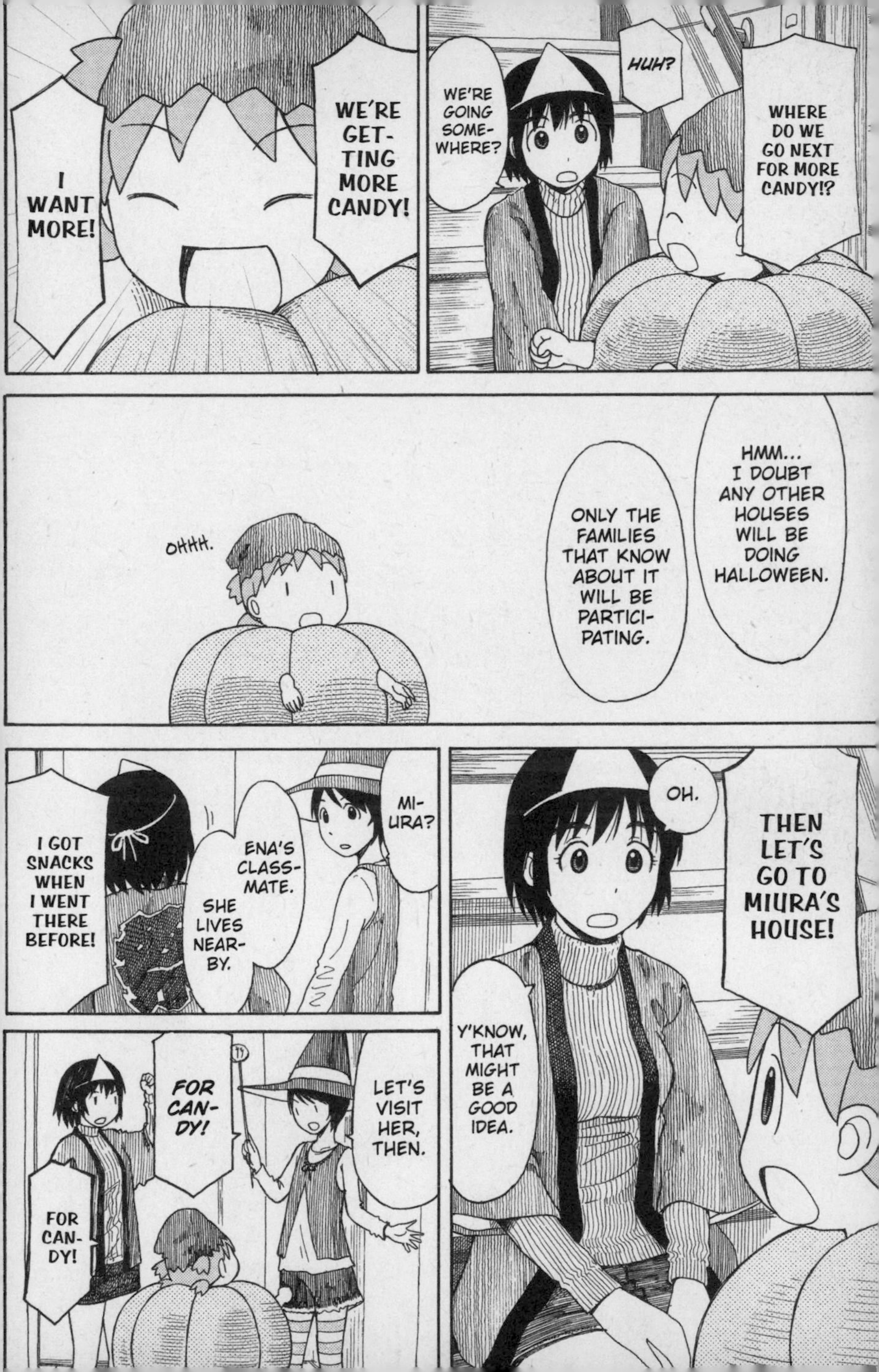
WHERE DO WE GO NEXT FOR MORE CANDY!?
HUH?
WE'RE GOING SOMEWHERE?
WE'RE GETTING MORE CANDY!
I WANT MORE!
HMM... I DOUBT ANY OTHER HOUSES WILL BE DOING HALLOWEEN.
ONLY THE FAMILIES THAT KNOW ABOUT IT WILL BE PARTICIPATING.
OHHH.
THEN LET'S GO TO MIURA'S HOUSE!
OH.
Y'KNOW, THAT MIGHT BE A GOOD IDEA.
MIURA?
ENA'S CLASSMATE.
SHE LIVES NEARBY.
I GOT SNACKS WHEN I WENT THERE BEFORE!
LET'S VISIT HER, THEN.
FOR CANDY!
FOR CANDY!

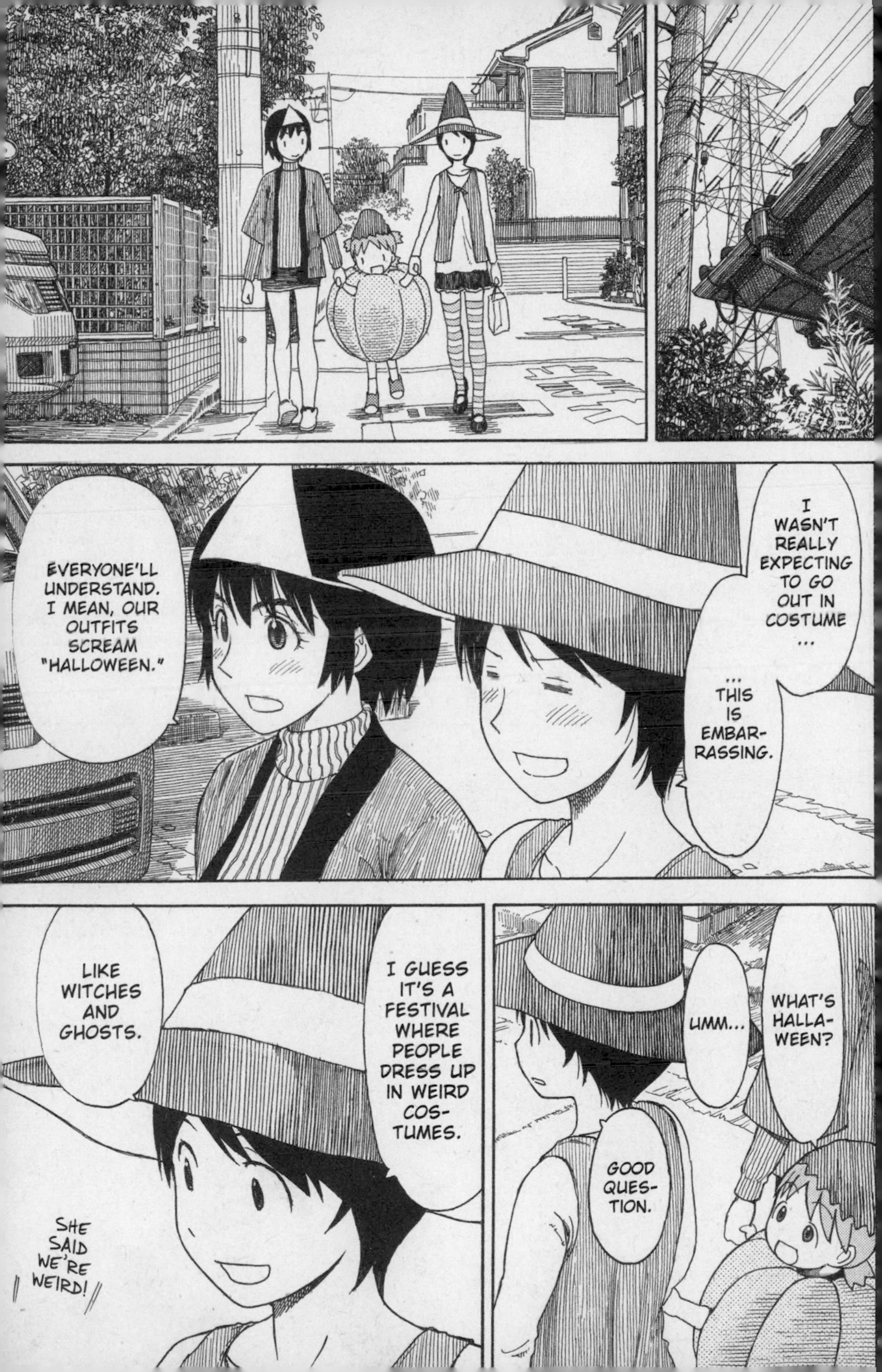
I WASN'T REALLY EXPECTING TO GO OUT IN COSTUME...
...THIS IS EMBARRASSING.
EVERYONE'LL UNDERSTAND. I MEAN, OUR OUTFITS SCREAM "HALLOWEEN."
WHAT'S HALLA-WEEN?
UMM...
GOOD QUES-TION.
I GUESS IT'S A FESTIVAL WHERE PEOPLE DRESS UP IN WEIRD COS-TUMES.
LIKE WITCHES AND GHOSTS.
SHE SAID WE'RE WEIRD!

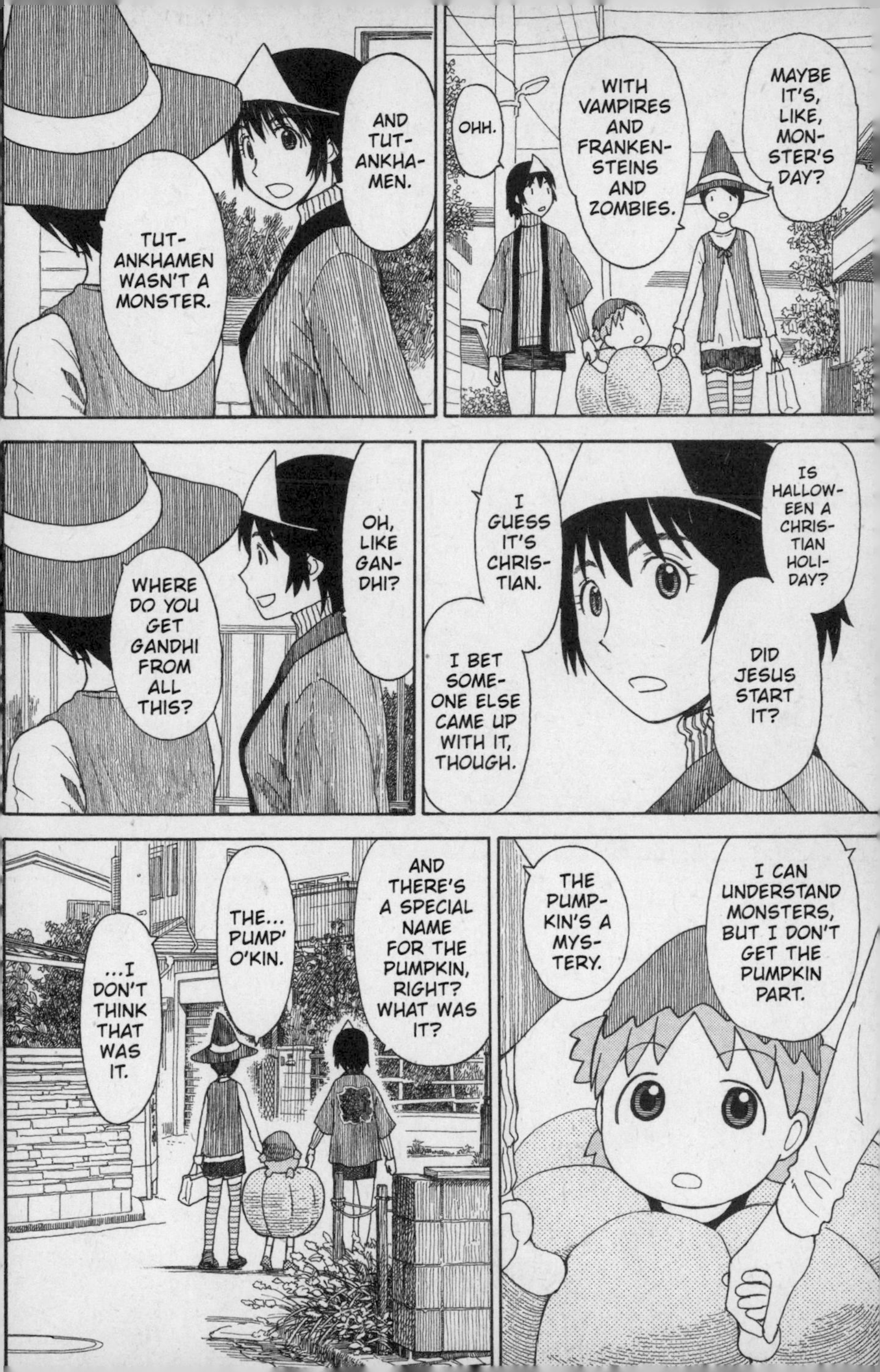
MAYBE IT'S, LIKE, MONSTER'S DAY?
WITH VAMPIRES AND FRANKENSTEINS AND ZOMBIES.
OHH.
AND TUTANKHAMEN.
TUTANKHAMEN WASN'T A MONSTER.
IS HALLOWEEN A CHRISTIAN HOLIDAY?
I GUESS IT'S CHRISTIAN.
DID JESUS START IT?
I BET SOMEONE ELSE CAME UP WITH IT, THOUGH.
OH, LIKE GANDHI?
WHERE DO YOU GET GANDHI FROM ALL THIS?
I CAN UNDERSTAND MONSTERS, BUT I DON'T GET THE PUMPKIN PART.
THE PUMPKIN'S A MYSTERY.
AND THERE'S A SPECIAL NAME FOR THE PUMPKIN, RIGHT? WHAT WAS IT?
THE... PUMP'O'KIN.
...I DON'T THINK THAT WAS IT.

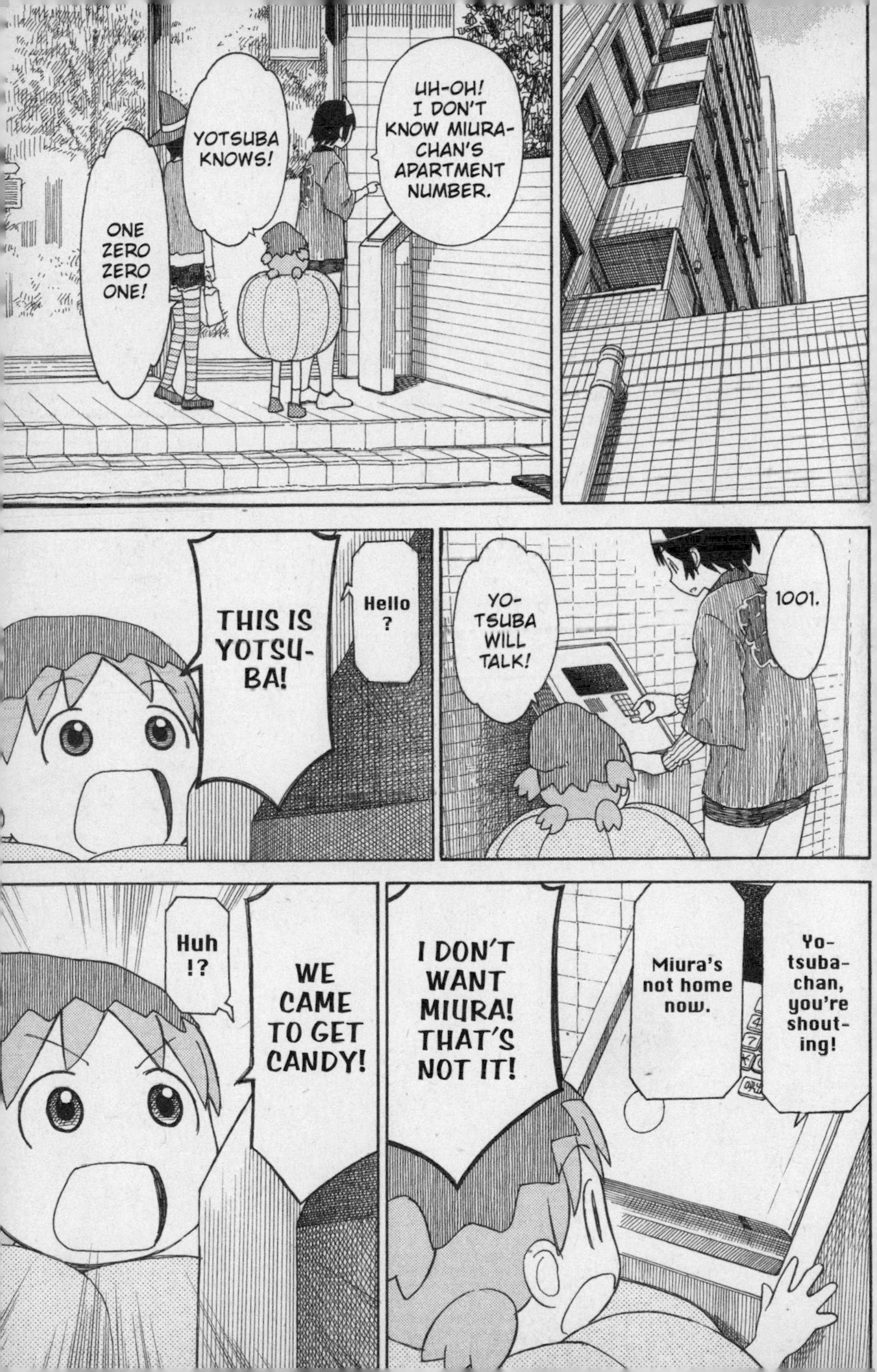
UH-OH! I DON'T KNOW MIURA-CHAN'S APARTMENT NUMBER.
YOTSUBA KNOWS!
ONE ZERO ZERO ONE!
1001.
YO-TSUBA WILL TALK!
Hello ?
THIS IS YOTSU-BA!
Yo-tsuba-chan, you're shout-ing!
Miura's not home now.
I DON'T WANT MIURA! THAT'S NOT IT!
WE CAME TO GET CANDY!
Huh !?

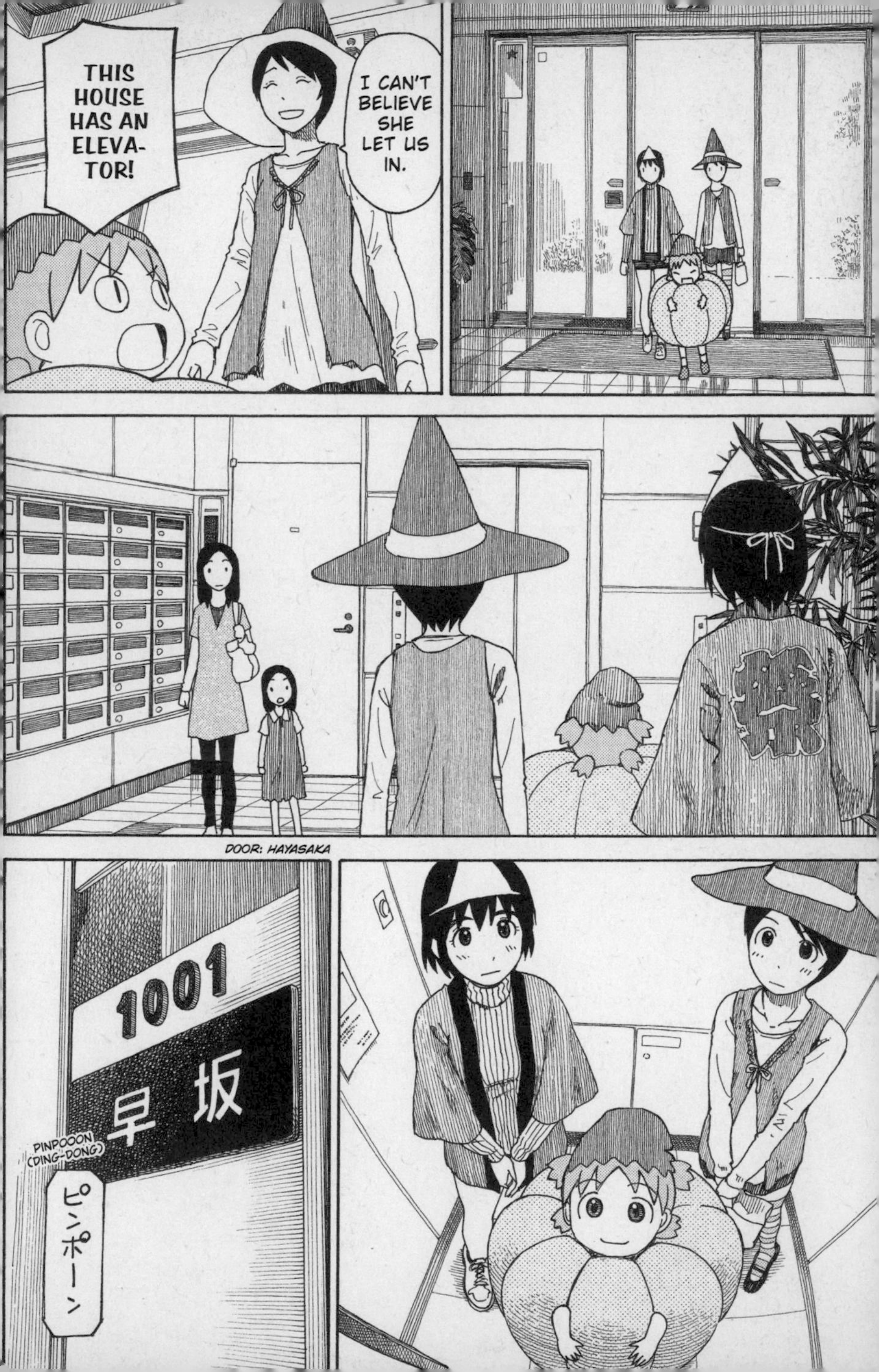
I CAN'T BELIEVE SHE LET US IN.
THIS HOUSE HAS AN ELEVATOR!
DOOR: HAYASAKA
1001
早坂
ピンポーン
PINPOOON (DING-DONG)

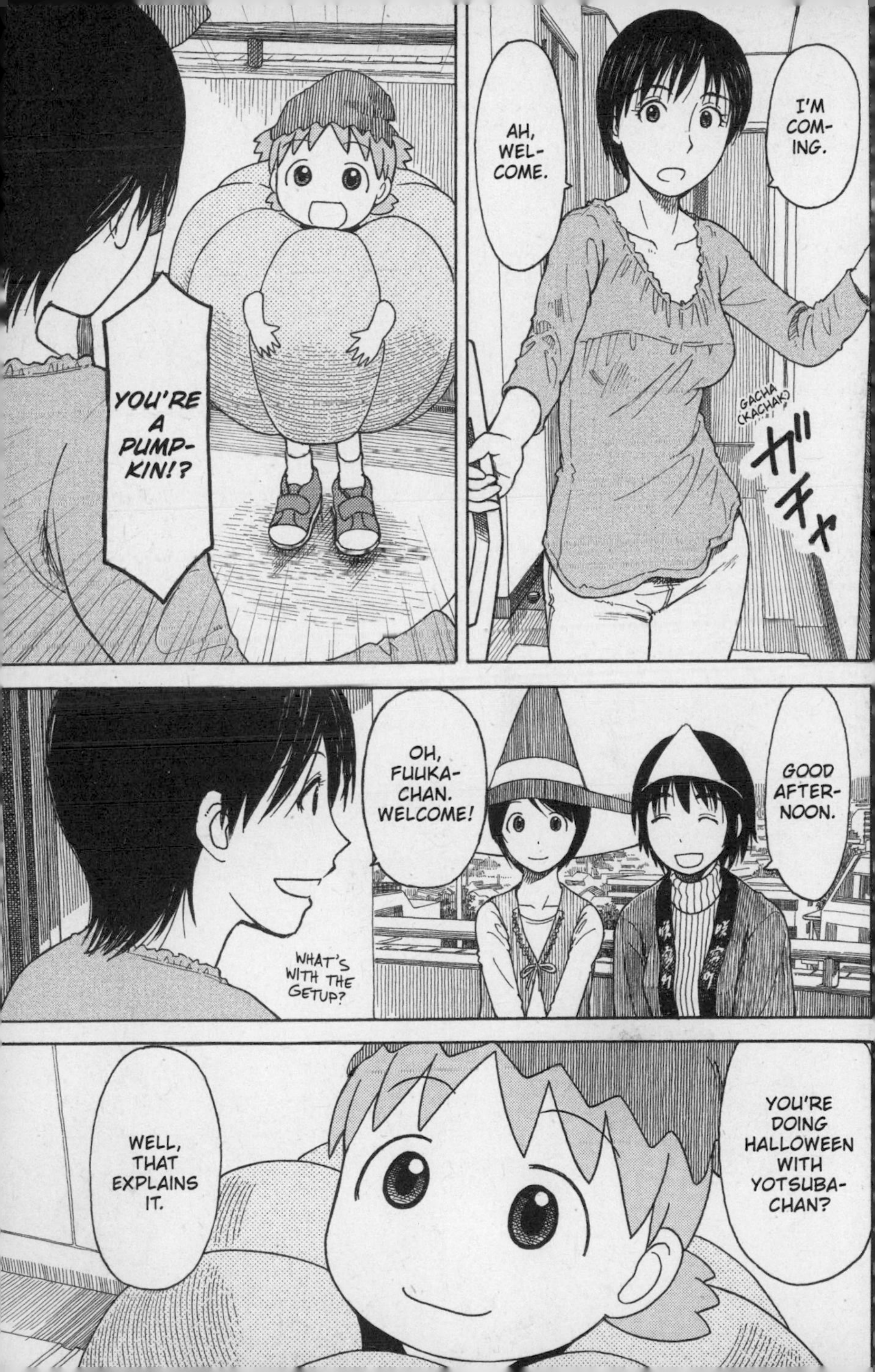
I'M COMING.
AH, WELCOME.
GACHA (KACHAK)
ガチャ
YOU'RE A PUMPKIN!?
GOOD AFTERNOON.
OH, FUUKA-CHAN. WELCOME!
WHAT'S WITH THE GETUP?
YOU'RE DOING HALLOWEEN WITH YOTSUBA-CHAN?
WELL, THAT EXPLAINS IT.

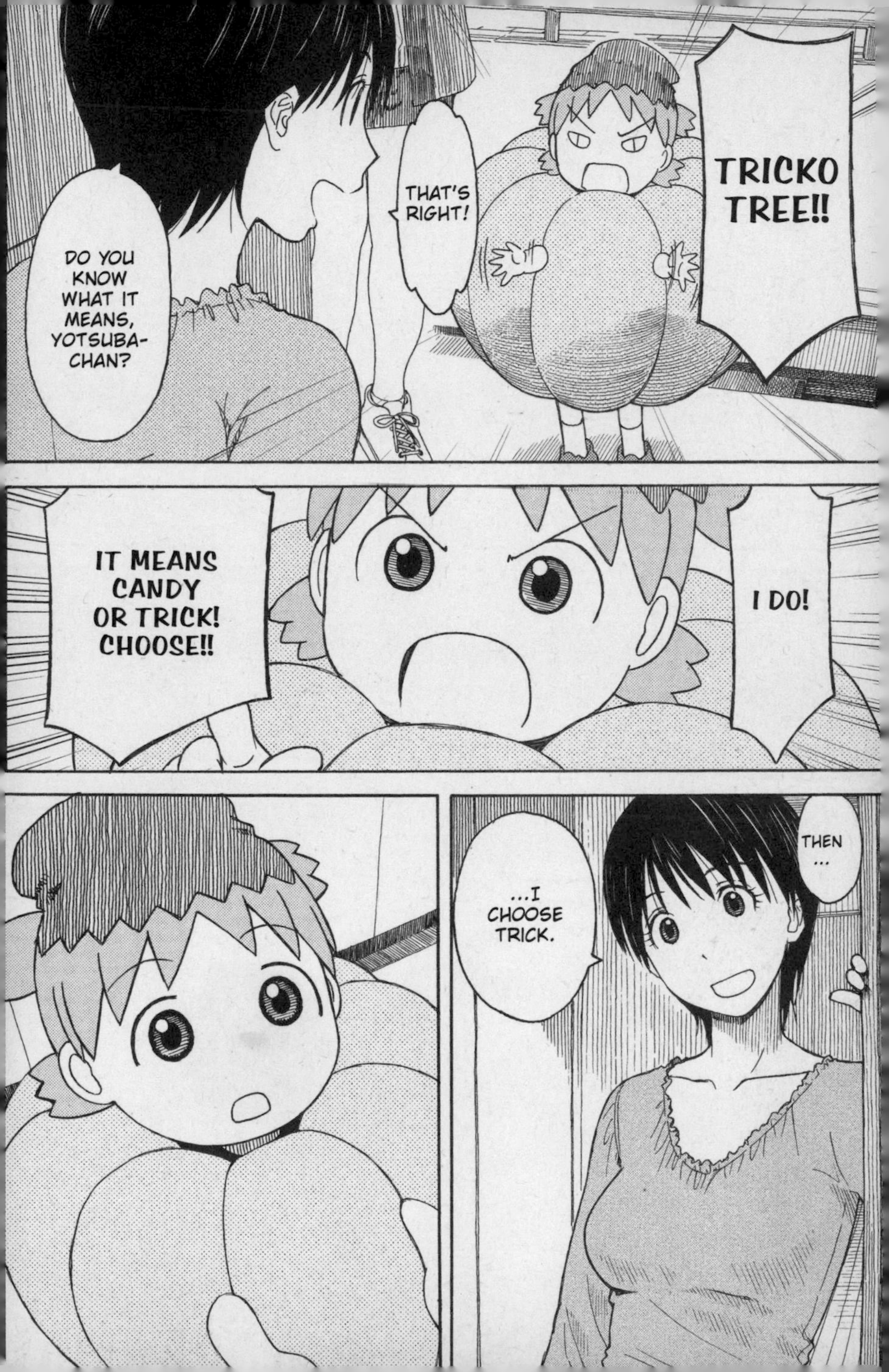
TRICKO TREE!!
THAT'S RIGHT!
DO YOU KNOW WHAT IT MEANS, YOTSUBA-CHAN?
I DO!
IT MEANS CANDY OR TRICK! CHOOSE!!
THEN ...
...I CHOOSE TRICK.

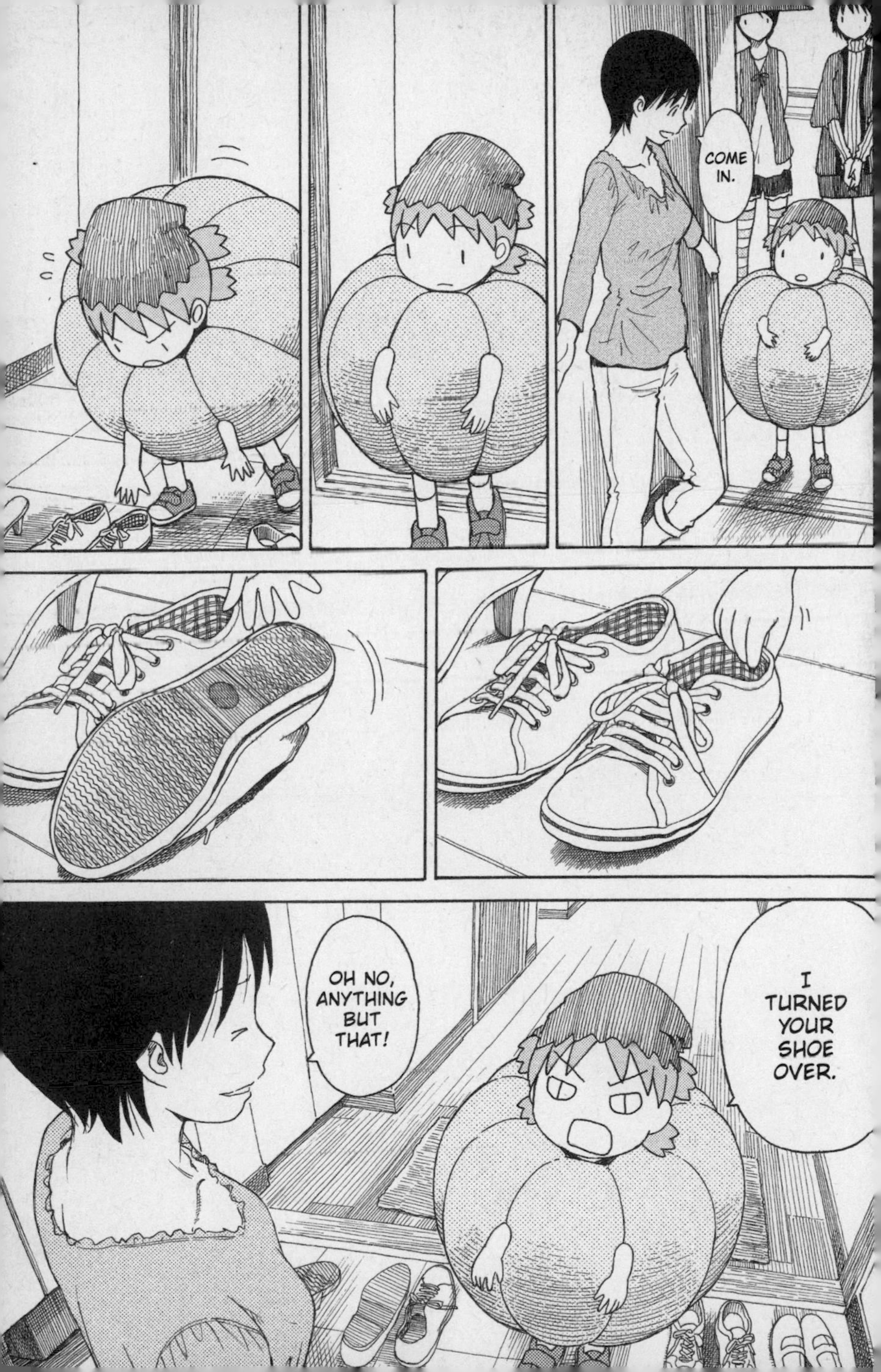
COME IN.
I TURNED YOUR SHOE OVER.
OH NO, ANYTHING BUT THAT!

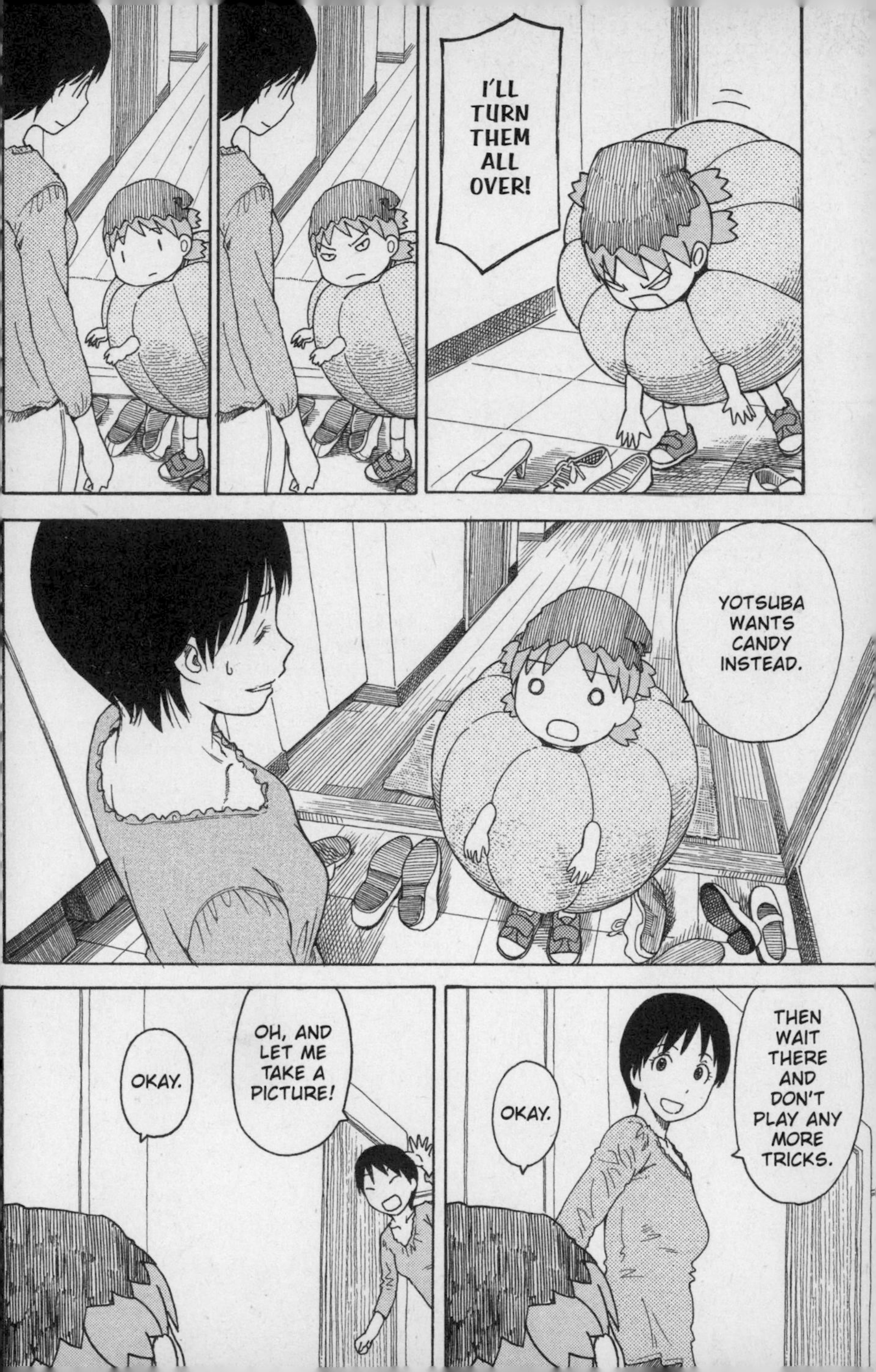
I'LL TURN THEM ALL OVER!
YOTSUBA WANTS CANDY INSTEAD.
THEN WAIT THERE AND DON'T PLAY ANY MORE TRICKS.
OKAY.
OH, AND LET ME TAKE A PICTURE!
OKAY.

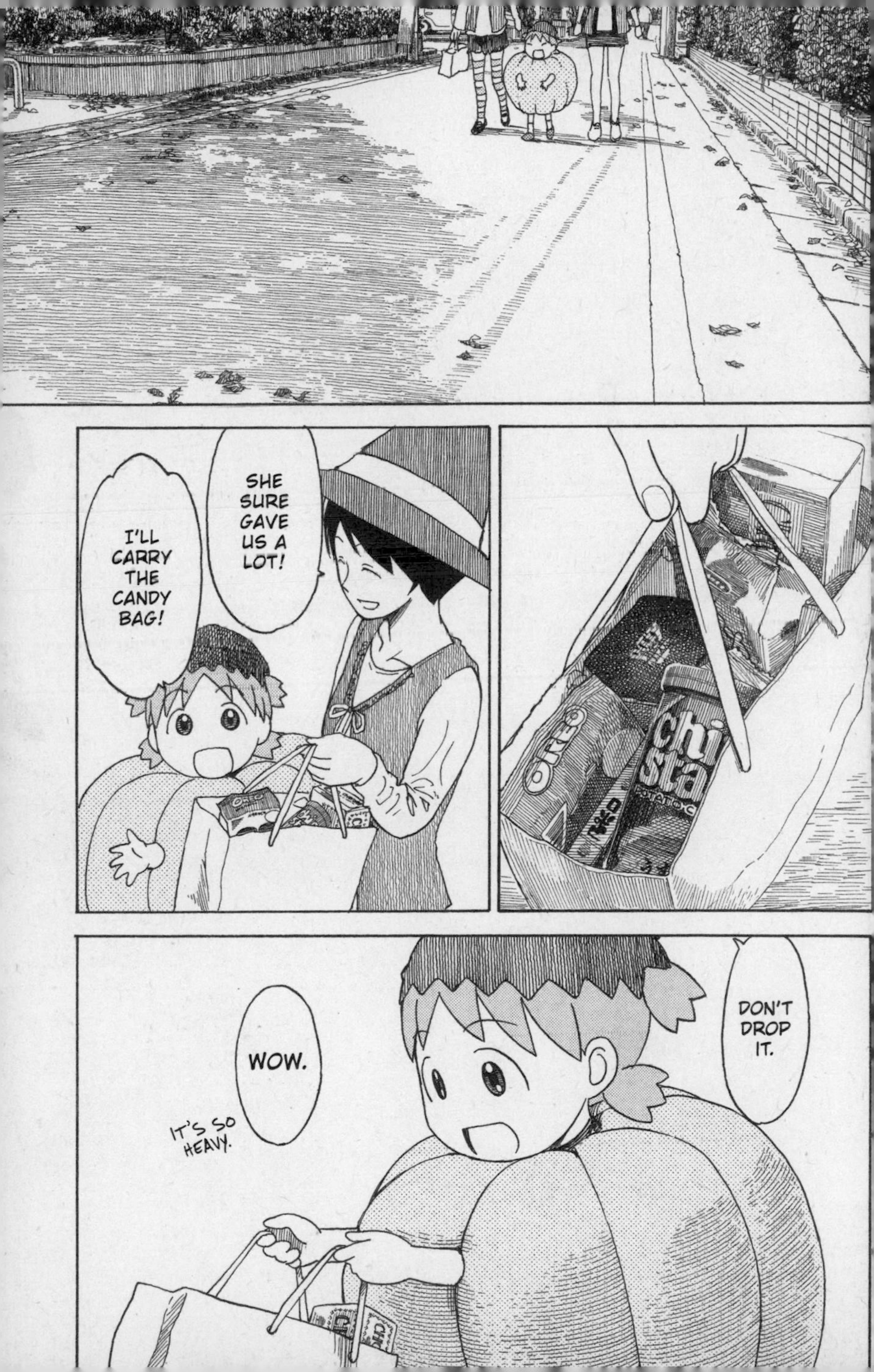
SHE SURE GAVE US A LOT!
I'LL CARRY THE CANDY BAG!
DON'T DROP IT.
WOW.
IT'S SO HEAVY.

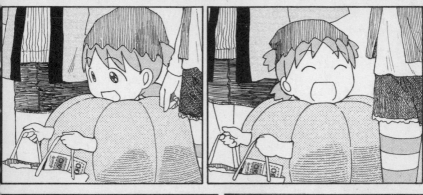

I AP-PROVE!

SHALL WE WALK DOWN TO THE PARK FOR SNACK TIME?

YOTSUBA&!

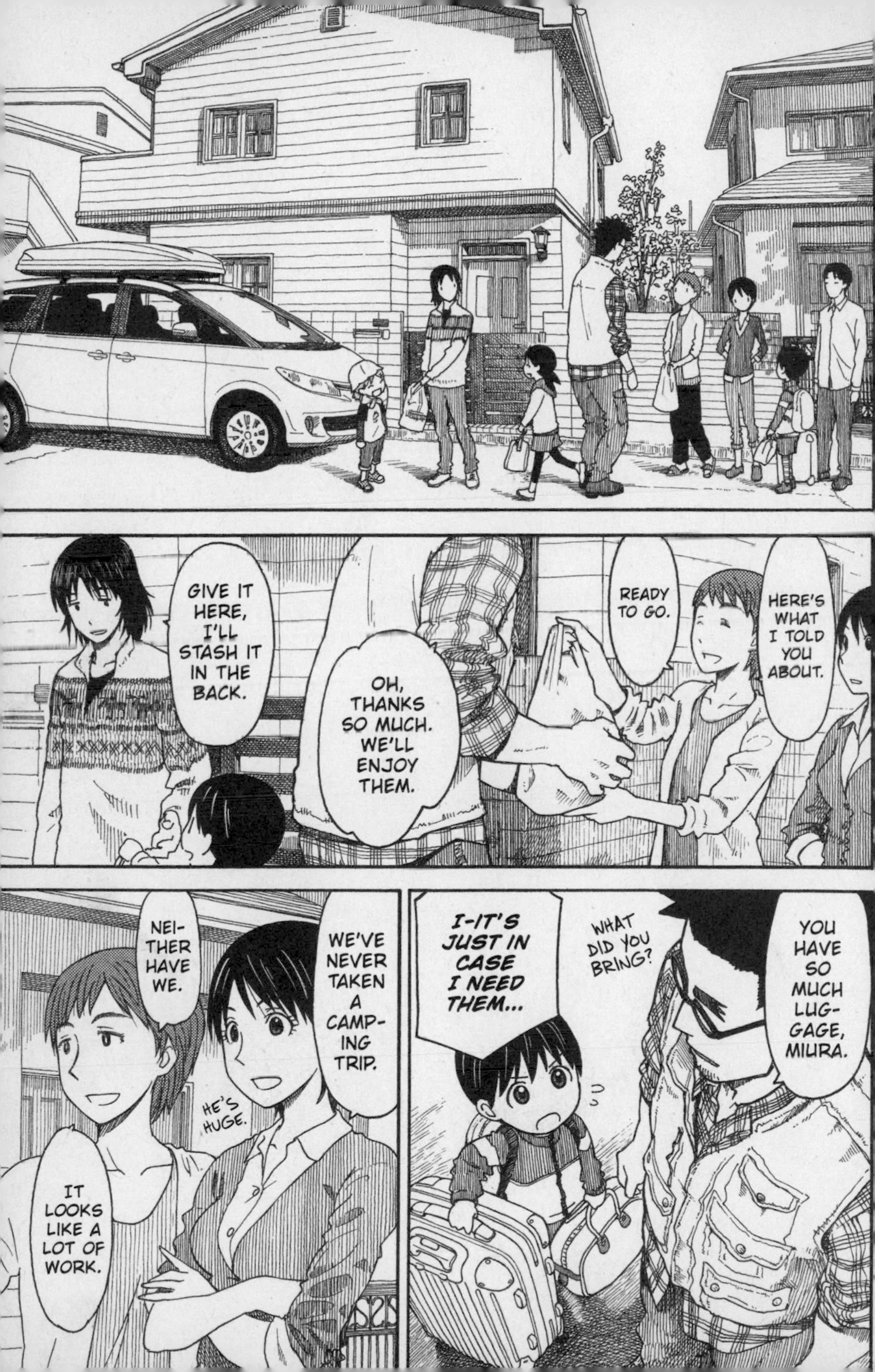

HERE'S WHAT I TOLD YOU ABOUT.
READY TO GO.
OH, THANKS SO MUCH. WE'LL ENJOY THEM.
GIVE IT HERE, I'LL STASH IT IN THE BACK.
YOU HAVE SO MUCH LUG-GAGE, MIURA.
WHAT DID YOU BRING?
I-IT'S JUST IN CASE I NEED THEM...
WE'VE NEVER TAKEN A CAMP-ING TRIP.
NEI-THER HAVE WE.
HE'S HUGE.
IT LOOKS LIKE A LOT OF WORK.

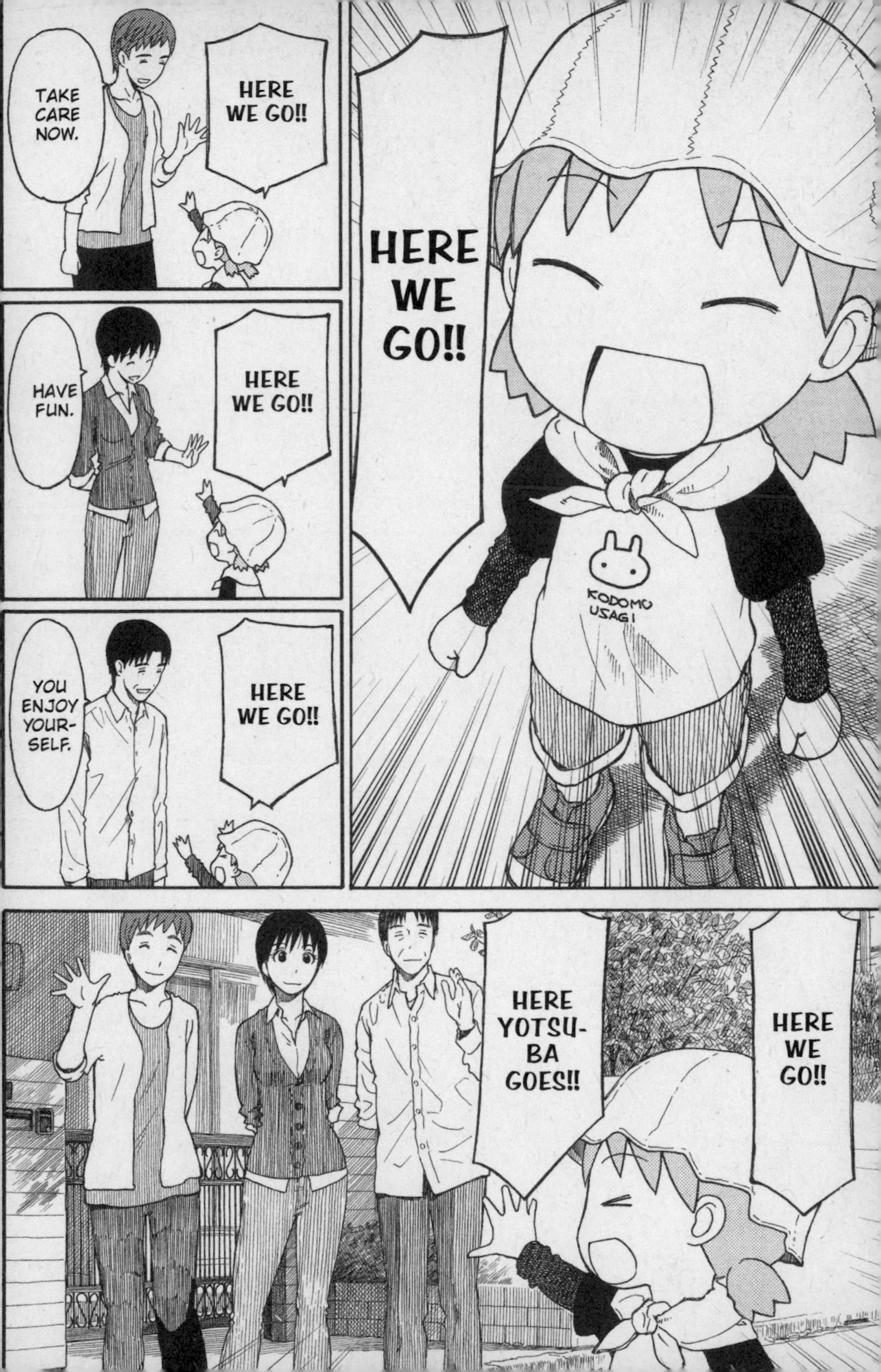
HERE WE GO!!
KODOMO USAGI
HERE WE GO!!
TAKE CARE NOW.
HERE WE GO!!
HAVE FUN.
HERE WE GO!!
YOU ENJOY YOUR-SELF.
HERE WE GO!!
HERE YOTSU-BA GOES!!

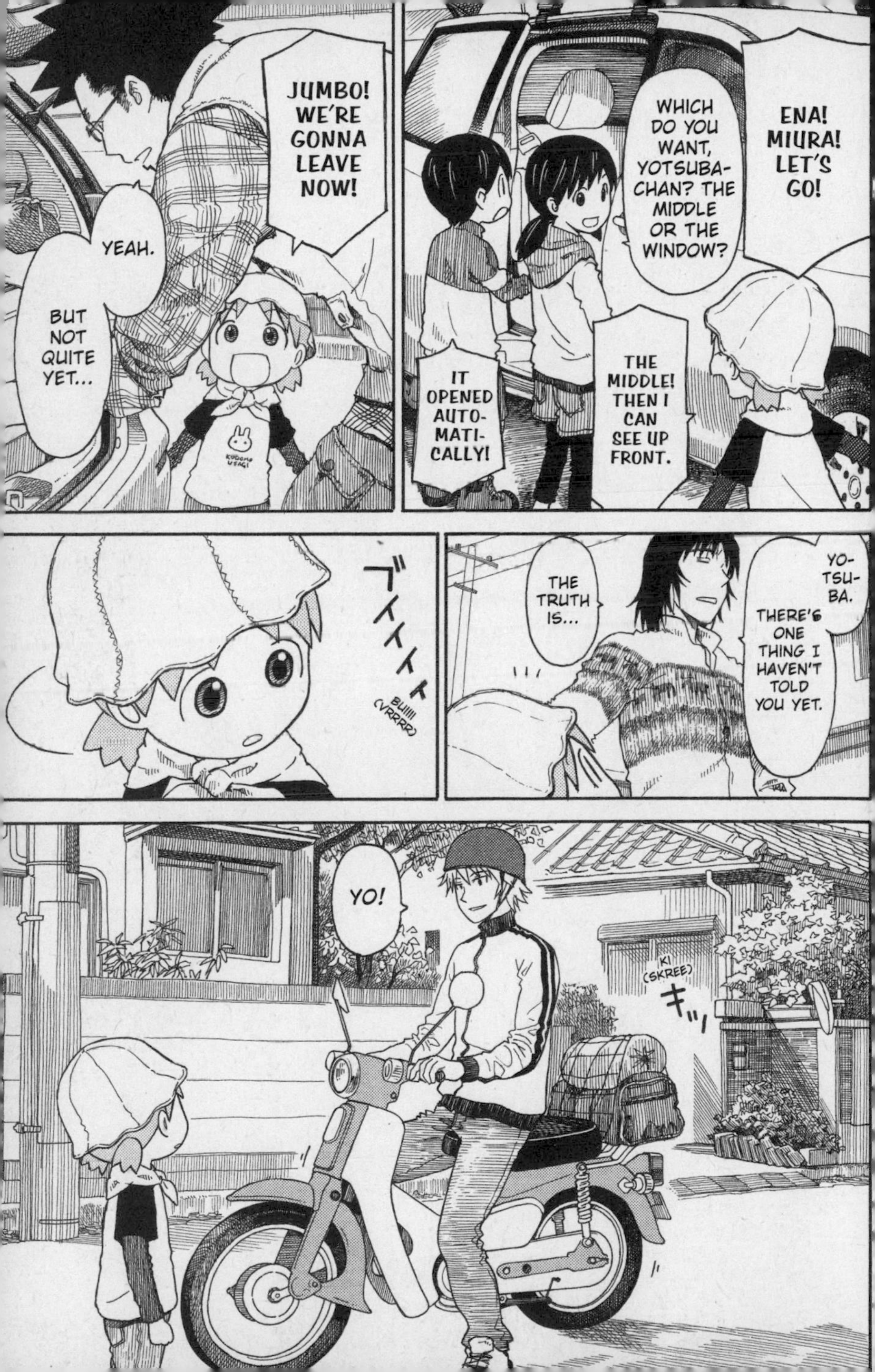
ENA! MIURA! LET'S GO!
WHICH DO YOU WANT, YOTSUBA-CHAN? THE MIDDLE OR THE WINDOW?
THE MIDDLE! THEN I CAN SEE UP FRONT.
IT OPENED AUTO-MATI-CALLY!
JUMBO! WE'RE GONNA LEAVE NOW!
YEAH.
BUT NOT QUITE YET...
YO-TSU-BA.
THERE'S ONE THING I HAVEN'T TOLD YOU YET.
THE TRUTH IS...
ブイイイイ
BUIIII (VRRRR)
KI (SKREE)
キッ
YO!

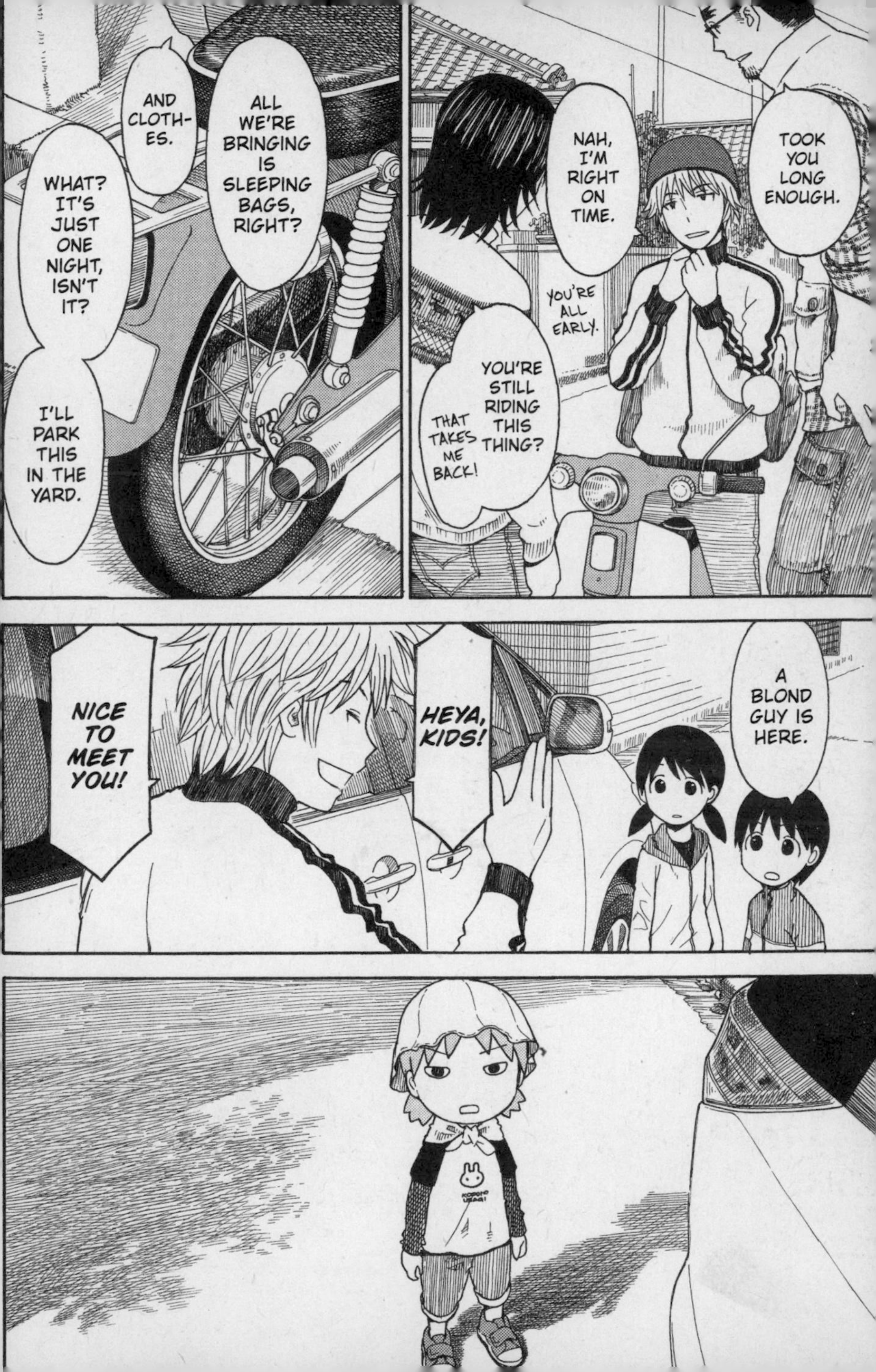
TOOK YOU LONG ENOUGH.
NAH, I'M RIGHT ON TIME.
YOU'RE ALL EARLY.
YOU'RE STILL RIDING THIS THING?
THAT TAKES ME BACK!
ALL WE'RE BRINGING IS SLEEPING BAGS, RIGHT?
AND CLOTH-ES.
WHAT? IT'S JUST ONE NIGHT, ISN'T IT?
I'LL PARK THIS IN THE YARD.
A BLOND GUY IS HERE.
HEYA, KIDS!
NICE TO MEET YOU!

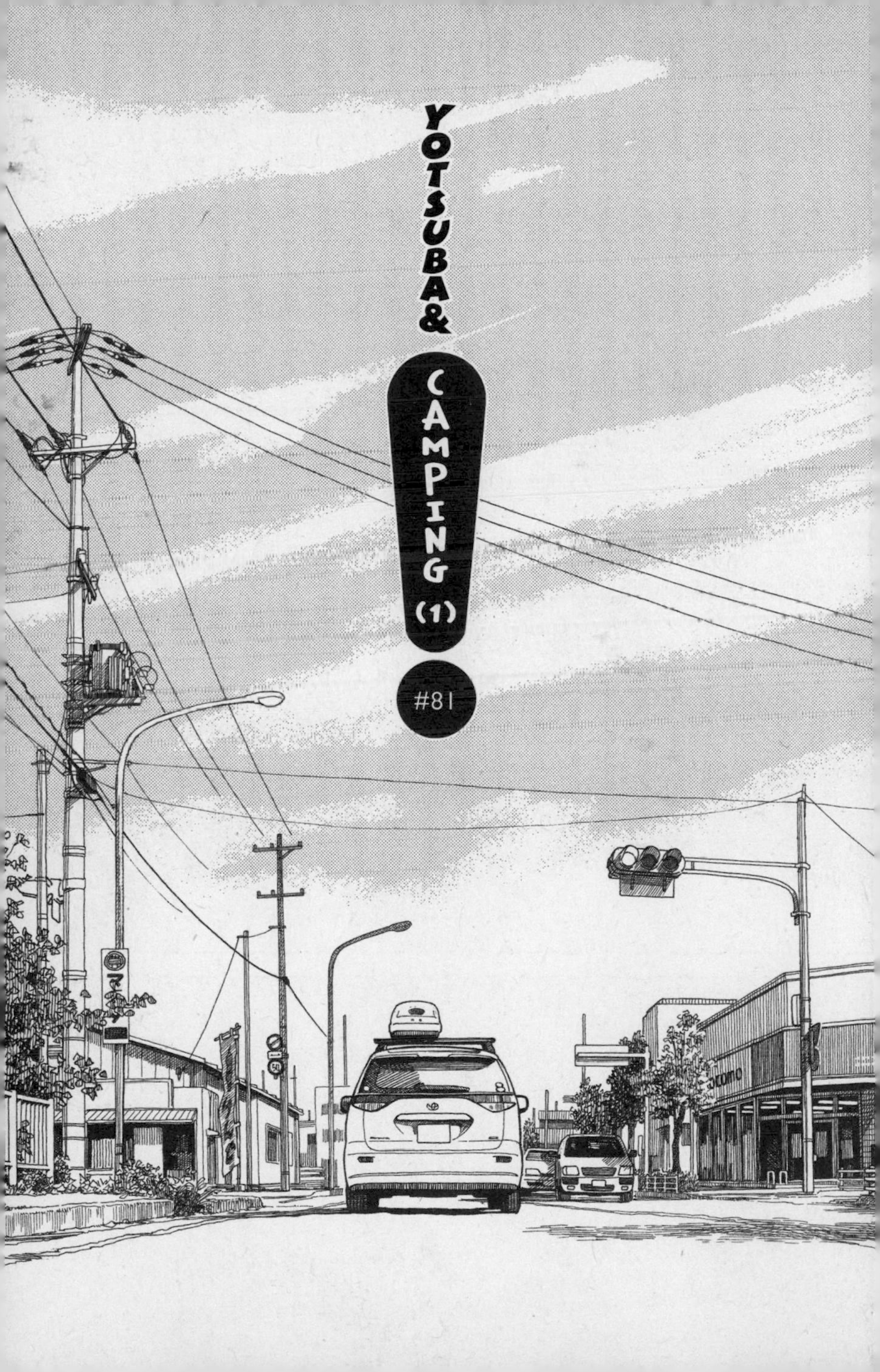
YOTSUBA&
CAMPING (1)
#81

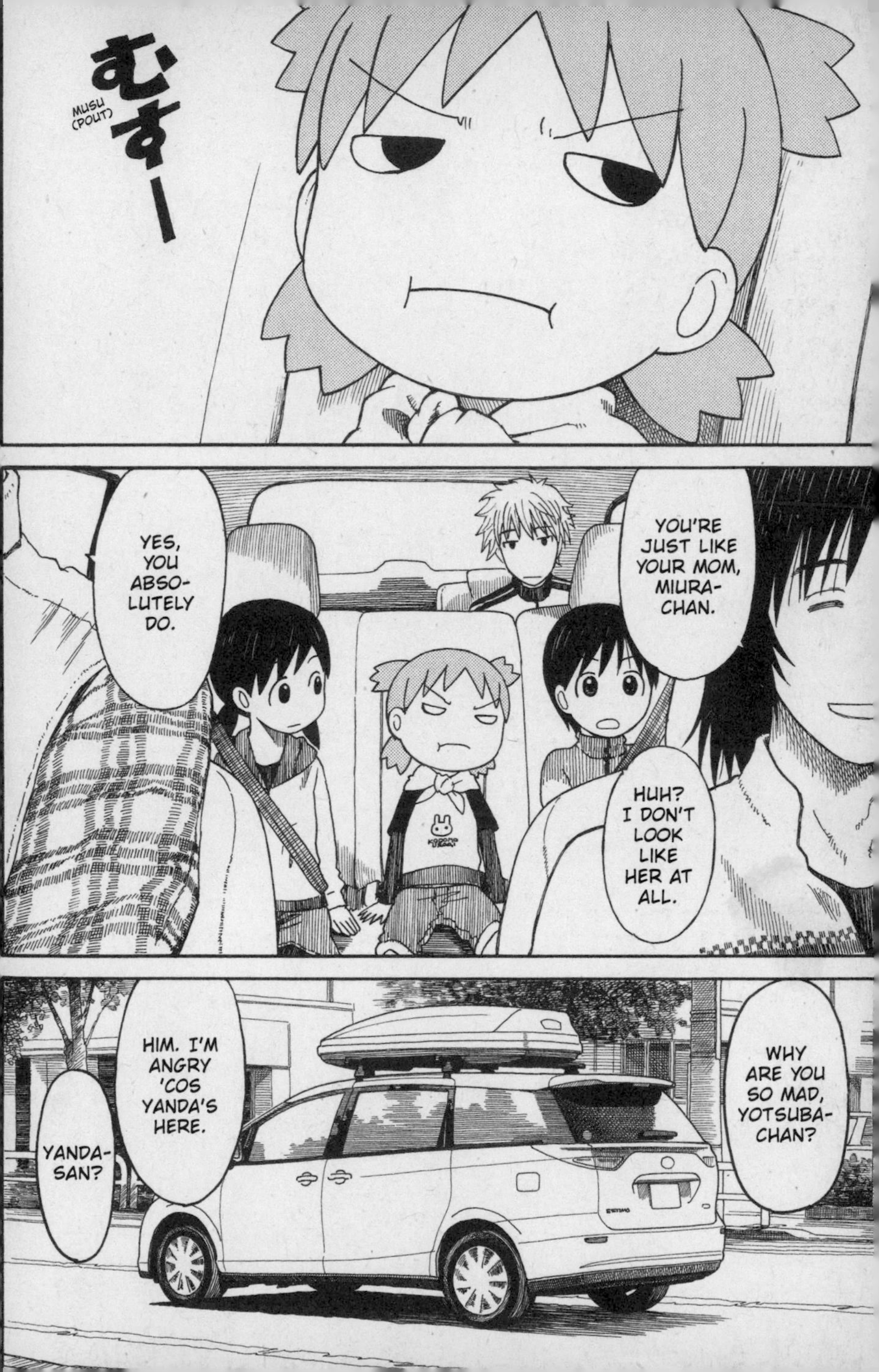
むすー
MUSU (POUT)
YOU'RE JUST LIKE YOUR MOM, MIURA-CHAN.
HUH? I DON'T LOOK LIKE HER AT ALL.
YES, YOU ABSOLUTELY DO.
WHY ARE YOU SO MAD, YOTSUBA-CHAN?
HIM. I'M ANGRY 'COS YANDA'S HERE.
YANDA-SAN?

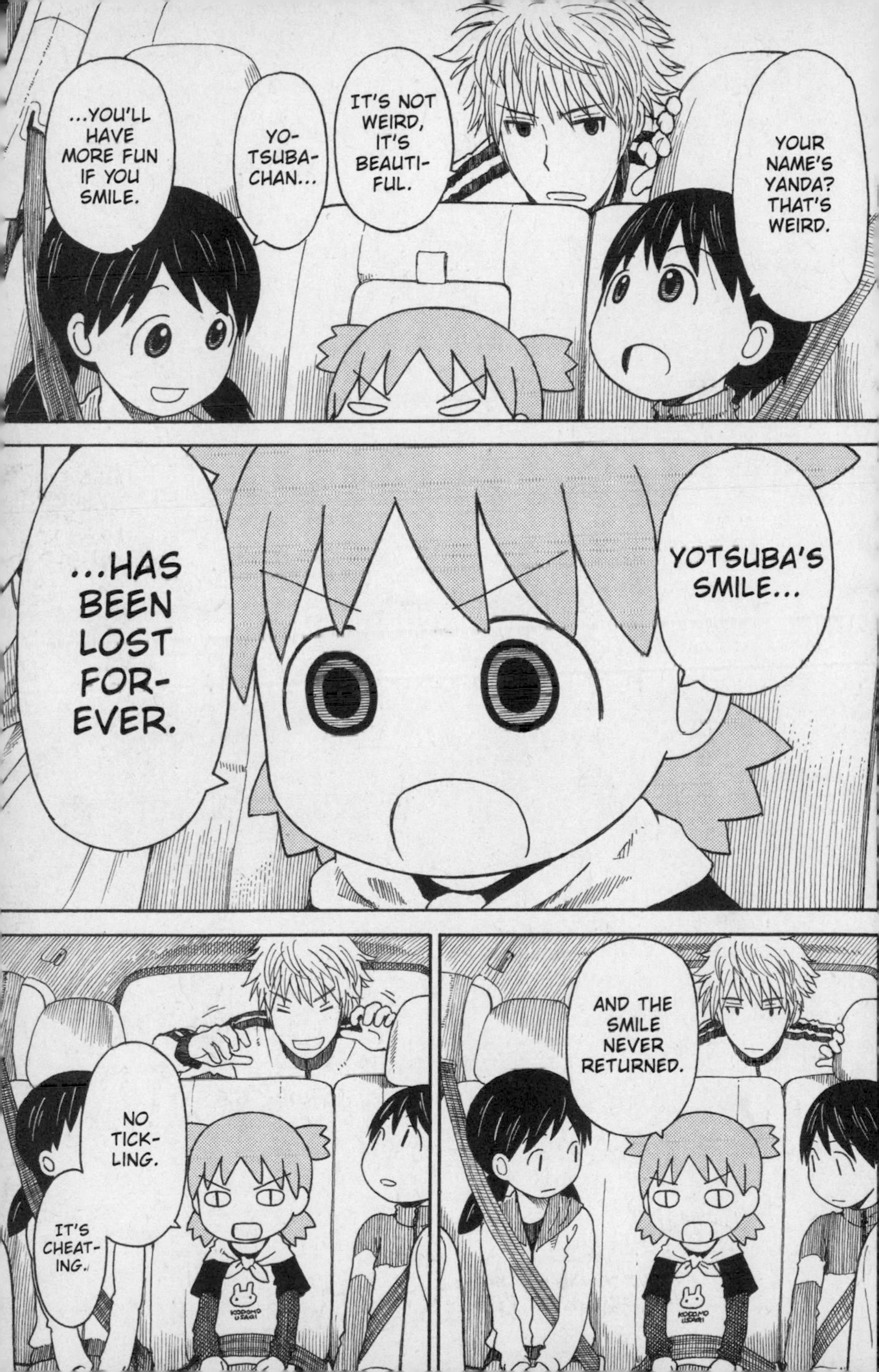
YOUR NAME'S YANDA? THAT'S WEIRD.
IT'S NOT WEIRD, IT'S BEAUTIFUL.
YOTSUBA-CHAN...
...YOU'LL HAVE MORE FUN IF YOU SMILE.
YOTSUBA'S SMILE...
...HAS BEEN LOST FOREVER.
AND THE SMILE NEVER RETURNED.
NO TICKLING.
IT'S CHEATING.

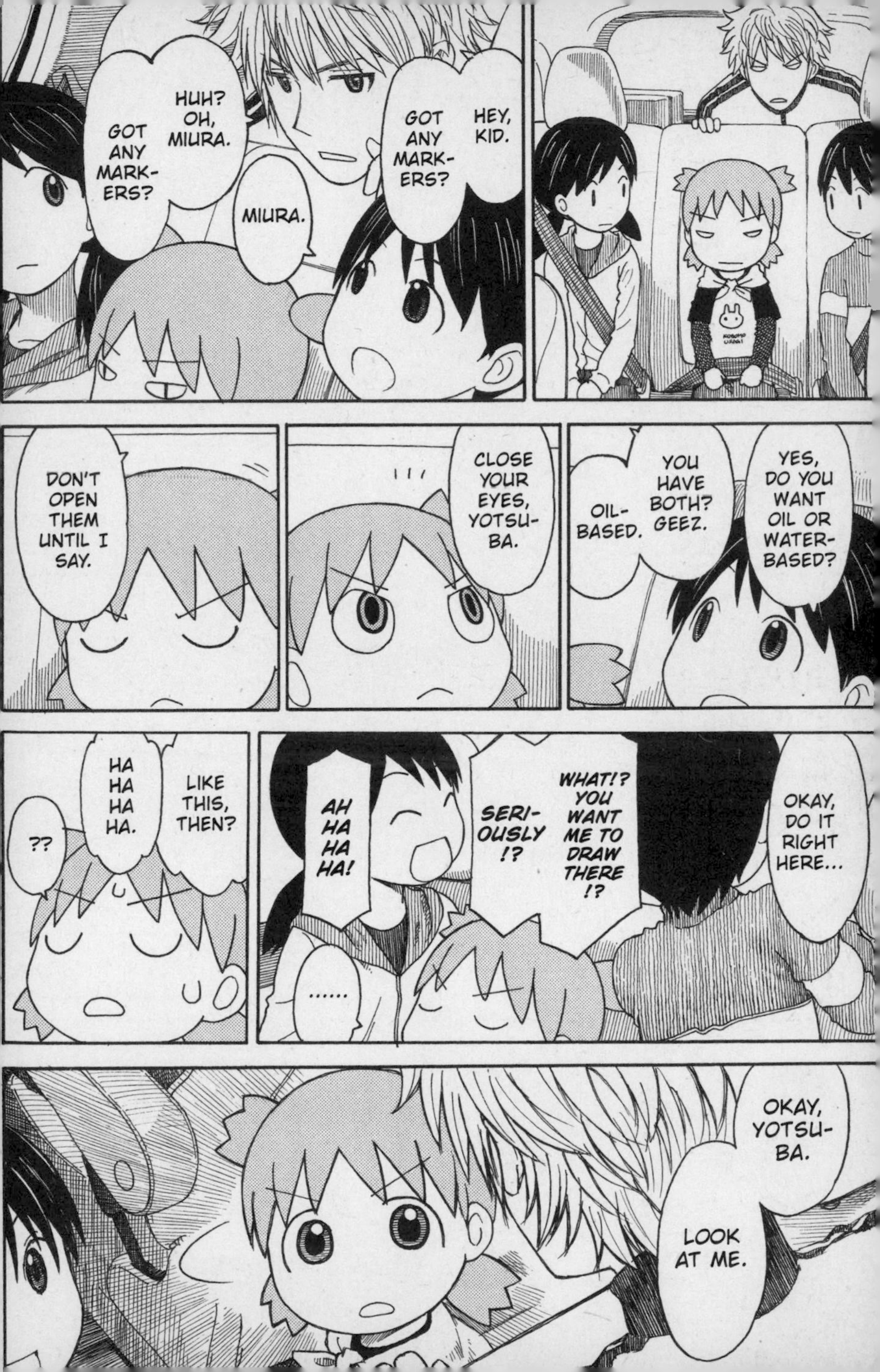
HEY, KID. GOT ANY MARKERS?
MIURA.
HUH? OH, MIURA. GOT ANY MARKERS?
YES, DO YOU WANT OIL OR WATER-BASED?
YOU HAVE BOTH? GEEZ. OIL-BASED.
CLOSE YOUR EYES, YOTSUBA.
DON'T OPEN THEM UNTIL I SAY.
OKAY, DO IT RIGHT HERE...
WHAT!? YOU WANT ME TO DRAW THERE!?
SERIOUSLY!?
AH HA HA HA!
......
LIKE THIS, THEN?
HA HA HA HA.
??
OKAY, YOTSUBA.
LOOK AT ME.

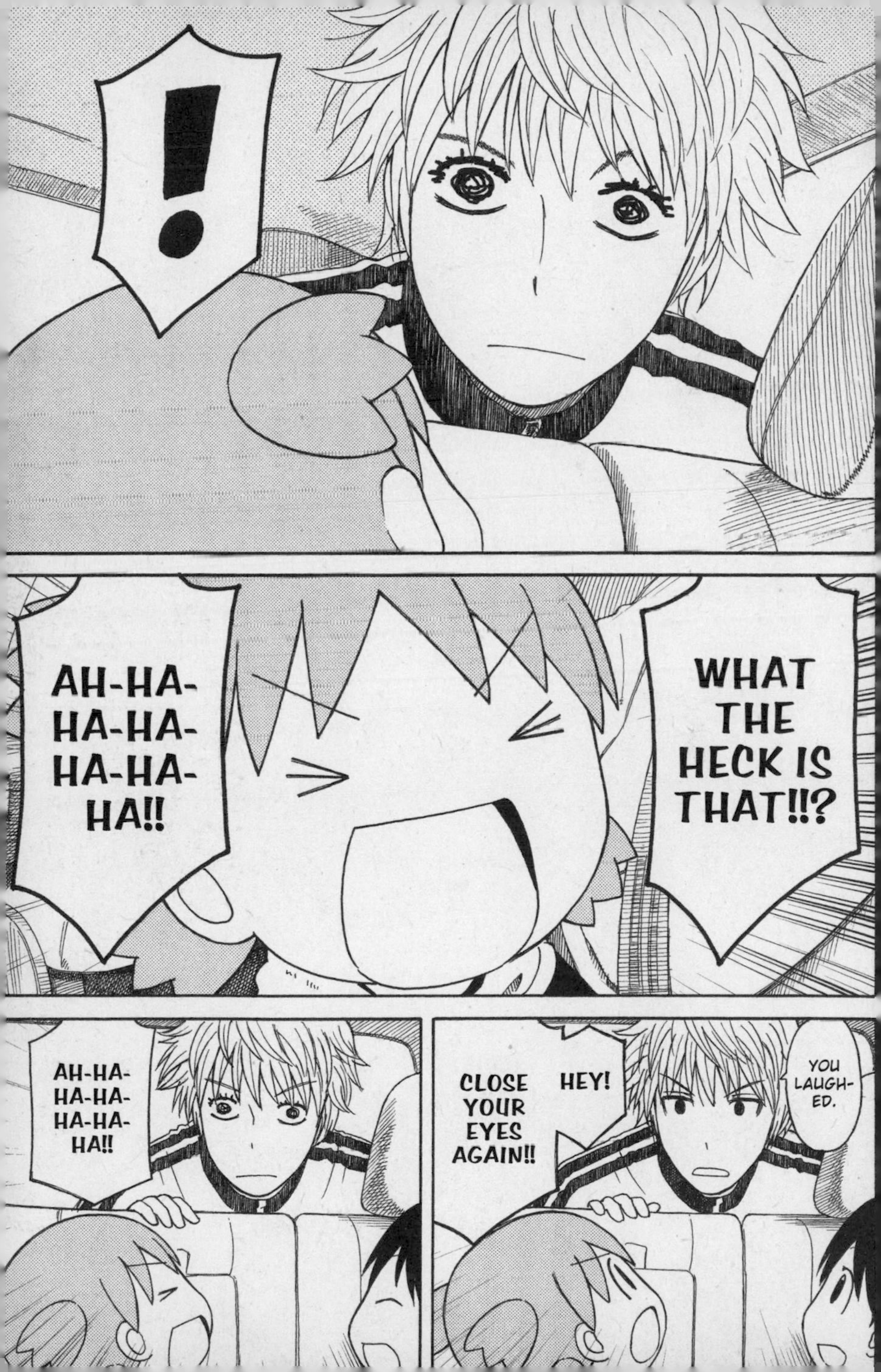
!
WHAT THE HECK IS THAT!!?
AH-HA-HA-HA-HA-HA-HA!!
YOU LAUGHED.
HEY! CLOSE YOUR EYES AGAIN!!
AH-HA-HA-HA-HA-HA-HA!!

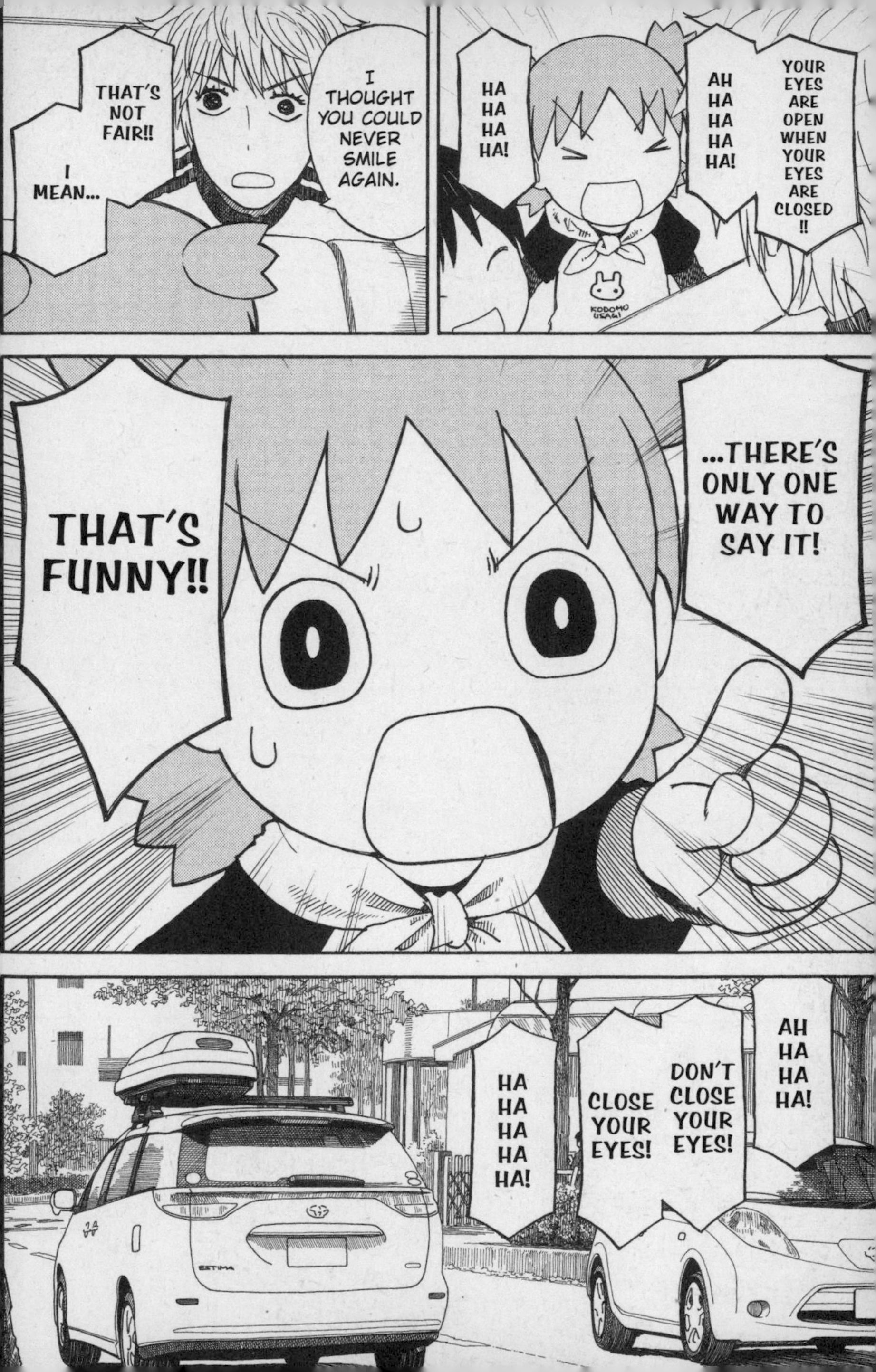
YOUR EYES ARE OPEN WHEN YOUR EYES ARE CLOSED!!
AH HA HA HA HA!
HA HA HA HA!
KODOMO USAGI
I THOUGHT YOU COULD NEVER SMILE AGAIN.
THAT'S NOT FAIR!!
I MEAN...
...THERE'S ONLY ONE WAY TO SAY IT!
THAT'S FUNNY!!
AH HA HA HA!
DON'T CLOSE YOUR EYES!
CLOSE YOUR EYES!
HA HA HA HA HA!

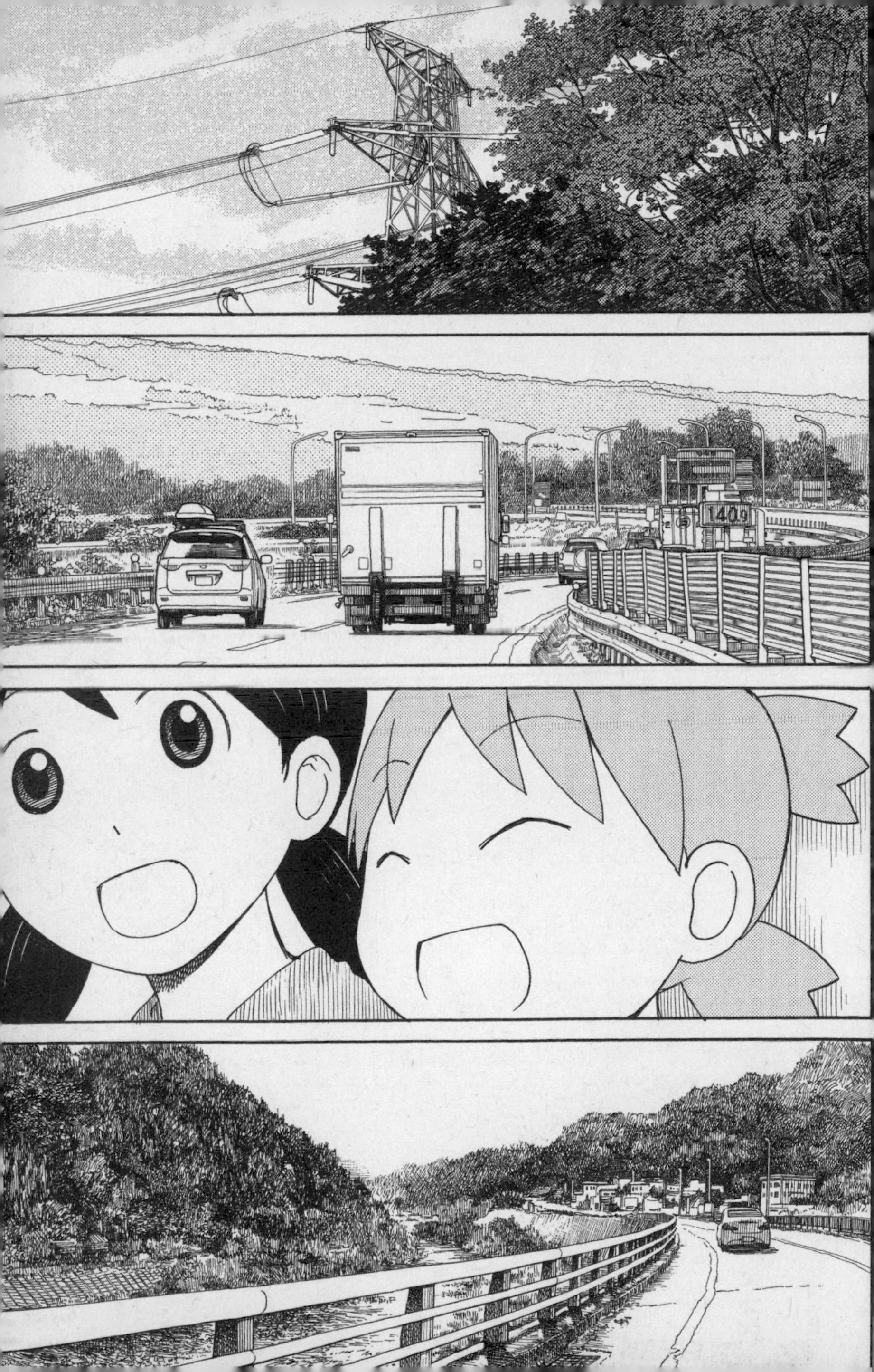

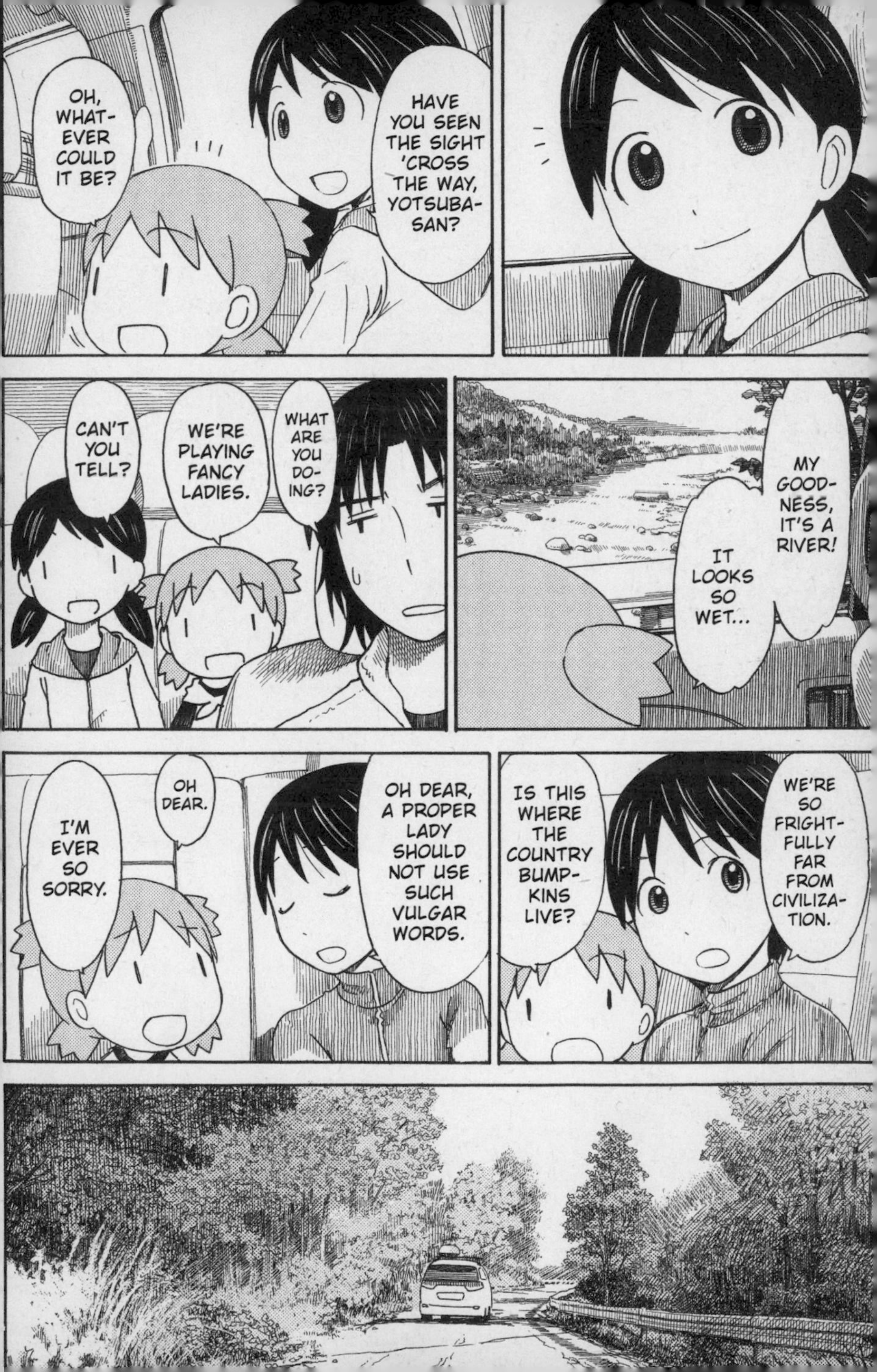
HAVE YOU SEEN THE SIGHT 'CROSS THE WAY, YOTSUBA-SAN?
OH, WHATEVER COULD IT BE?
MY GOODNESS, IT'S A RIVER!
IT LOOKS SO WET...
WHAT ARE YOU DOING?
WE'RE PLAYING FANCY LADIES.
CAN'T YOU TELL?
WE'RE SO FRIGHTFULLY FAR FROM CIVILIZATION.
IS THIS WHERE THE COUNTRY BUMPKINS LIVE?
OH DEAR, A PROPER LADY SHOULD NOT USE SUCH VULGAR WORDS.
OH DEAR.
I'M EVER SO SORRY.

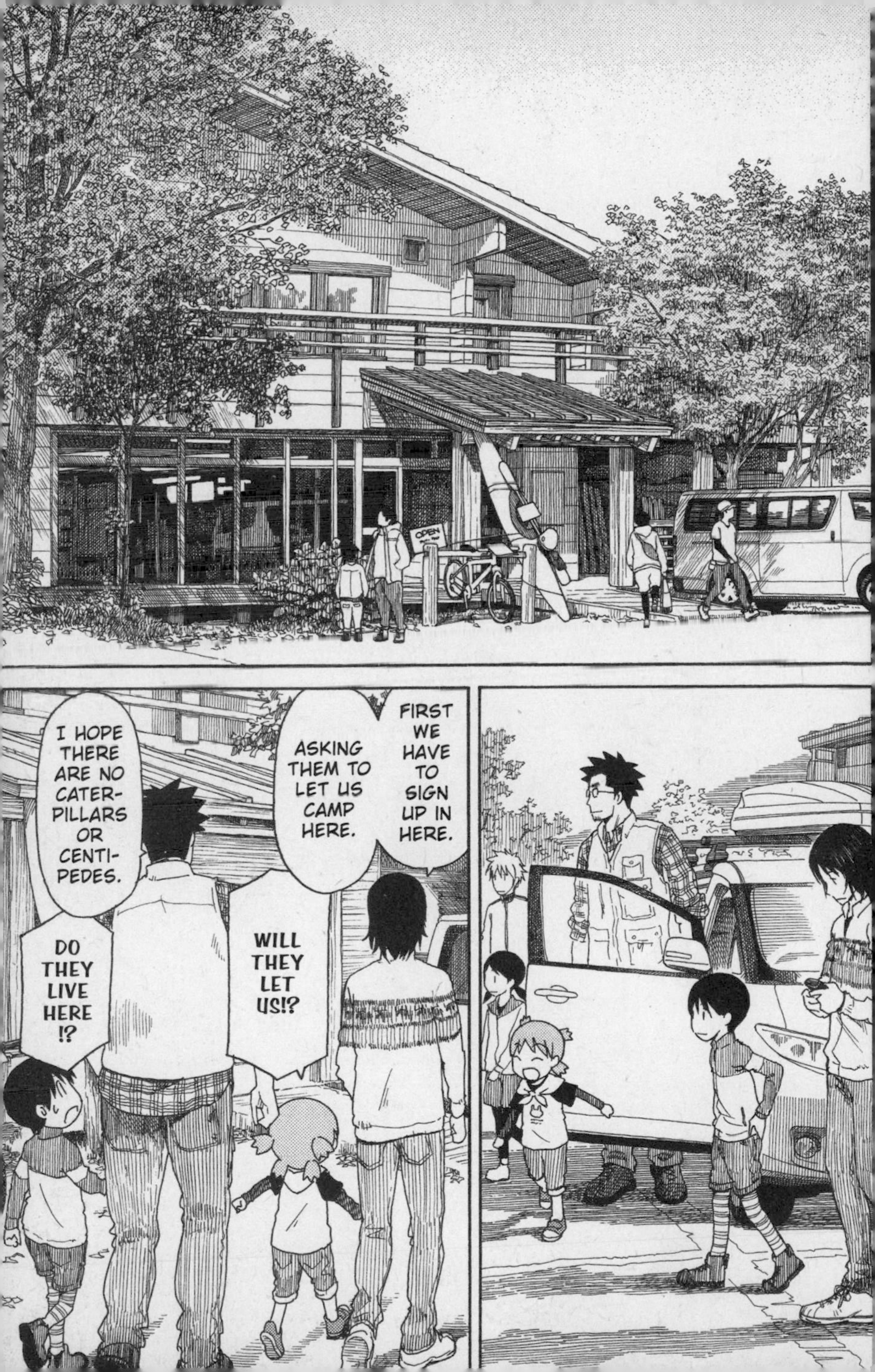

OPEN
FIRST WE HAVE TO SIGN UP IN HERE.
ASKING THEM TO LET US CAMP HERE.
I HOPE THERE ARE NO CATER-PILLARS OR CENTI-PEDES.
WILL THEY LET US!?
DO THEY LIVE HERE !?

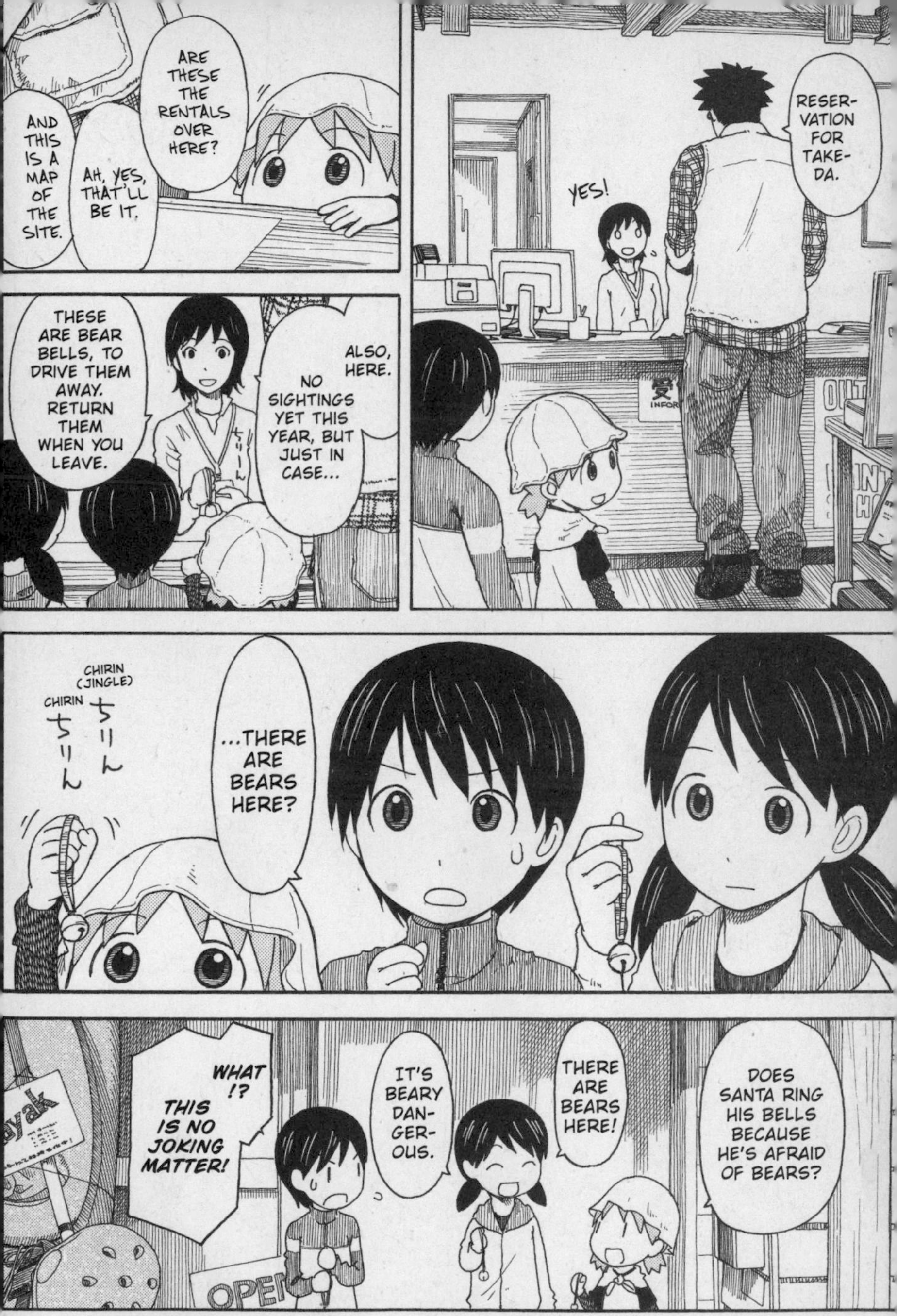
RESER-VATION FOR TAKE-DA.
YES!
ARE THESE THE RENTALS OVER HERE?
AH, YES, THAT'LL BE IT.
AND THIS IS A MAP OF THE SITE.
ALSO, HERE.
NO SIGHTINGS YET THIS YEAR, BUT JUST IN CASE...
THESE ARE BEAR BELLS, TO DRIVE THEM AWAY. RETURN THEM WHEN YOU LEAVE.
...THERE ARE BEARS HERE?
CHIRIN (JINGLE) ちりん
CHIRIN ちりん
DOES SANTA RING HIS BELLS BECAUSE HE'S AFRAID OF BEARS?
THERE ARE BEARS HERE!
IT'S BEARY DAN-GER-OUS.
WHAT!? THIS IS NO JOKING MATTER!
OPEN

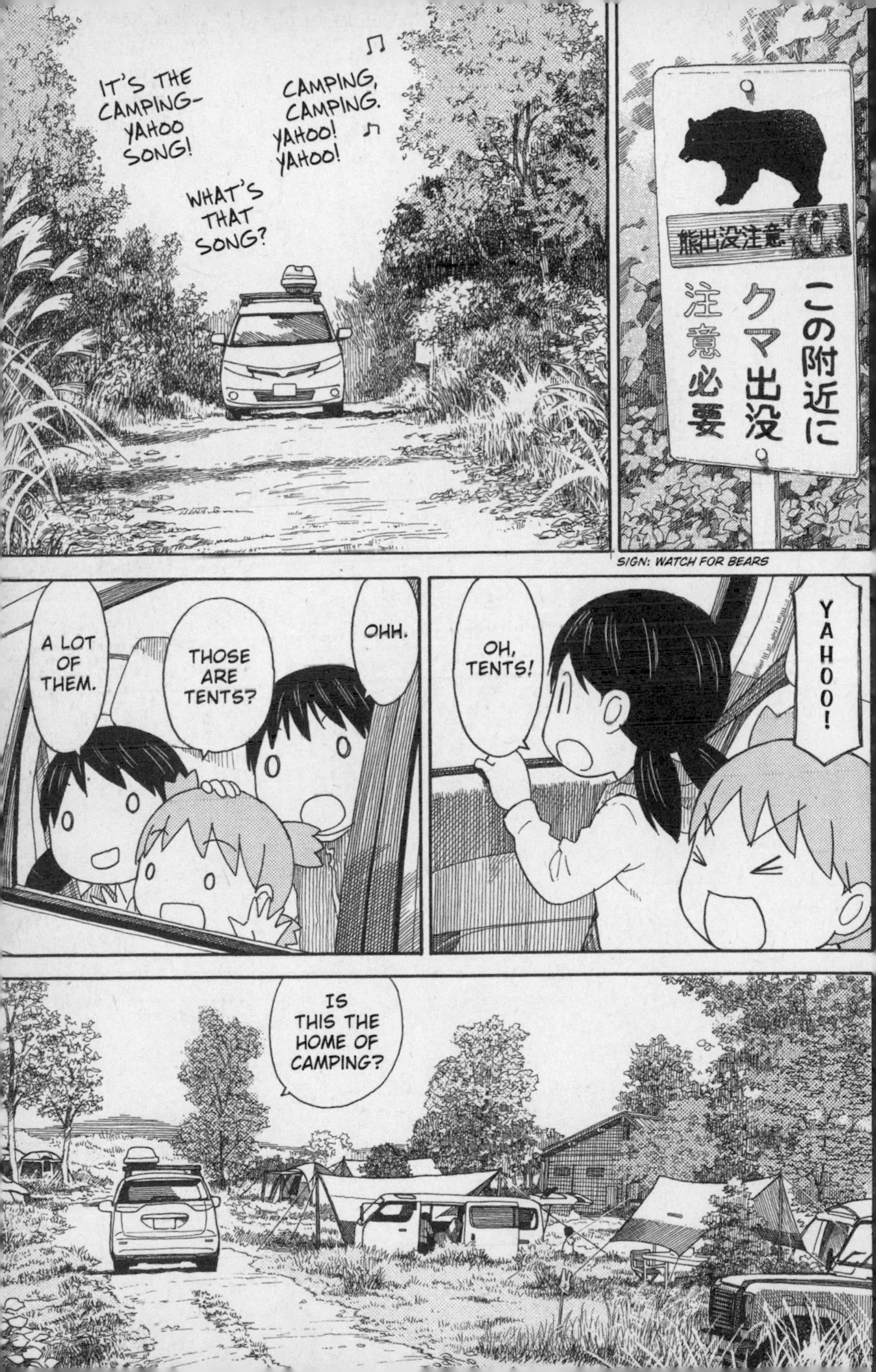
熊出没注意
この附近に
クマ出没
注意必要
SIGN: WATCH FOR BEARS
CAMPING, CAMPING. YAHOO! YAHOO!
IT'S THE CAMPING-YAHOO SONG!
WHAT'S THAT SONG?
YAHOO!
OH, TENTS!
OHH.
THOSE ARE TENTS?
A LOT OF THEM.
IS THIS THE HOME OF CAMPING?

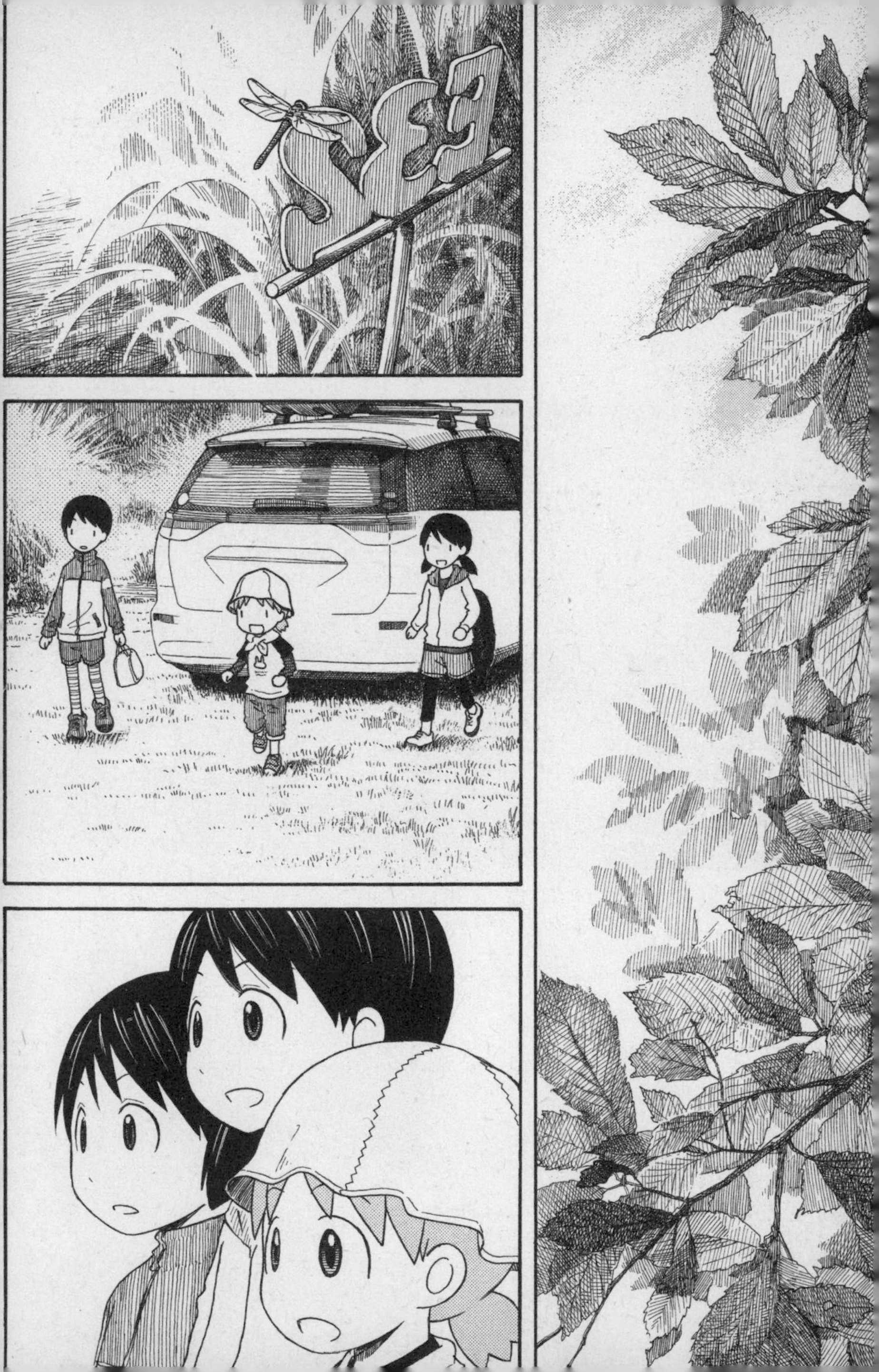

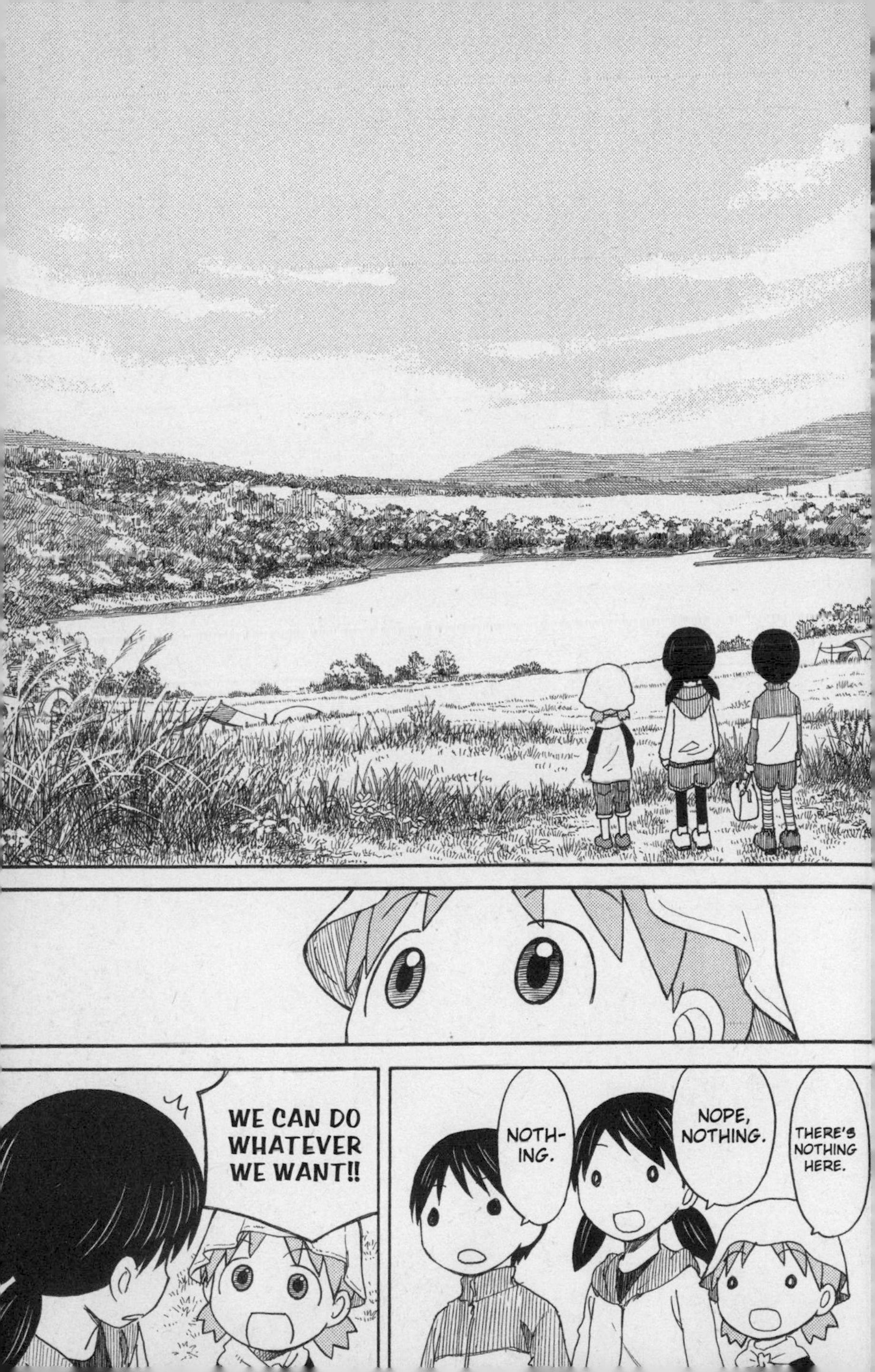
THERE'S NOTHING HERE.
NOPE, NOTHING.
NOTH-ING.
WE CAN DO WHATEVER WE WANT!!

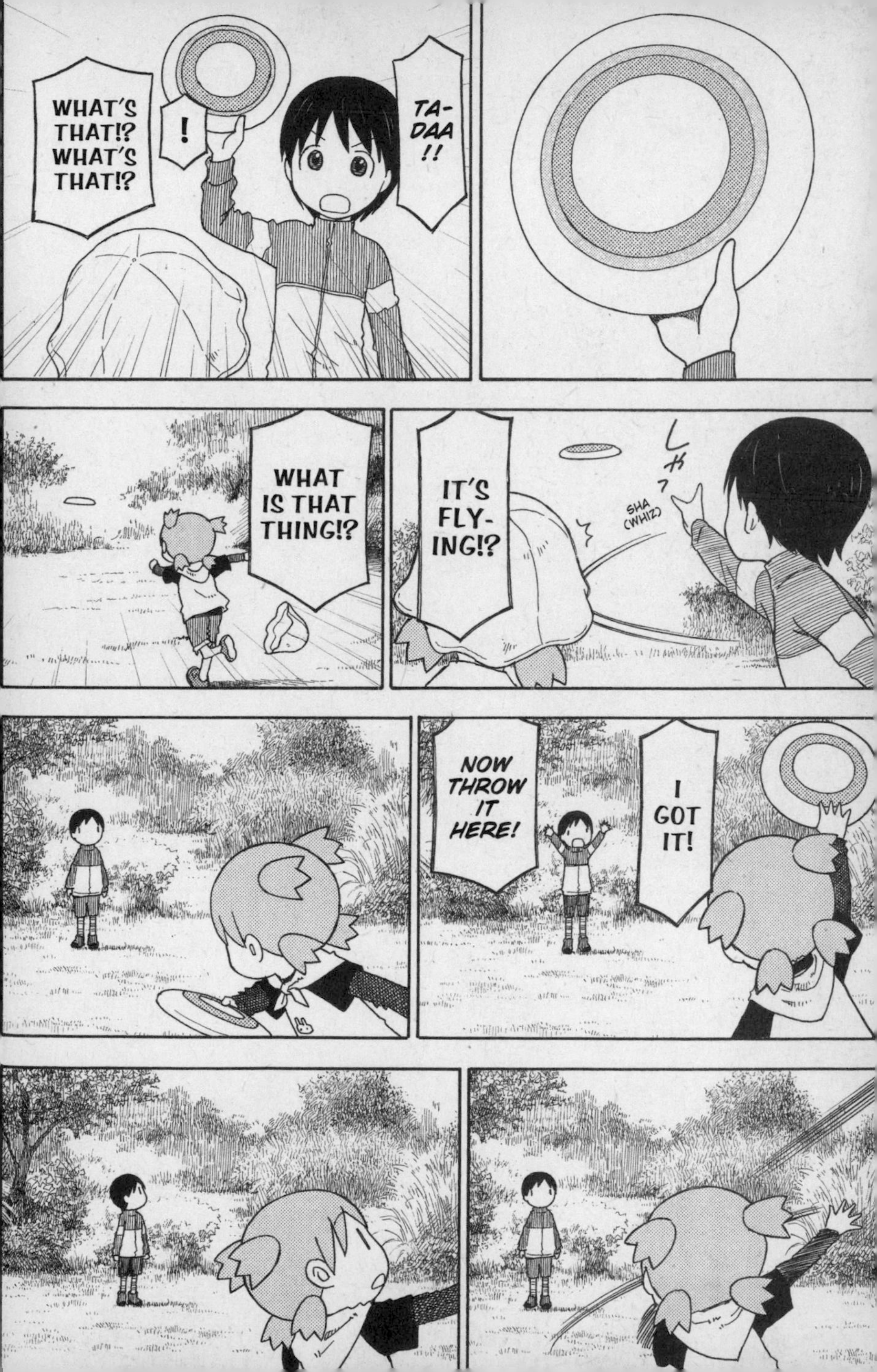
TA-DAA!!
!
WHAT'S THAT!? WHAT'S THAT!?
SHA (WHIZ)
IT'S FLY-ING!?
WHAT IS THAT THING!?
I GOT IT!
NOW THROW IT HERE!

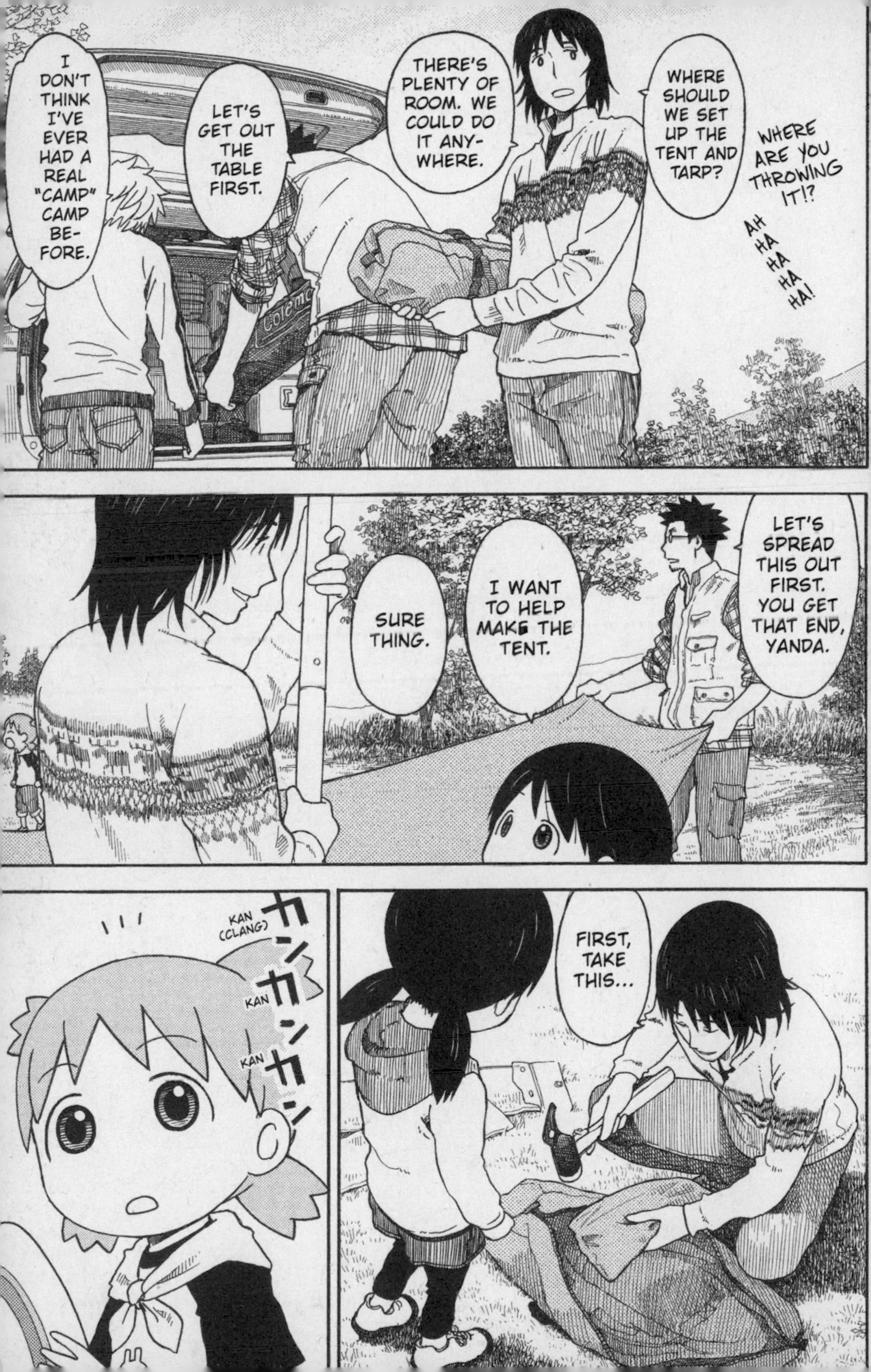
WHERE ARE YOU THROWING IT!?
AH HA HA HA HA!
WHERE SHOULD WE SET UP THE TENT AND TARP?
THERE'S PLENTY OF ROOM. WE COULD DO IT ANY-WHERE.
LET'S GET OUT THE TABLE FIRST.
I DON'T THINK I'VE EVER HAD A REAL "CAMP" CAMP BE-FORE.
LET'S SPREAD THIS OUT FIRST. YOU GET THAT END, YANDA.
I WANT TO HELP MAKE THE TENT.
SURE THING.
FIRST, TAKE THIS...
KAN (CLANG)
KAN
KAN

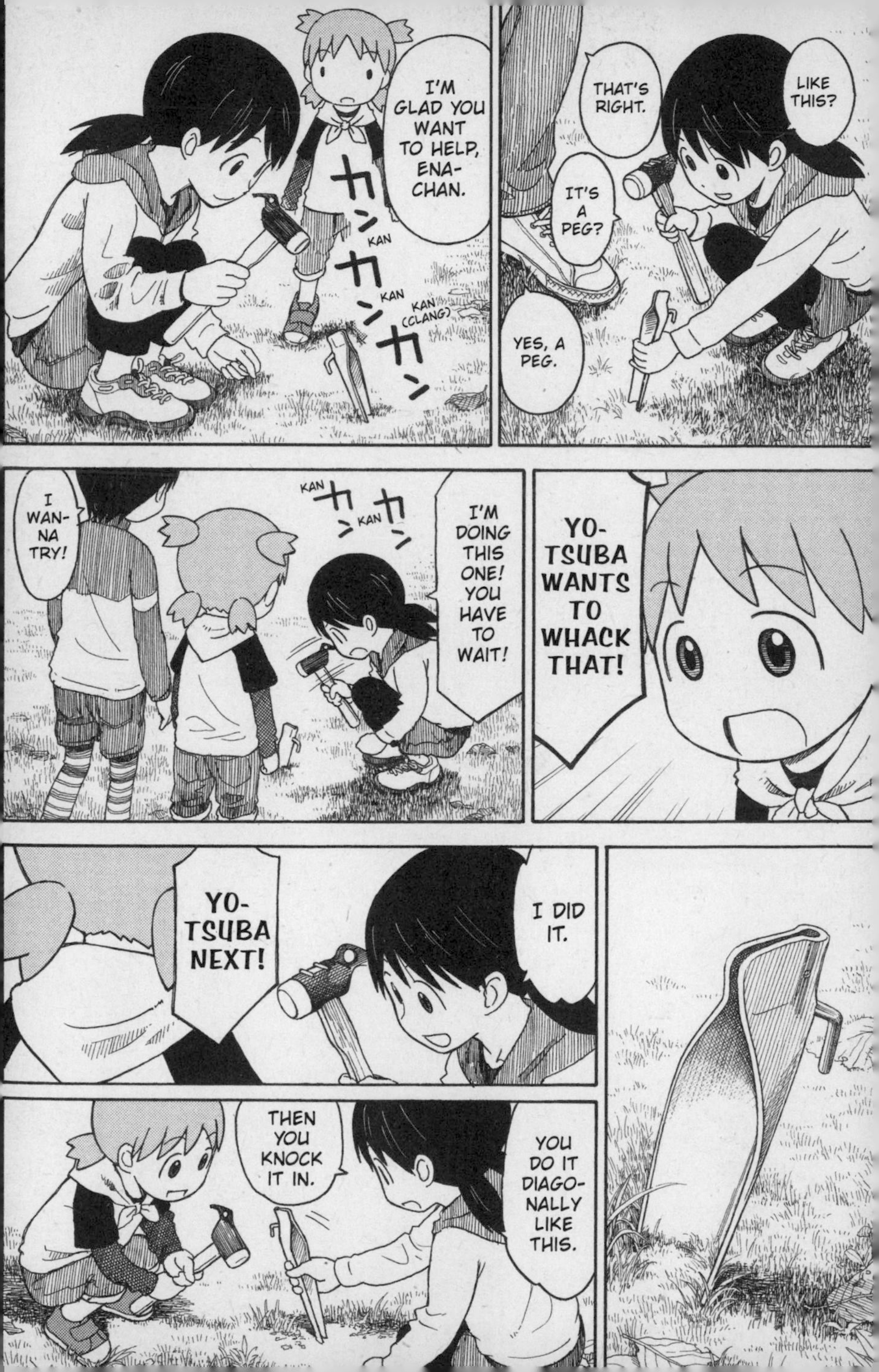

LIKE THIS?
THAT'S RIGHT.
IT'S A PEG?
YES, A PEG.
I'M GLAD YOU WANT TO HELP, ENA-CHAN.
カン KAN
カン KAN
カン KAN (CLANG)
YO-TSUBA WANTS TO WHACK THAT!
I'M DOING THIS ONE! YOU HAVE TO WAIT!
カン KAN
カン KAN
I WAN-NA TRY!
I DID IT.
YO-TSUBA NEXT!
YOU DO IT DIAGO-NALLY LIKE THIS.
THEN YOU KNOCK IT IN.

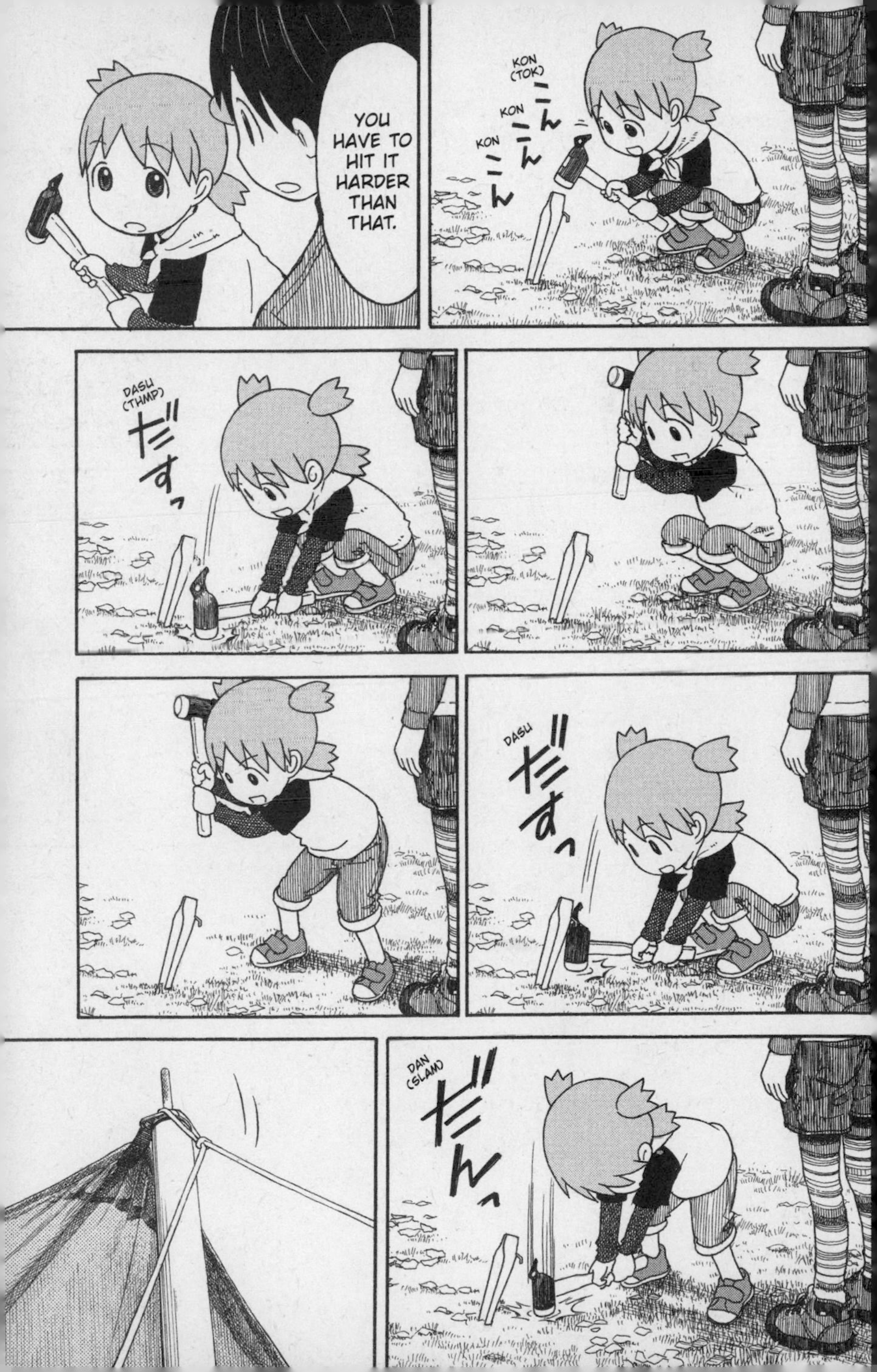
KON (TOK)
こん
KON
こん
KON
こん
YOU HAVE TO HIT IT HARDER THAN THAT.
DASU (THMP)
だすっ
DASU
だすっ
DAN (SLAM)
だんっ

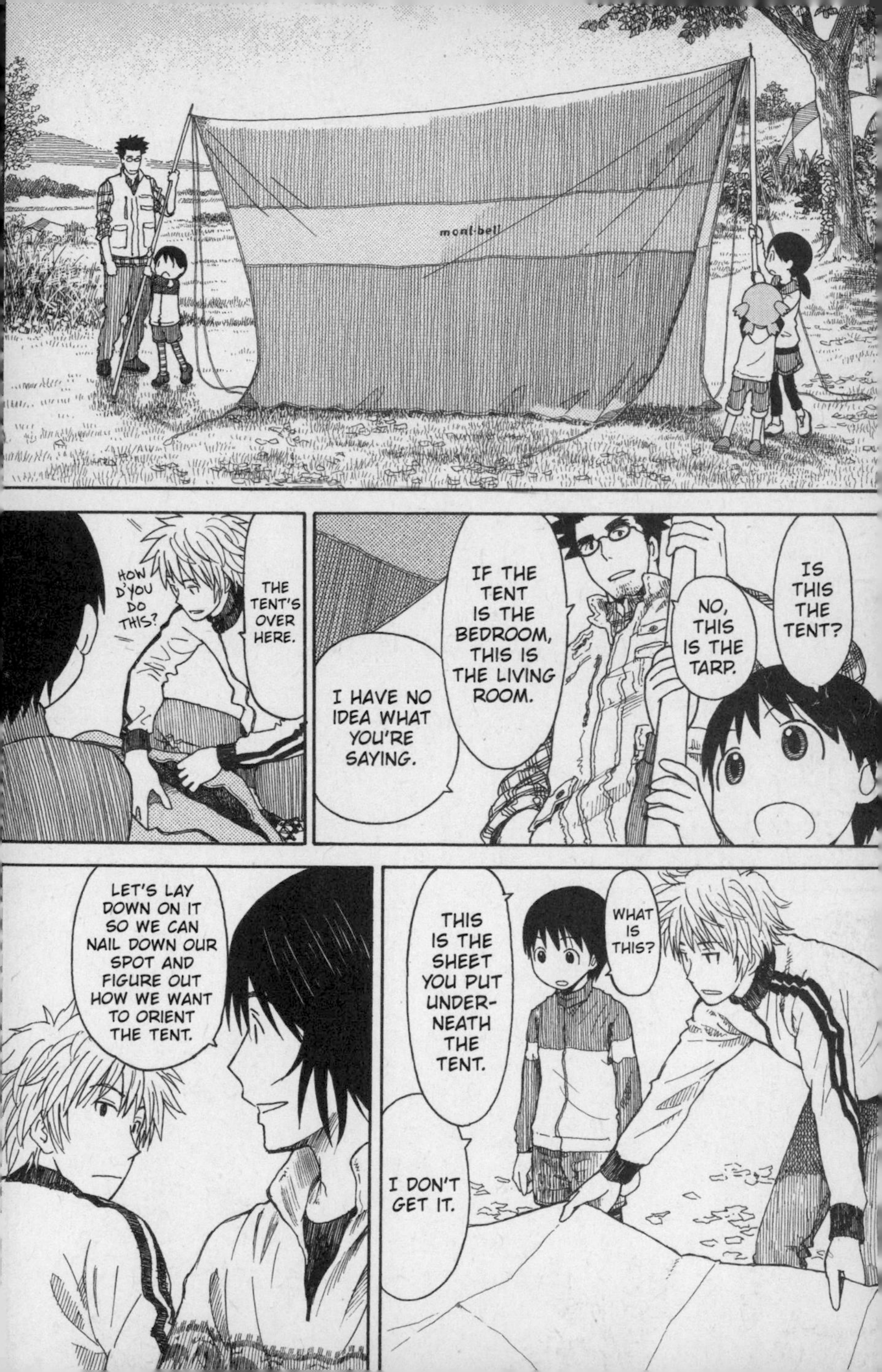
mont·bell
IS THIS THE TENT?
NO, THIS IS THE TARP.
IF THE TENT IS THE BEDROOM, THIS IS THE LIVING ROOM.
I HAVE NO IDEA WHAT YOU'RE SAYING.
THE TENT'S OVER HERE.
HOW D'YOU DO THIS?
WHAT IS THIS?
THIS IS THE SHEET YOU PUT UNDER-NEATH THE TENT.
I DON'T GET IT.
LET'S LAY DOWN ON IT SO WE CAN NAIL DOWN OUR SPOT AND FIGURE OUT HOW WE WANT TO ORIENT THE TENT.

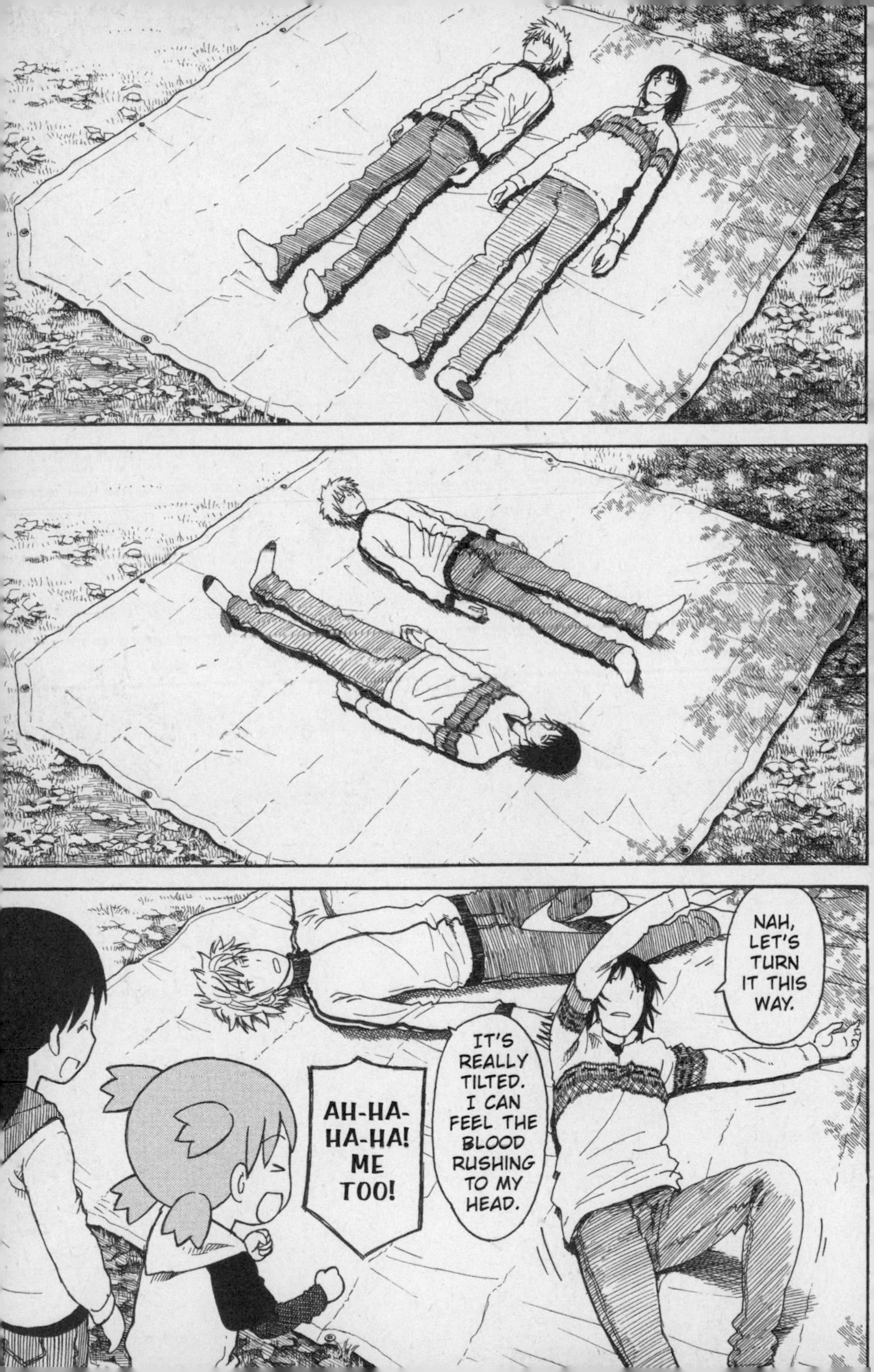
NAH, LET'S TURN IT THIS WAY.
IT'S REALLY TILTED. I CAN FEEL THE BLOOD RUSHING TO MY HEAD.
AH-HA-HA-HA! ME TOO!

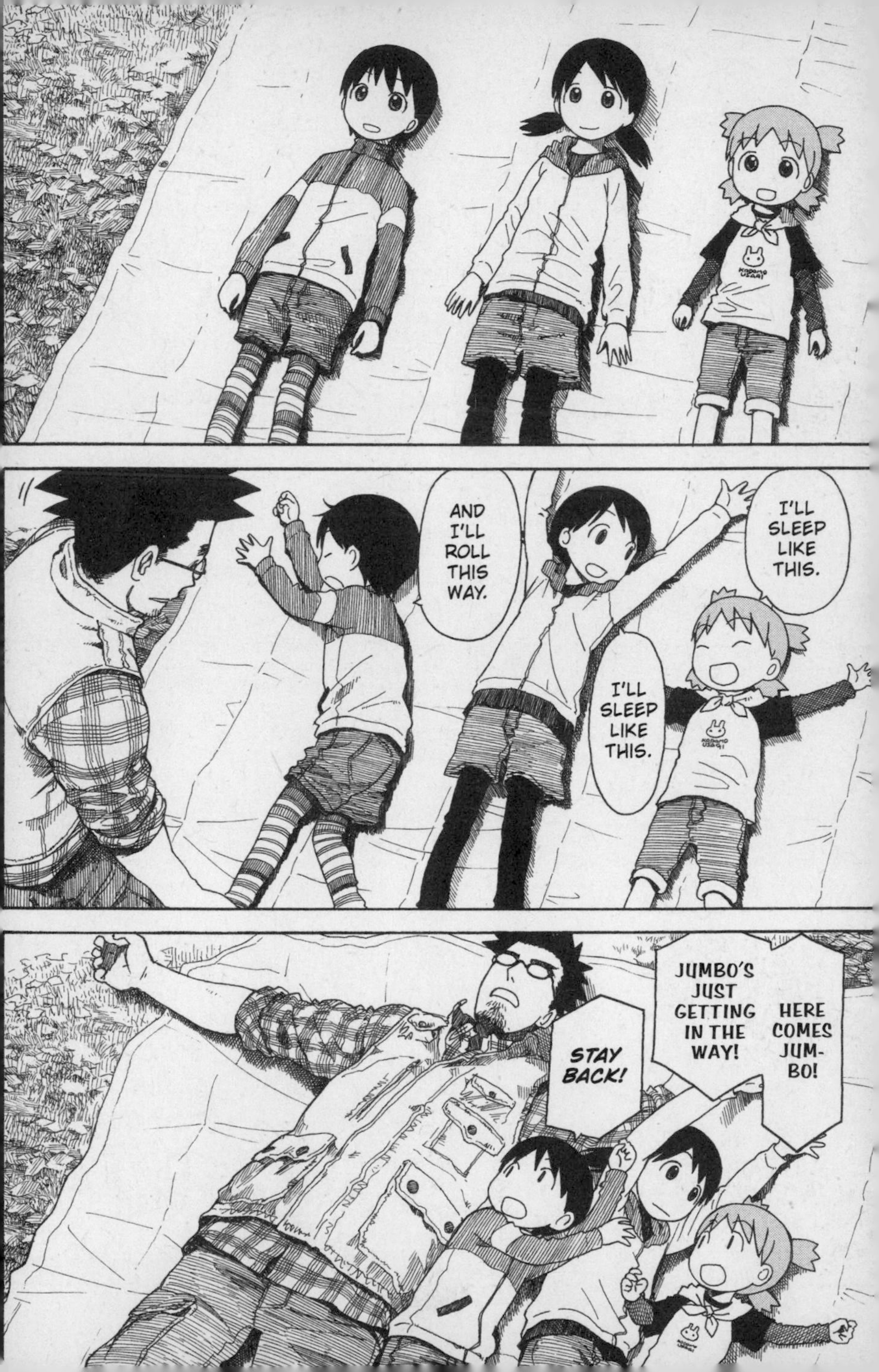
I'LL SLEEP LIKE THIS.
I'LL SLEEP LIKE THIS.
AND I'LL ROLL THIS WAY.
HERE COMES JUM-BO!
JUMBO'S JUST GETTING IN THE WAY!
STAY BACK!

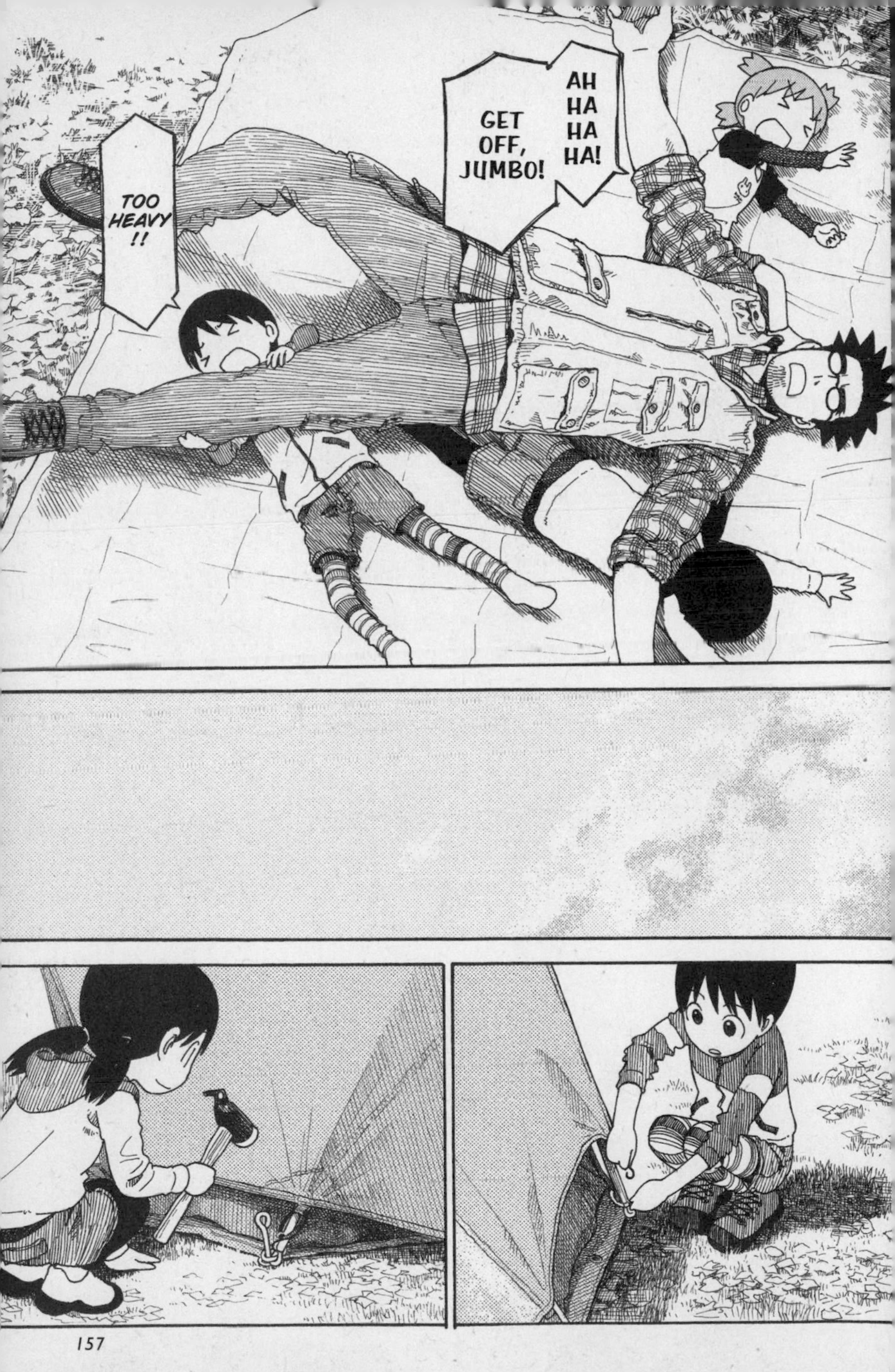
AH HA HA HA!
GET OFF, JUMBO!
TOO HEAVY !!

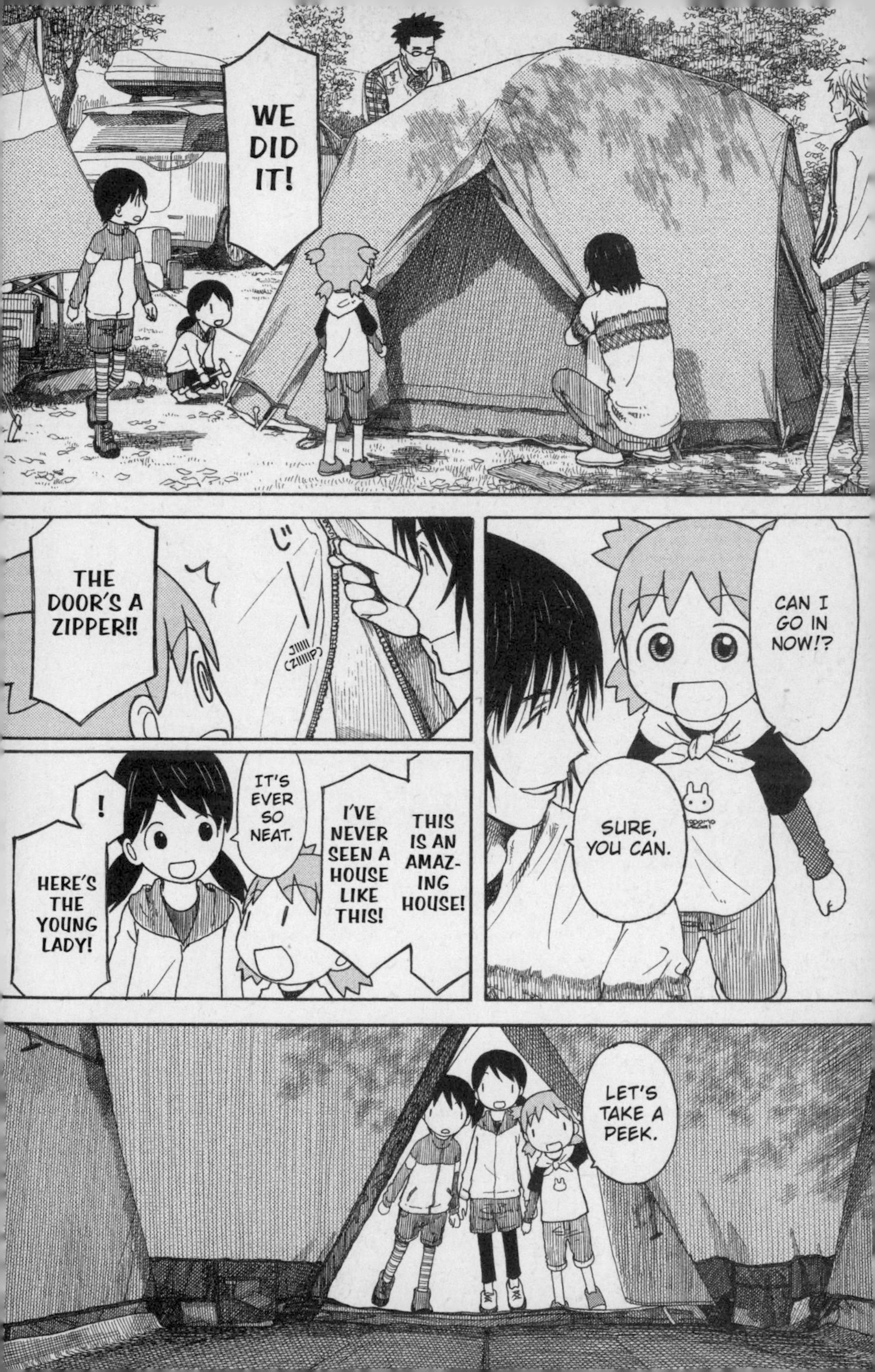

WE DID IT!
CAN I GO IN NOW!?
SURE, YOU CAN.
THE DOOR'S A ZIPPER!!
じ
JIIIII (ZIIIIIP)
THIS IS AN AMAZ-ING HOUSE!
I'VE NEVER SEEN A HOUSE LIKE THIS!
IT'S EVER SO NEAT.
!
HERE'S THE YOUNG LADY!
LET'S TAKE A PEEK.

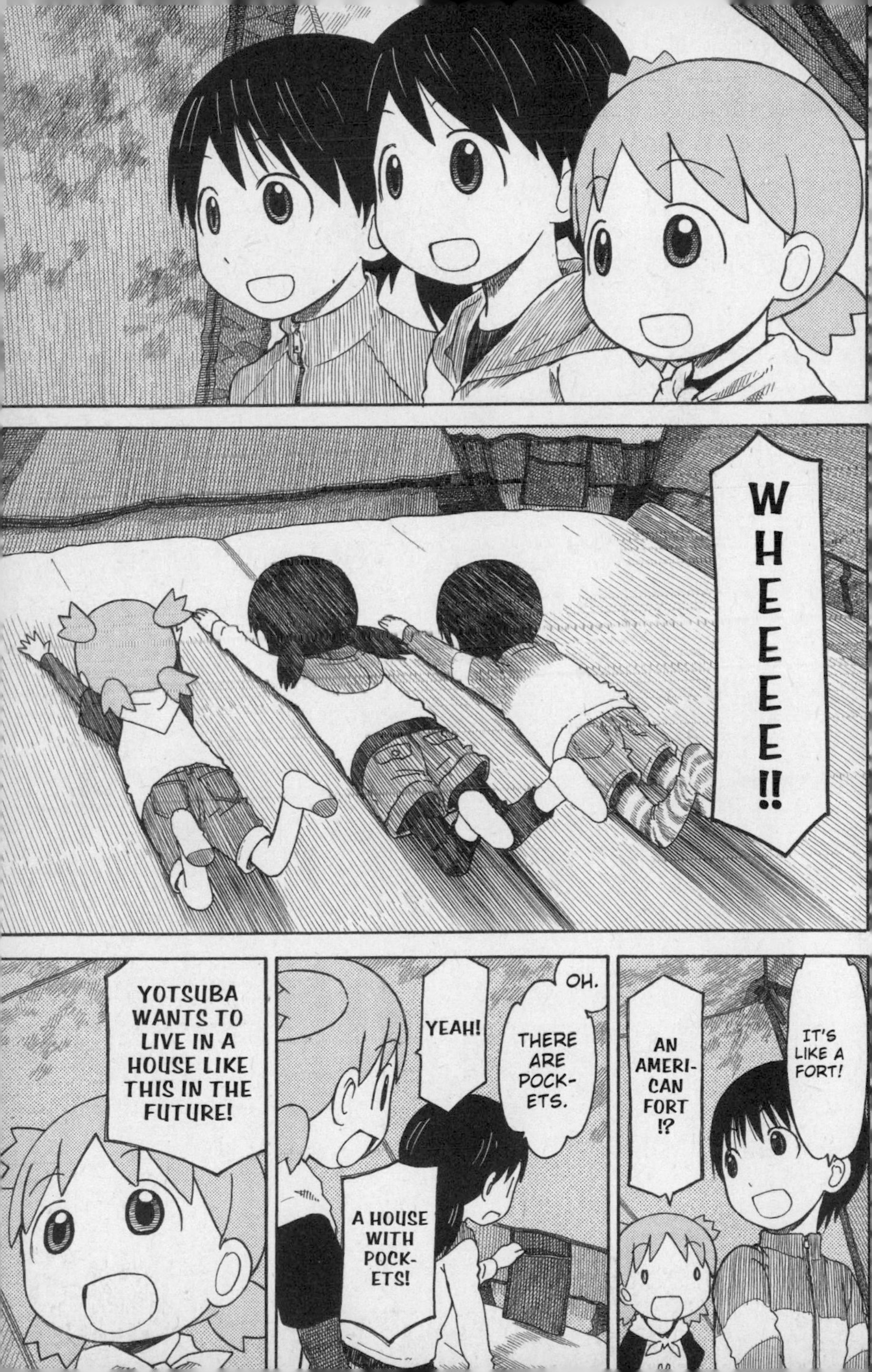
WHEEEEE!!
IT'S LIKE A FORT!
AN AMERICAN FORT!?
OH.
THERE ARE POCKETS.
YEAH!
A HOUSE WITH POCKETS!
YOTSUBA WANTS TO LIVE IN A HOUSE LIKE THIS IN THE FUTURE!

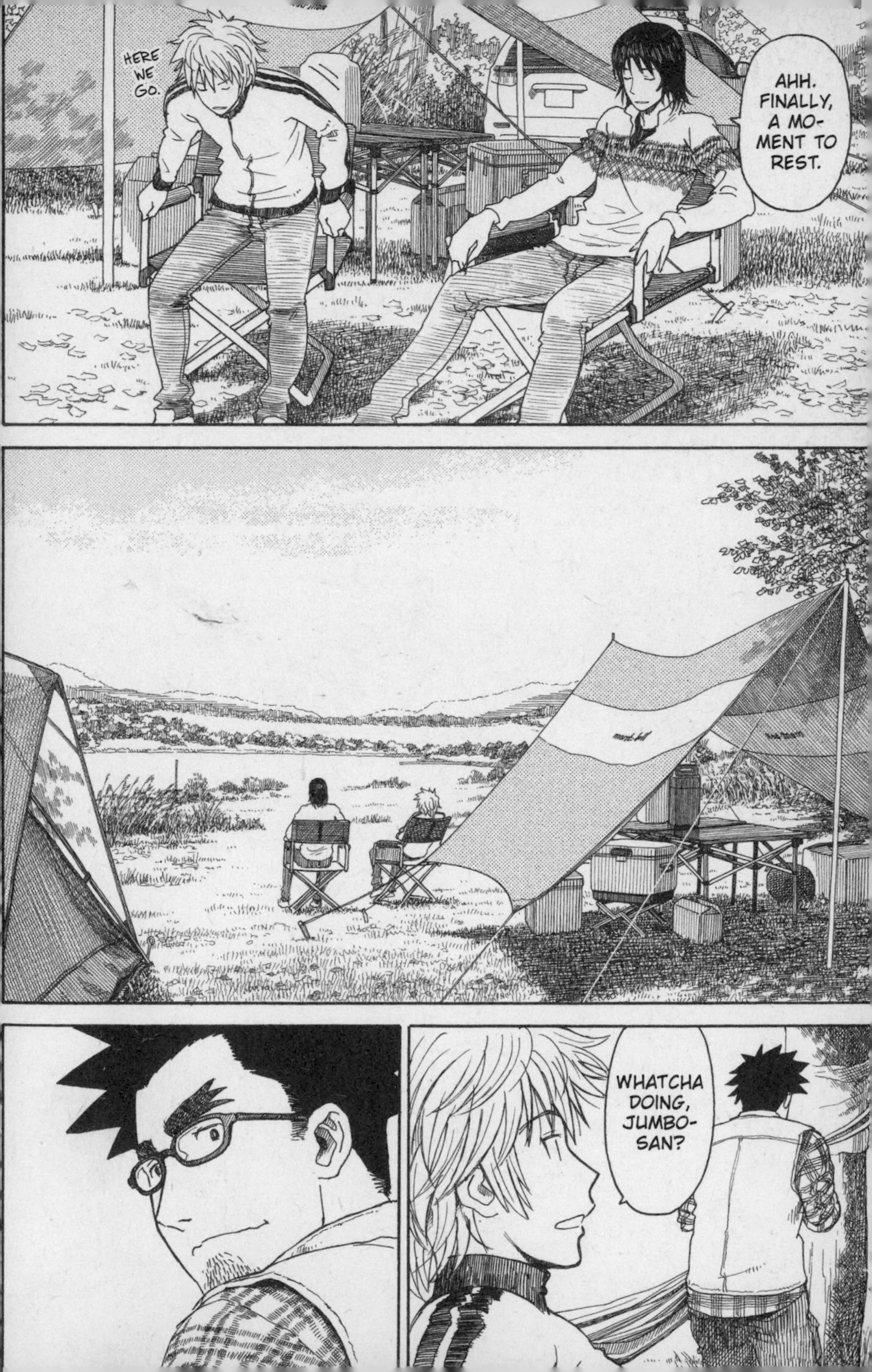
AHH. FINALLY, A MO- MENT TO REST.
HERE WE GO.
WHATCHA DOING, JUMBO-SAN?

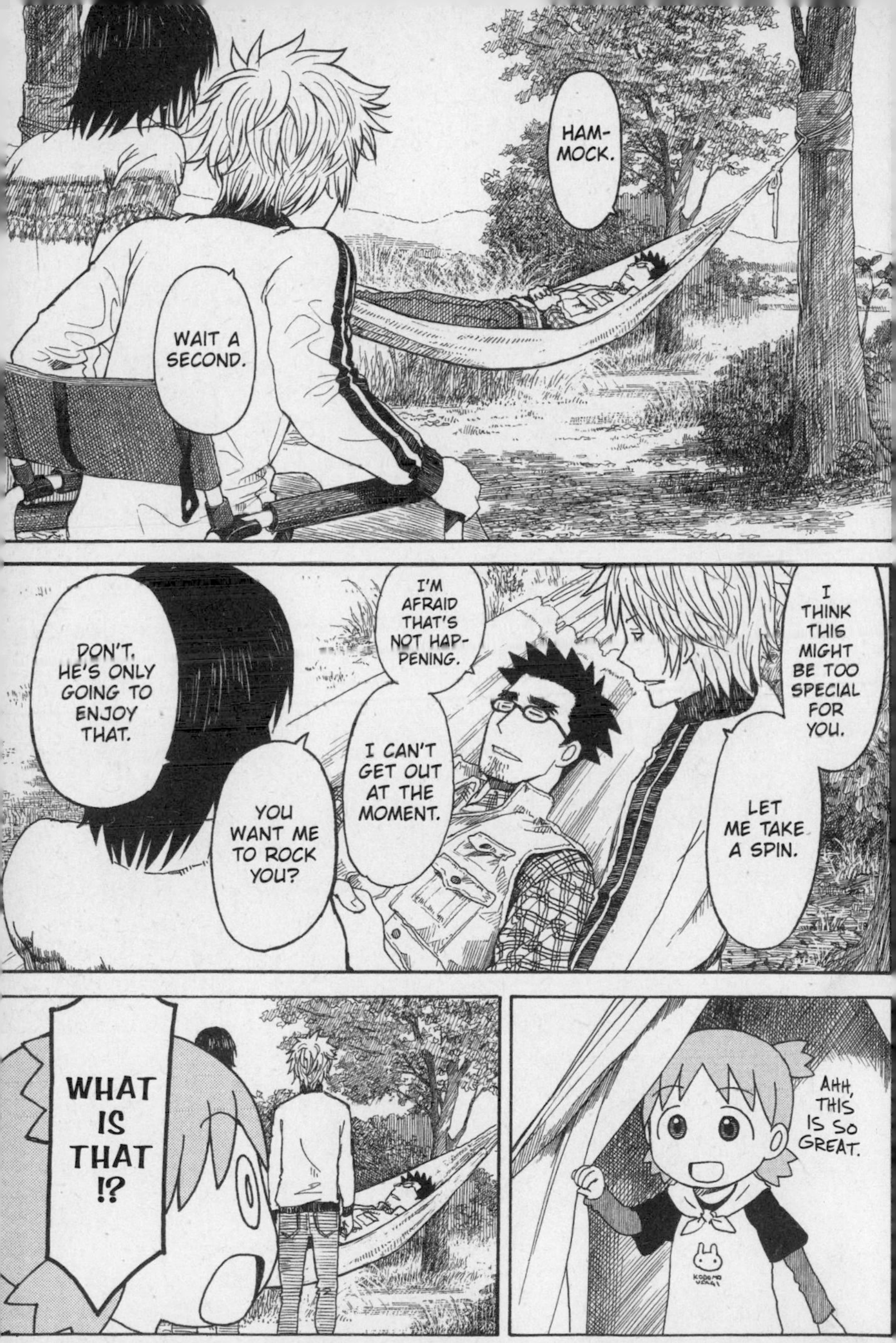
HAM-MOCK.
WAIT A SECOND.
I THINK THIS MIGHT BE TOO SPECIAL FOR YOU.
LET ME TAKE A SPIN.
I'M AFRAID THAT'S NOT HAP-PENING.
I CAN'T GET OUT AT THE MOMENT.
YOU WANT ME TO ROCK YOU?
DON'T. HE'S ONLY GOING TO ENJOY THAT.
AHH, THIS IS SO GREAT.
WHAT IS THAT!?

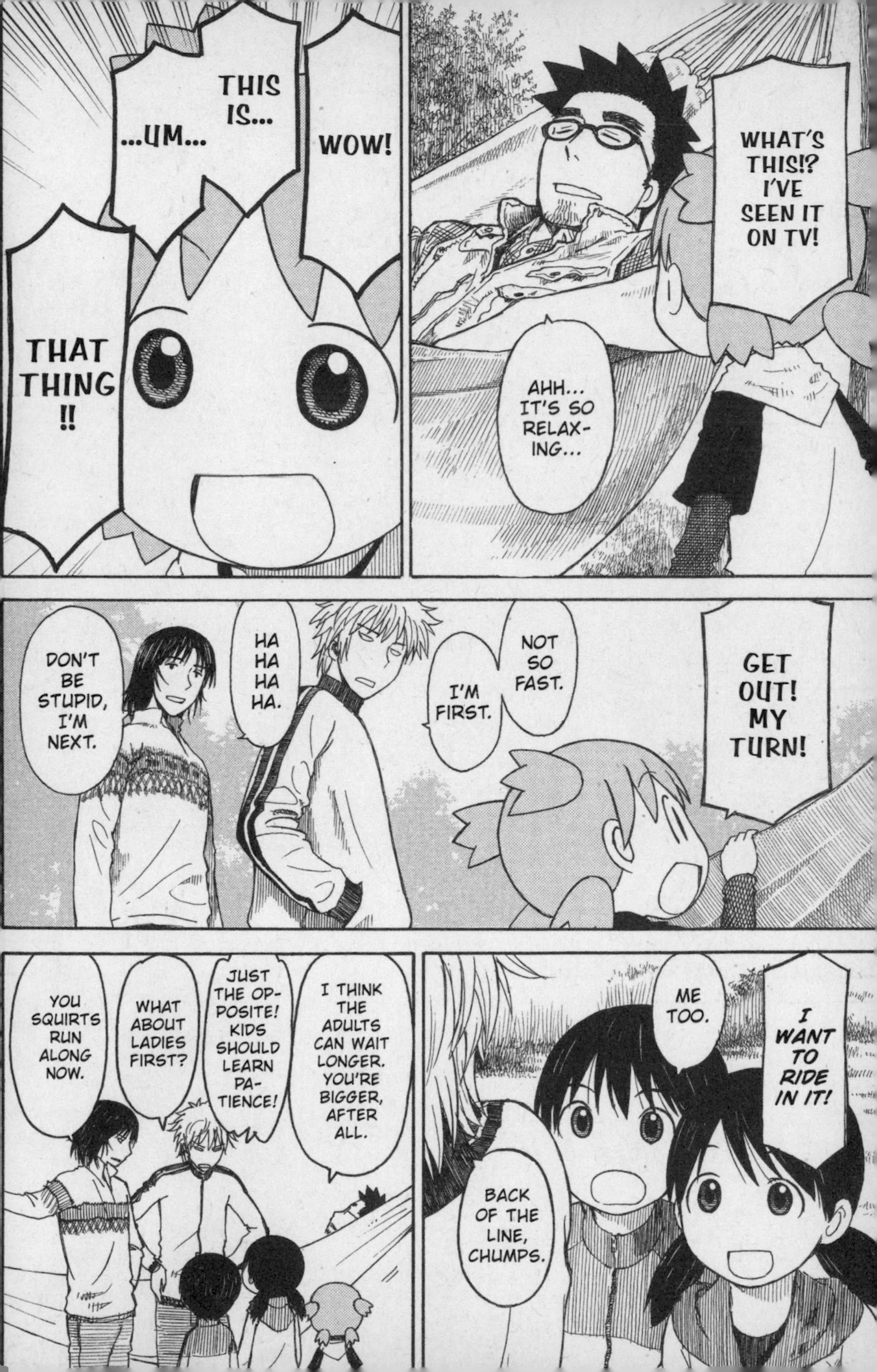
WHAT'S THIS!? I'VE SEEN IT ON TV!
AHH... IT'S SO RELAX-ING...
WOW!
THIS IS...
...UM...
THAT THING!!
GET OUT! MY TURN!
NOT SO FAST.
I'M FIRST.
HA HA HA HA.
DON'T BE STUPID, I'M NEXT.
I WANT TO RIDE IN IT!
ME TOO.
BACK OF THE LINE, CHUMPS.
I THINK THE ADULTS CAN WAIT LONGER. YOU'RE BIGGER, AFTER ALL.
JUST THE OP-POSITE! KIDS SHOULD LEARN PA-TIENCE!
WHAT ABOUT LADIES FIRST?
YOU SQUIRTS RUN ALONG NOW.

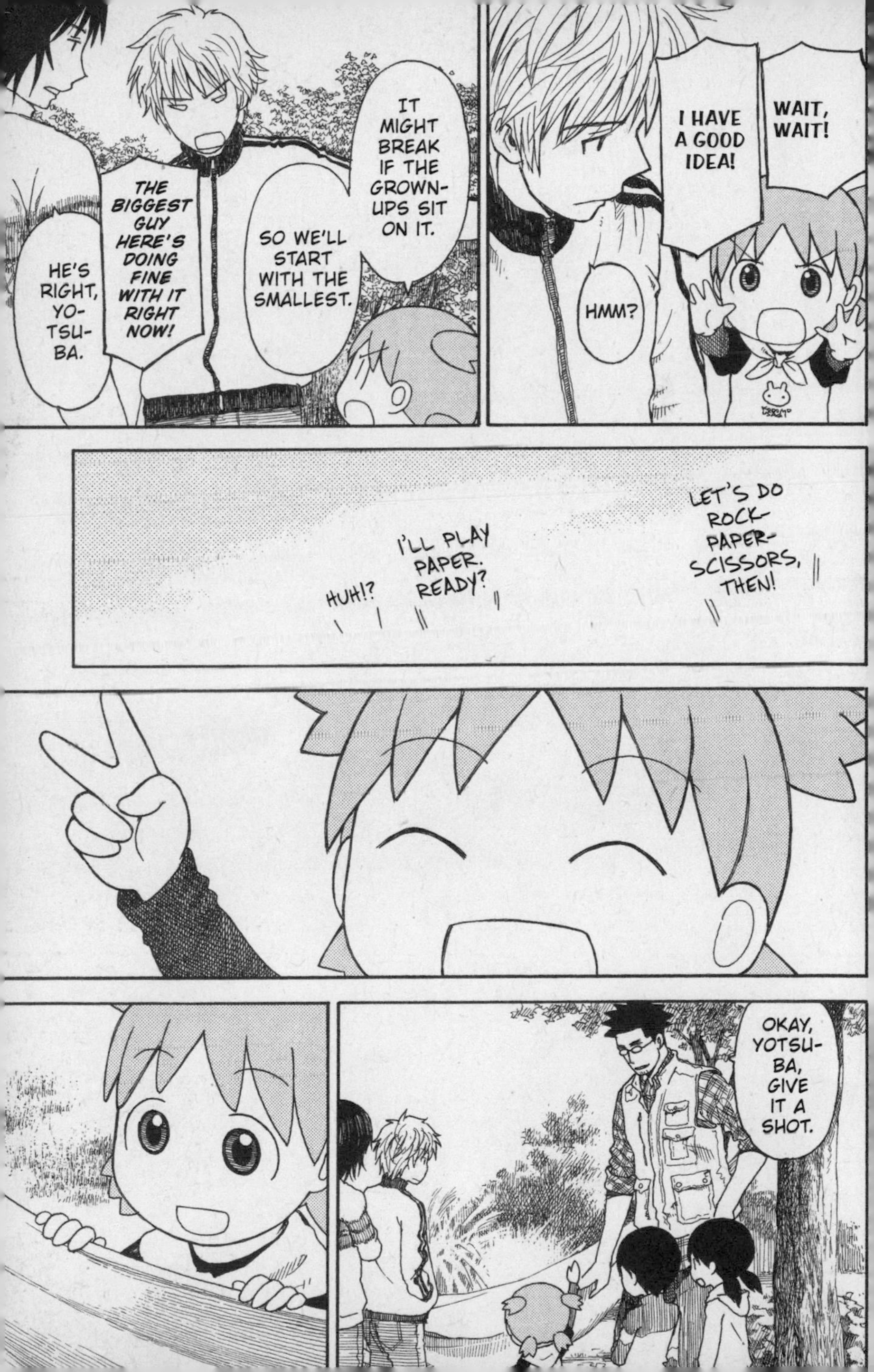
WAIT, WAIT!
I HAVE A GOOD IDEA!
HMM?
IT MIGHT BREAK IF THE GROWN-UPS SIT ON IT.
SO WE'LL START WITH THE SMALLEST.
THE BIGGEST GUY HERE'S DOING FINE WITH IT RIGHT NOW!
HE'S RIGHT, YOTSUBA.
LET'S DO ROCK-PAPER-SCISSORS, THEN!
I'LL PLAY PAPER. READY?
HUH!?
OKAY, YOTSUBA, GIVE IT A SHOT.

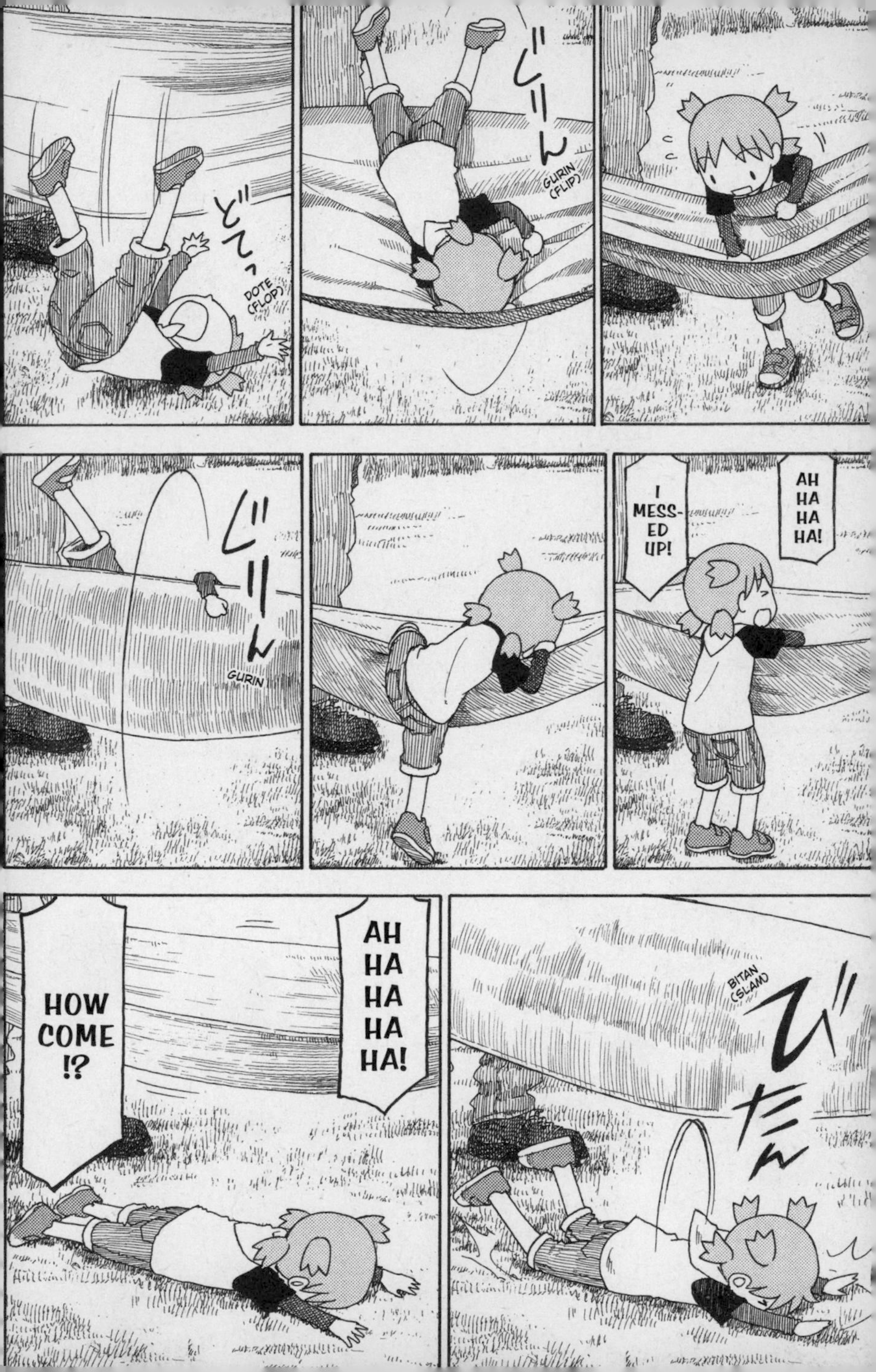
GURIN (FLIP)
DOTE (FLOP)
AH HA HA HA!
I MESS-ED UP!
GURIN
BITAN (SLAM)
AH HA HA HA HA!
HOW COME !?

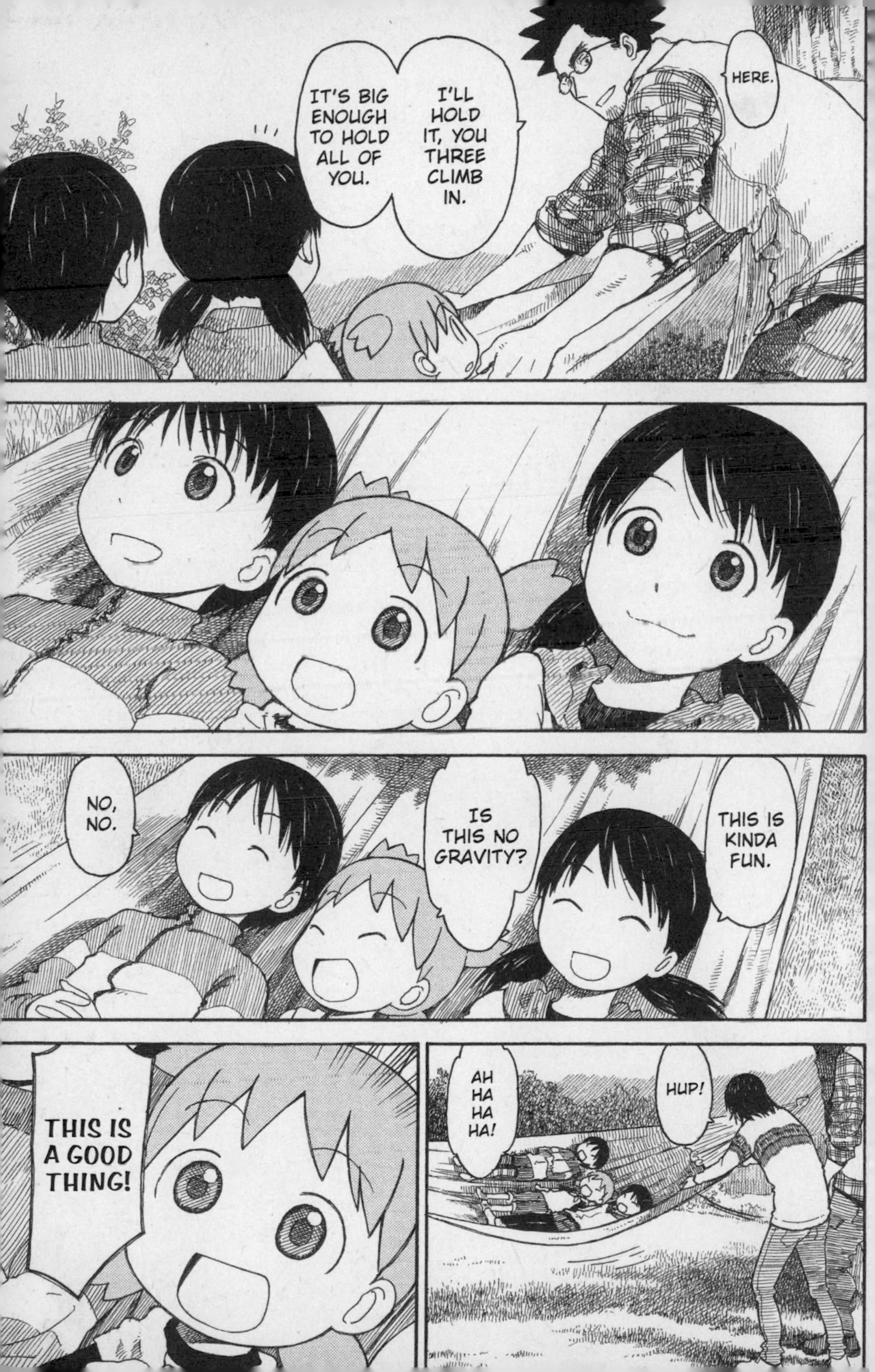
HERE.
I'LL HOLD IT, YOU THREE CLIMB IN.
IT'S BIG ENOUGH TO HOLD ALL OF YOU.
THIS IS KINDA FUN.
IS THIS NO GRAVITY?
NO, NO.
HUP!
AH HA HA HA!
THIS IS A GOOD THING!

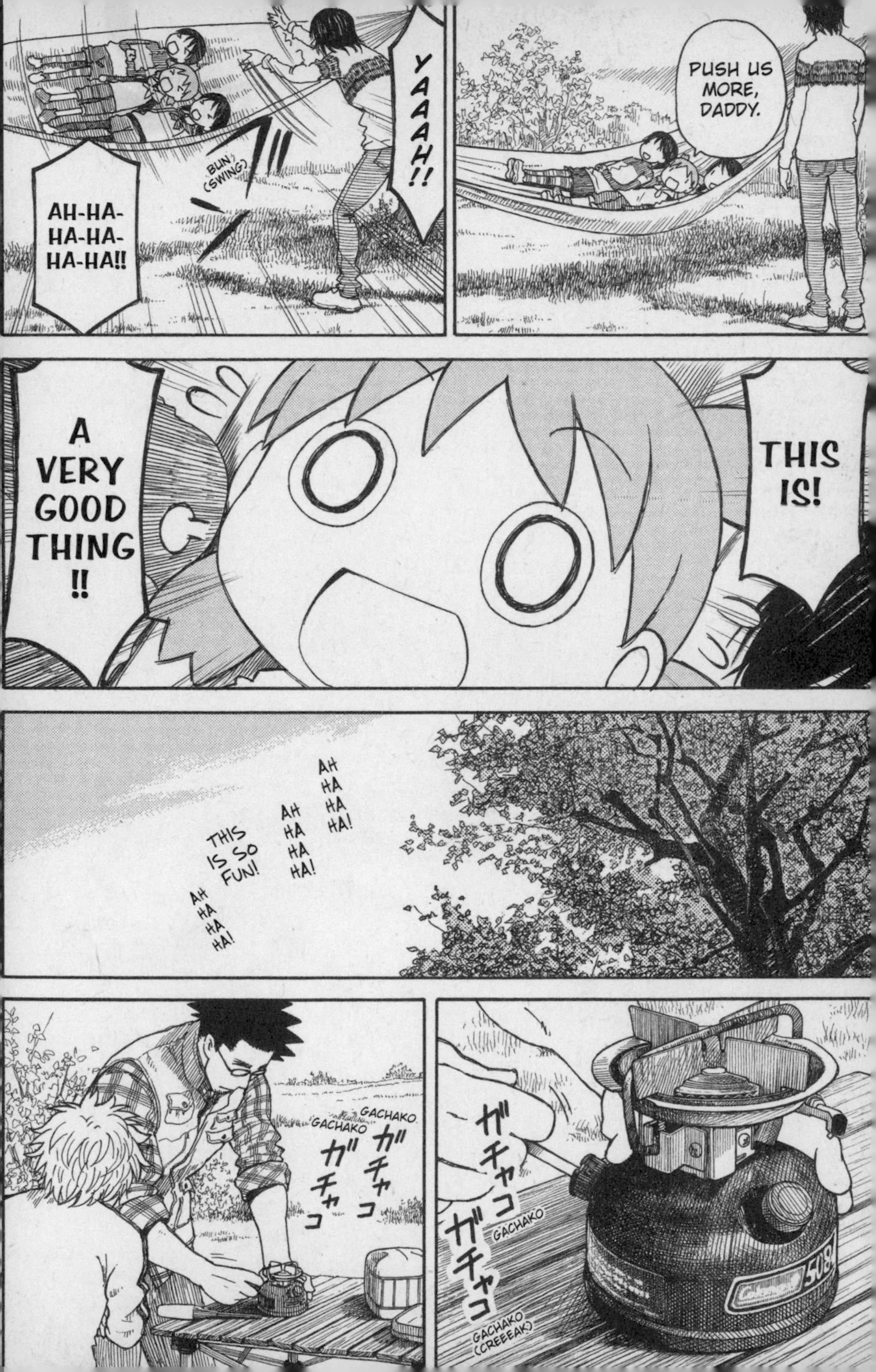
PUSH US MORE, DADDY.
YAAAAH!!
BUN (SWING)
AH-HA-HA-HA-HA-HA!!
THIS IS!
A VERY GOOD THING!!
AH HA HA HA!
AH HA HA HA!
THIS IS SO FUN!
AH HA HA HA!
ガチャコ
GACHAKO
ガチャコ
GACHAKO (CREEEAK)
ガチャコ
GACHAKO
ガチャコ
GACHAKO

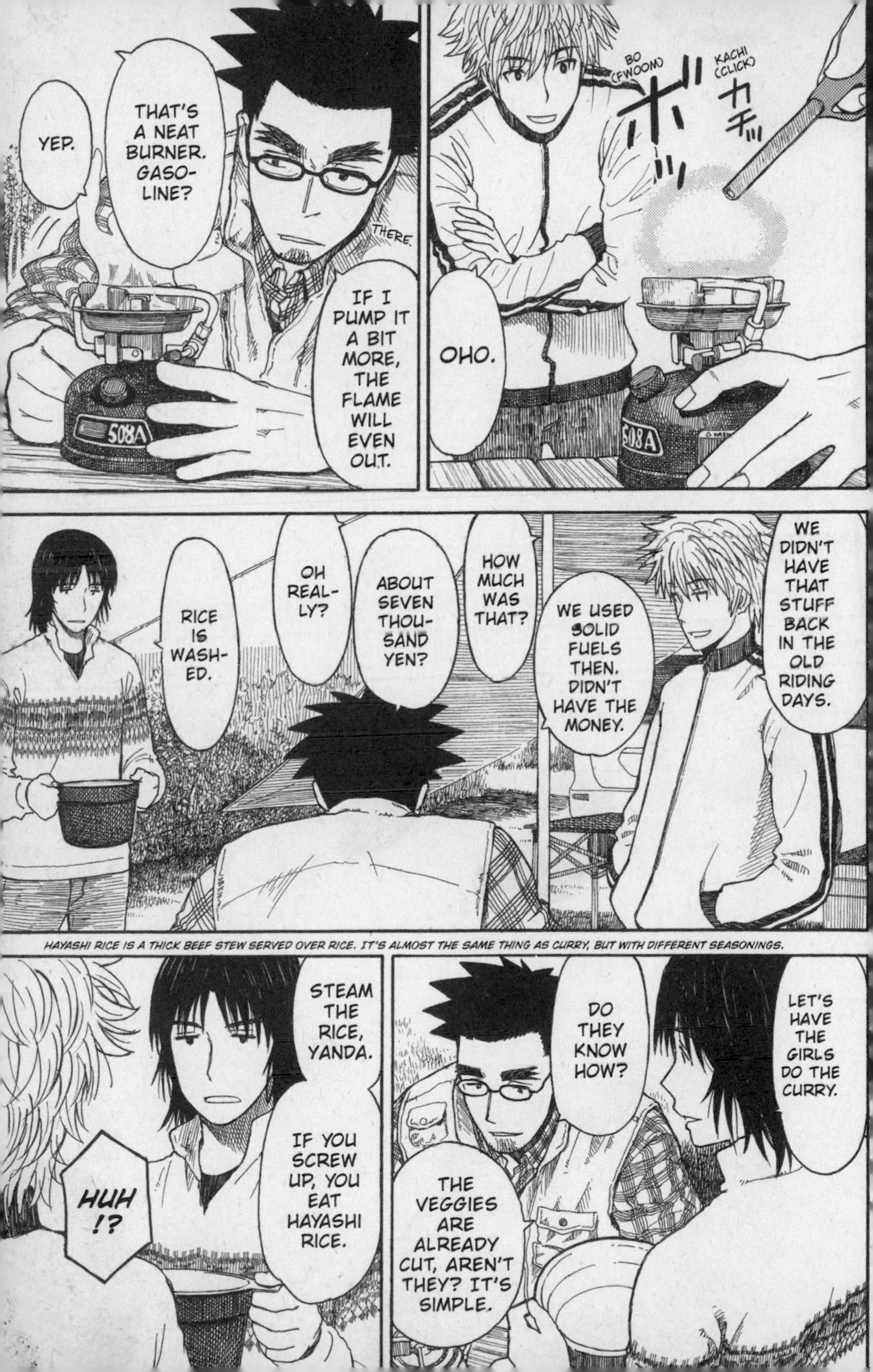
KACHI (CLICK)
BO (FWOOM)
OHO.
THAT'S A NEAT BURNER. GASO-LINE?
YEP.
THERE.
IF I PUMP IT A BIT MORE, THE FLAME WILL EVEN OUT.
508A
WE DIDN'T HAVE THAT STUFF BACK IN THE OLD RIDING DAYS.
WE USED SOLID FUELS THEN. DIDN'T HAVE THE MONEY.
HOW MUCH WAS THAT?
ABOUT SEVEN THOU-SAND YEN?
OH REAL-LY?
RICE IS WASH-ED.
HAYASHI RICE IS A THICK BEEF STEW SERVED OVER RICE. IT'S ALMOST THE SAME THING AS CURRY, BUT WITH DIFFERENT SEASONINGS.
LET'S HAVE THE GIRLS DO THE CURRY.
DO THEY KNOW HOW?
THE VEGGIES ARE ALREADY CUT, AREN'T THEY? IT'S SIMPLE.
STEAM THE RICE, YANDA.
IF YOU SCREW UP, YOU EAT HAYASHI RICE.
HUH!?

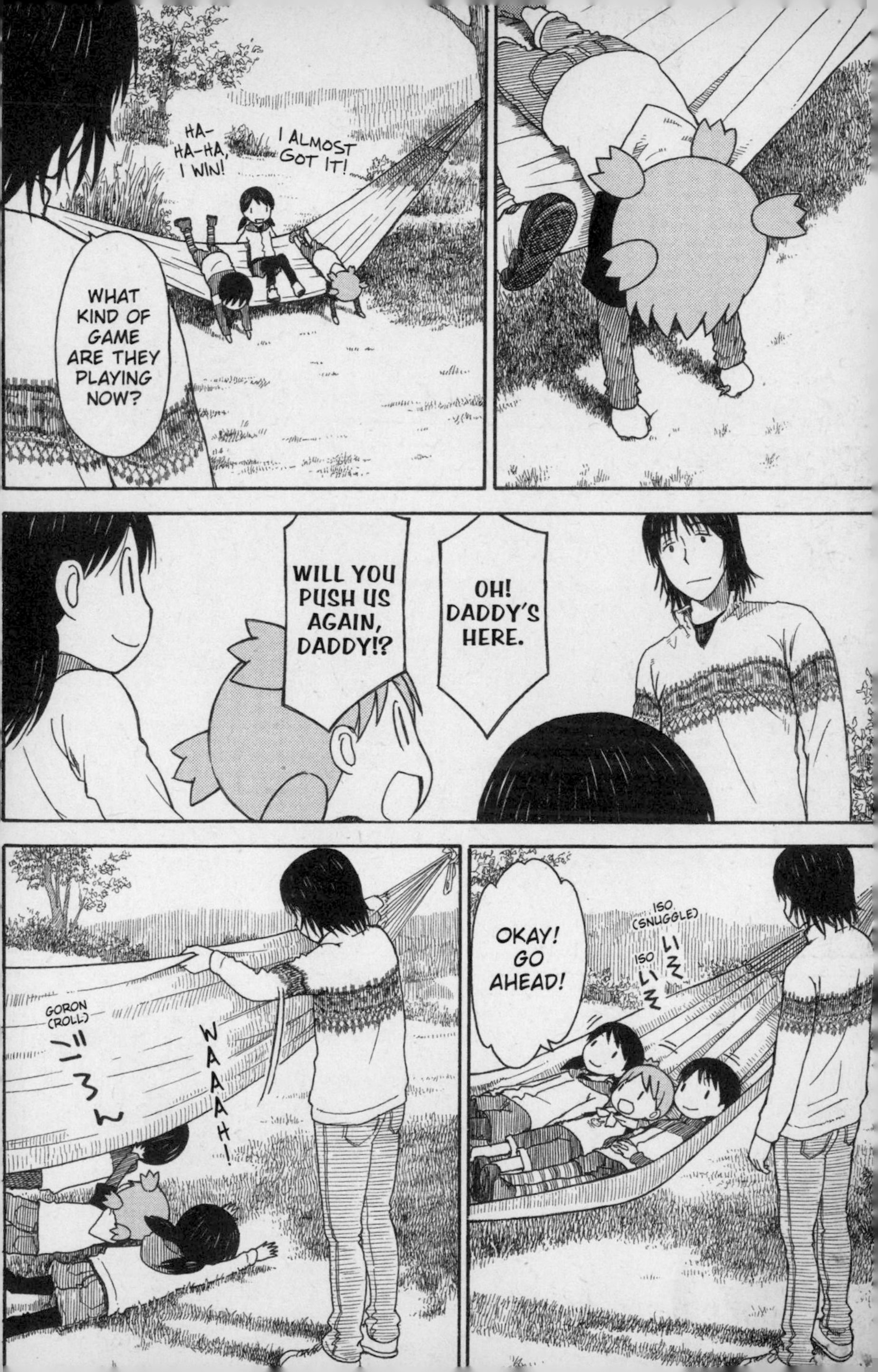
I ALMOST GOT IT!
HA-HA-HA, I WIN!
WHAT KIND OF GAME ARE THEY PLAYING NOW?
OH! DADDY'S HERE.
WILL YOU PUSH US AGAIN, DADDY!?
ISO ISO (SNUGGLE)
いそ いそ
OKAY! GO AHEAD!
WAAAAH!
GORON (ROLL)
ごろん

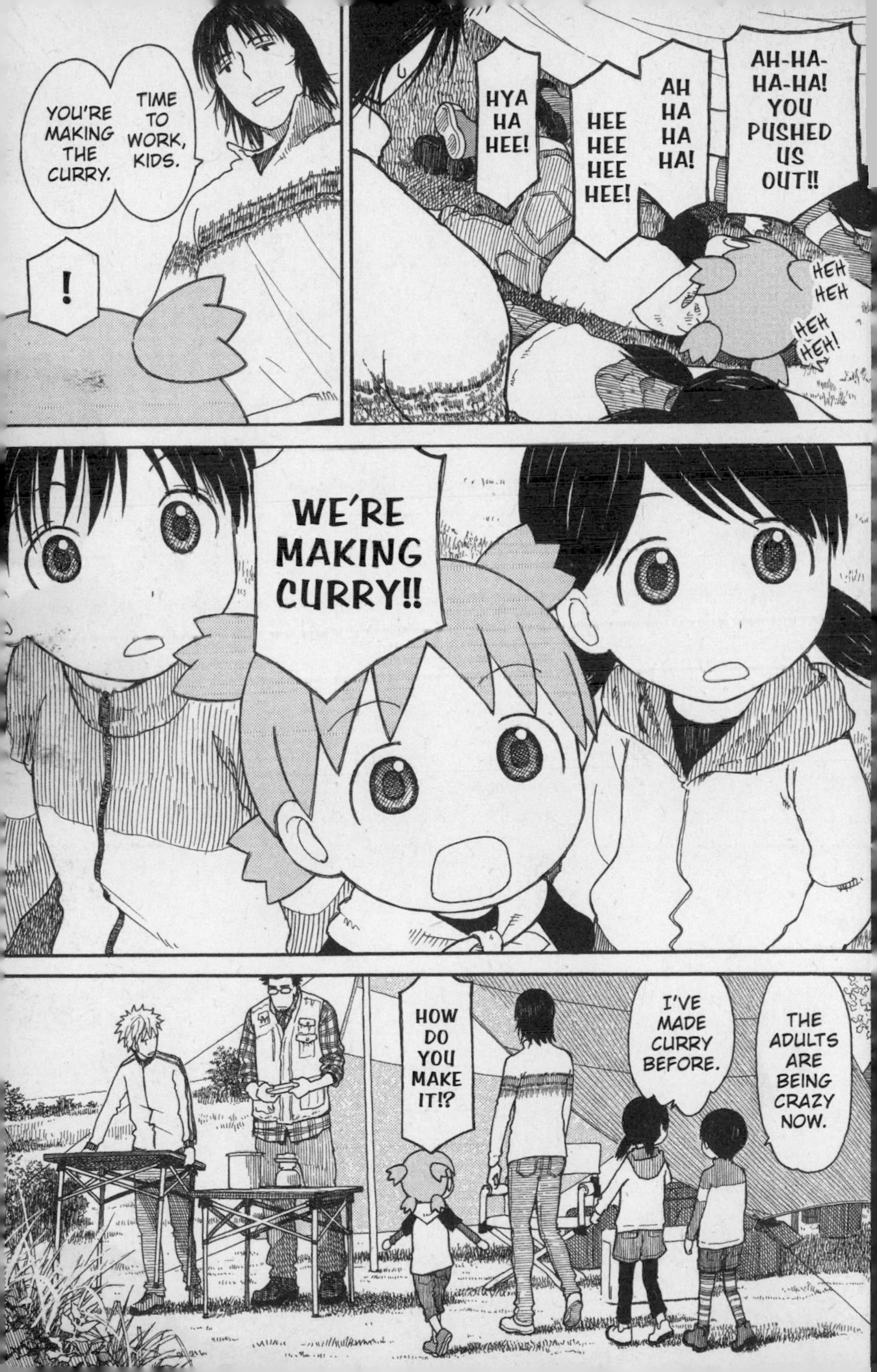
AH-HA-HA-HA! YOU PUSHED US OUT!!
AH HA HA HA!
HEE HEE HEE HEE!
HYA HA HEE!
HEH HEH HEH HEH!
TIME TO WORK, KIDS.
YOU'RE MAKING THE CURRY.
!
WE'RE MAKING CURRY!!
THE ADULTS ARE BEING CRAZY NOW.
I'VE MADE CURRY BEFORE.
HOW DO YOU MAKE IT!?

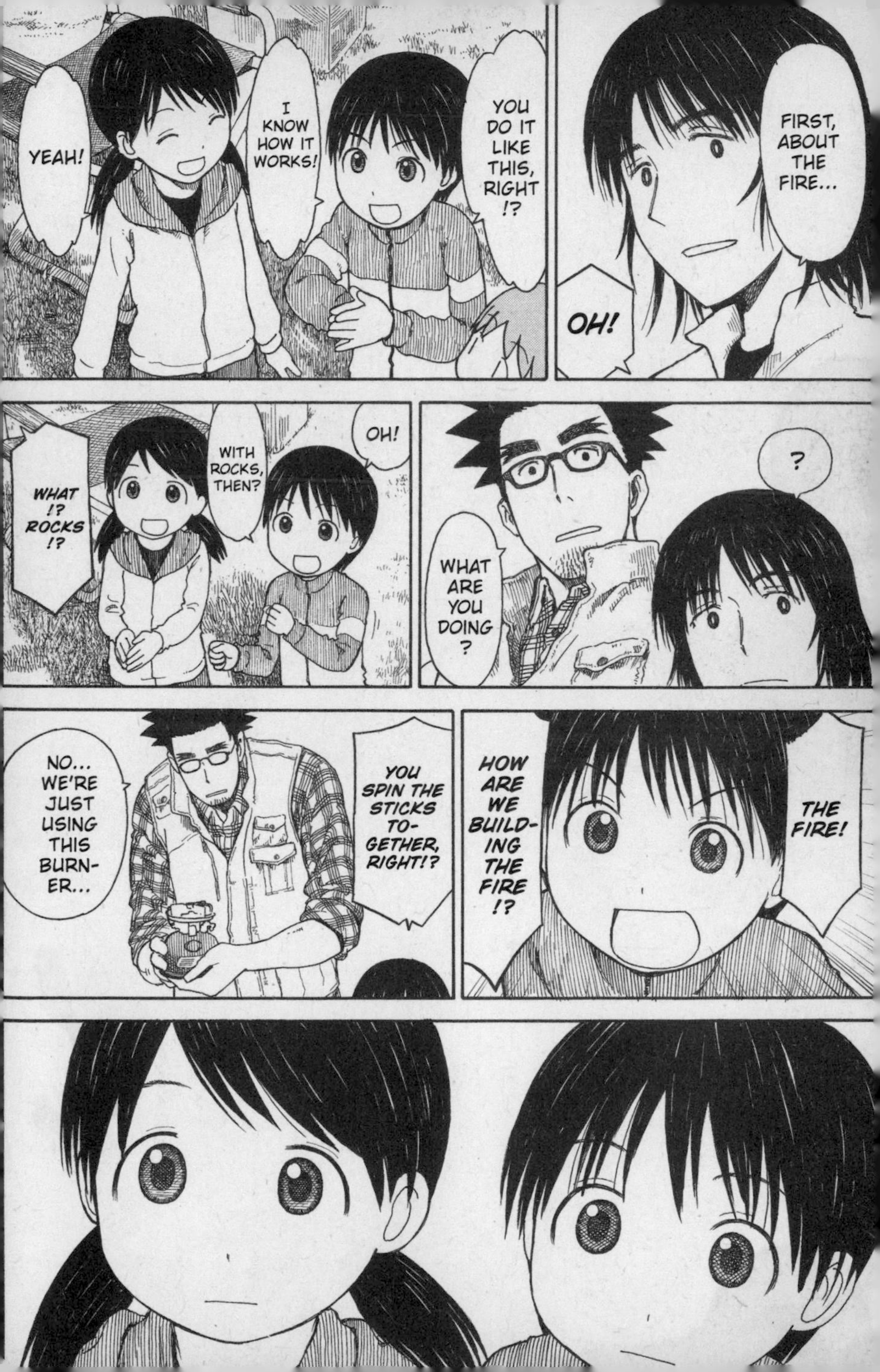
FIRST, ABOUT THE FIRE...
OH!
YOU DO IT LIKE THIS, RIGHT!?
I KNOW HOW IT WORKS!
YEAH!
?
WHAT ARE YOU DOING?
OH!
WITH ROCKS, THEN?
WHAT!? ROCKS!?
THE FIRE!
HOW ARE WE BUILDING THE FIRE!?
YOU SPIN THE STICKS TOGETHER, RIGHT!?
NO... WE'RE JUST USING THIS BURNER...

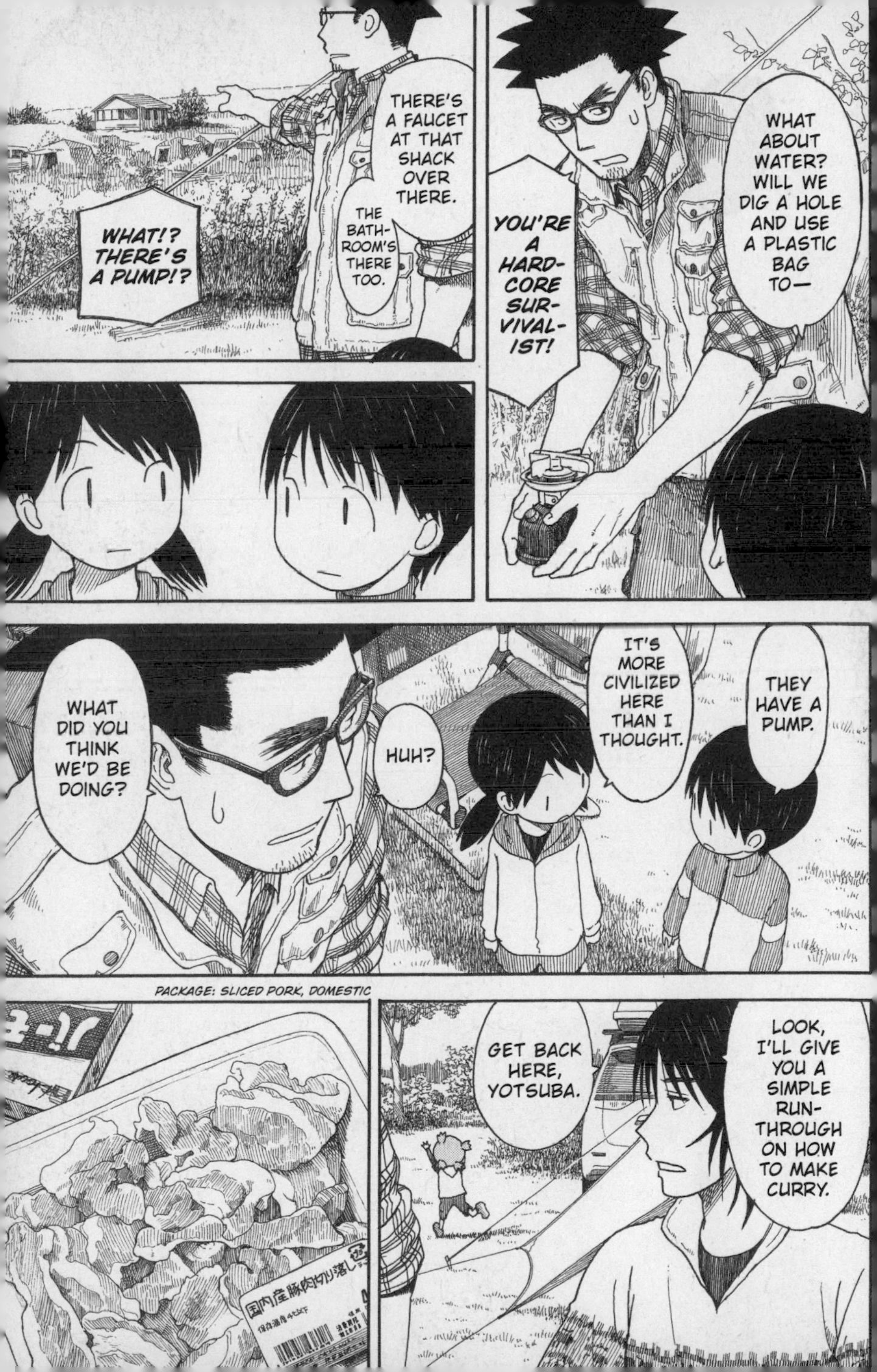
WHAT ABOUT WATER? WILL WE DIG A HOLE AND USE A PLASTIC BAG TO—
YOU'RE A HARD-CORE SURVIVALIST!
THERE'S A FAUCET AT THAT SHACK OVER THERE.
THE BATHROOM'S THERE TOO.
WHAT!? THERE'S A PUMP!?
THEY HAVE A PUMP.
IT'S MORE CIVILIZED HERE THAN I THOUGHT.
HUH?
WHAT DID YOU THINK WE'D BE DOING?
LOOK, I'LL GIVE YOU A SIMPLE RUN-THROUGH ON HOW TO MAKE CURRY.
GET BACK HERE, YOTSUBA.
PACKAGE: SLICED PORK, DOMESTIC
国内産豚肉切り落し

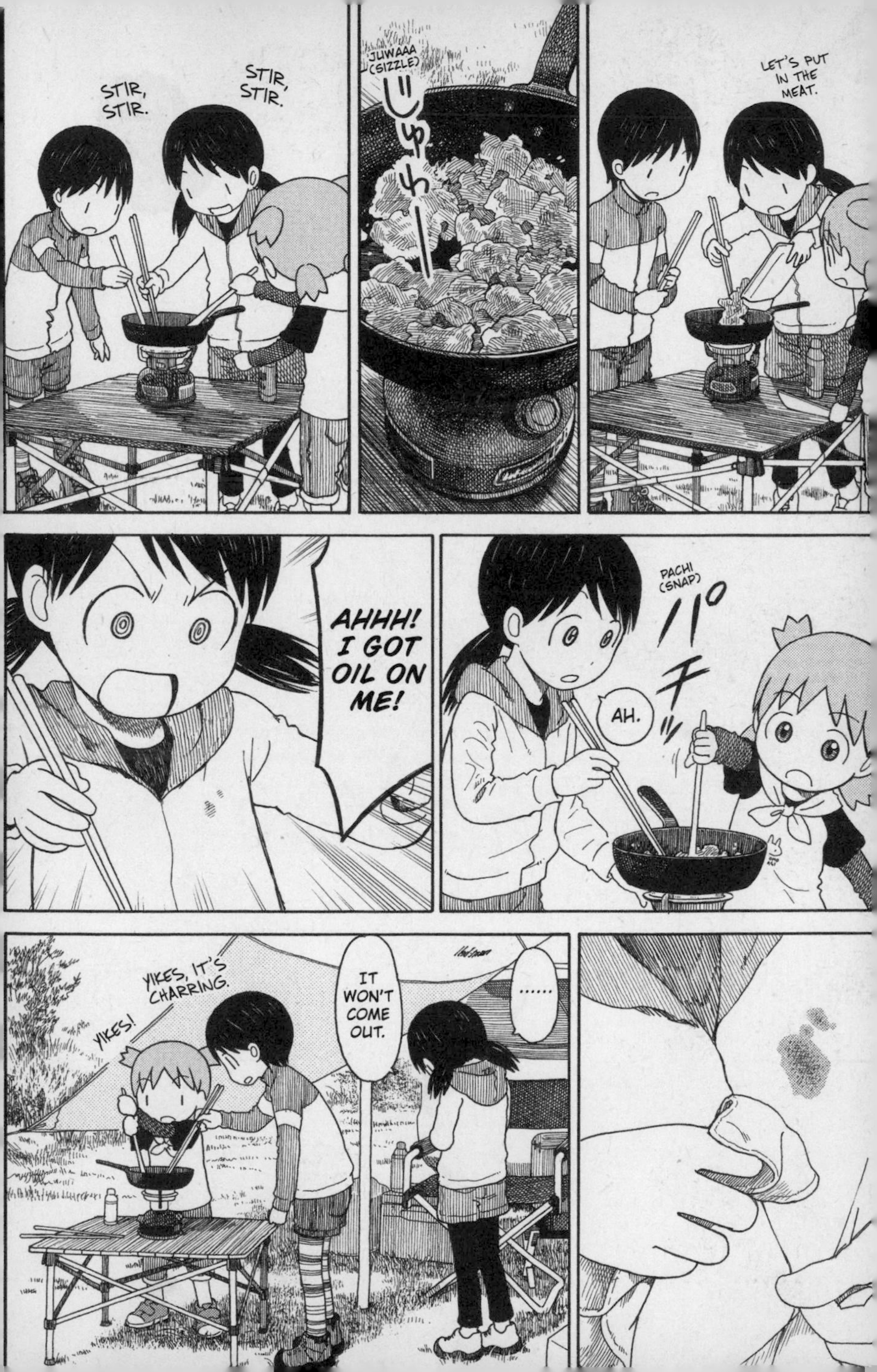
LET'S PUT IN THE MEAT.
JUWAAA (SIZZLE)
じゅわー
STIR, STIR.
STIR, STIR.
PACHI (SNAP)
パチッ
AH.
AHHH! I GOT OIL ON ME!
......
IT WON'T COME OUT.
YIKES, IT'S CHARRING.
YIKES!

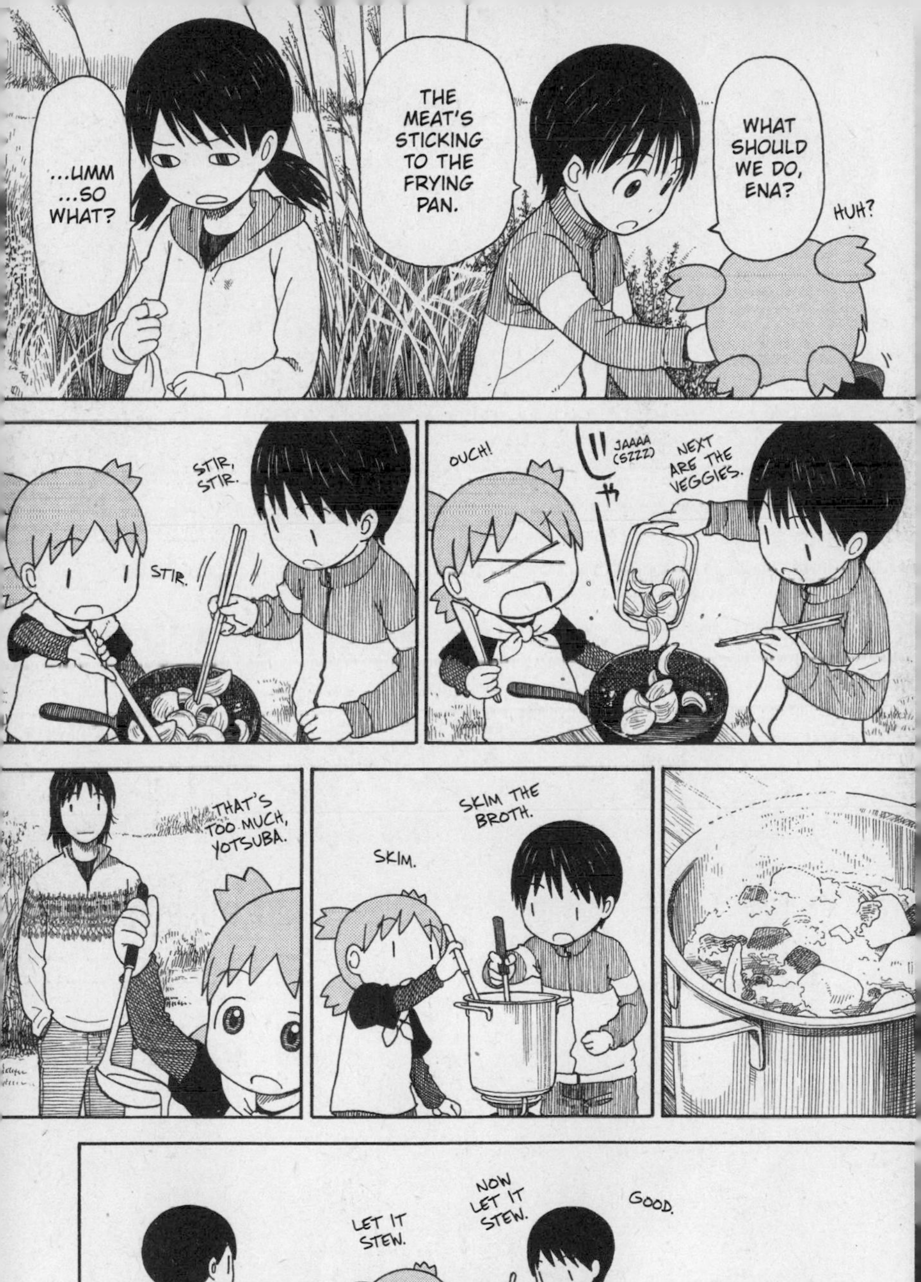
WHAT SHOULD WE DO, ENA?
HUH?
THE MEAT'S STICKING TO THE FRYING PAN.
...UMM ...SO WHAT?
NEXT ARE THE VEGGIES.
JAAAA (SZZZ)
OUCH!
STIR, STIR.
STIR.
SKIM THE BROTH.
SKIM.
THAT'S TOO MUCH, YOTSUBA.
GOOD.
NOW LET IT STEW.
LET IT STEW.

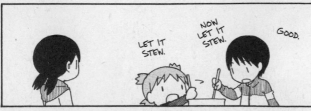

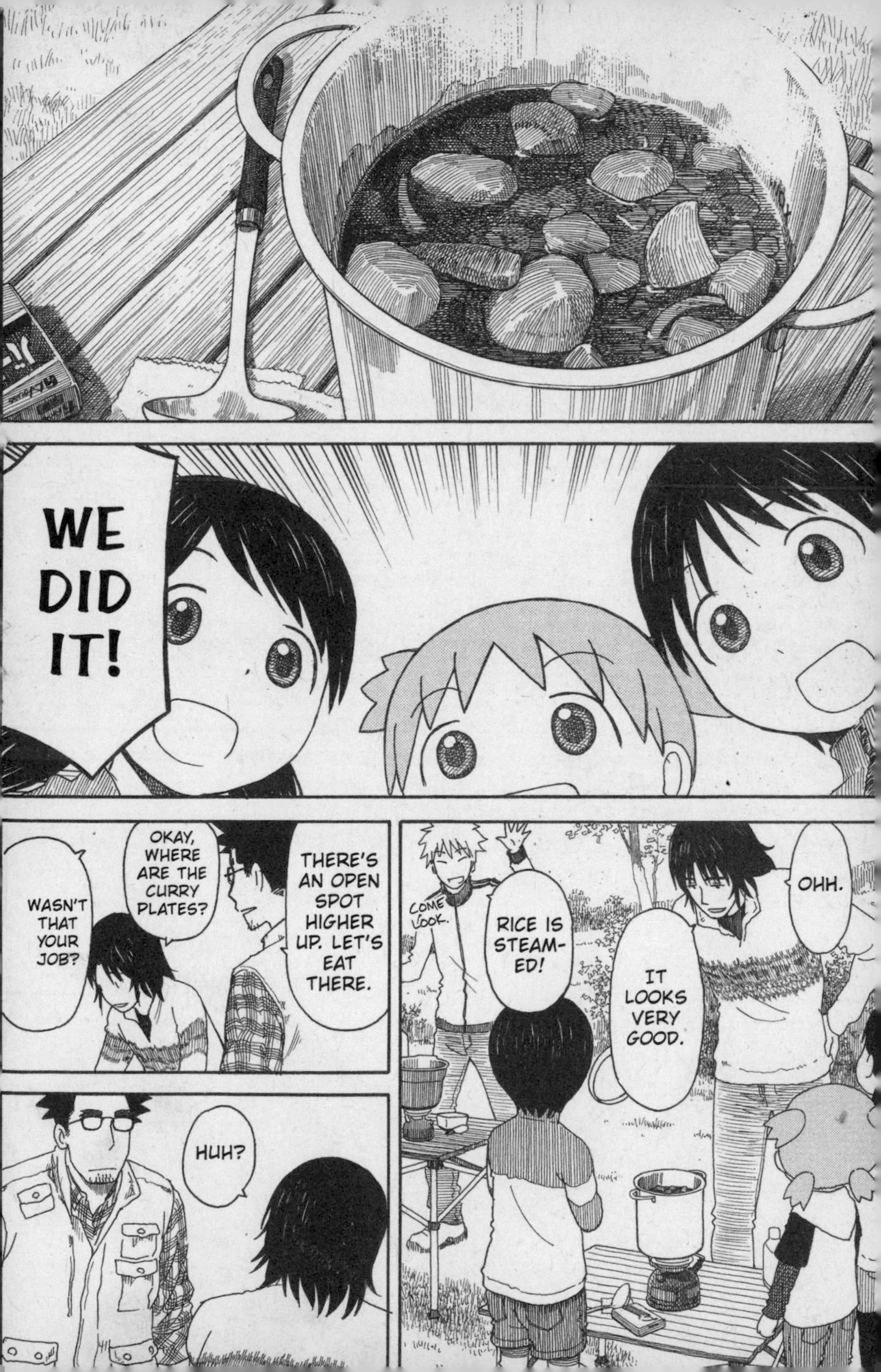
WE DID IT!
OHH.
RICE IS STEAM-ED!
IT LOOKS VERY GOOD.
COME LOOK.
THERE'S AN OPEN SPOT HIGHER UP. LET'S EAT THERE.
OKAY, WHERE ARE THE CURRY PLATES?
WASN'T THAT YOUR JOB?
HUH?

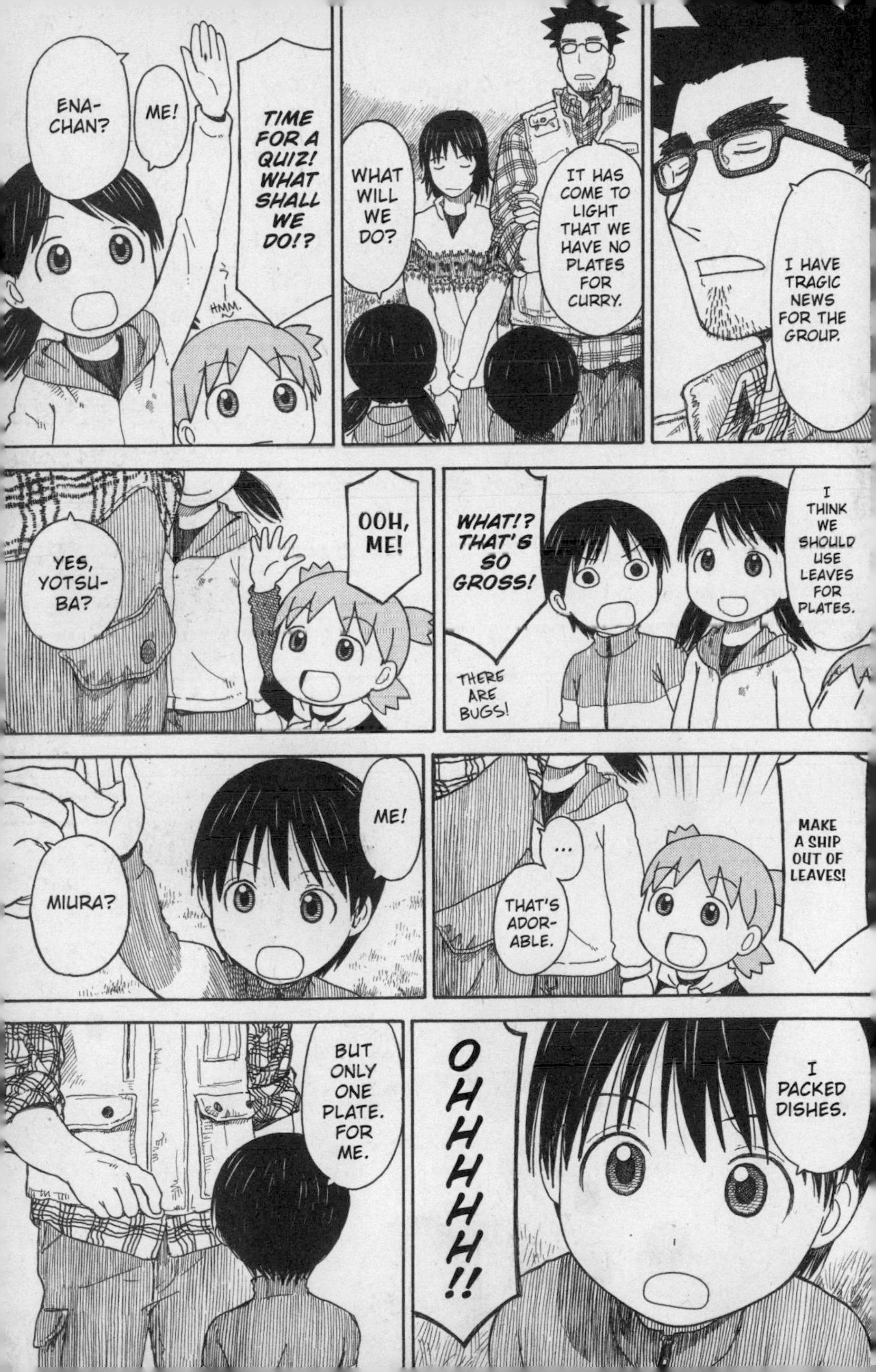
I HAVE TRAGIC NEWS FOR THE GROUP.
IT HAS COME TO LIGHT THAT WE HAVE NO PLATES FOR CURRY.
WHAT WILL WE DO?
TIME FOR A QUIZ! WHAT SHALL WE DO!?
HMM.
ME!
ENA-CHAN?
I THINK WE SHOULD USE LEAVES FOR PLATES.
WHAT!? THAT'S SO GROSS!
THERE ARE BUGS!
OOH, ME!
YES, YOTSU-BA?
MAKE A SHIP OUT OF LEAVES!
...
THAT'S ADOR-ABLE.
ME!
MIURA?
I PACKED DISHES.
OHHHHHH!!
BUT ONLY ONE PLATE. FOR ME.

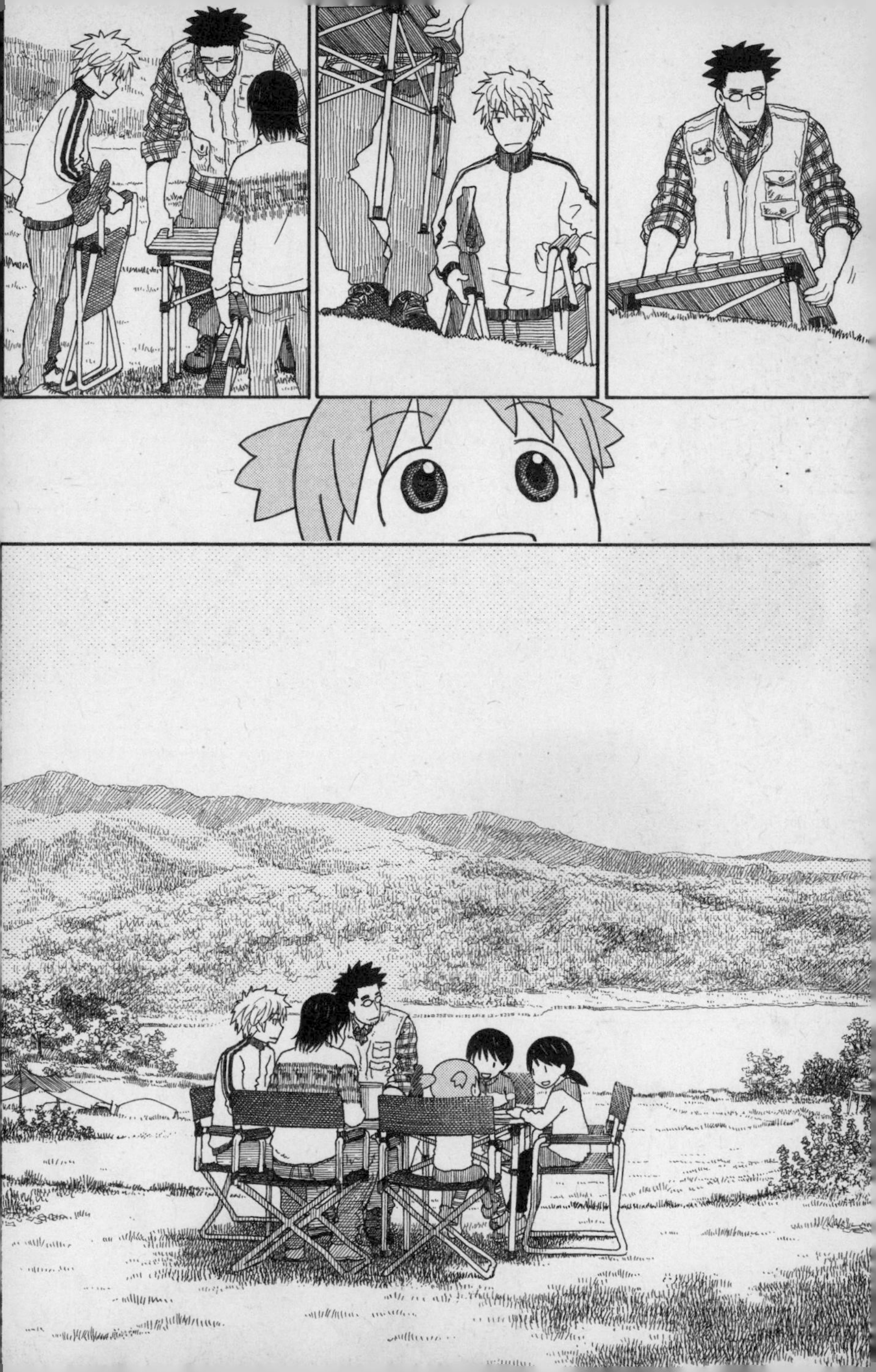

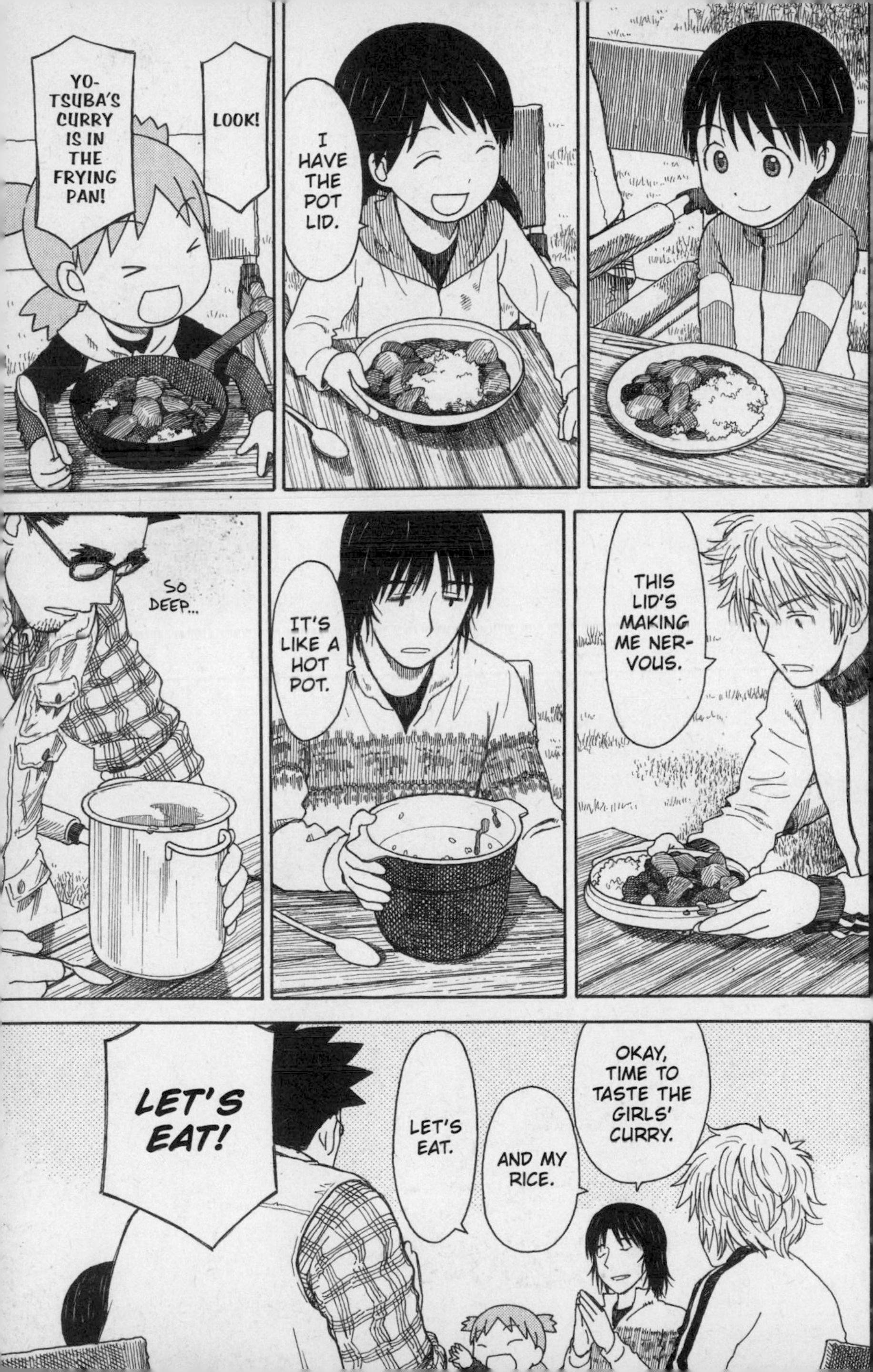
I HAVE THE POT LID.
LOOK!
YOTSUBA'S CURRY IS IN THE FRYING PAN!
THIS LID'S MAKING ME NERVOUS.
IT'S LIKE A HOT POT.
SO DEEP...
OKAY, TIME TO TASTE THE GIRLS' CURRY.
AND MY RICE.
LET'S EAT.
LET'S EAT!

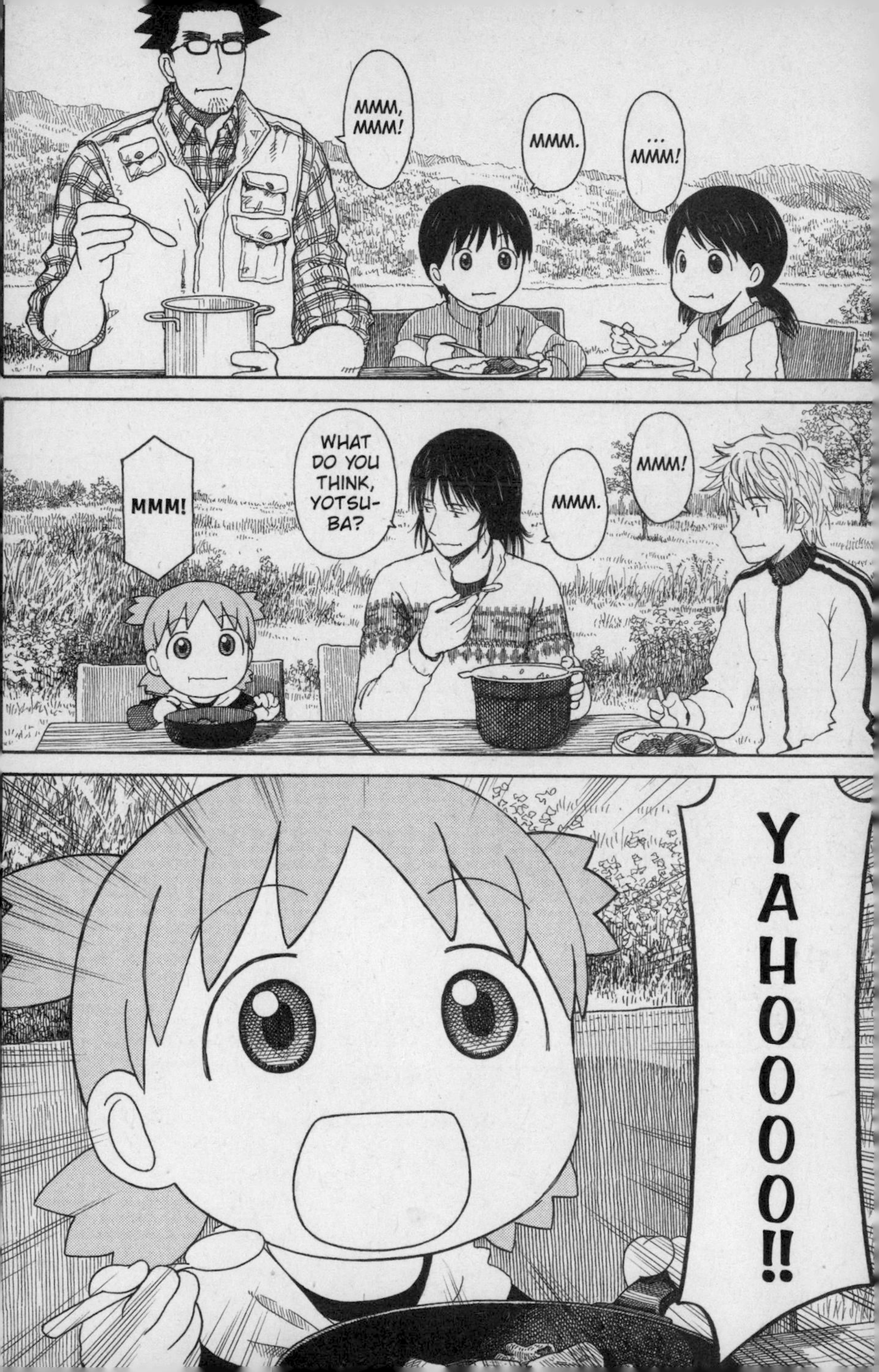

... MMM!
MMM.
MMM, MMM!
MMM!
MMM.
WHAT DO YOU THINK, YOTSU-BA?
MMM!
YAHOOOO!!

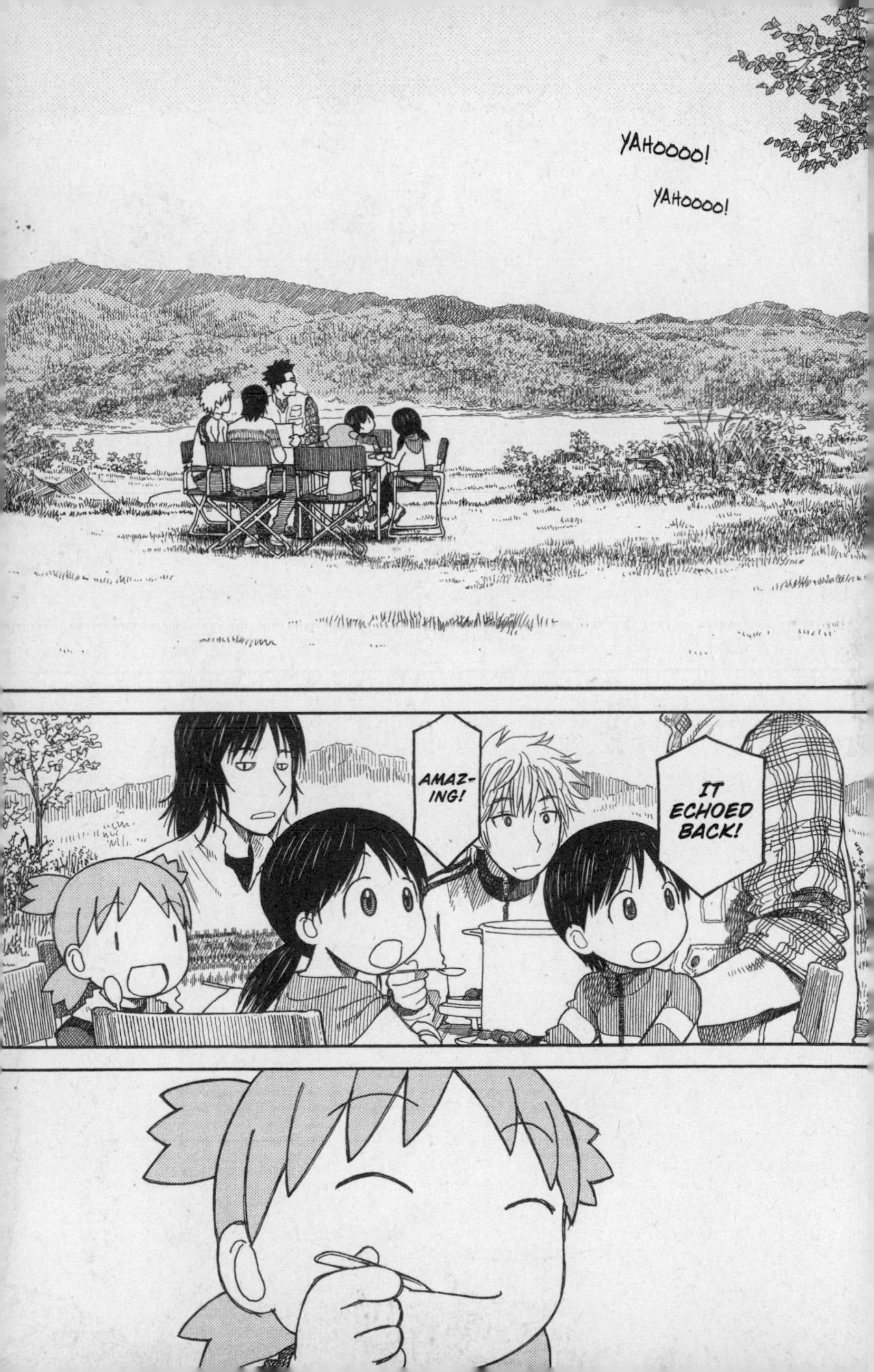
YAHOOOO!
YAHOOOO!
IT ECHOED BACK!
AMAZ-ING!

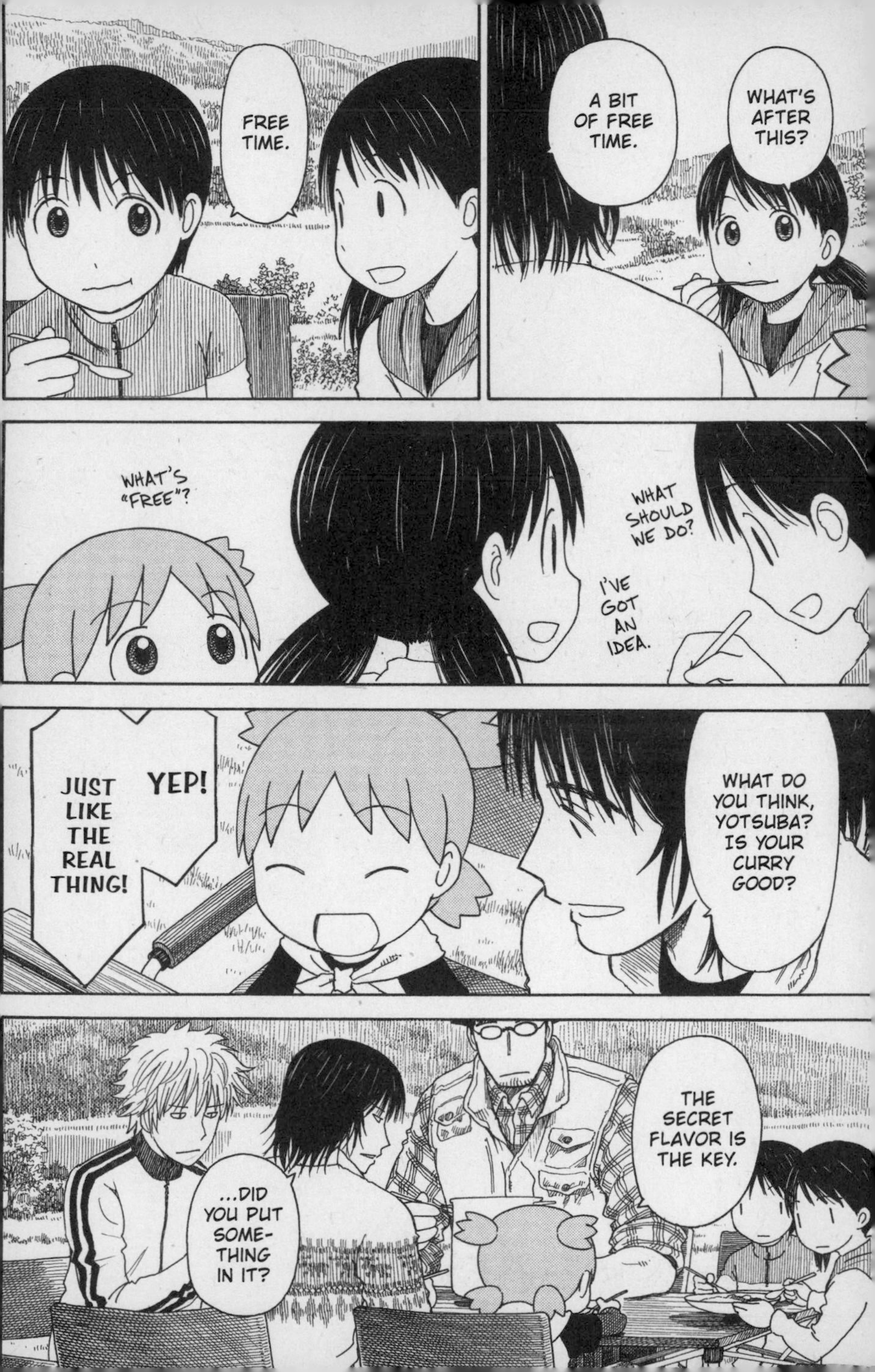
WHAT'S AFTER THIS?
A BIT OF FREE TIME.
FREE TIME.
WHAT SHOULD WE DO?
I'VE GOT AN IDEA.
WHAT'S "FREE"?
WHAT DO YOU THINK, YOTSUBA? IS YOUR CURRY GOOD?
YEP!
JUST LIKE THE REAL THING!
THE SECRET FLAVOR IS THE KEY.
...DID YOU PUT SOME-THING IN IT?

**YOTSUBA&!**

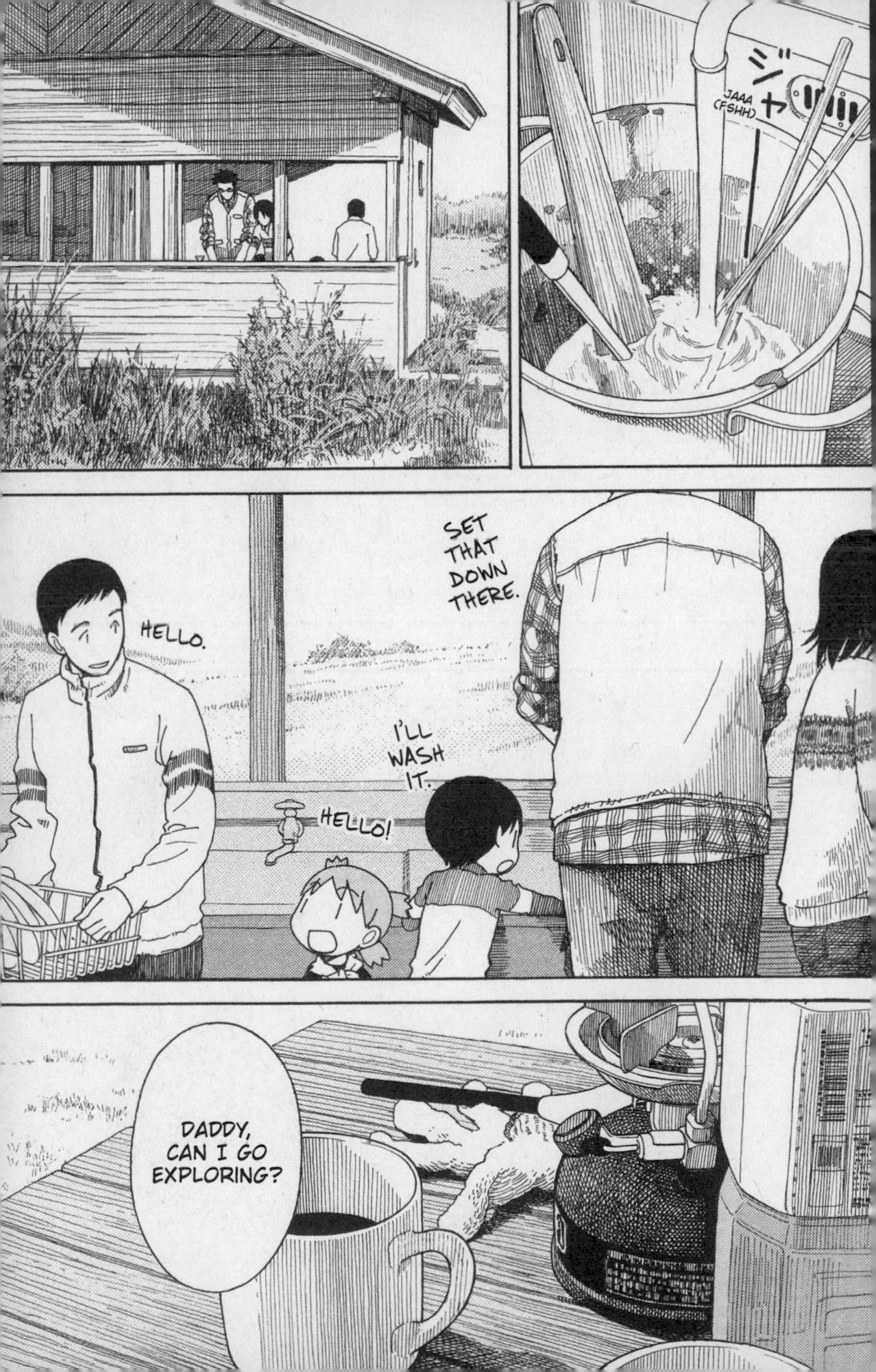
ジャー
JAAA (FSHH)
SET THAT DOWN THERE.
I'LL WASH IT.
HELLO!
HELLO.
DADDY, CAN I GO EXPLORING?

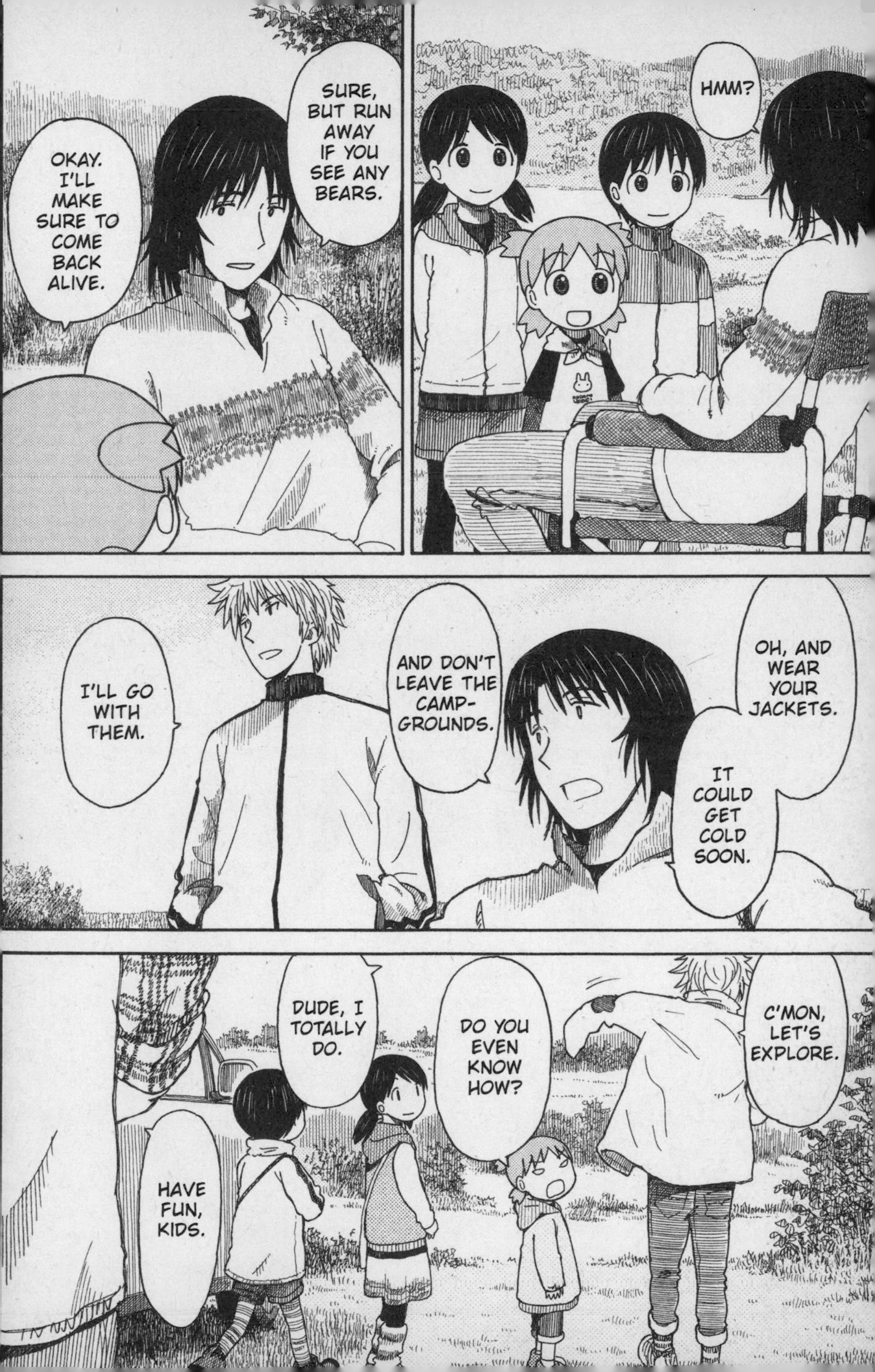
HMM?
SURE, BUT RUN AWAY IF YOU SEE ANY BEARS.
OKAY. I'LL MAKE SURE TO COME BACK ALIVE.
OH, AND WEAR YOUR JACKETS.
IT COULD GET COLD SOON.
AND DON'T LEAVE THE CAMP-GROUNDS.
I'LL GO WITH THEM.
C'MON, LET'S EXPLORE.
DO YOU EVEN KNOW HOW?
DUDE, I TOTALLY DO.
HAVE FUN, KIDS.

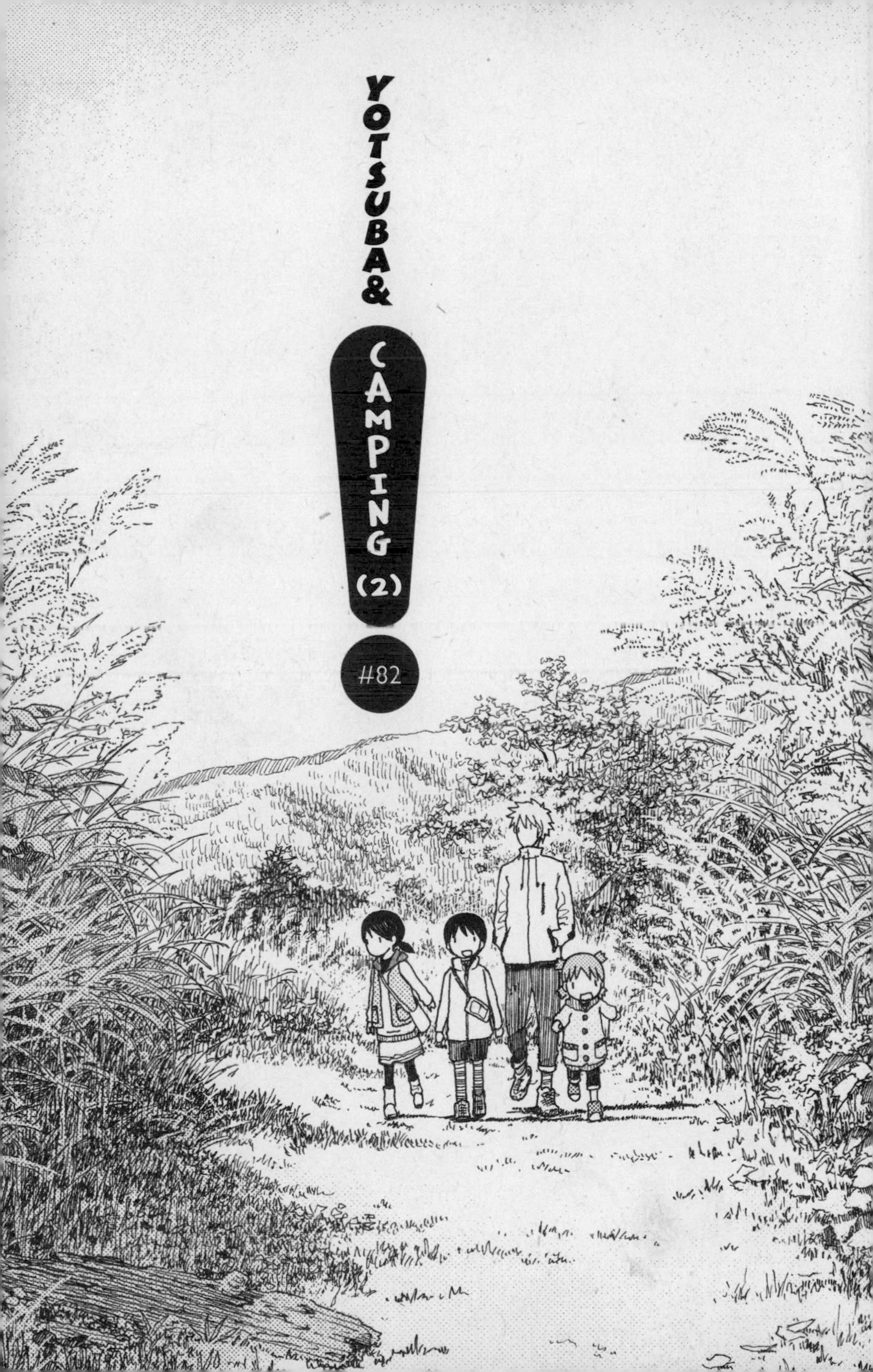
YOTSUBA&
CAMPING (2)
#82

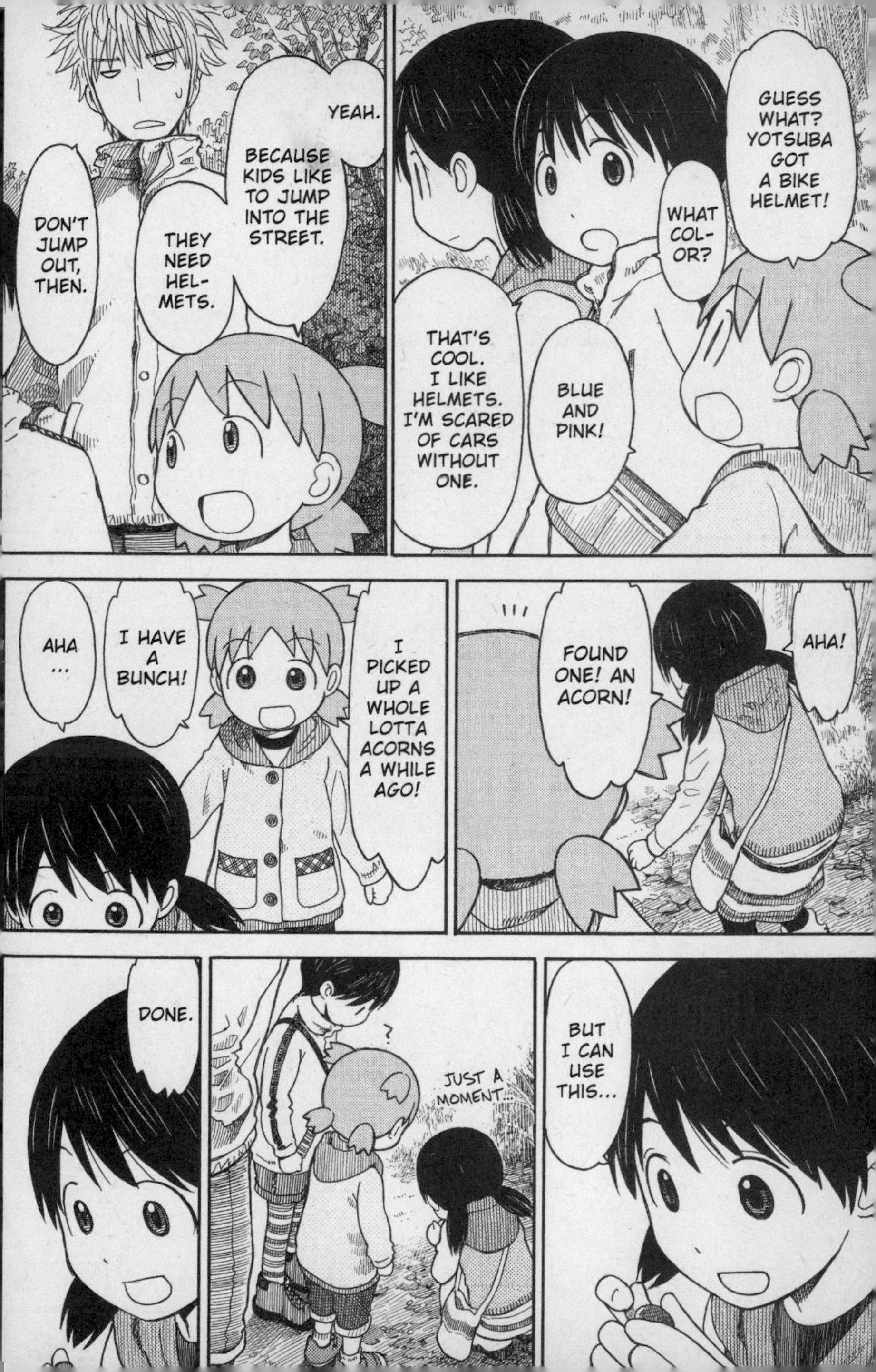
GUESS WHAT? YOTSUBA GOT A BIKE HELMET!
WHAT COL-OR?
BLUE AND PINK!
THAT'S COOL. I LIKE HELMETS. I'M SCARED OF CARS WITHOUT ONE.
YEAH.
BECAUSE KIDS LIKE TO JUMP INTO THE STREET.
THEY NEED HEL-METS.
DON'T JUMP OUT, THEN.
AHA!
FOUND ONE! AN ACORN!
I PICKED UP A WHOLE LOTTA ACORNS A WHILE AGO!
I HAVE A BUNCH!
AHA ...
BUT I CAN USE THIS...
?
JUST A MOMENT...
DONE.

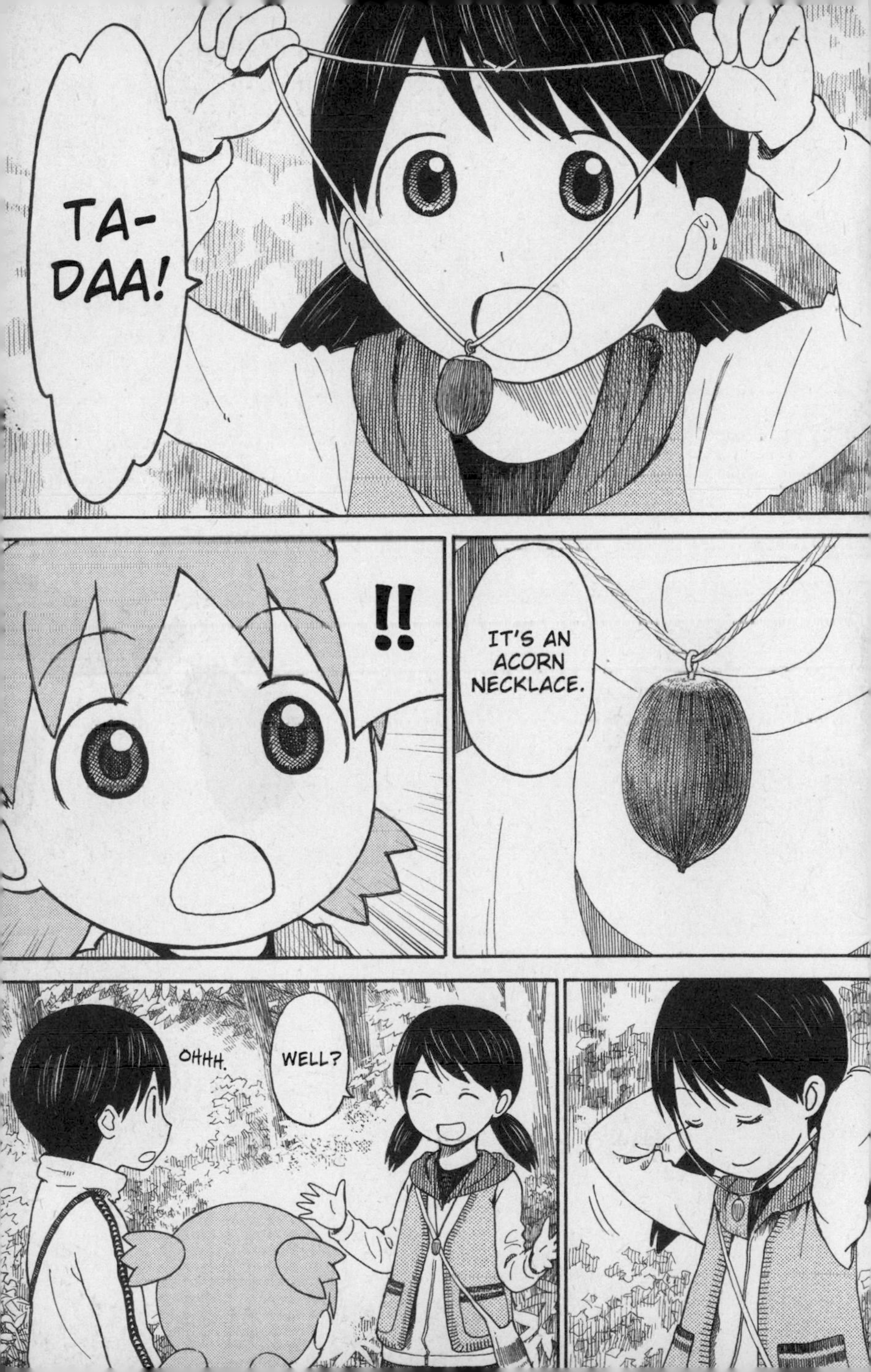
TA-DAA!
IT'S AN ACORN NECKLACE.
!!
WELL?
OHHH.

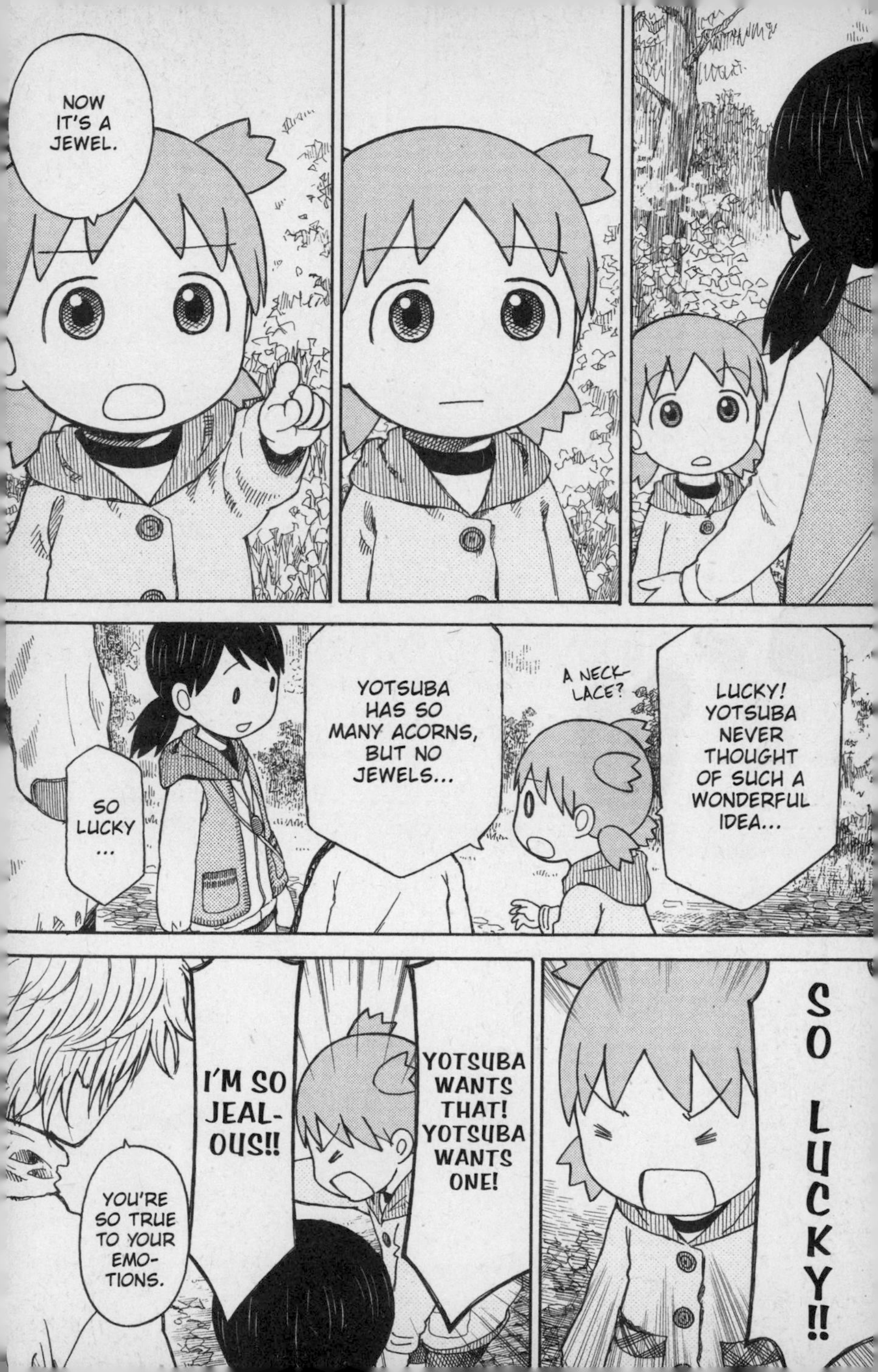
NOW IT'S A JEWEL.
LUCKY! YOTSUBA NEVER THOUGHT OF SUCH A WONDERFUL IDEA...
A NECK LACE?
YOTSUBA HAS SO MANY ACORNS, BUT NO JEWELS...
SO LUCKY ...
SO LUCKY!!
YOTSUBA WANTS THAT! YOTSUBA WANTS ONE!
I'M SO JEAL- OUS!!
YOU'RE SO TRUE TO YOUR EMO- TIONS.

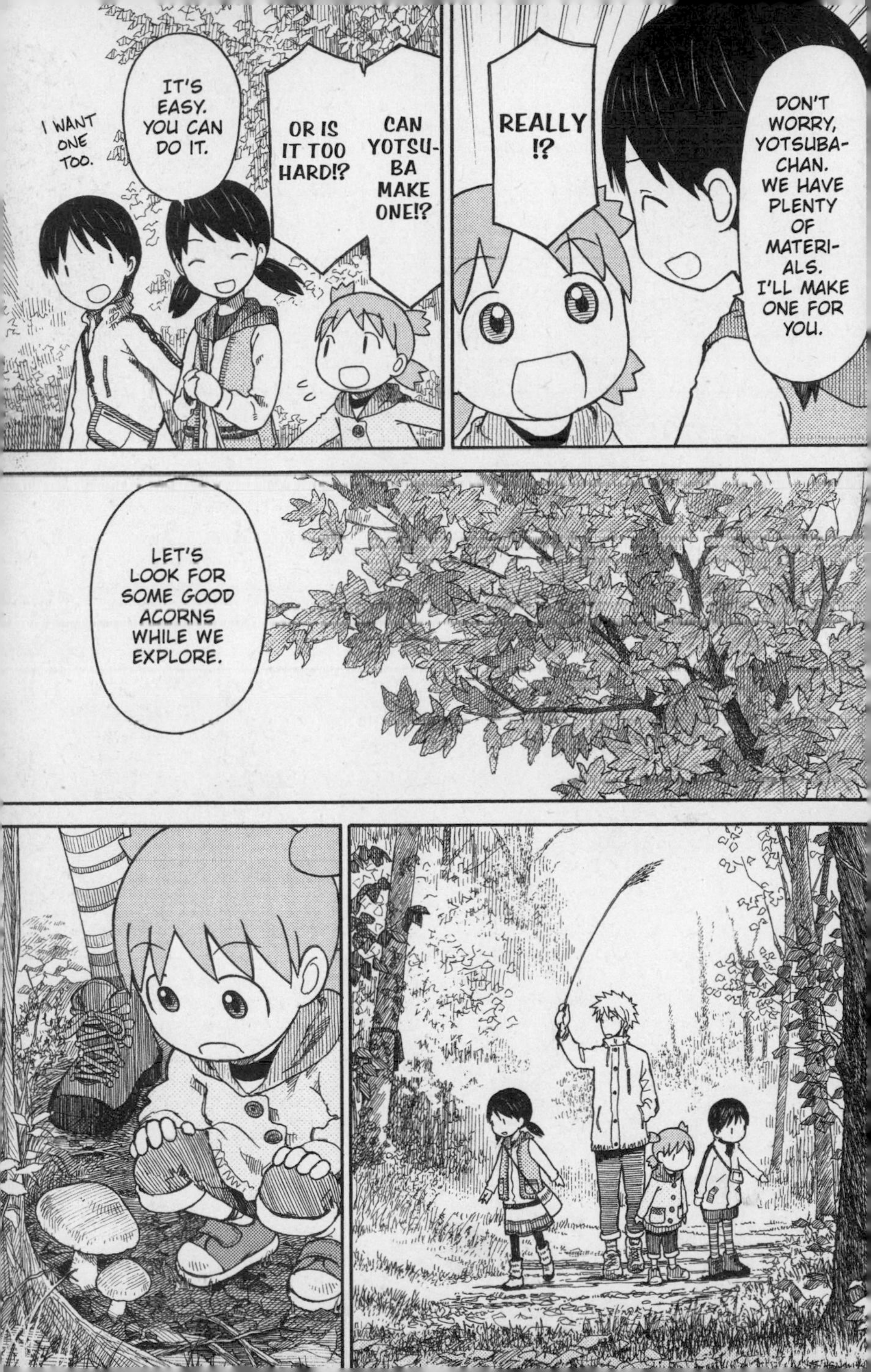
DON'T WORRY, YOTSUBA-CHAN. WE HAVE PLENTY OF MATERIALS. I'LL MAKE ONE FOR YOU.
REALLY !?
CAN YOTSUBA MAKE ONE!?
OR IS IT TOO HARD!?
IT'S EASY. YOU CAN DO IT.
I WANT ONE TOO.
LET'S LOOK FOR SOME GOOD ACORNS WHILE WE EXPLORE.

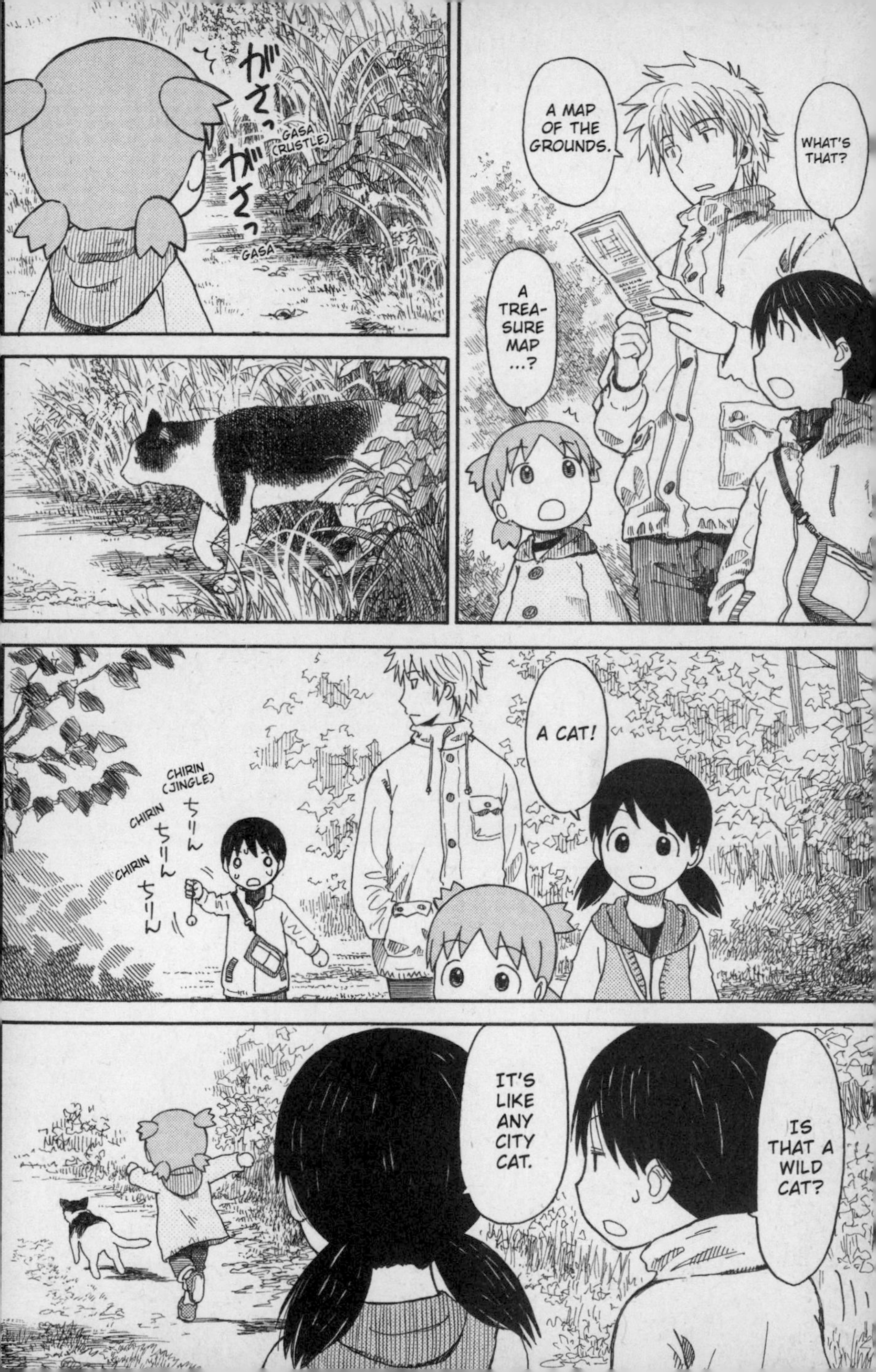
WHAT'S THAT?
A MAP OF THE GROUNDS.
A TREASURE MAP ...?
がさっ
GASA (RUSTLE)
がさっ
GASA
A CAT!
ちりん
CHIRIN (JINGLE)
ちりん
CHIRIN
ちりん
CHIRIN
IS THAT A WILD CAT?
IT'S LIKE ANY CITY CAT.

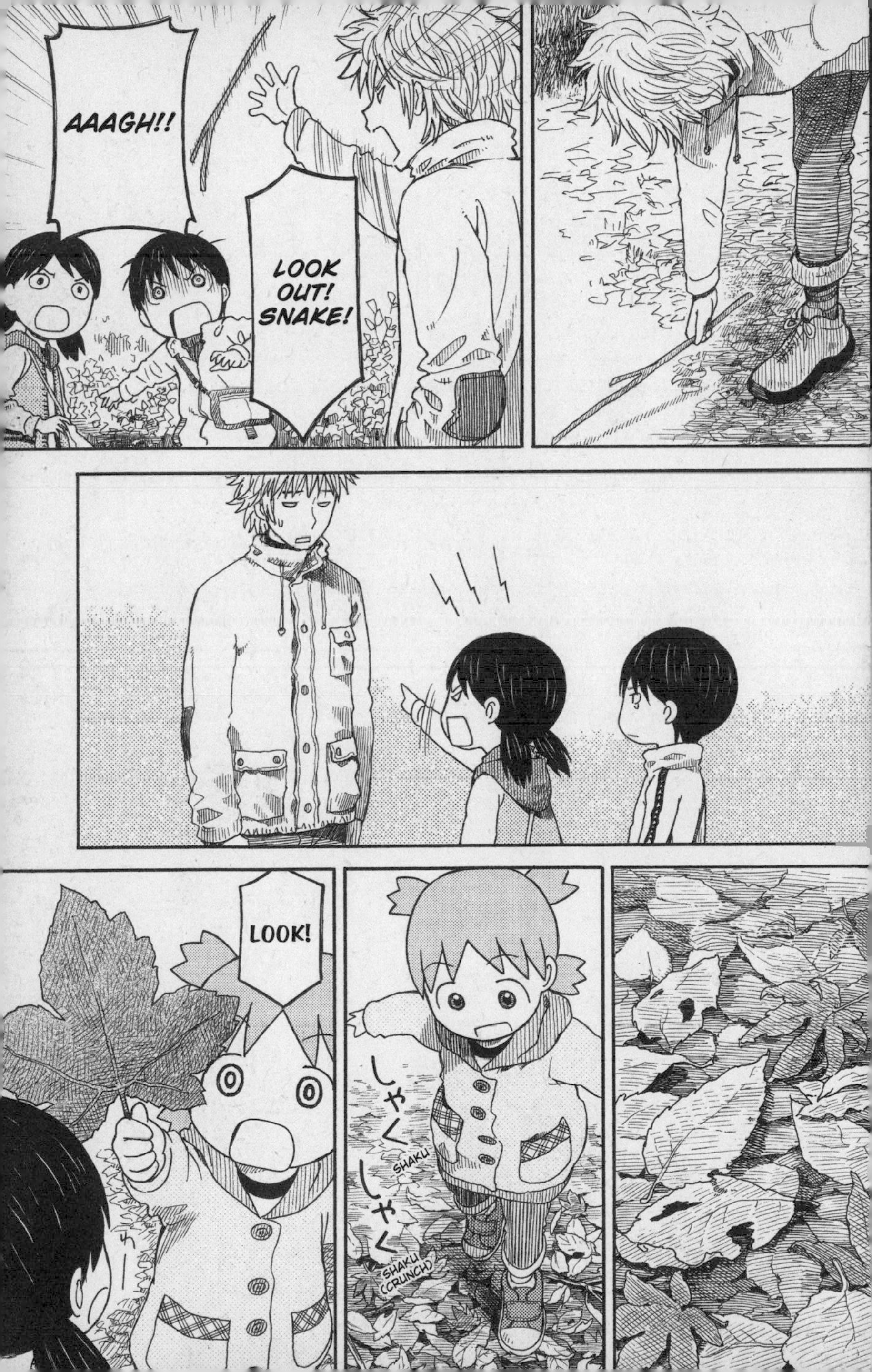
LOOK OUT! SNAKE!
AAAGH!!
しゃく
SHAKU
しゃく
SHAKU (CRUNCH)
LOOK!

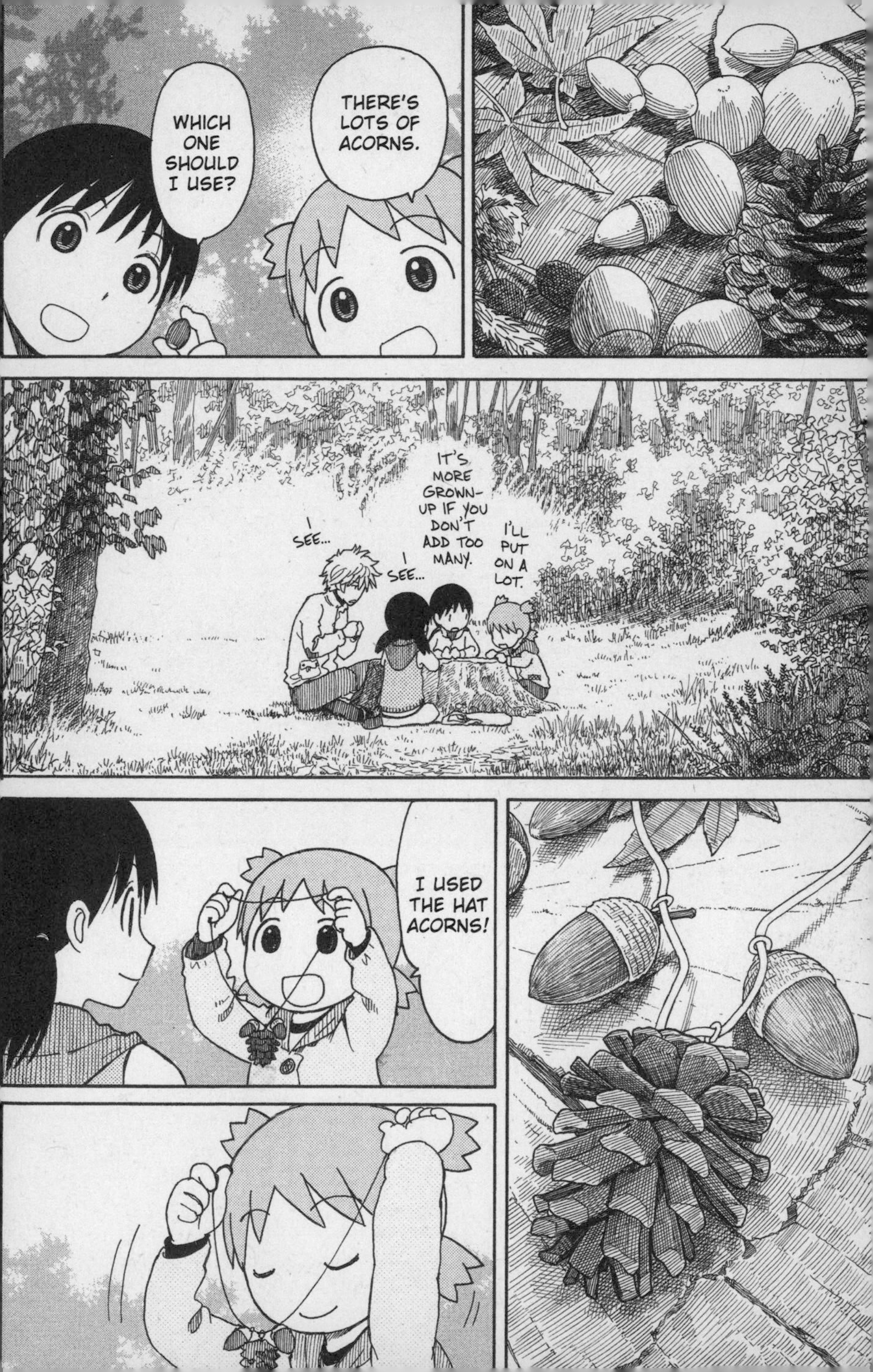
THERE'S LOTS OF ACORNS.
WHICH ONE SHOULD I USE?
I'LL PUT ON A LOT.
IT'S MORE GROWN-UP IF YOU DON'T ADD TOO MANY.
I SEE...
I SEE...
I USED THE HAT ACORNS!

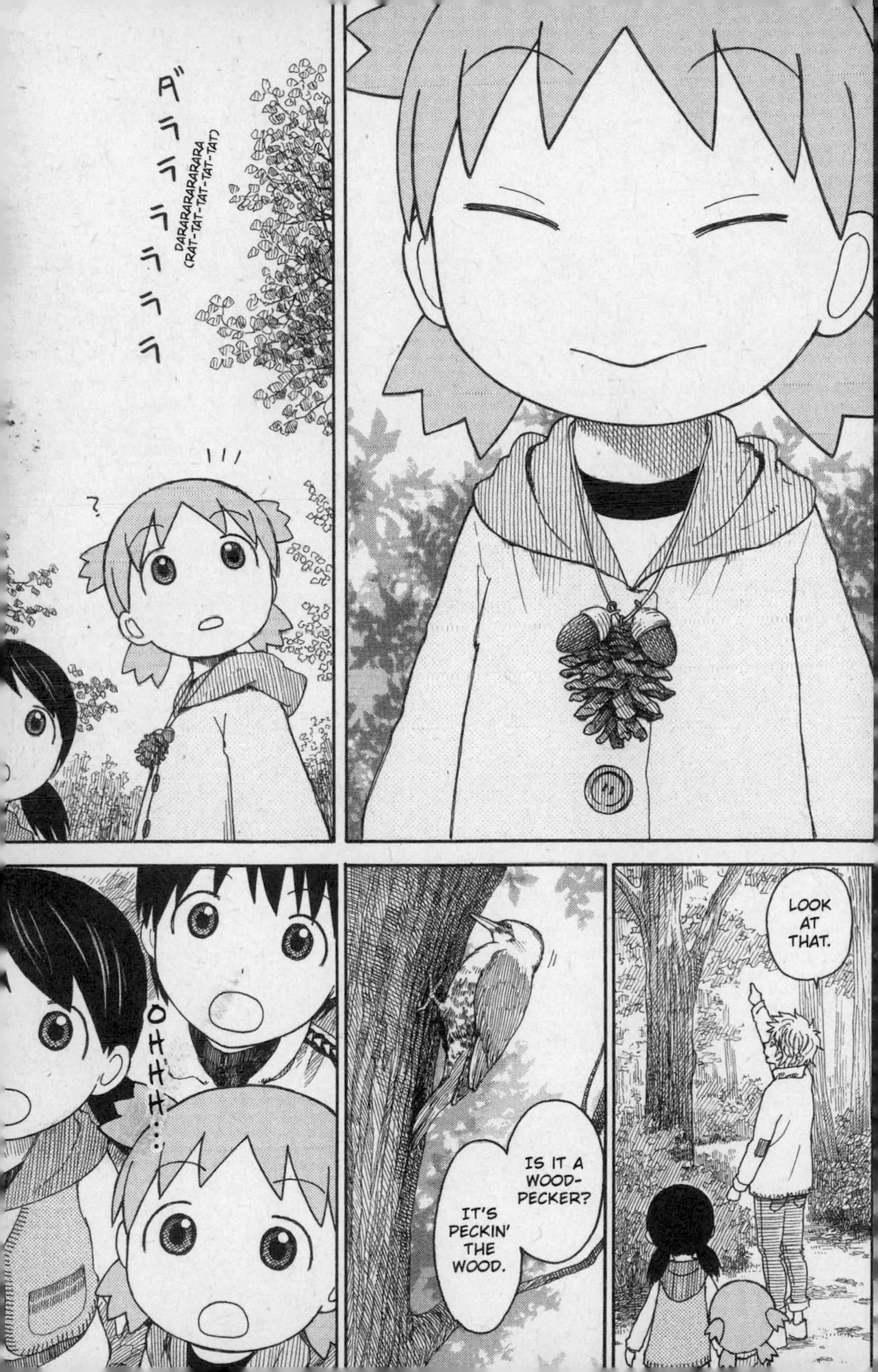
ダラララララ
DARARARARARA (RAT-TAT-TAT-TAT)
?
LOOK AT THAT.
IS IT A WOOD-PECKER?
IT'S PECKIN' THE WOOD.
OHHH...

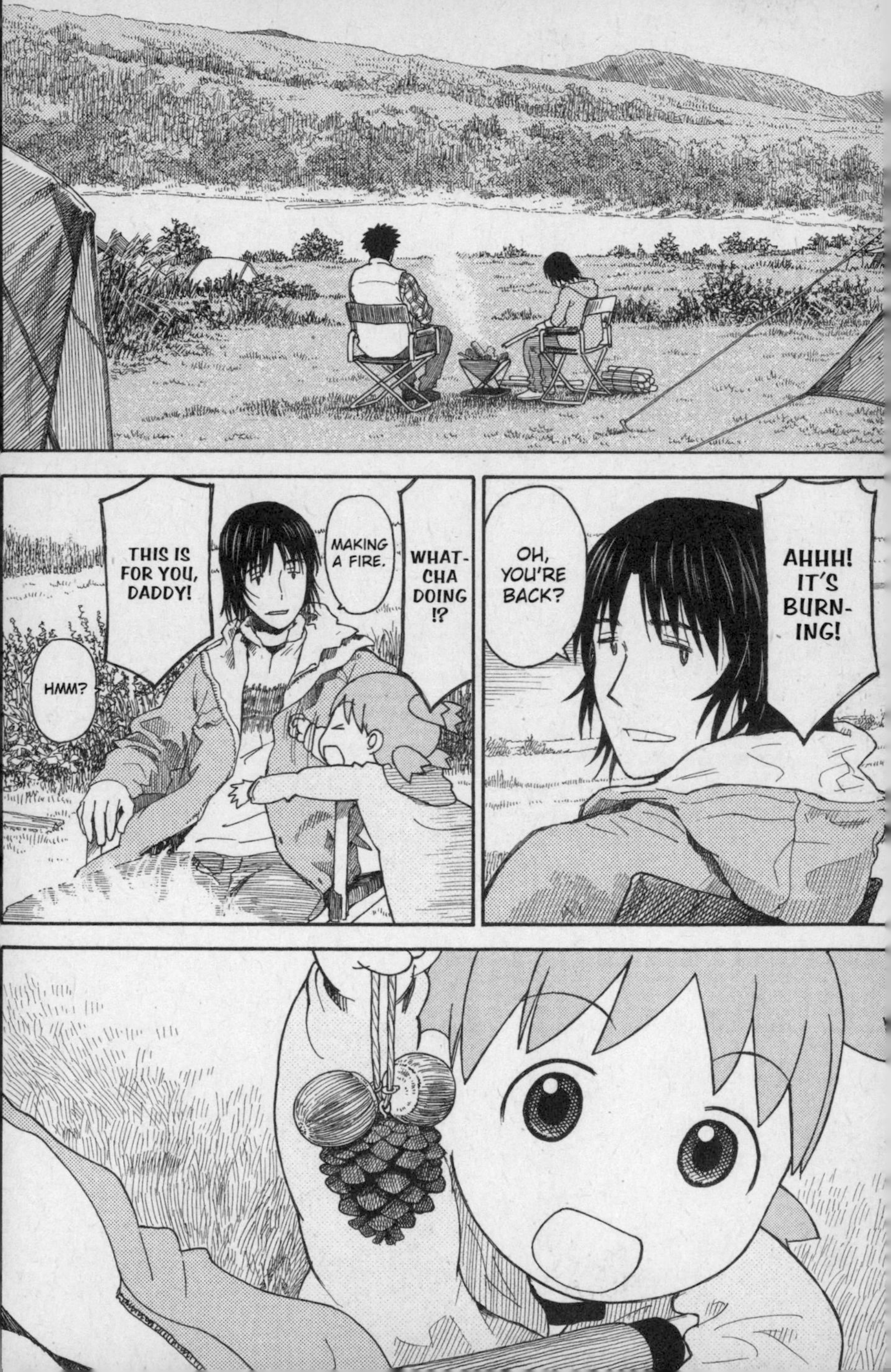
AHHH! IT'S BURNING!
OH, YOU'RE BACK?
WHAT-CHA DOING!?
MAKING A FIRE.
THIS IS FOR YOU, DADDY!
HMM?

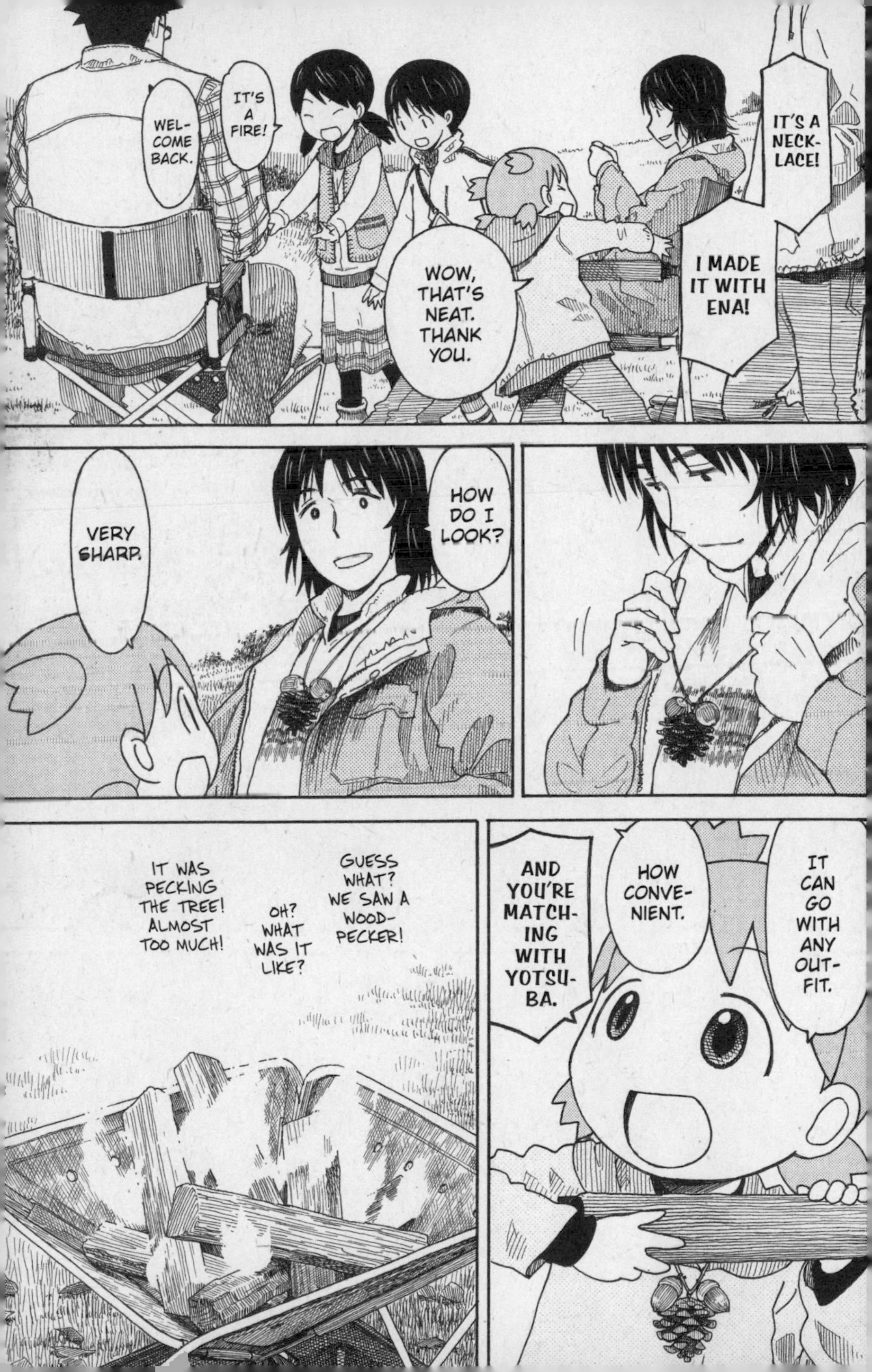
IT'S A NECKLACE!
I MADE IT WITH ENA!
WOW, THAT'S NEAT. THANK YOU.
IT'S A FIRE!
WELCOME BACK.
HOW DO I LOOK?
VERY SHARP.
IT CAN GO WITH ANY OUTFIT.
HOW CONVENIENT.
AND YOU'RE MATCHING WITH YOTSUBA.
GUESS WHAT? WE SAW A WOODPECKER!
OH? WHAT WAS IT LIKE?
IT WAS PECKING THE TREE! ALMOST TOO MUCH!

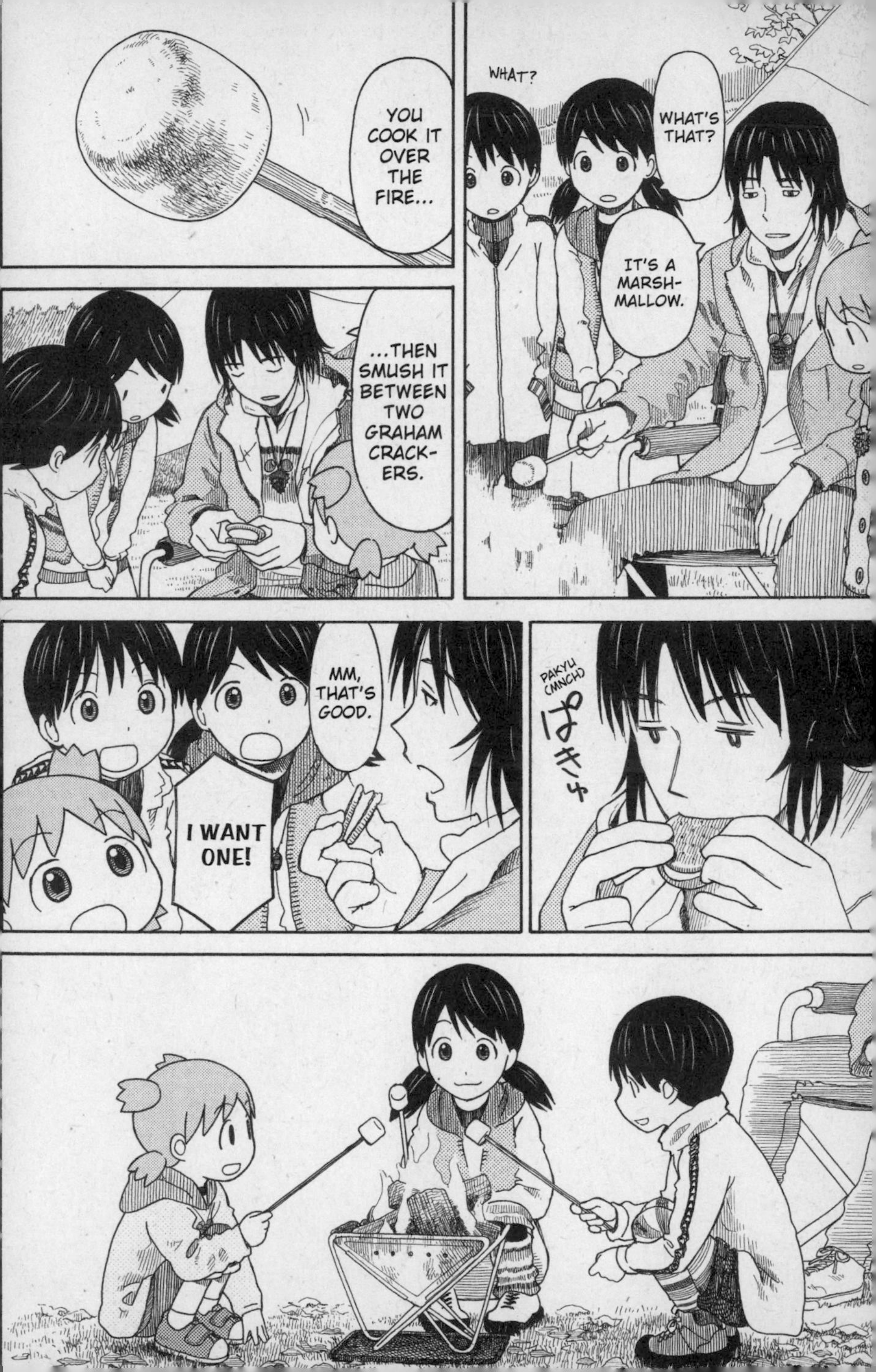
WHAT'S THAT?
WHAT?
IT'S A MARSH-MALLOW.
YOU COOK IT OVER THE FIRE...
...THEN SMUSH IT BETWEEN TWO GRAHAM CRACK-ERS.
PAKYU (MNCH)
ぱきゅ
MM, THAT'S GOOD.
I WANT ONE!

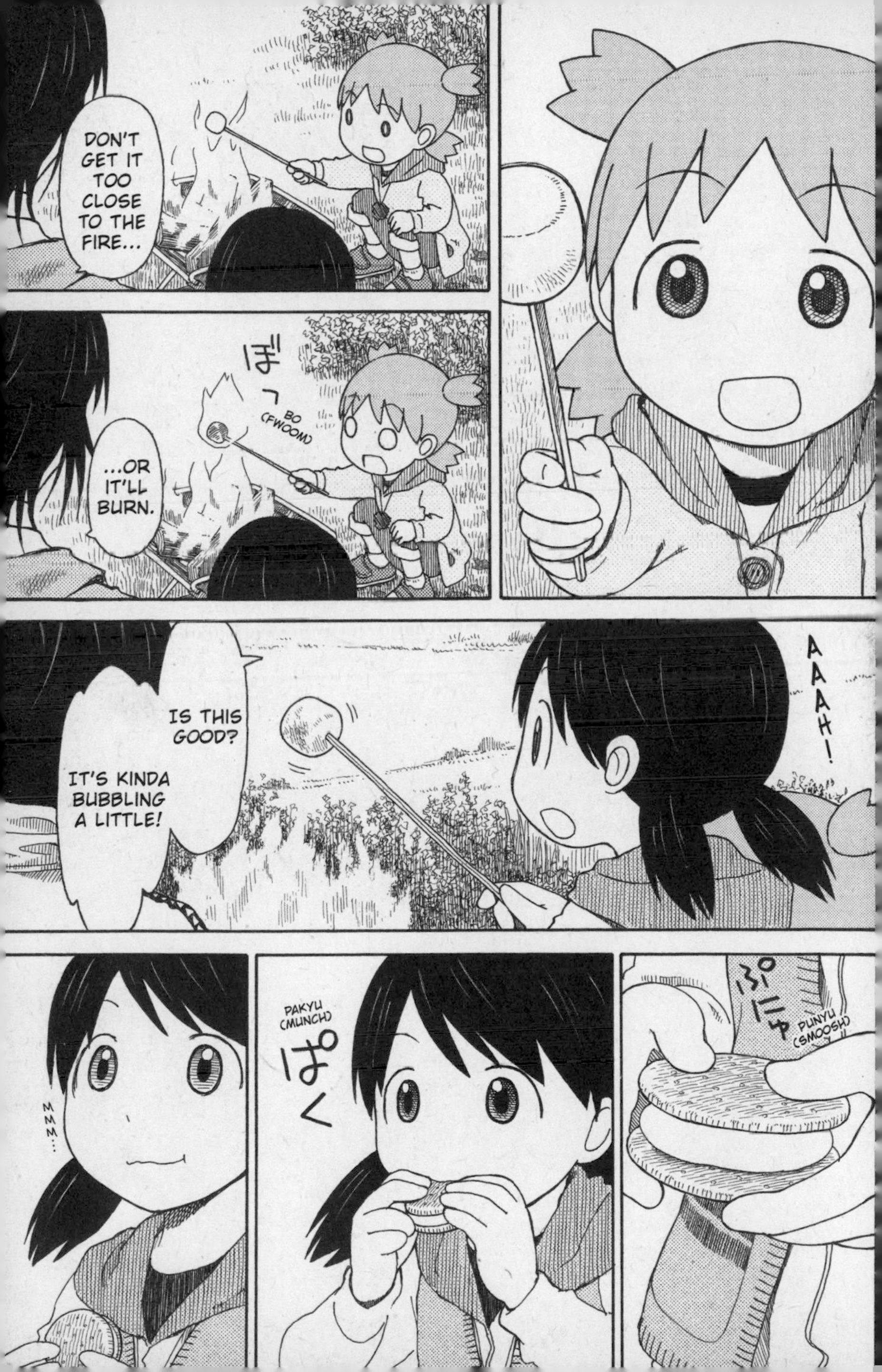
DON'T GET IT TOO CLOSE TO THE FIRE...
ぼっ
BO (FWOOM)
...OR IT'LL BURN.
AAAH!
IS THIS GOOD?
IT'S KINDA BUBBLING A LITTLE!
ぷにゃ
PUNYU (SMOOSH)
PAKYU (MUNCH)
ぱく
MMM...

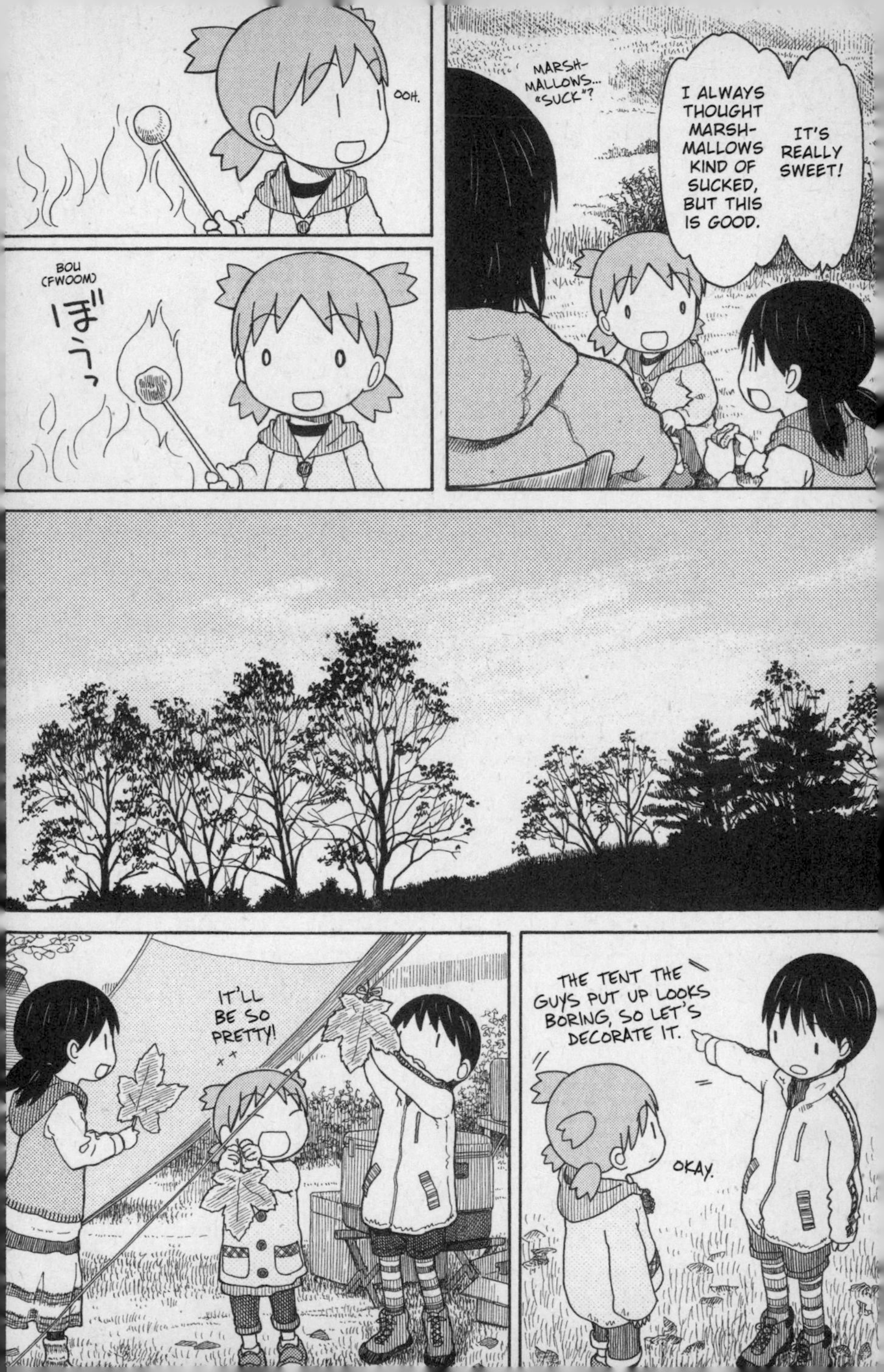
IT'S REALLY SWEET!
I ALWAYS THOUGHT MARSH-MALLOWS KIND OF SUCKED, BUT THIS IS GOOD.
MARSH-MALLOWS... "SUCK"?
OOH.
BOU (FWOOM)
ぼうっ
THE TENT THE GUYS PUT UP LOOKS BORING, SO LET'S DECORATE IT.
OKAY.
IT'LL BE SO PRETTY!

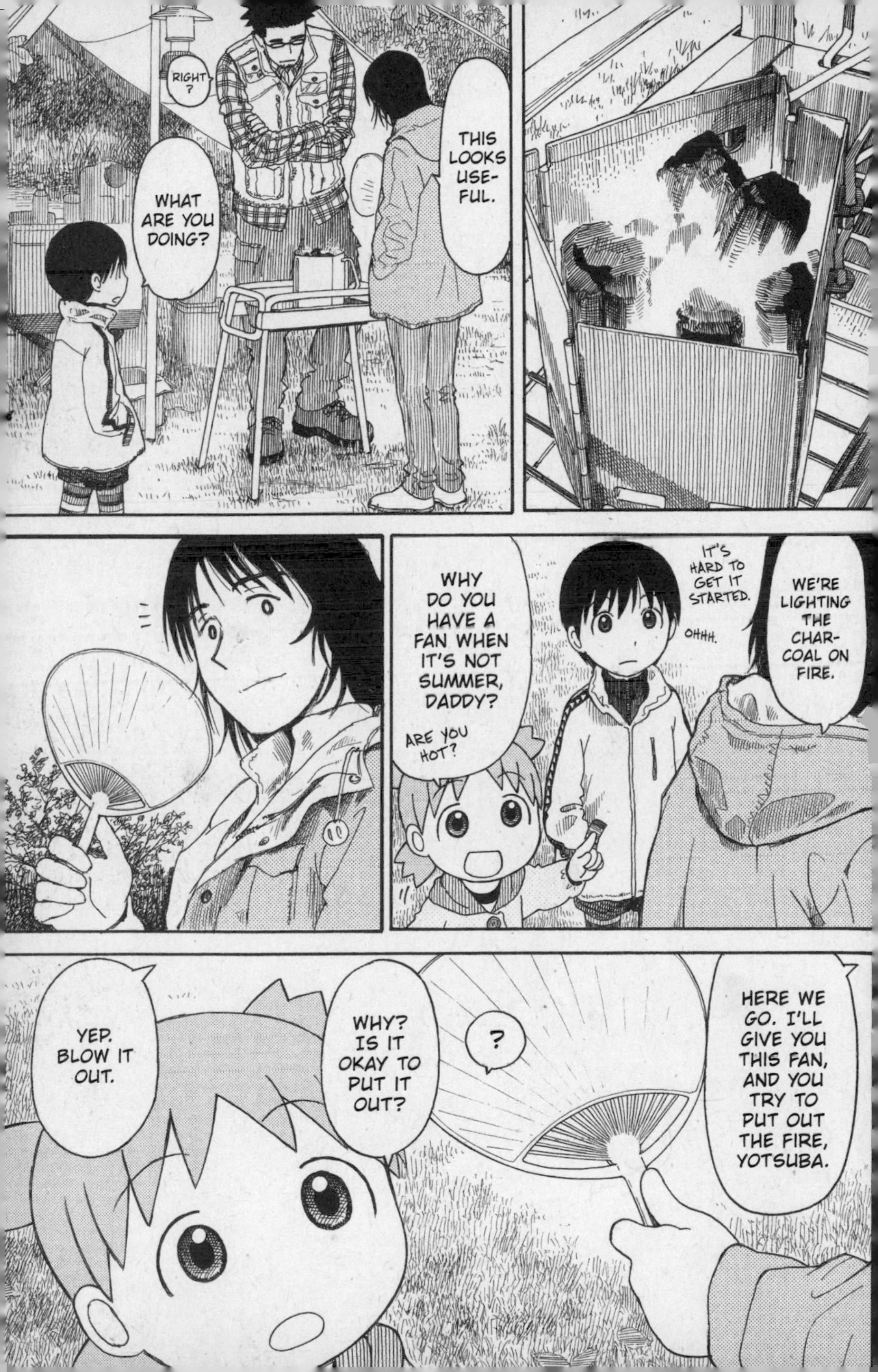
THIS LOOKS USE-FUL.
RIGHT?
WHAT ARE YOU DOING?
WE'RE LIGHTING THE CHAR-COAL ON FIRE.
IT'S HARD TO GET IT STARTED.
OHHH.
WHY DO YOU HAVE A FAN WHEN IT'S NOT SUMMER, DADDY?
ARE YOU HOT?
HERE WE GO. I'LL GIVE YOU THIS FAN, AND YOU TRY TO PUT OUT THE FIRE, YOTSUBA.
?
WHY? IS IT OKAY TO PUT IT OUT?
YEP. BLOW IT OUT.

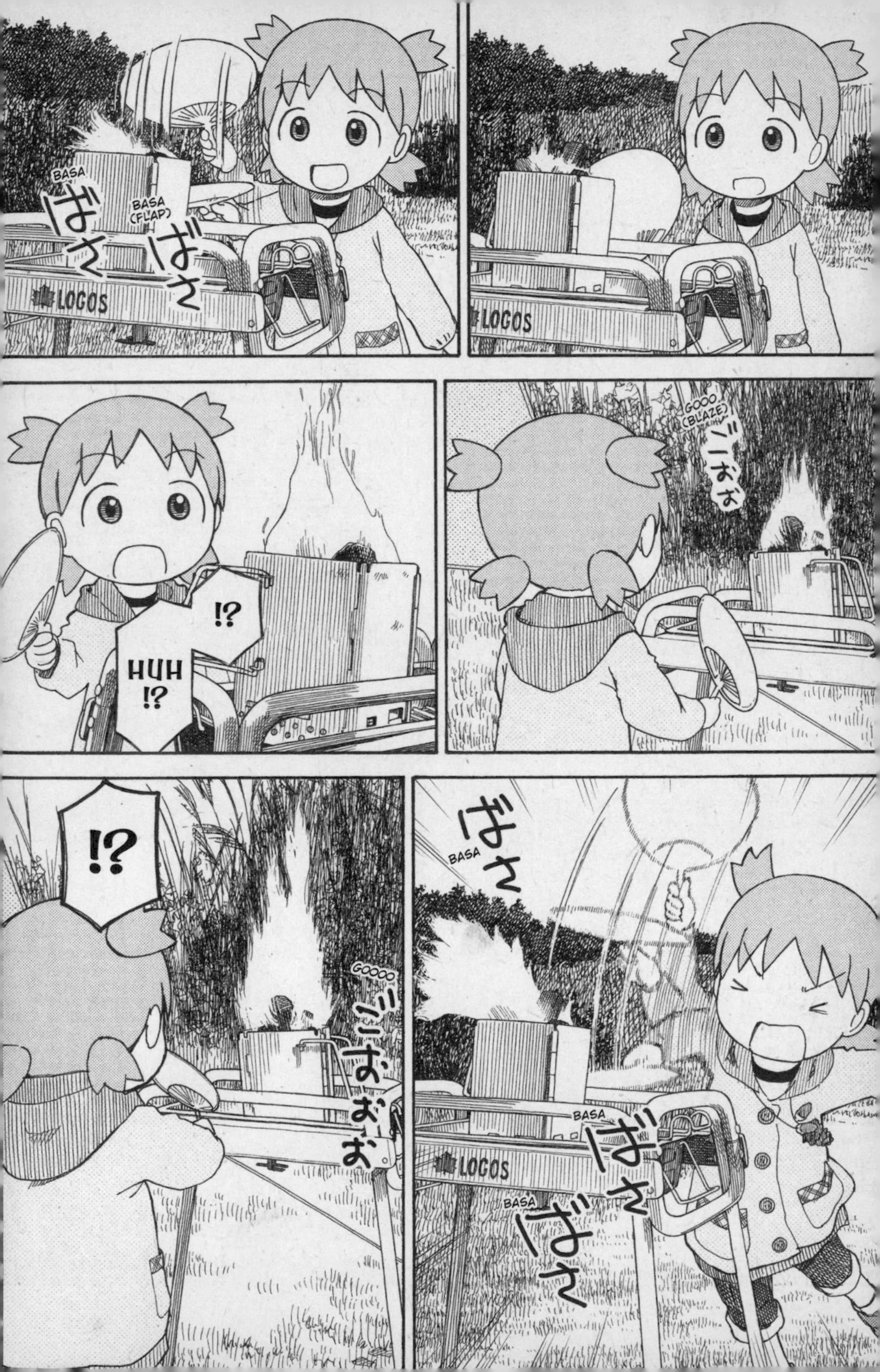
BASA
ばさ
BASA (FLAP)
ばさ
GOOO (BLAZE)
ごおお
!?
HUH !?
BASA
ばさ
BASA
ばさ
BASA
ばさ
!?
GOOOO
ごおおお

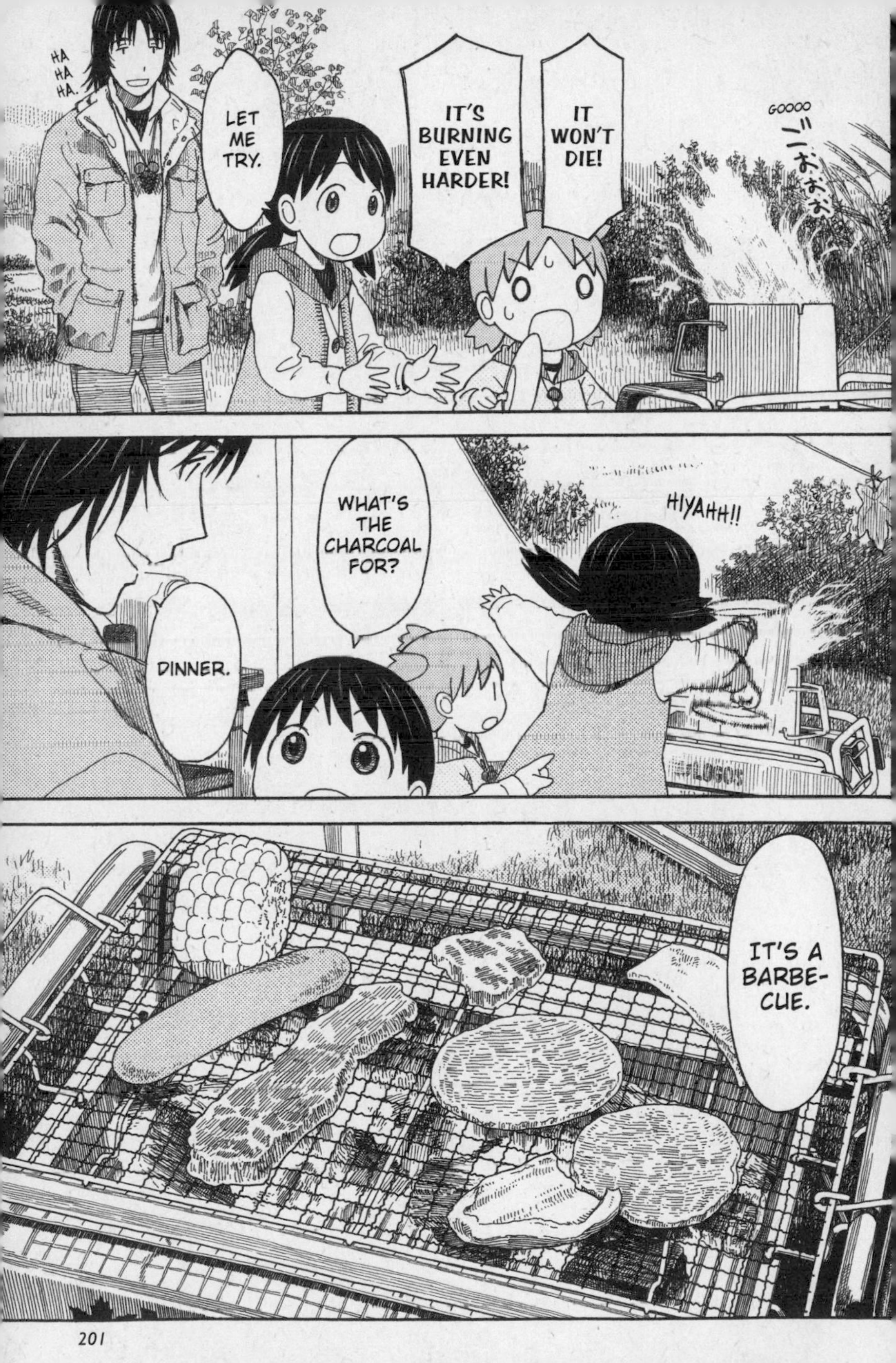
GOOOO
ゴおおお
IT WON'T DIE!
IT'S BURNING EVEN HARDER!
LET ME TRY.
HA HA HA.
HIYAHH!!
WHAT'S THE CHARCOAL FOR?
DINNER.
IT'S A BARBECUE.

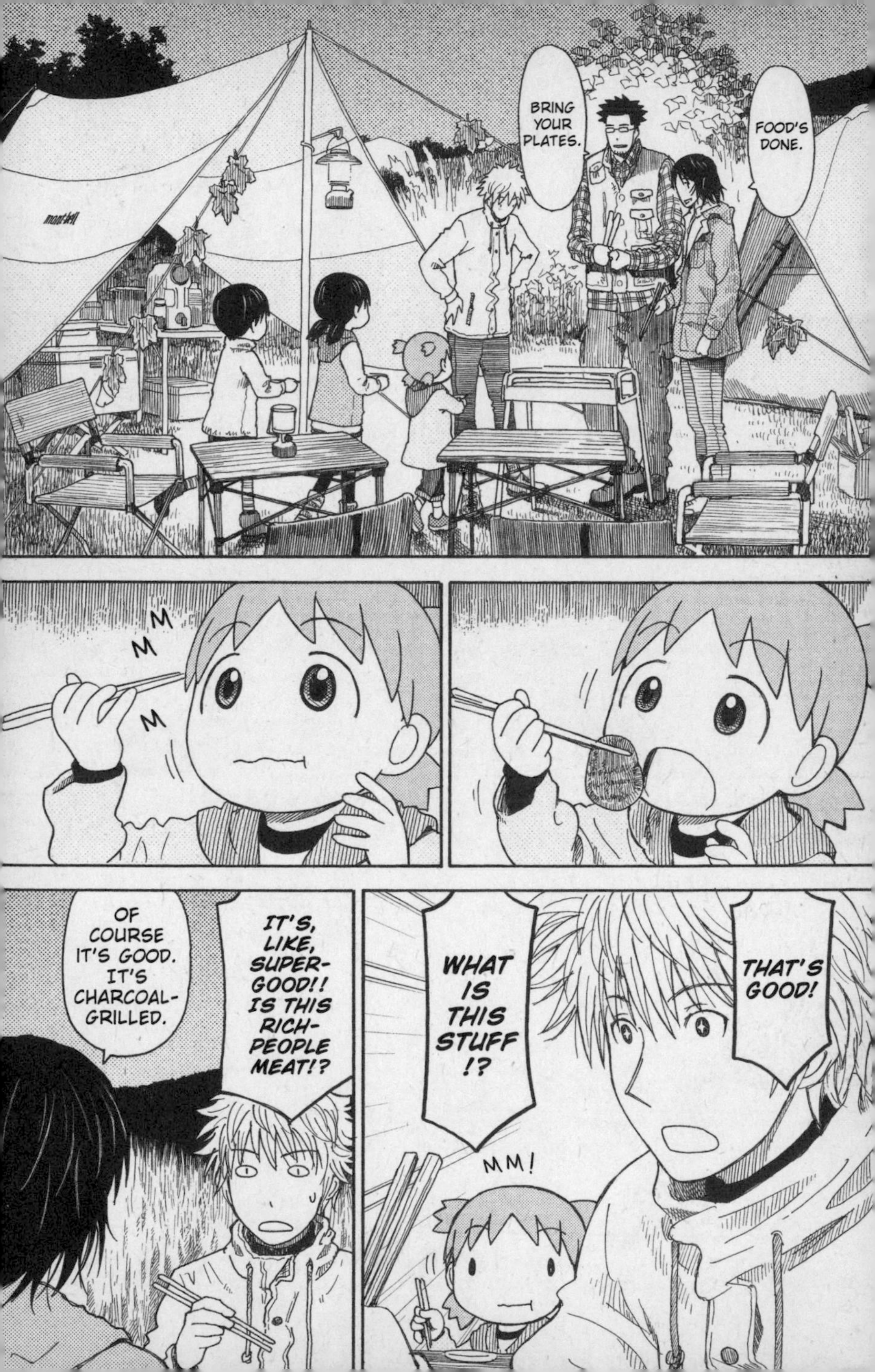
FOOD'S DONE.
BRING YOUR PLATES.
M M M
THAT'S GOOD!
WHAT IS THIS STUFF !?
MM!
IT'S, LIKE, SUPER-GOOD!! IS THIS RICH-PEOPLE MEAT!?
OF COURSE IT'S GOOD. IT'S CHARCOAL-GRILLED.

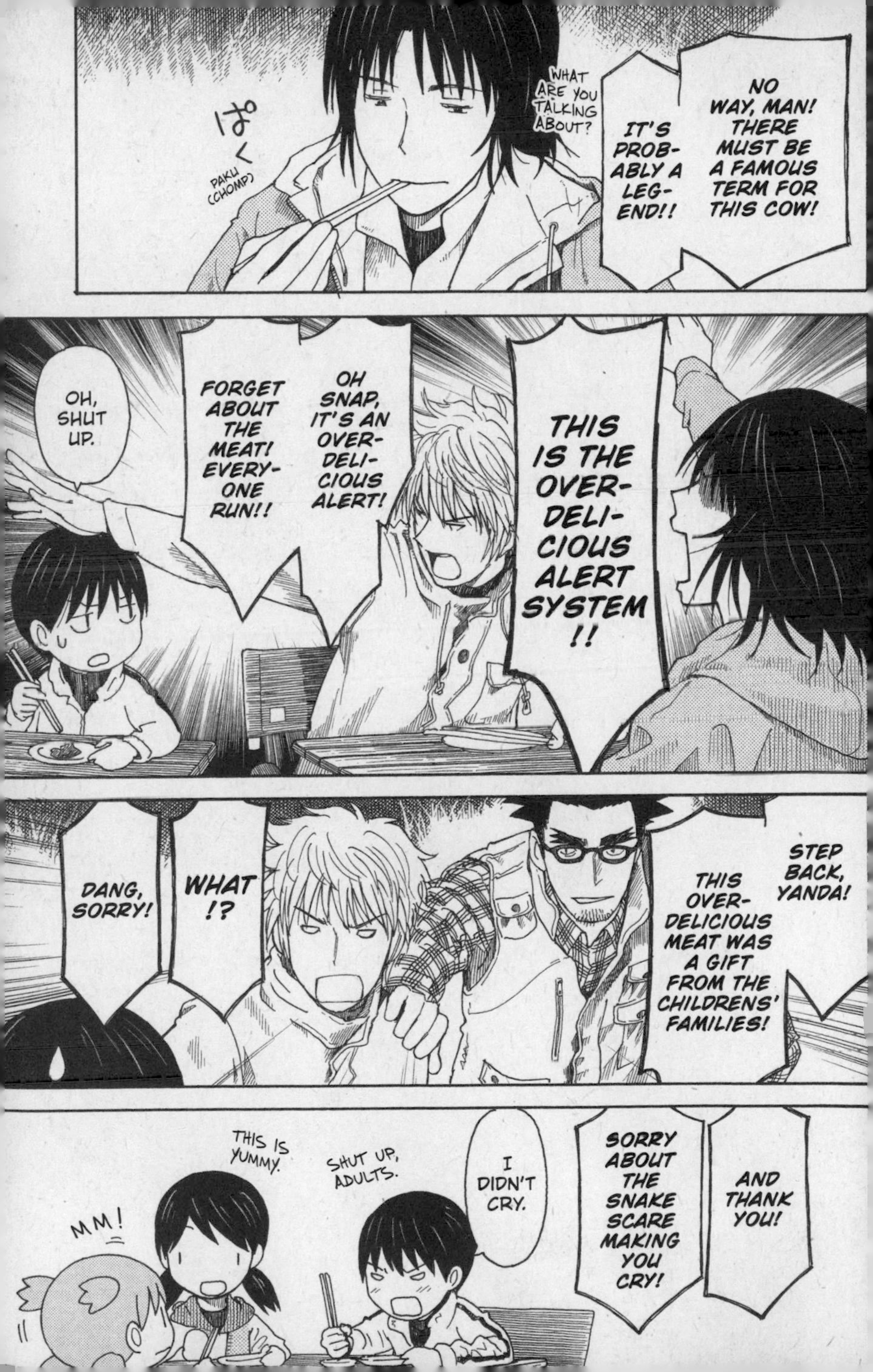
NO WAY, MAN! THERE MUST BE A FAMOUS TERM FOR THIS COW!
IT'S PROBABLY A LEGEND!!
WHAT ARE YOU TALKING ABOUT?
ぱく
PAKU (CHOMP)
THIS IS THE OVER-DELICIOUS ALERT SYSTEM!!
OH SNAP, IT'S AN OVER-DELICIOUS ALERT!
FORGET ABOUT THE MEAT! EVERYONE RUN!!
OH, SHUT UP.
STEP BACK, YANDA!
THIS OVER-DELICIOUS MEAT WAS A GIFT FROM THE CHILDRENS' FAMILIES!
WHAT!?
DANG, SORRY!
AND THANK YOU!
SORRY ABOUT THE SNAKE SCARE MAKING YOU CRY!
I DIDN'T CRY.
SHUT UP, ADULTS.
THIS IS YUMMY.
MM!

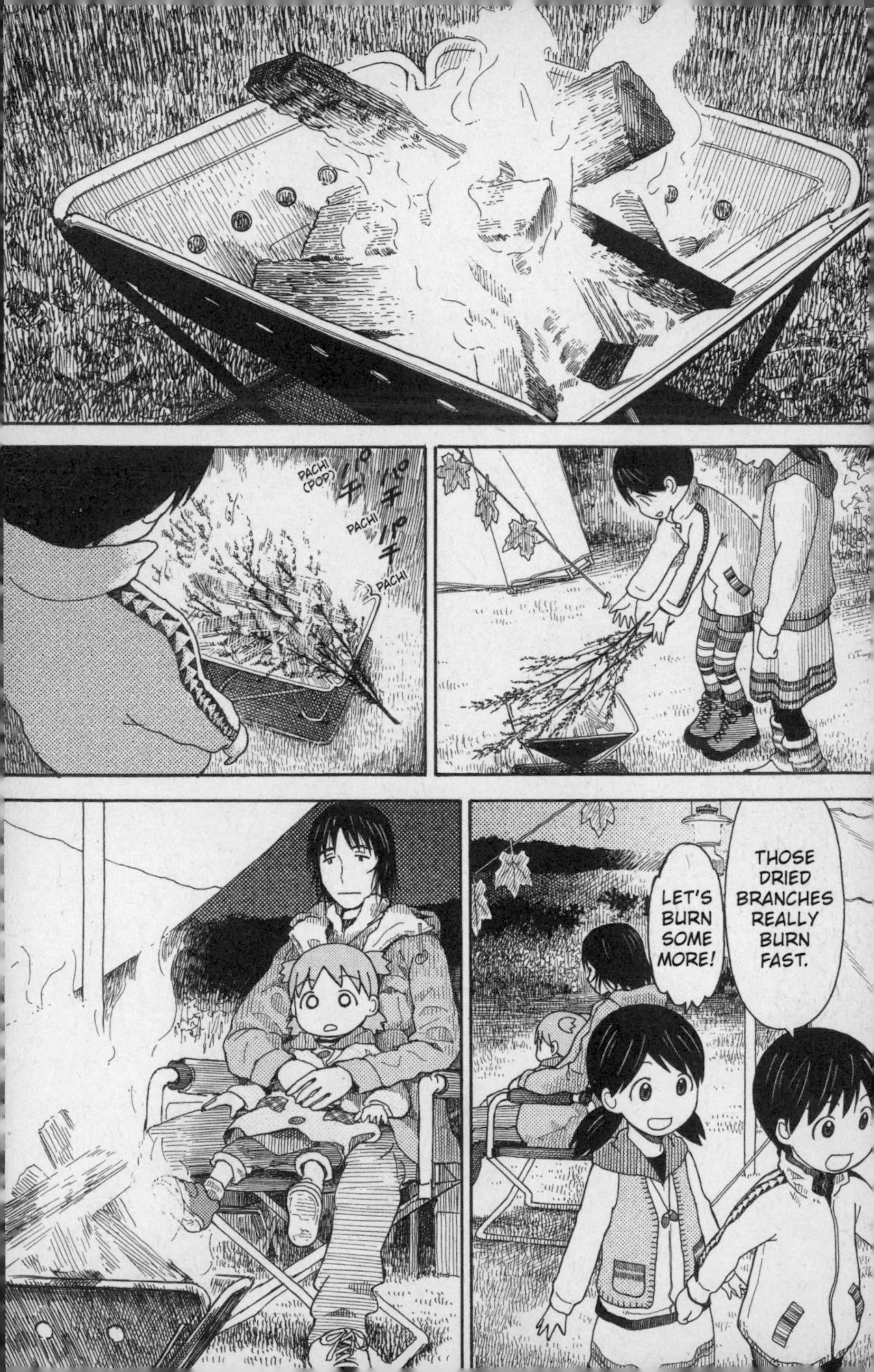
PACHI (POP)
PACHI
PACHI
THOSE DRIED BRANCHES REALLY BURN FAST.
LET'S BURN SOME MORE!

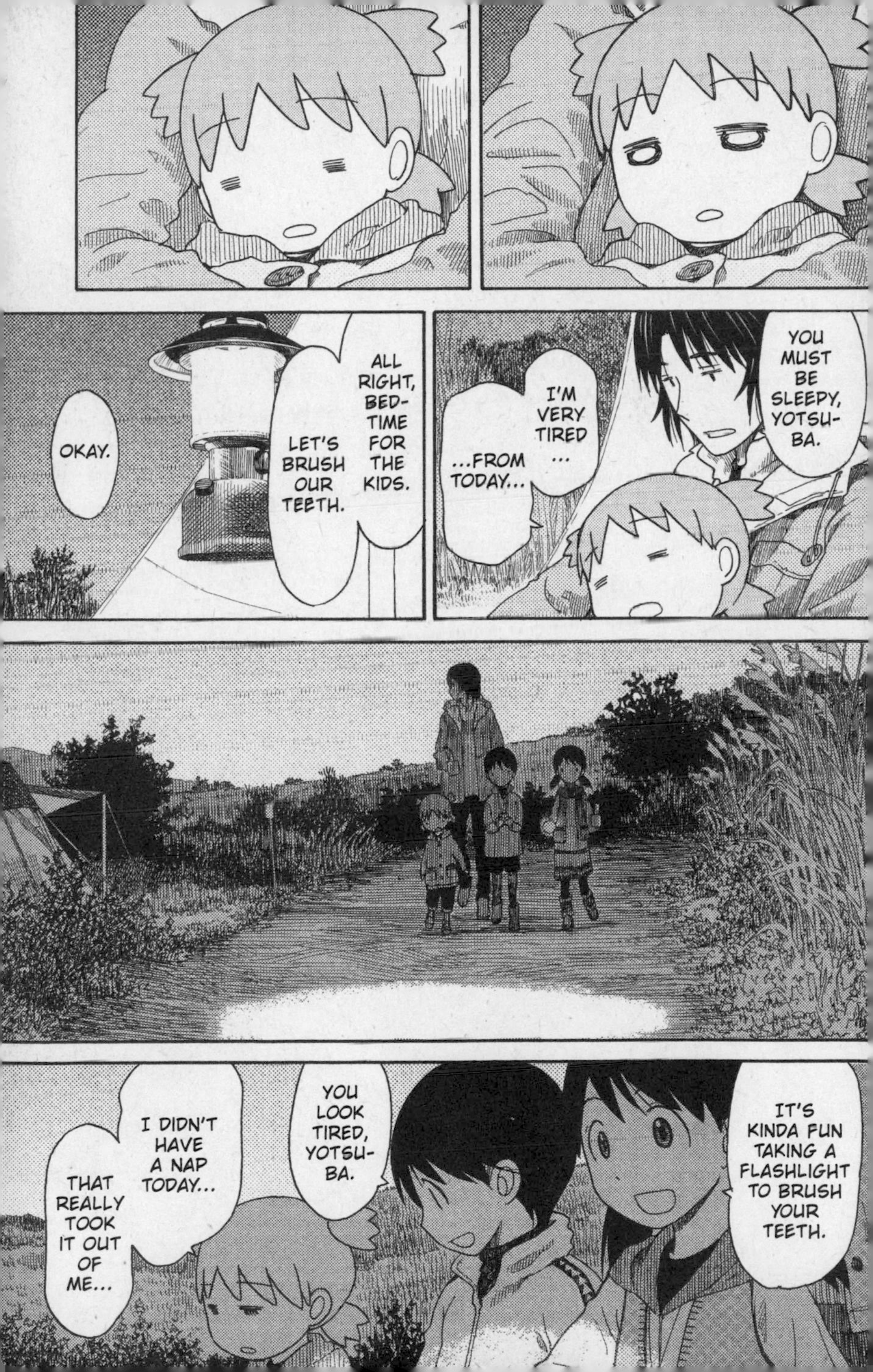
YOU MUST BE SLEEPY, YOTSUBA.
I'M VERY TIRED…
…FROM TODAY…
ALL RIGHT, BEDTIME FOR THE KIDS.
LET'S BRUSH OUR TEETH.
OKAY.
IT'S KINDA FUN TAKING A FLASHLIGHT TO BRUSH YOUR TEETH.
YOU LOOK TIRED, YOTSUBA.
I DIDN'T HAVE A NAP TODAY…
THAT REALLY TOOK IT OUT OF ME…

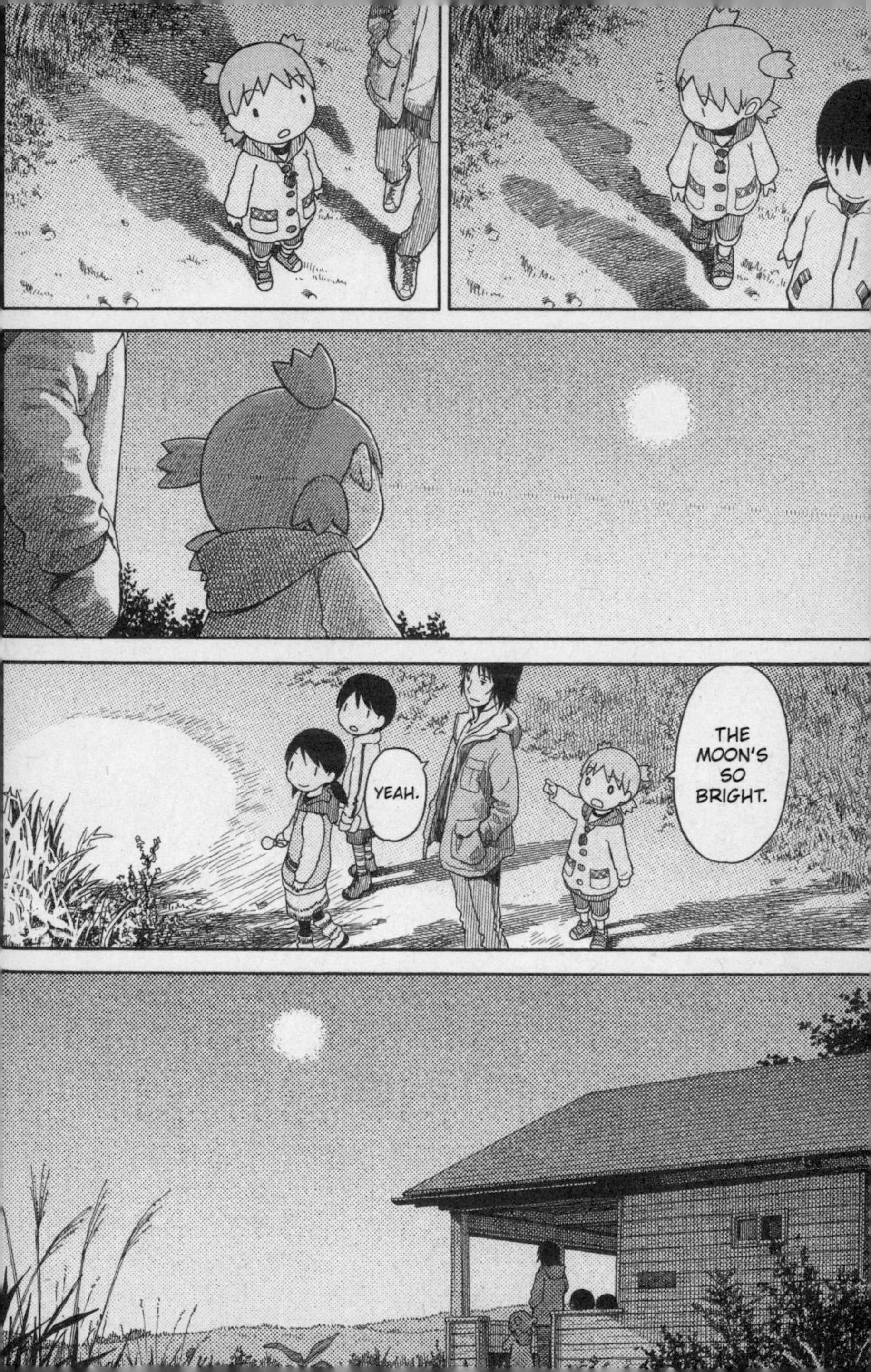
THE MOON'S SO BRIGHT.
YEAH.

CHIIIIII
(ZIIIIIP)

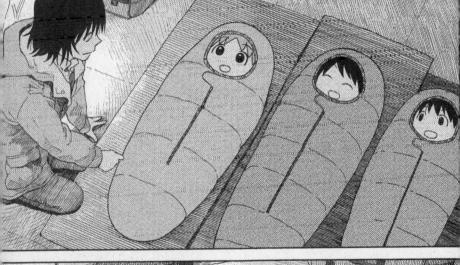

YEAH.

THIS IS
KINDA
FUNNY

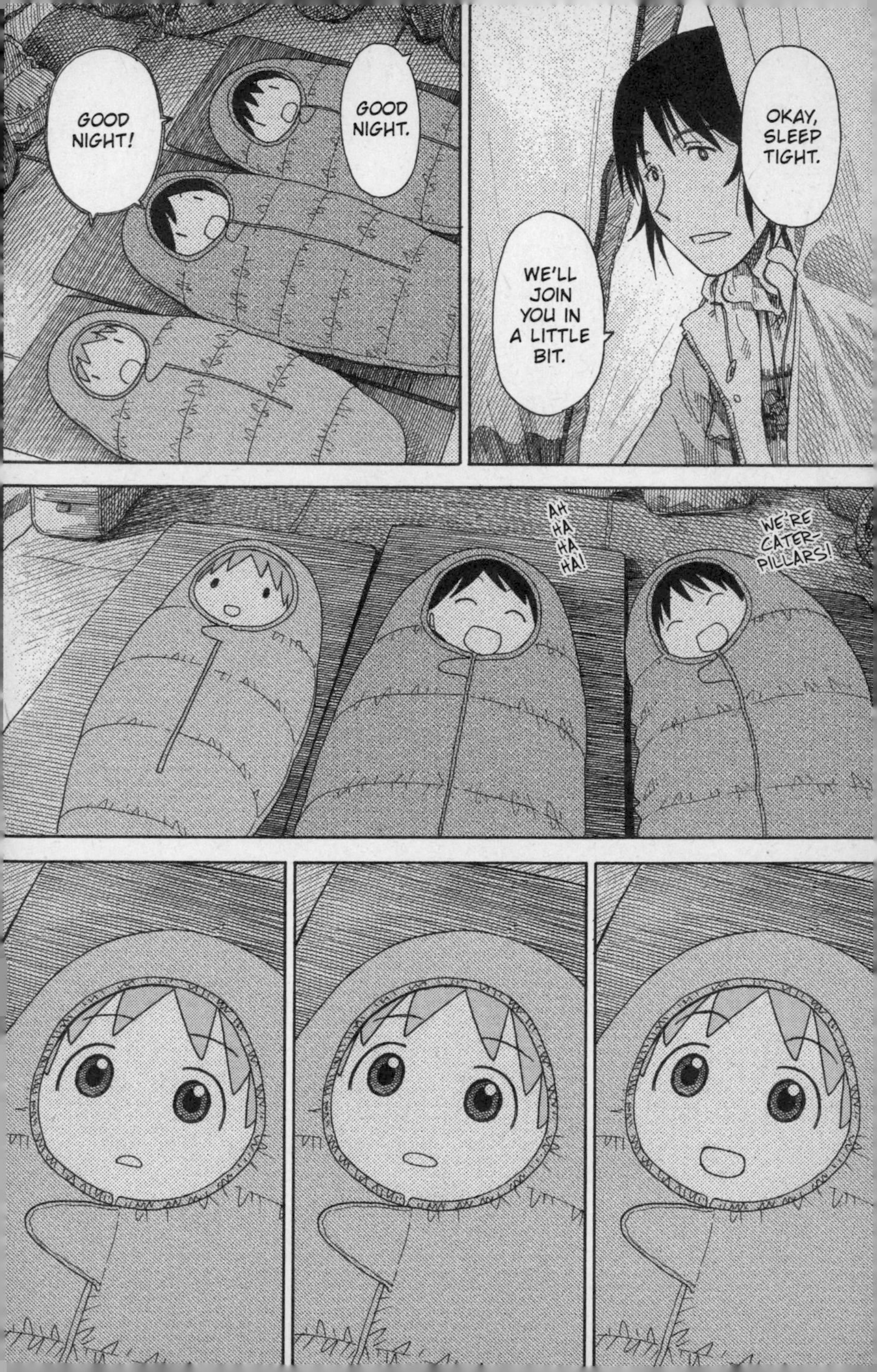
OKAY, SLEEP TIGHT.
WE'LL JOIN YOU IN A LITTLE BIT.
GOOD NIGHT.
GOOD NIGHT!
WE'RE CATER-PILLARS!
AH HA HA HA!

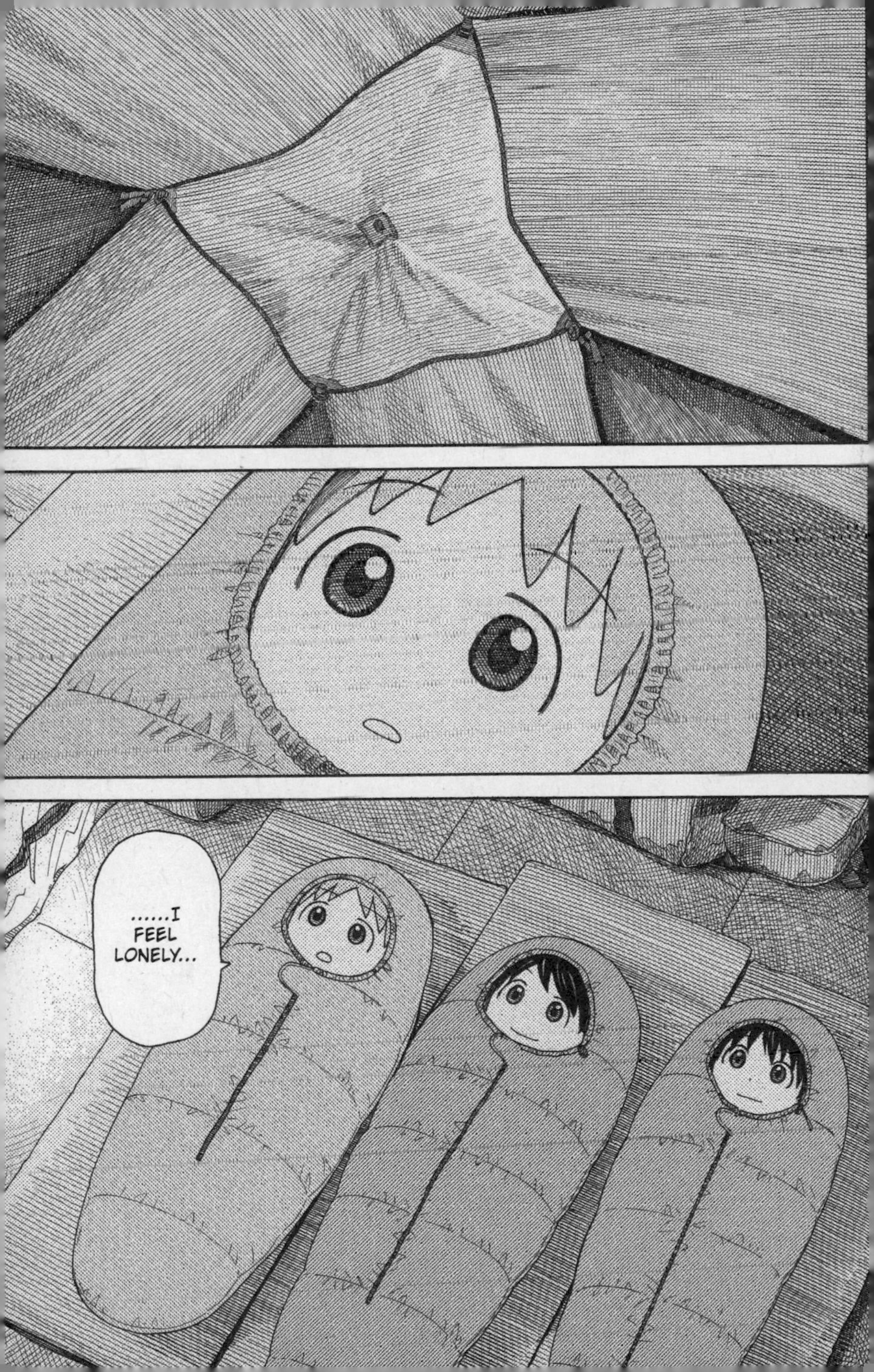
......I FEEL LONELY...

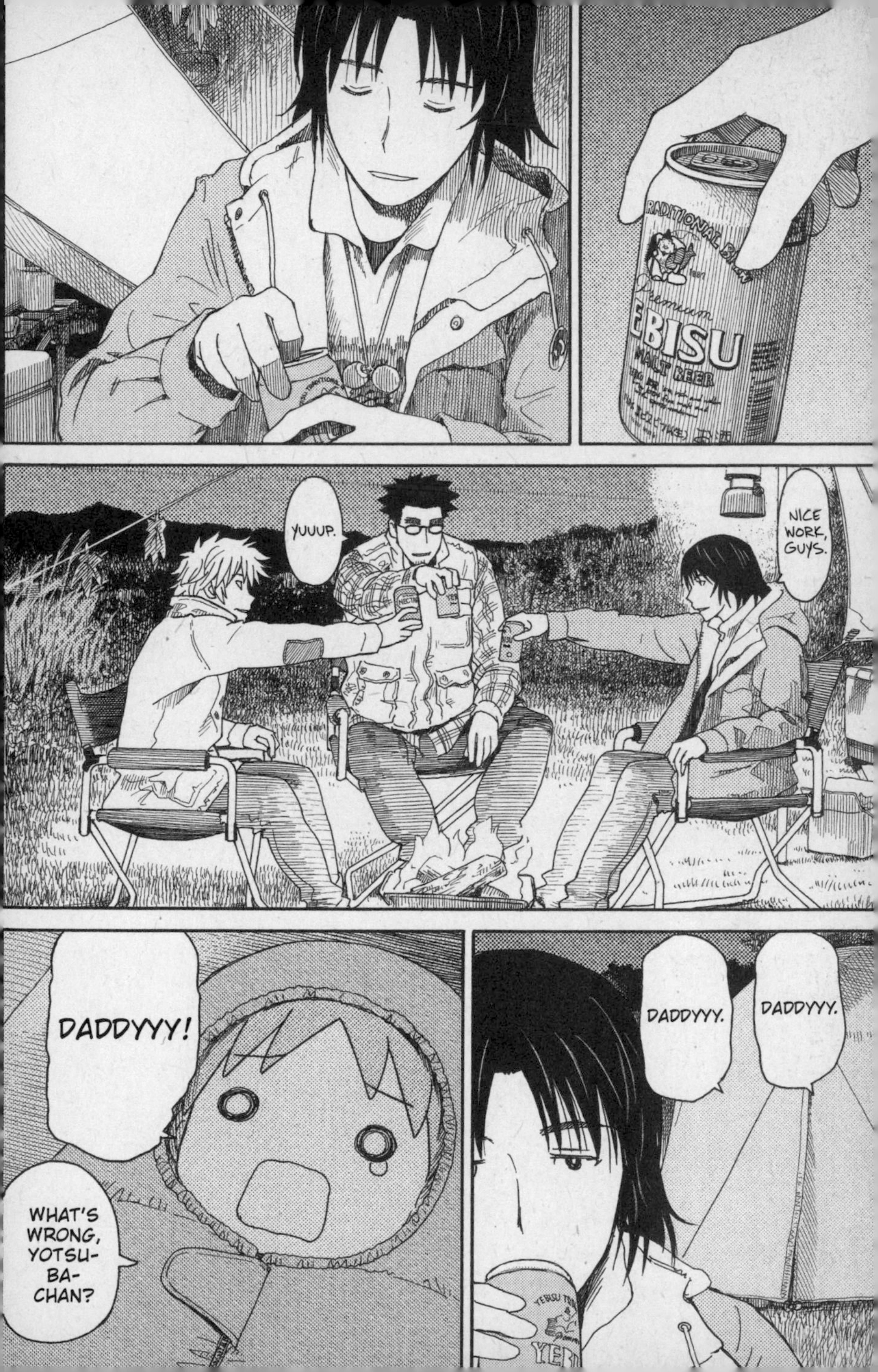
Premium
EBISU
MALT BEER
NICE WORK, GUYS.
YUUUP.
DADDYYY.
DADDYYY.
DADDYYY!
WHAT'S WRONG, YOTSUBA-CHAN?

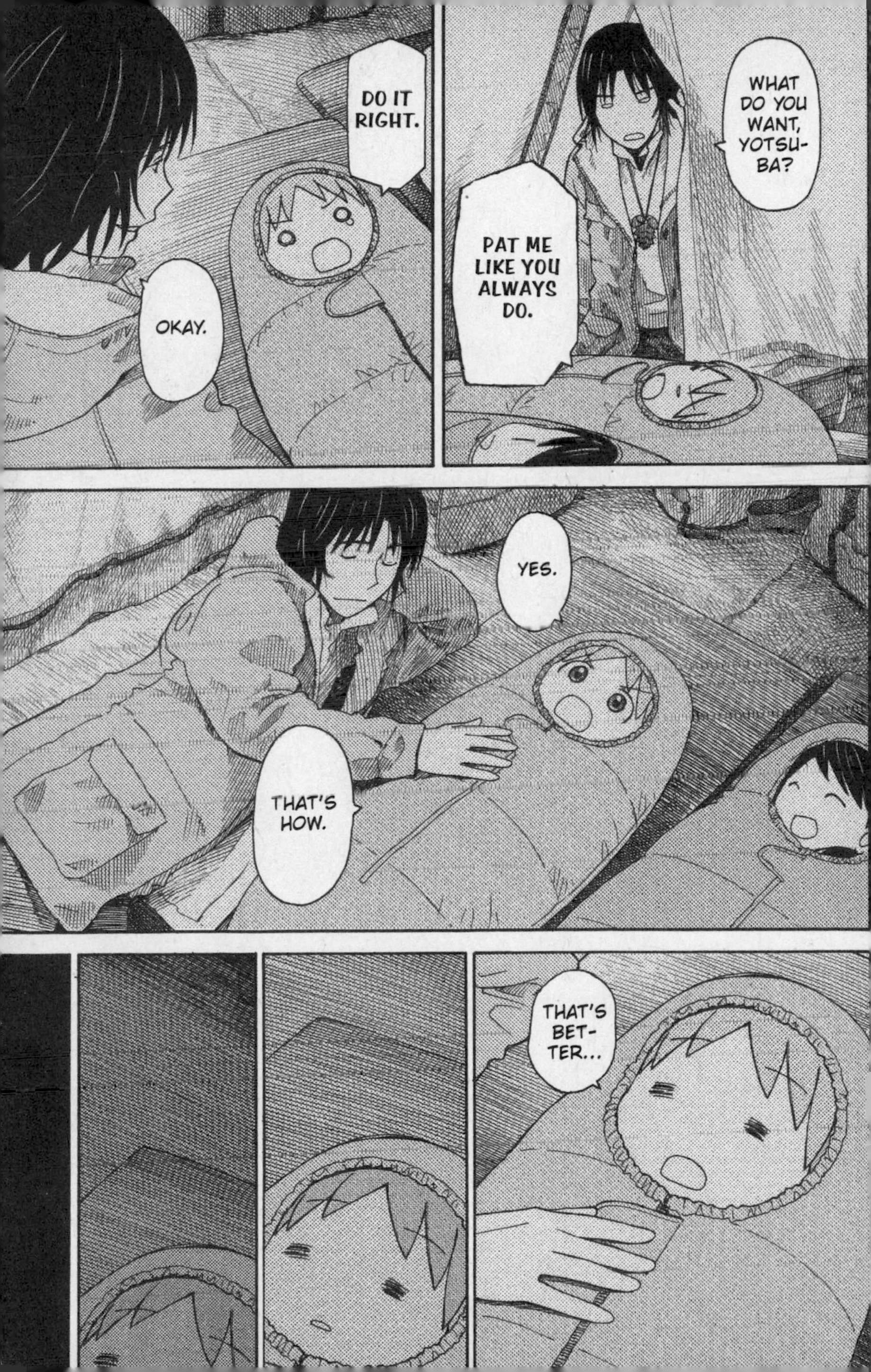
WHAT DO YOU WANT, YOTSU-BA?
PAT ME LIKE YOU ALWAYS DO.
DO IT RIGHT.
OKAY.
YES.
THAT'S HOW.
THAT'S BET-TER...

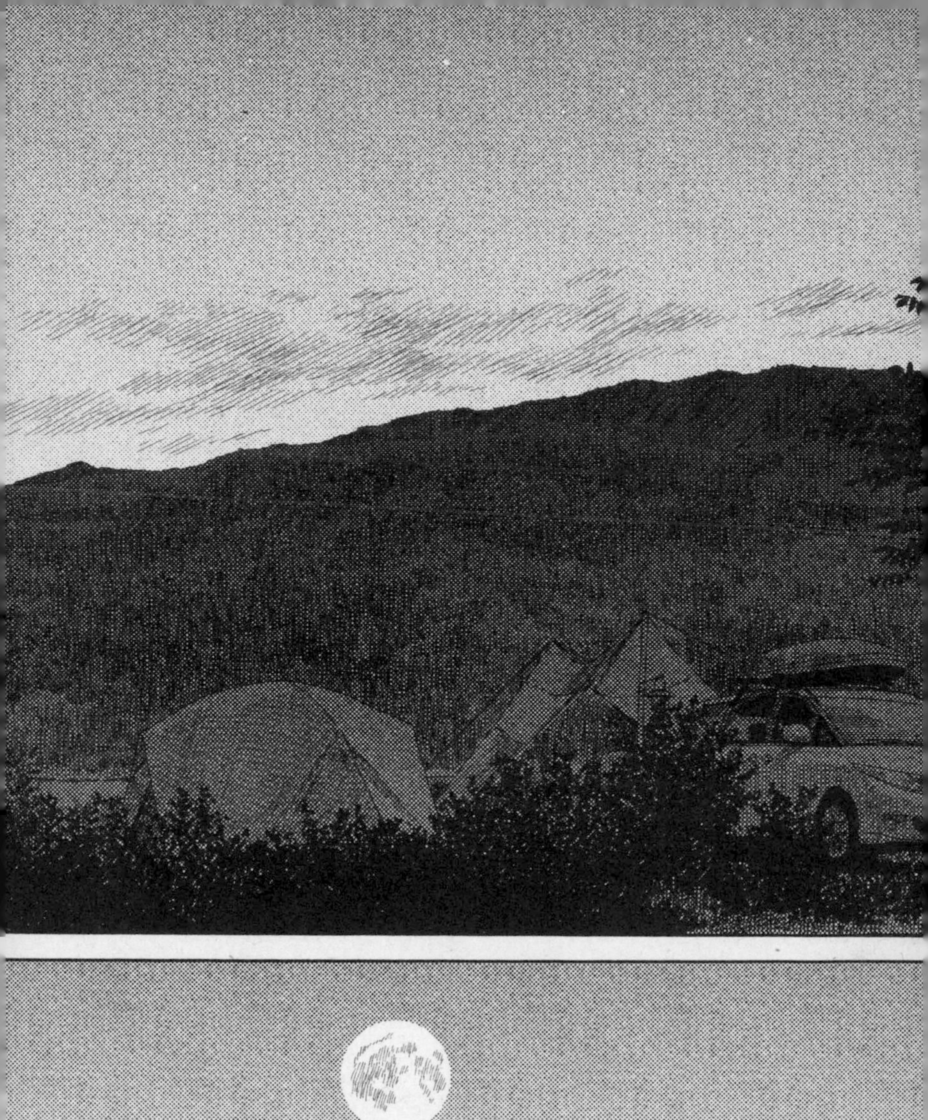
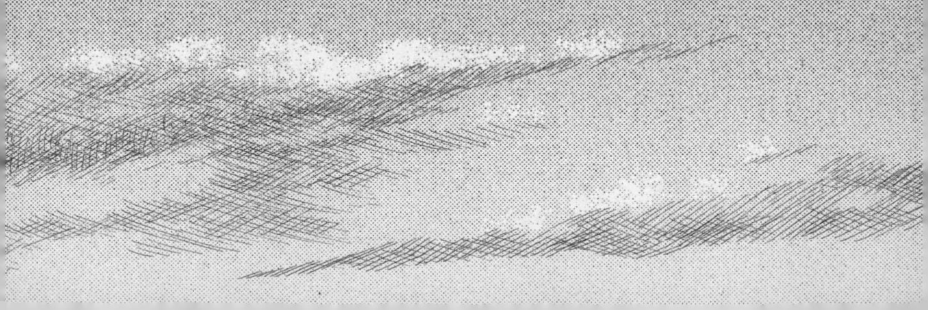

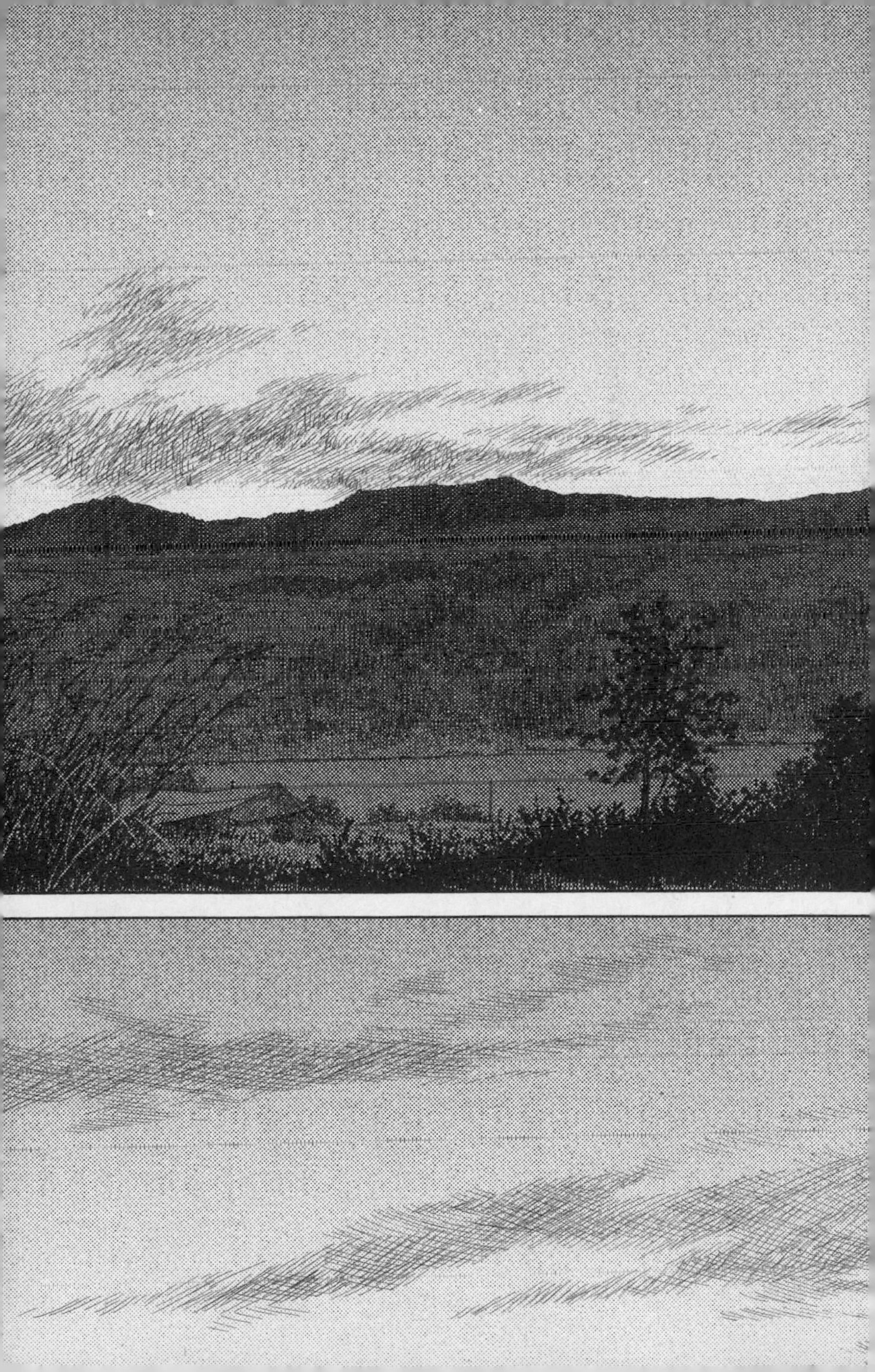

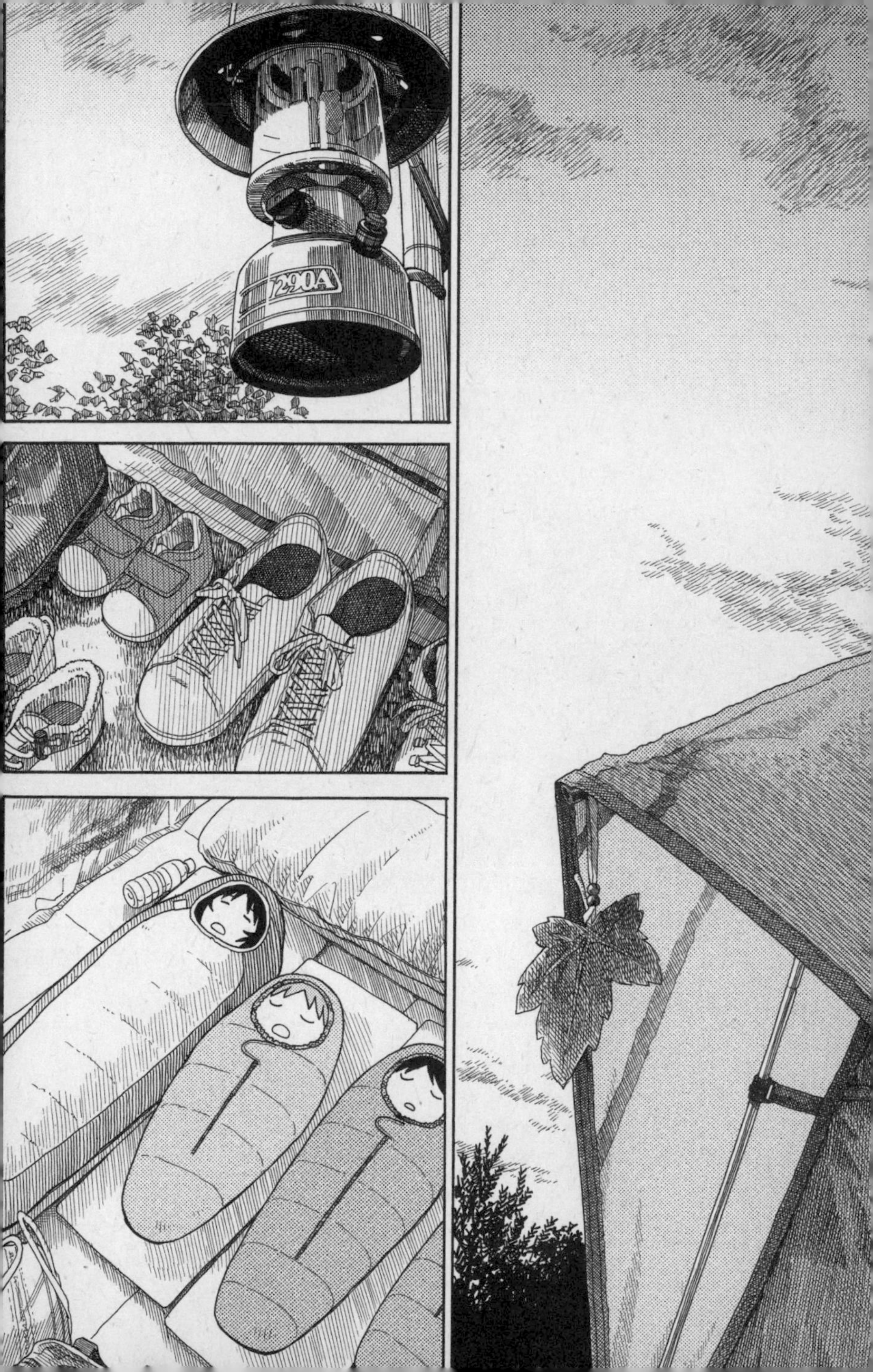
290A

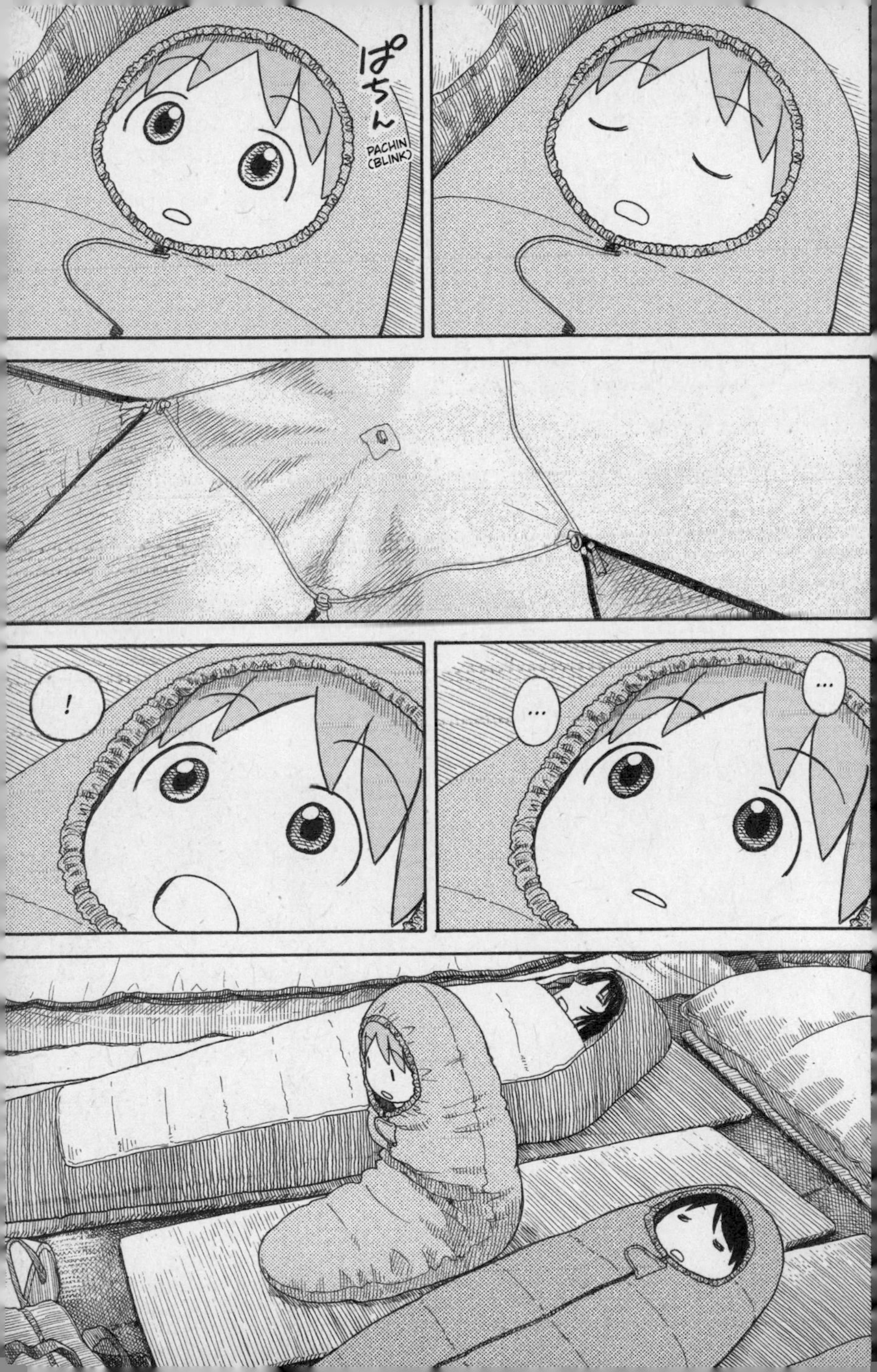
ぱちん
PACHIN (BLINK)
...
...
!

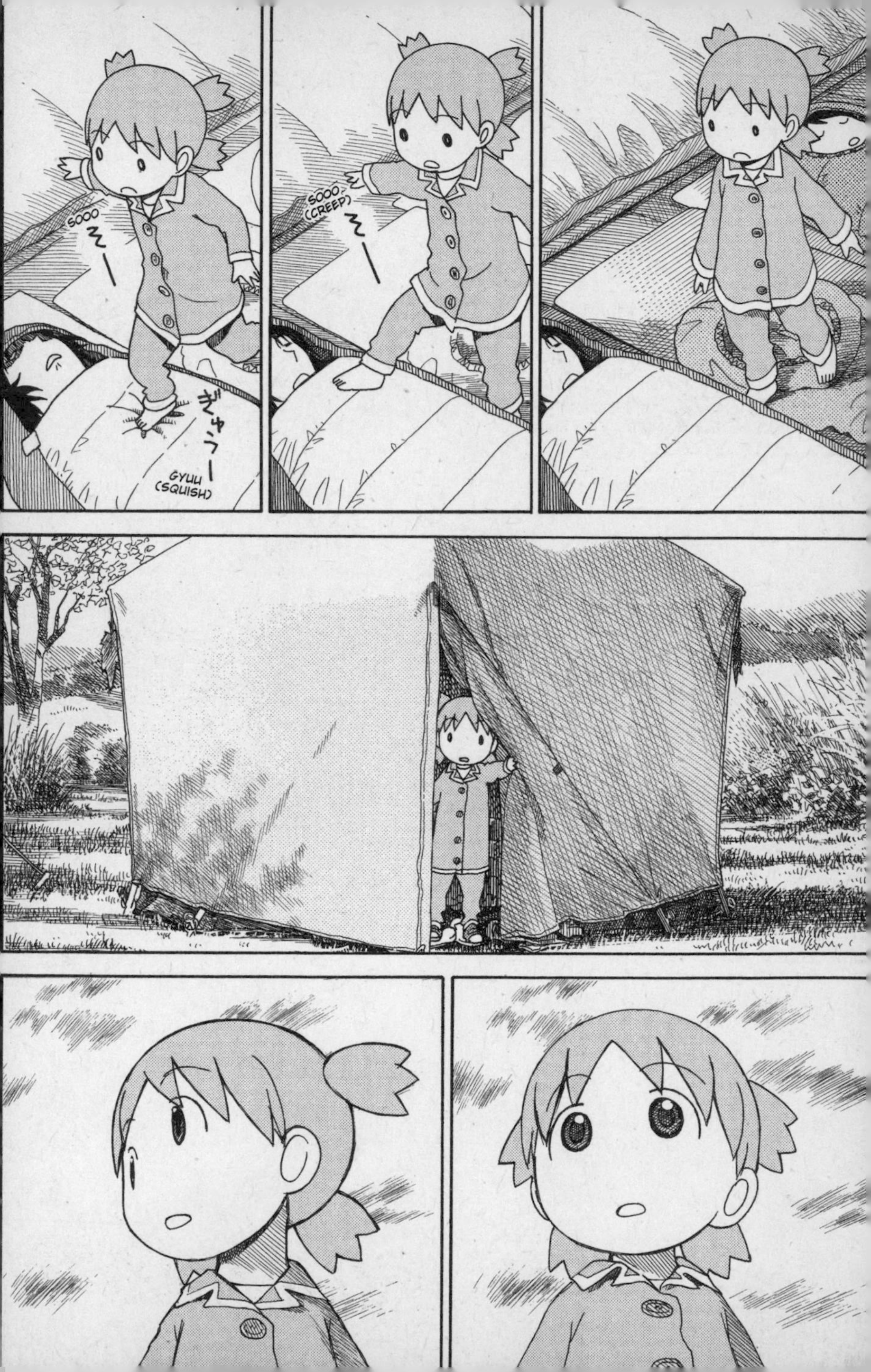

SOOO (CREEP)
そー
SOOO
そー
ぎゅうー
GYUU (SQUISH)

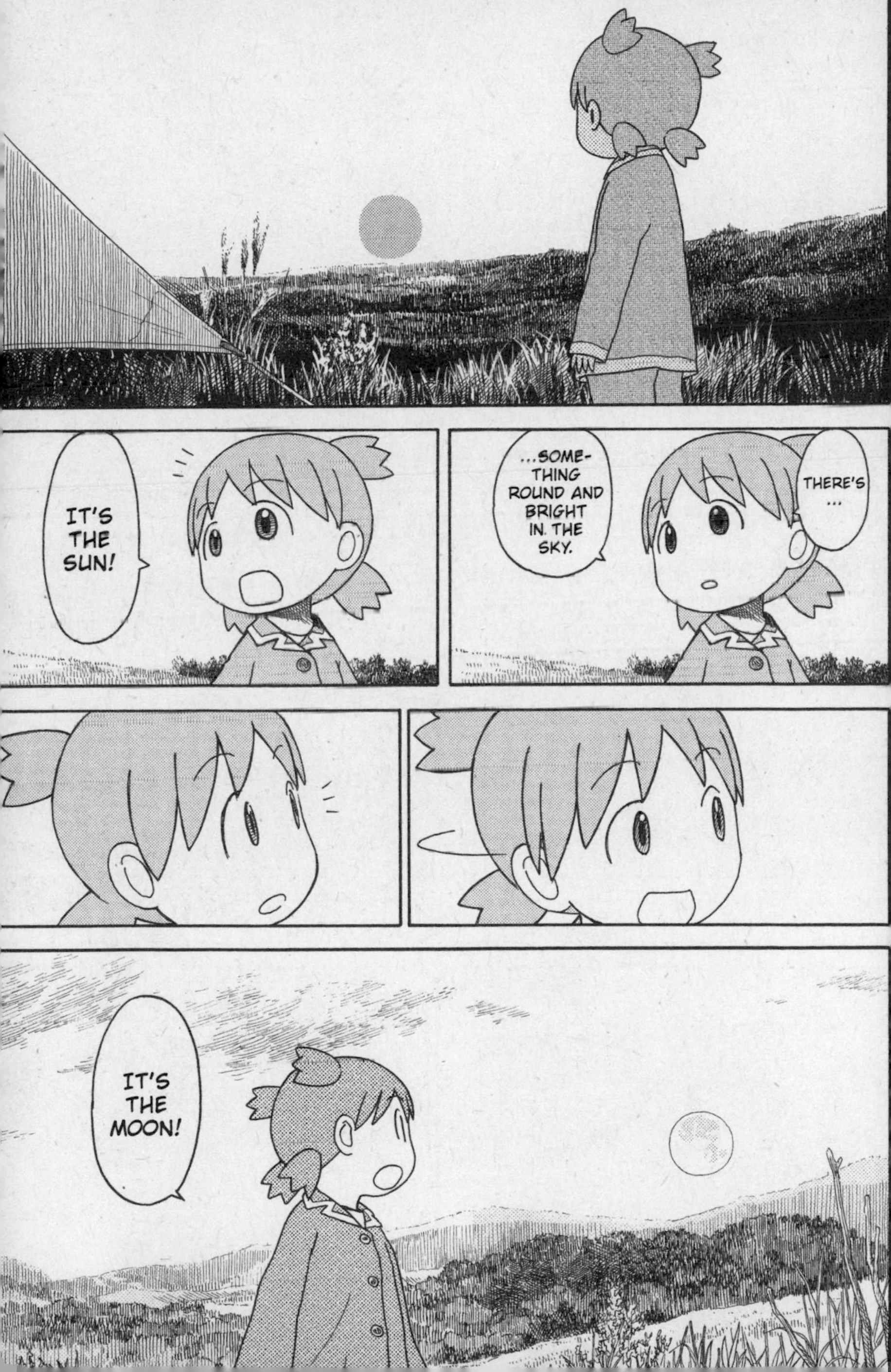
THERE'S ...
...SOME-THING ROUND AND BRIGHT IN THE SKY.
IT'S THE SUN!
IT'S THE MOON!

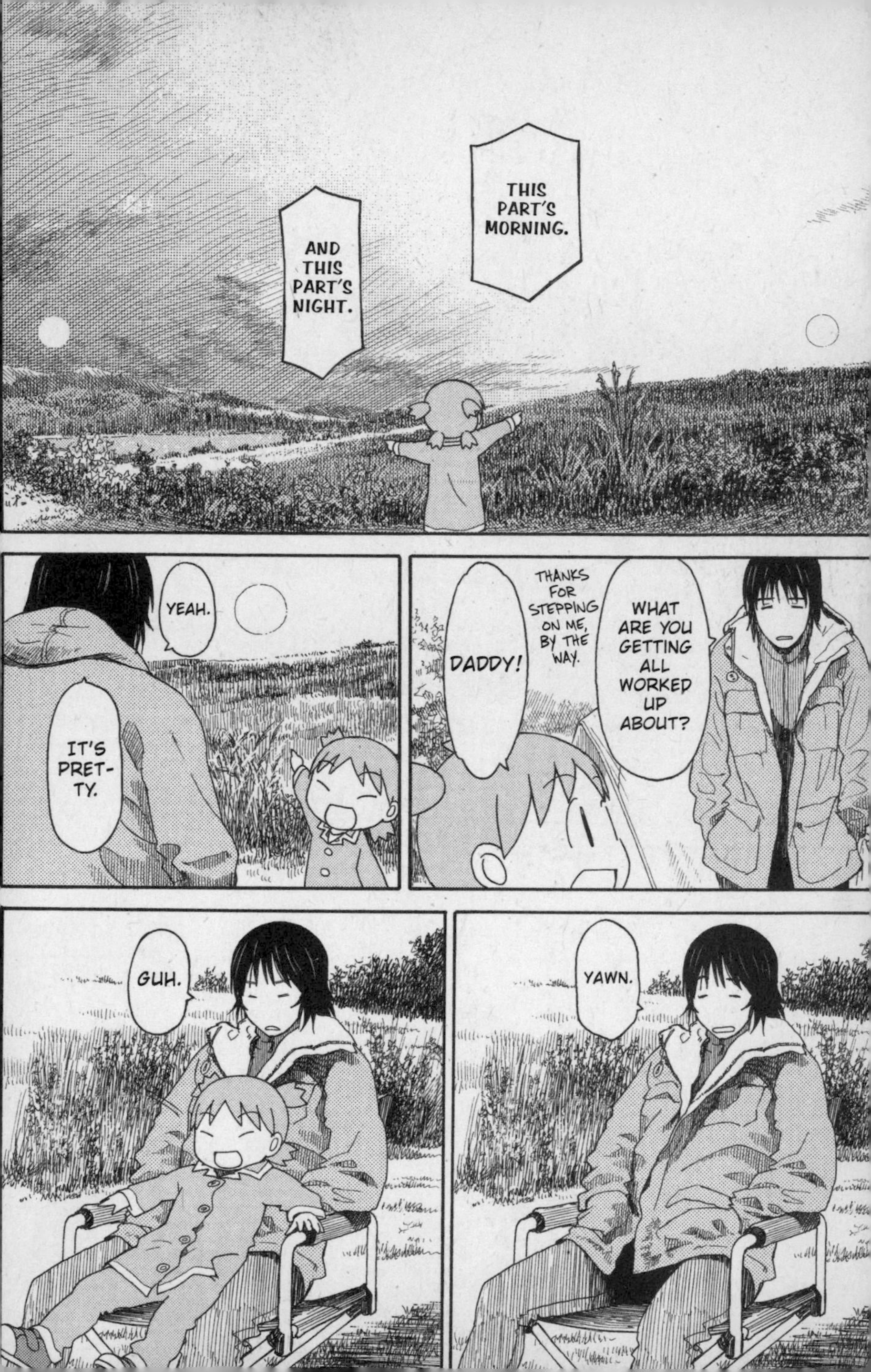
THIS PART'S MORNING.
AND THIS PART'S NIGHT.
WHAT ARE YOU GETTING ALL WORKED UP ABOUT?
THANKS FOR STEPPING ON ME, BY THE WAY.
DADDY!
YEAH.
IT'S PRET-TY.
YAWN.
GUH.

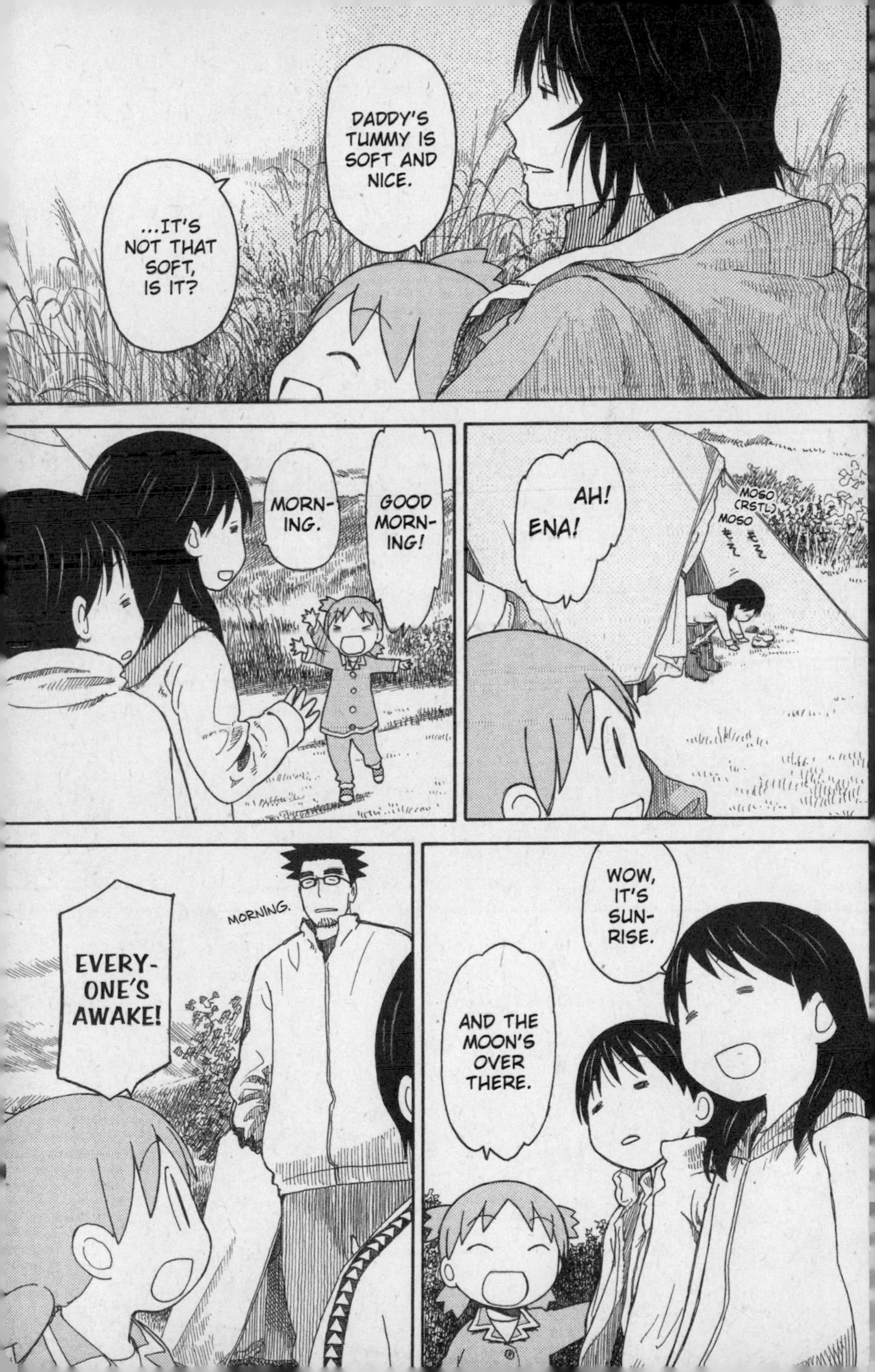
DADDY'S TUMMY IS SOFT AND NICE.
...IT'S NOT THAT SOFT, IS IT?
AH! ENA!
MOSO (RSTL) MOSO
もそ もそ
GOOD MORN-ING!
MORN-ING.
WOW, IT'S SUN-RISE.
AND THE MOON'S OVER THERE.
MORNING.
EVERY-ONE'S AWAKE!

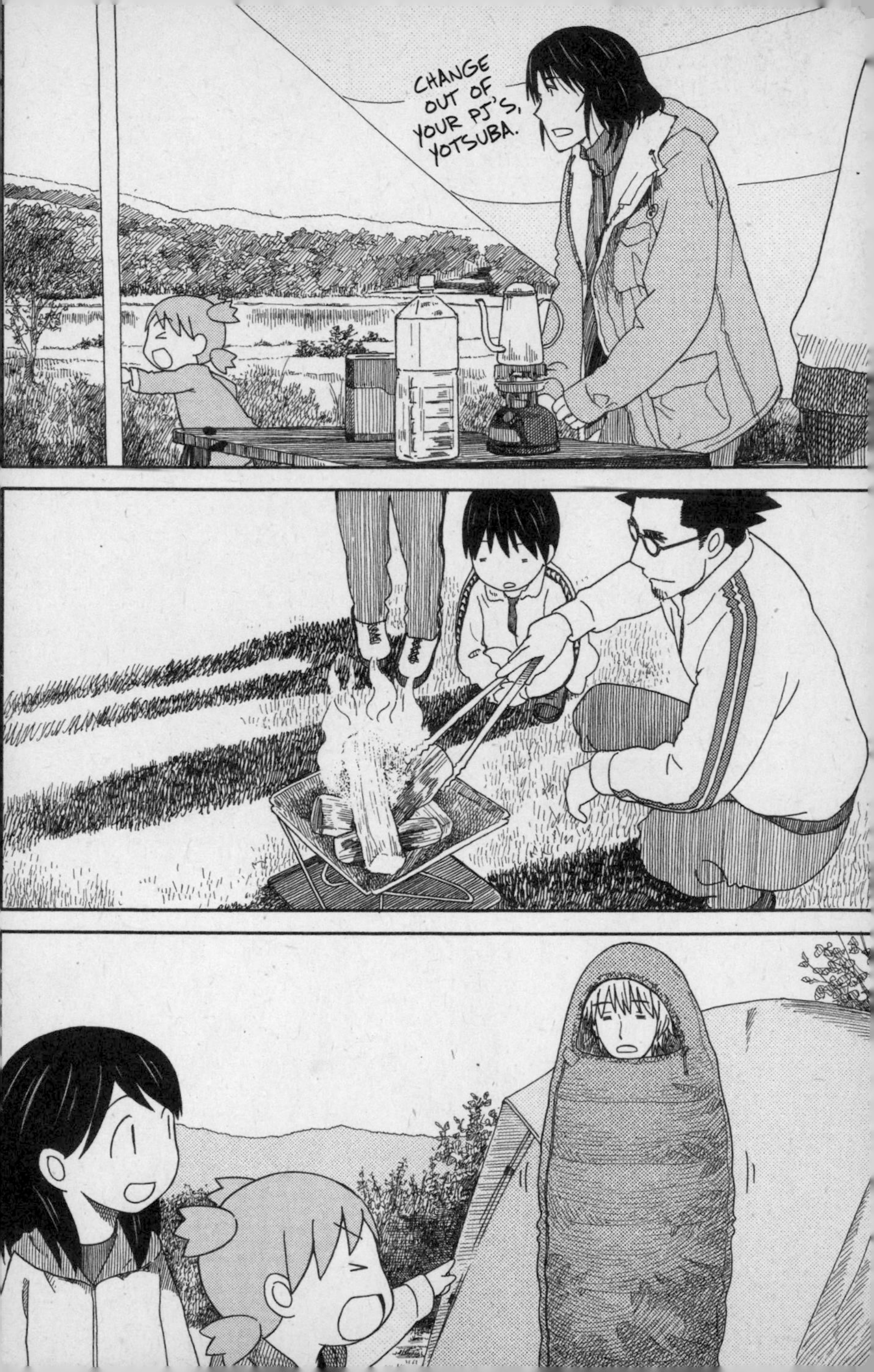
CHANGE OUT OF YOUR PJ'S, YOTSUBA.

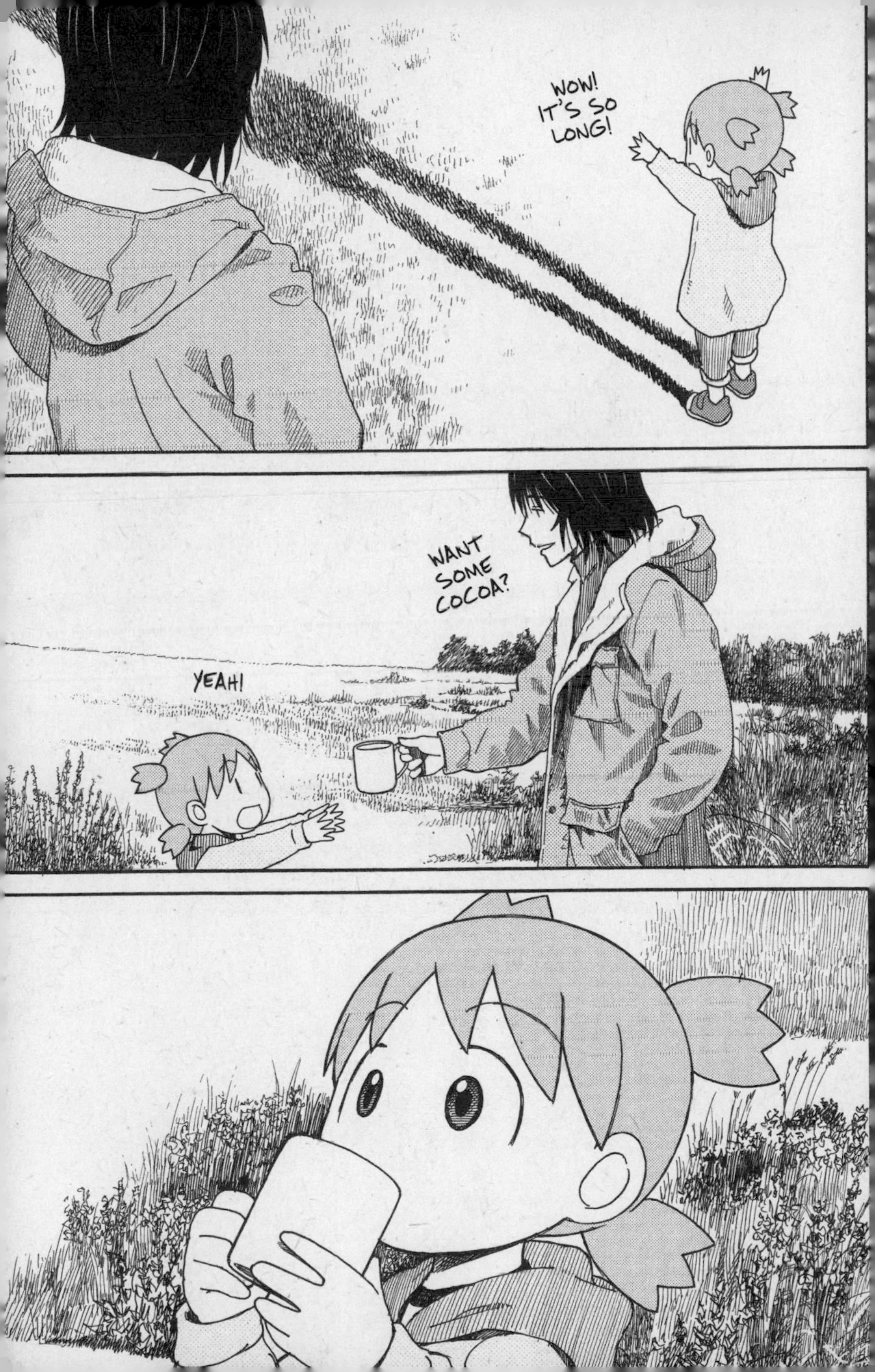
WOW! IT'S SO LONG!
WANT SOME COCOA?
YEAH!

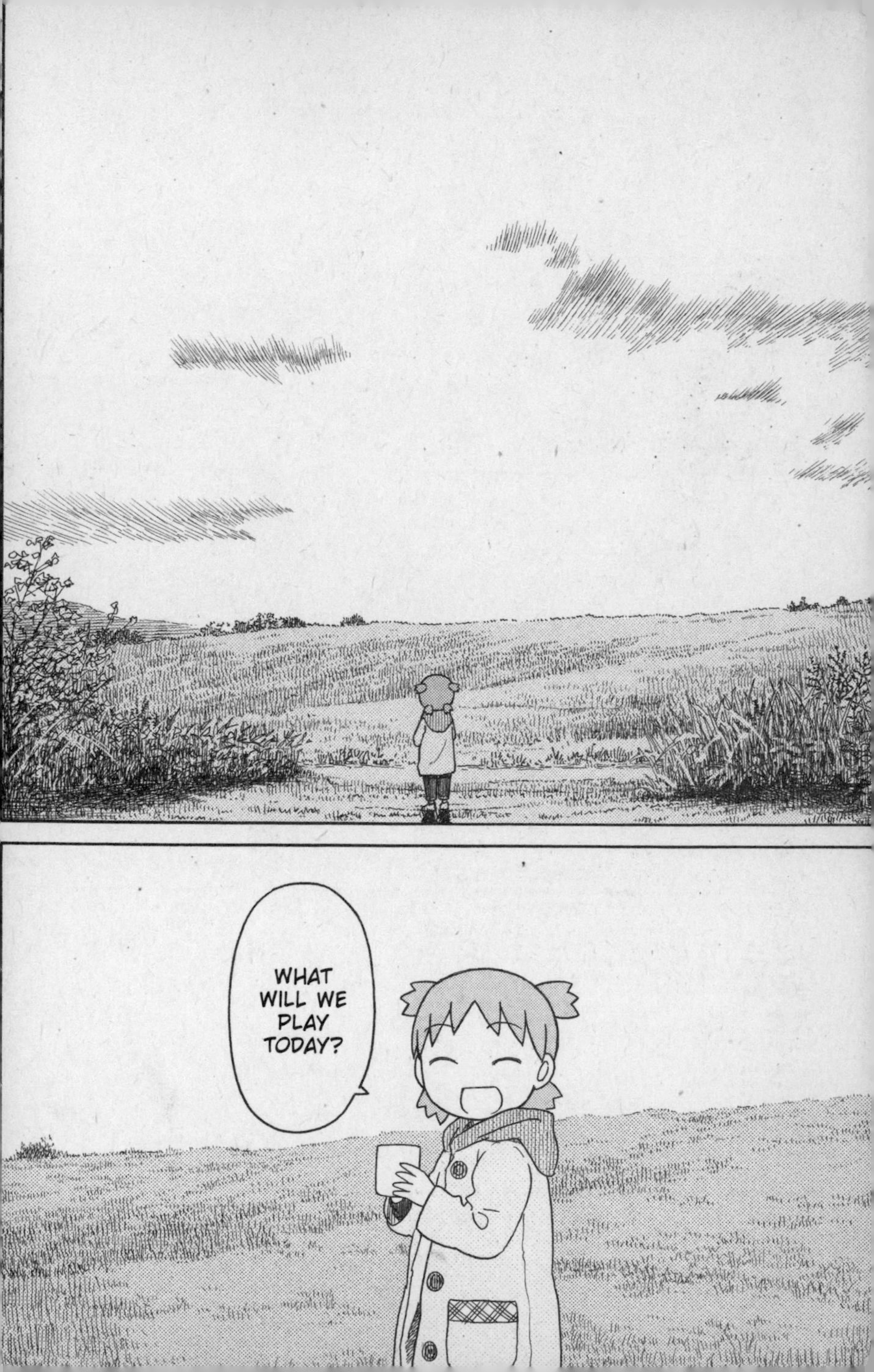
WHAT WILL WE PLAY TODAY?

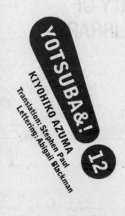

YOTSUBA&! 12

KIYOHIKO AZUMA

Translation: Stephen Paul
Lettering: Abigail Blackman



YOTSUBA&! Vol. 12

Edited by ASCII MEDIA WORKS
First published in Japan in 2013 by
KADOKAWA CORPORATION, Tokyo.
English translation rights arranged with
KADOKAWA CORPORATION, Tokyo,
through Tuttle-Mori Agency, Inc., Tokyo.



Yen Press
1290 Avenue of the Americas
New York, NY 10104

Visit us at yenpress.com
facebook.com/yenpress
twitter.com/yenpress
yenpress.tumblr.com
instagram.com/yenpress

First Yen Press Edition: November 2013

Yen Press is an imprint of Yen Press, LLC.
The Yen Press name and logo are trademarks of Yen Press, LLC.

The publisher is not responsible for websites (or their content) that are not owned by the publisher.

ISBN: 978-0-316-32232-4

10

WOR

Printed in the United States of America

# YOTSUBA&!

**ENJOY EVERYTHING.**

# TO BE CONTINUED!